DEMON SACRED

Vol. 4

By Natsumi Itsuki

HAMBURG // LONDON // LOS ANGELES // TOKYO

Demon Sacred Volume 4
Created by Natsumi Itsuki

Translation - Yuko Fukami
English Adaptation - Ysabet MacFarlane
Retouch and Lettering - Star Print Brokers
Graphic Designer - Marguerite DuLac

Editor - Jill Bentley
Print Production Manager - Lucas Rivera
Managing Editor - Vy Nguyen
Senior Designer - Louis Csontos
Art Director - Al-Insan Lashley
Director of Sales and Manufacturing - Allyson De Simone
Senior Vice President - Mike Kiley
President and C.O.O. - John Parker
C.E.O. and Chief Creative Officer - Stu Levy

A  Manga

TOKYOPOP Inc.
5900 Wilshire Blvd. Suite 2000
Los Angeles, CA 90036

E-mail: info@TOKYOPOP.com
Come visit us online at www.TOKYOPOP.com

DEMON SACRED by Natsumi Itsuki © 2003, 2004, 2011
by ITSUKI NATSUMI ART, Inc. All rights reserved.
First published in Japan in 2004 by HAKUSENSHA, INC., Tokyo
English language translation rights in the United States of
America and Canada arranged with HAKUSENSHA, INC.,
Tokyo through Tuttle-Mori Agency Inc., Tokyo
English text copyright © 2011 TOKYOPOP Inc.

ISBN: 978-1-4278-1392-3

First TOKYOPOP printing: March 2011
10 9 8 7 6 5 4 3 2 1
Printed in the USA

DEMON SACRED

VOLUME 4

NATSUMI ITSUKI

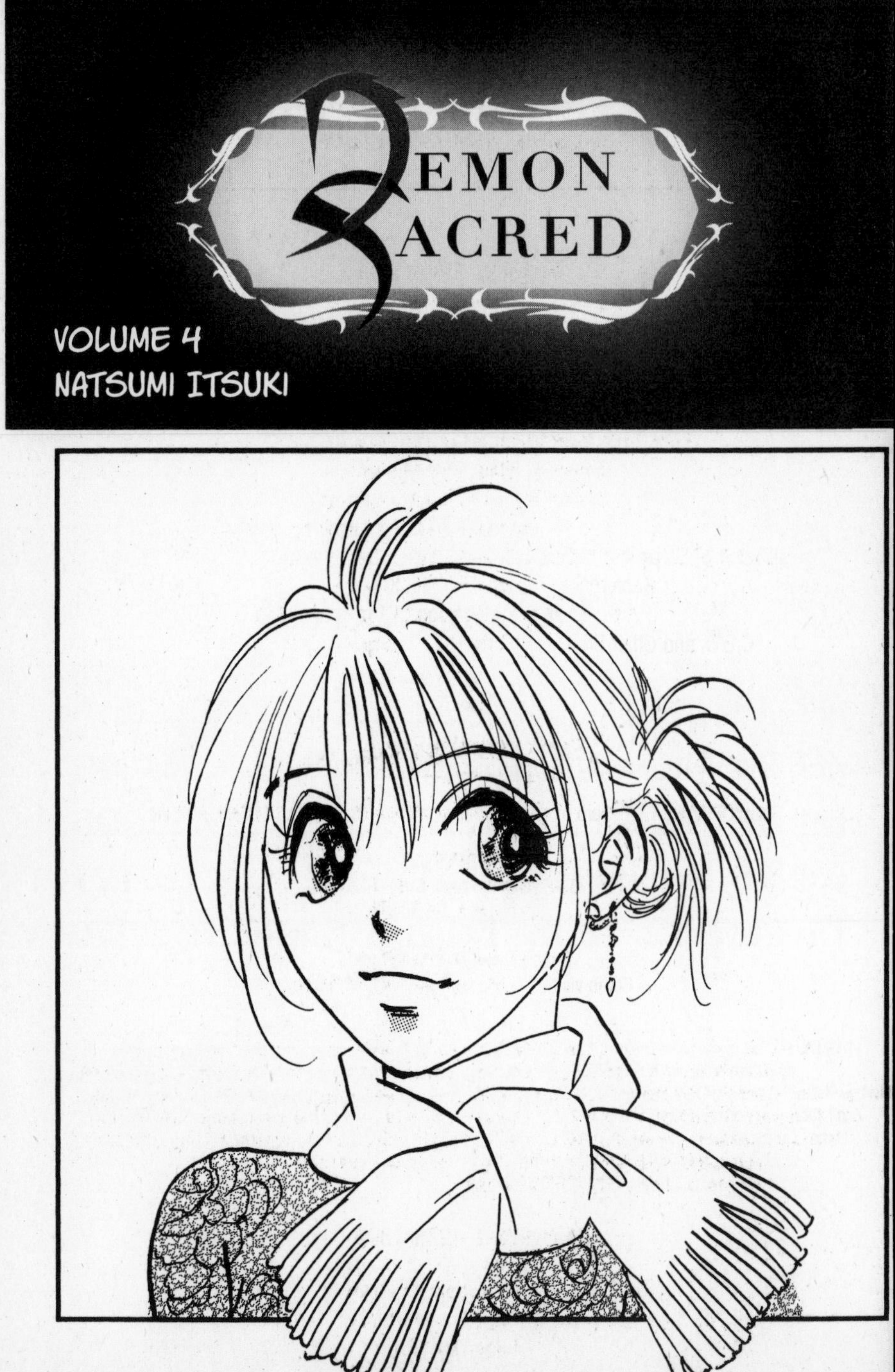

Contents

Demon Sacred

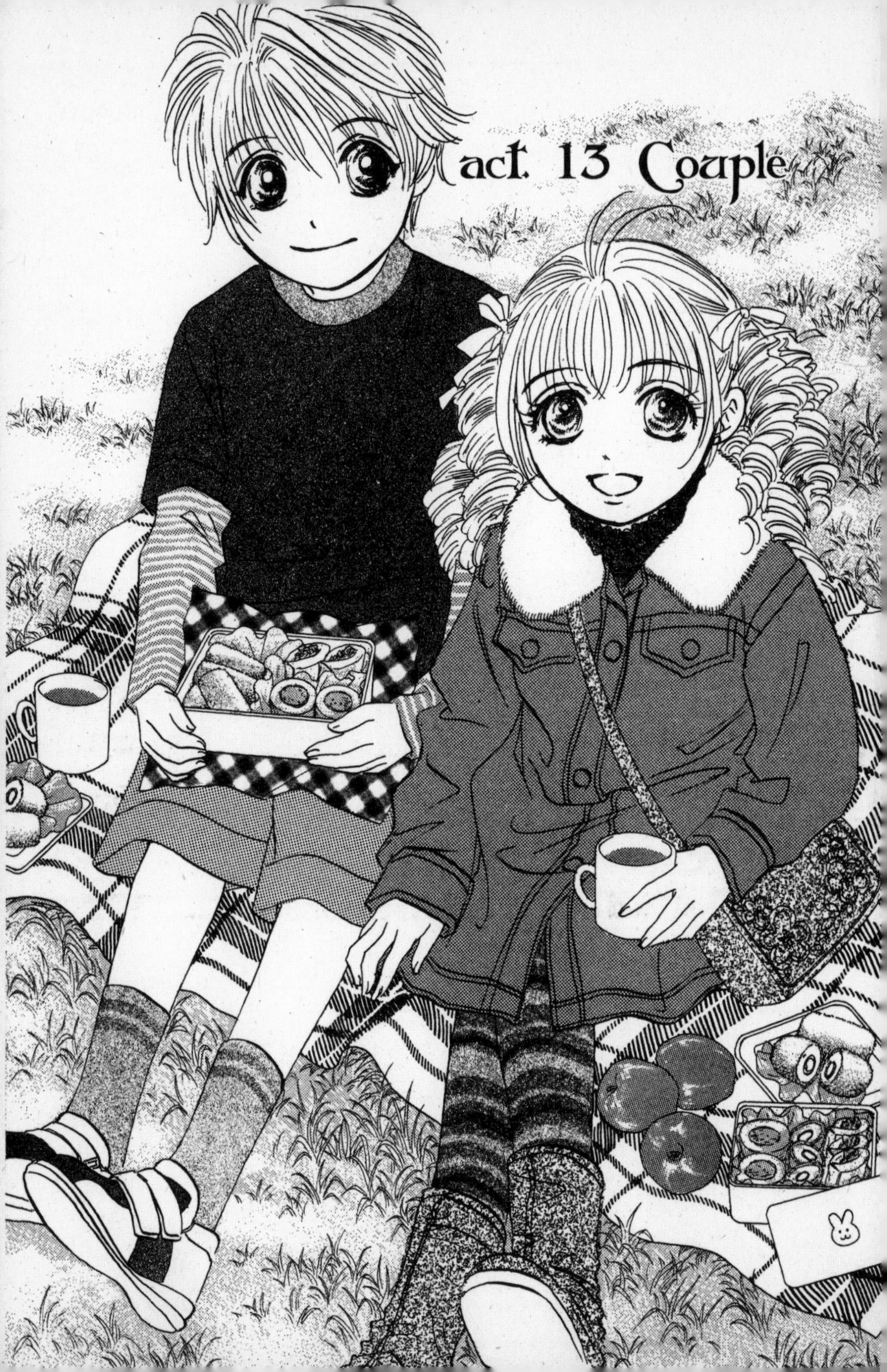
act. 13 Couple

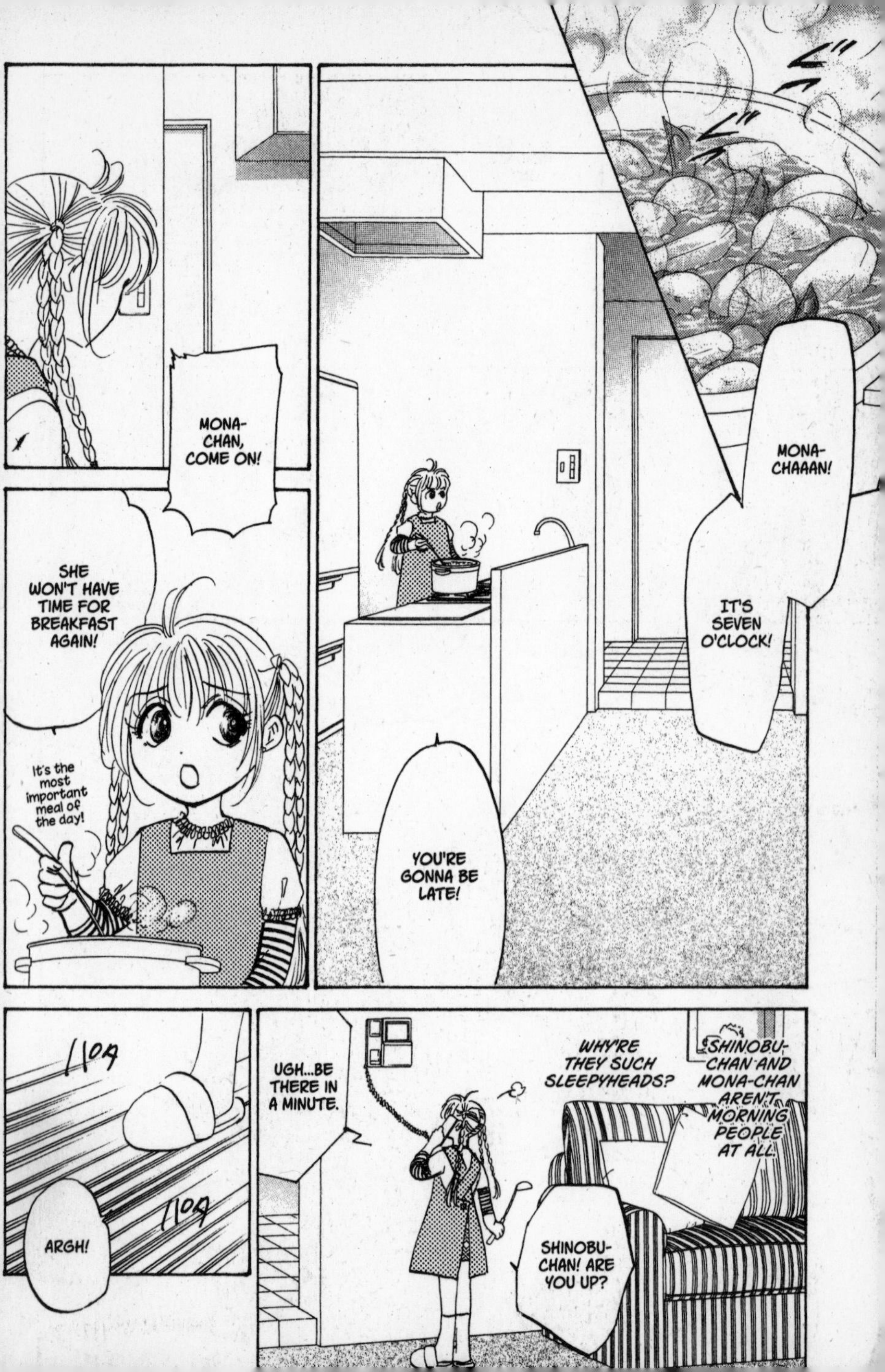
MONA-CHAAAN!
IT'S SEVEN O'CLOCK!
YOU'RE GONNA BE LATE!
MONA-CHAN, COME ON!
SHE WON'T HAVE TIME FOR BREAKFAST AGAIN!
It's the most important meal of the day!
SHINOBU-CHAN AND MONA-CHAN AREN'T MORNING PEOPLE AT ALL.
WHY'RE THEY SUCH SLEEPYHEADS?
SHINOBU-CHAN! ARE YOU UP?
UGH...BE THERE IN A MINUTE.
ARGH!

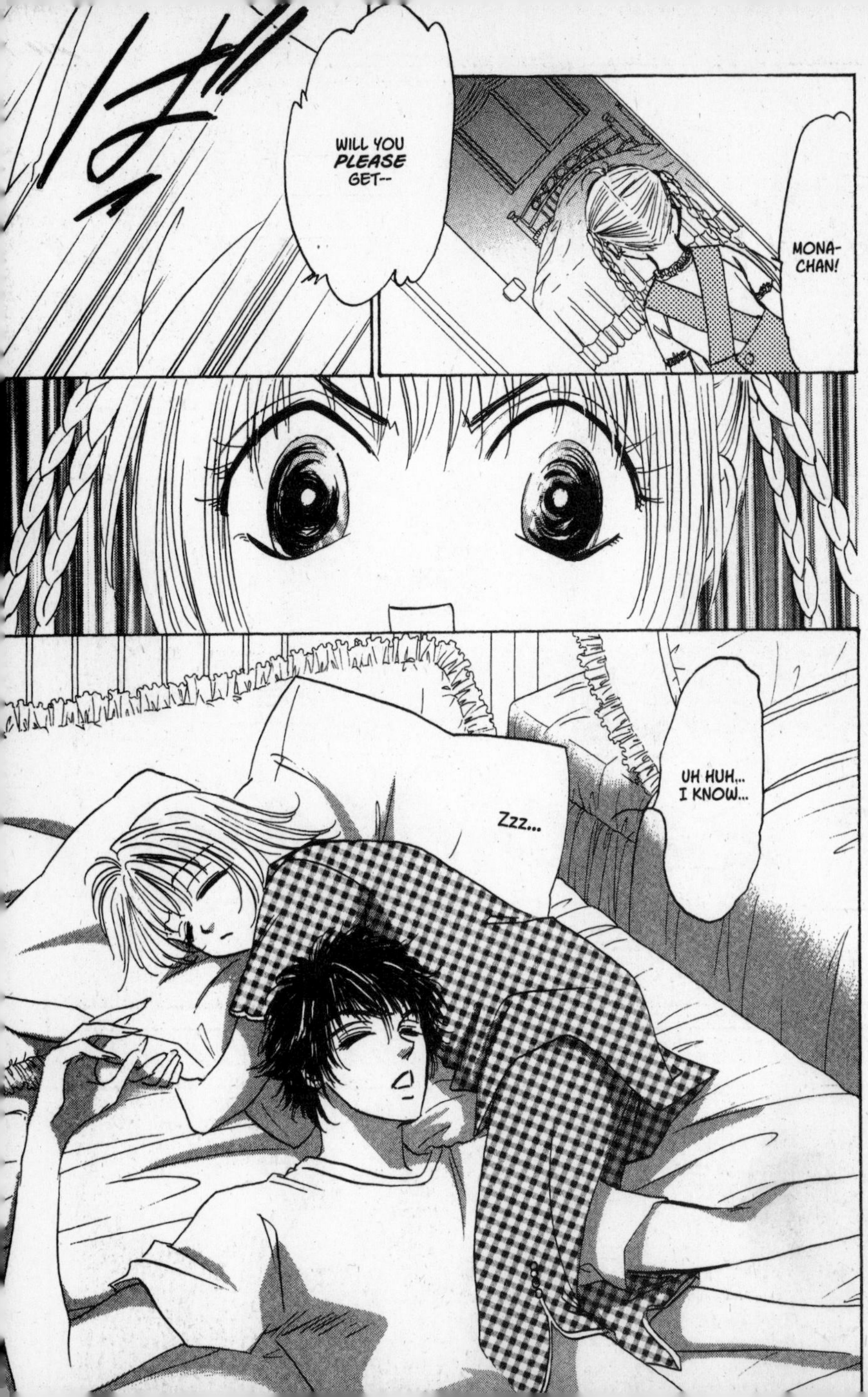
MONA-CHAN!
WILL YOU PLEASE GET--
UH HUH... I KNOW...
Zzz...

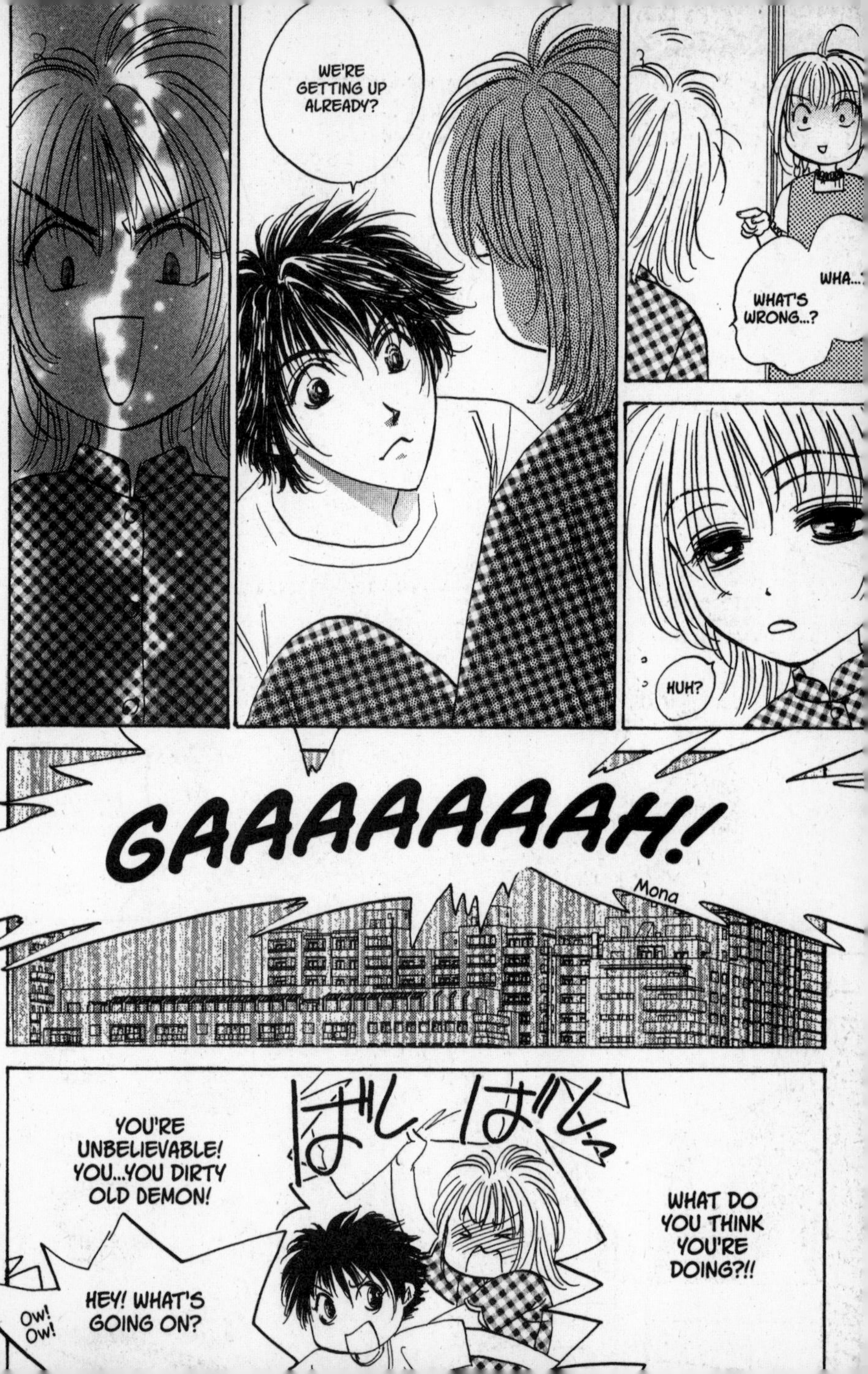
WHA...
WHAT'S WRONG...?
HUH?
WE'RE GETTING UP ALREADY?
GAAAAAAAH!
Mona
ばし ばしっ
WHAT DO YOU THINK YOU'RE DOING?!!
YOU'RE UNBELIEVABLE! YOU...YOU DIRTY OLD DEMON!
HEY! WHAT'S GOING ON?
OW! OW!

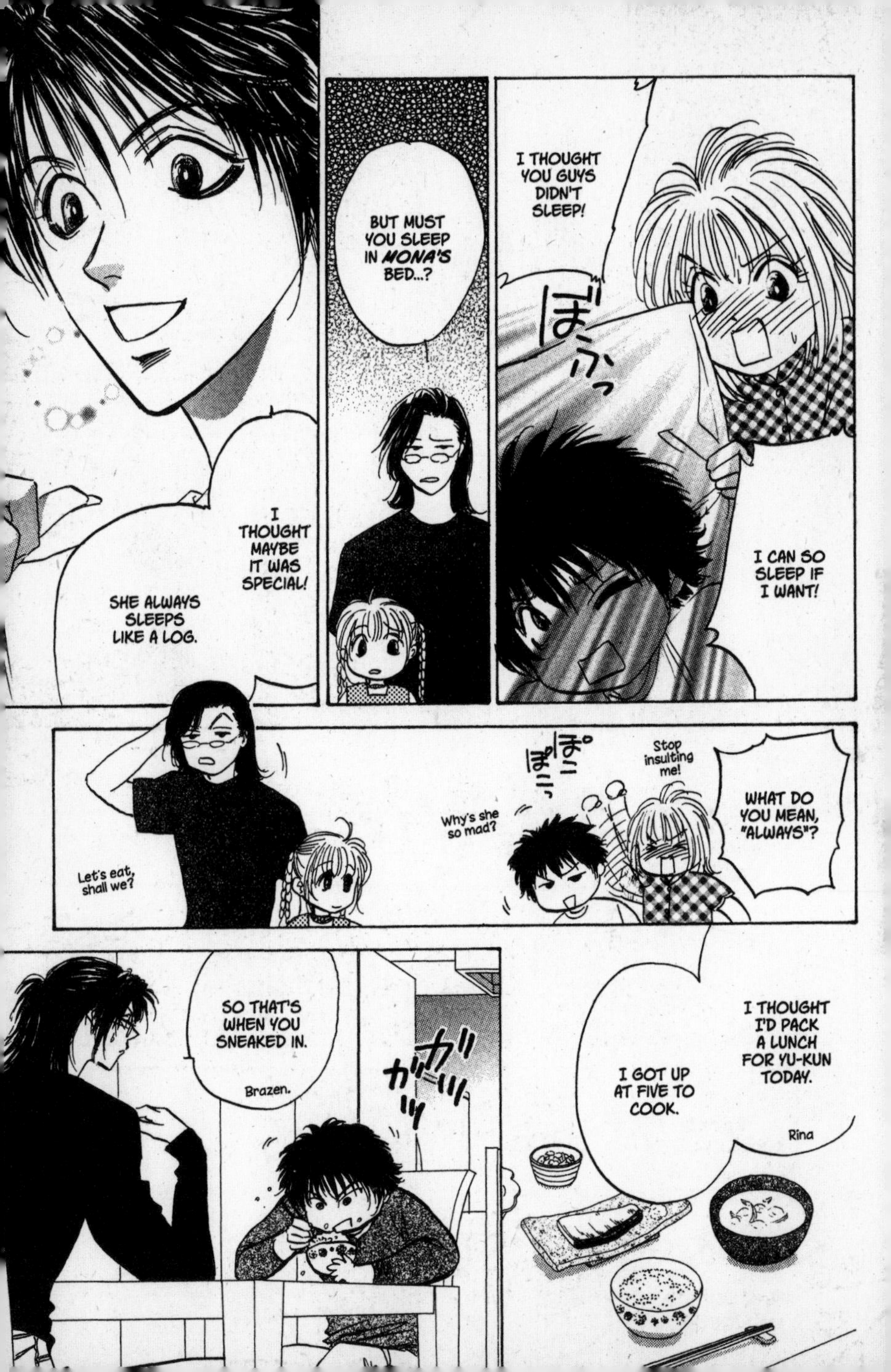
I THOUGHT YOU GUYS DIDN'T SLEEP!
ぼふっ
I CAN SO SLEEP IF I WANT!
BUT MUST YOU SLEEP IN *MONA'S* BED...?
I THOUGHT MAYBE IT WAS SPECIAL!
SHE ALWAYS SLEEPS LIKE A LOG.
WHAT DO YOU MEAN, "ALWAYS"?
Stop insulting me!
ぽこぽこ
Why's she so mad?
Let's eat, shall we?
I THOUGHT I'D PACK A LUNCH FOR YU-KUN TODAY.
I GOT UP AT FIVE TO COOK.
Rina
ガツガツ
SO THAT'S WHEN YOU SNEAKED IN.
Brazen.

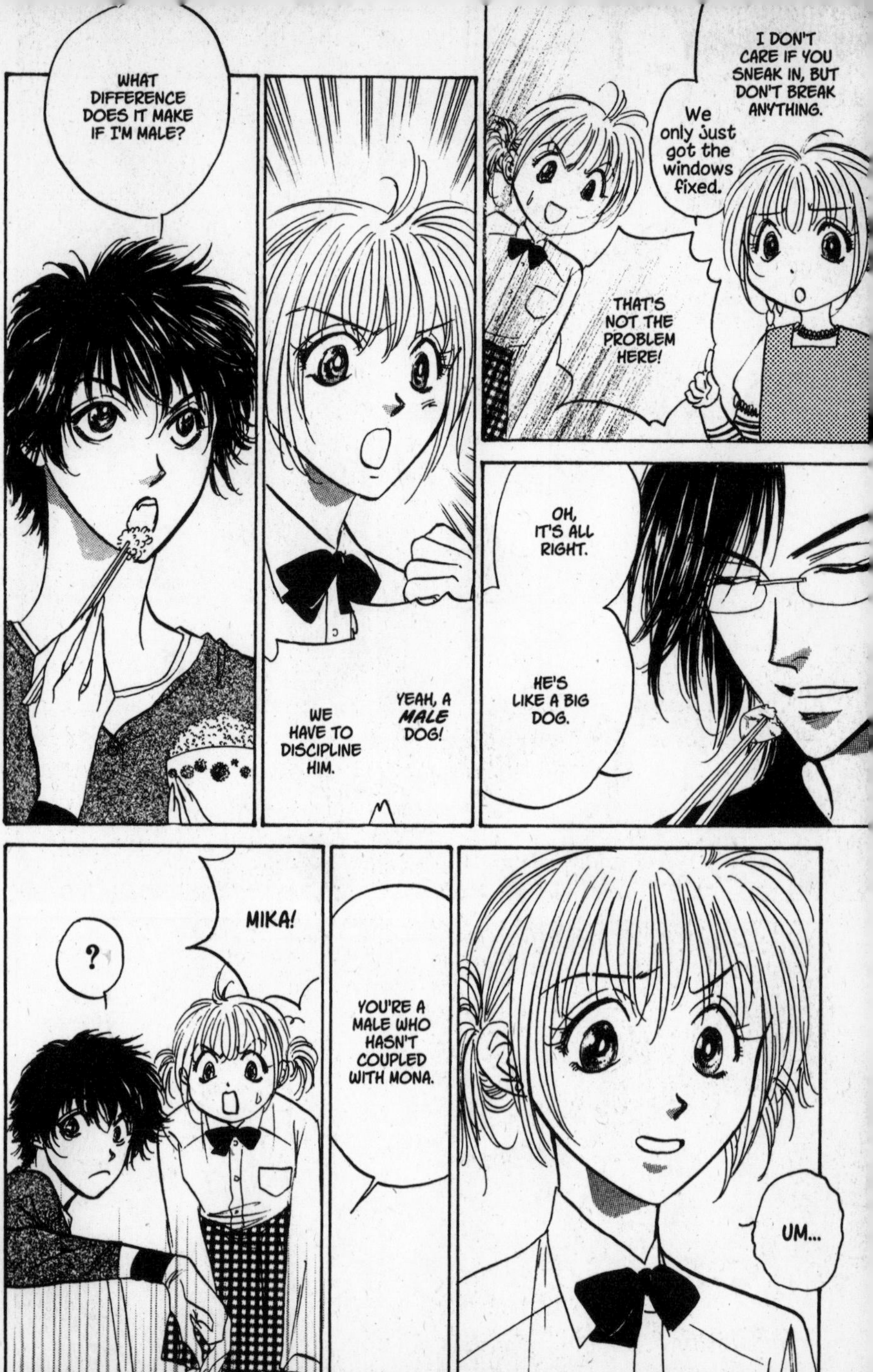
I DON'T CARE IF YOU SNEAK IN, BUT DON'T BREAK ANYTHING.
We only just got the windows fixed.
THAT'S NOT THE PROBLEM HERE!
OH, IT'S ALL RIGHT.
HE'S LIKE A BIG DOG.
YEAH, A *MALE* DOG!
WE HAVE TO DISCIPLINE HIM.
WHAT DIFFERENCE DOES IT MAKE IF I'M MALE?
UM...
YOU'RE A MALE WHO HASN'T COUPLED WITH MONA.
MIKA!
?

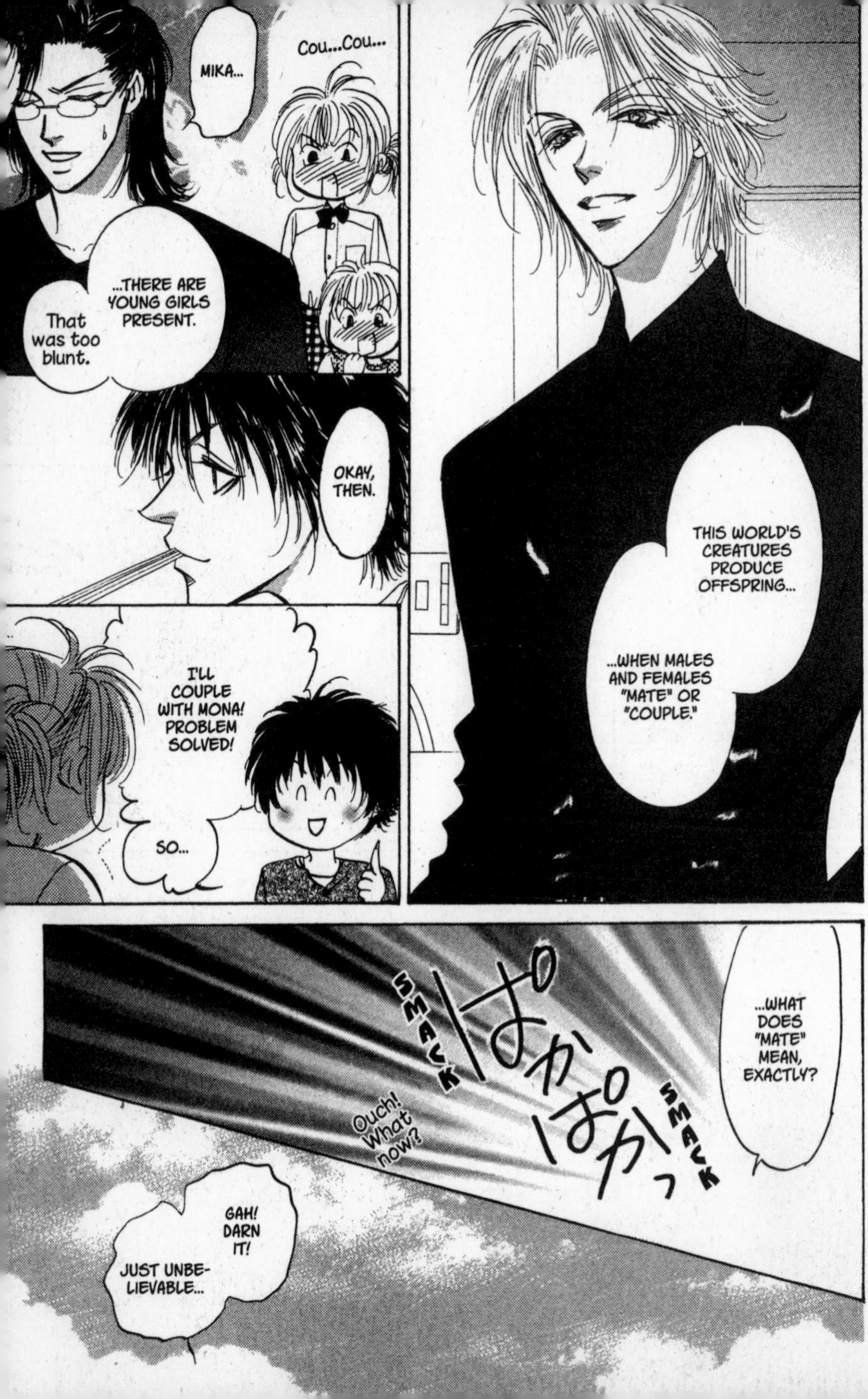
THIS WORLD'S CREATURES PRODUCE OFFSPRING...
...WHEN MALES AND FEMALES "MATE" OR "COUPLE."
Cou...Cou...
MIKA...
...THERE ARE YOUNG GIRLS PRESENT.
That was too blunt.
OKAY, THEN.
I'LL COUPLE WITH MONA! PROBLEM SOLVED!
SO...
...WHAT DOES "MATE" MEAN, EXACTLY?
ぱかぱかっ
SMACK
SMACK
Ouch! What now?
GAH! DARN IT!
JUST UNBELIEVABLE...

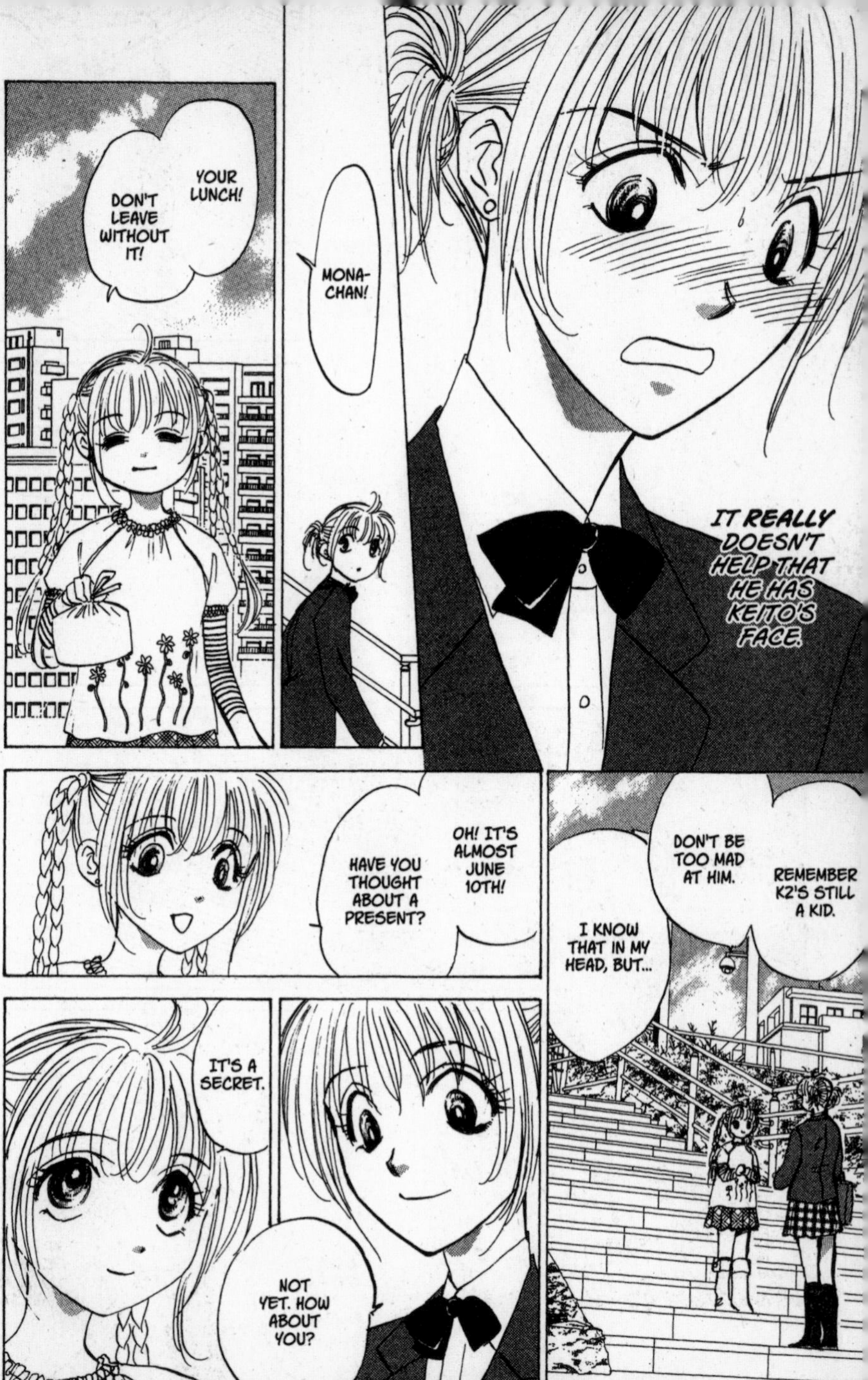
IT REALLY DOESN'T HELP THAT HE HAS KEITO'S FACE.
MONA-CHAN!
YOUR LUNCH! DON'T LEAVE WITHOUT IT!
DON'T BE TOO MAD AT HIM. REMEMBER K2'S STILL A KID.
I KNOW THAT IN MY HEAD, BUT...
OH! IT'S ALMOST JUNE 10TH! HAVE YOU THOUGHT ABOUT A PRESENT?
NOT YET. HOW ABOUT YOU?
IT'S A SECRET.

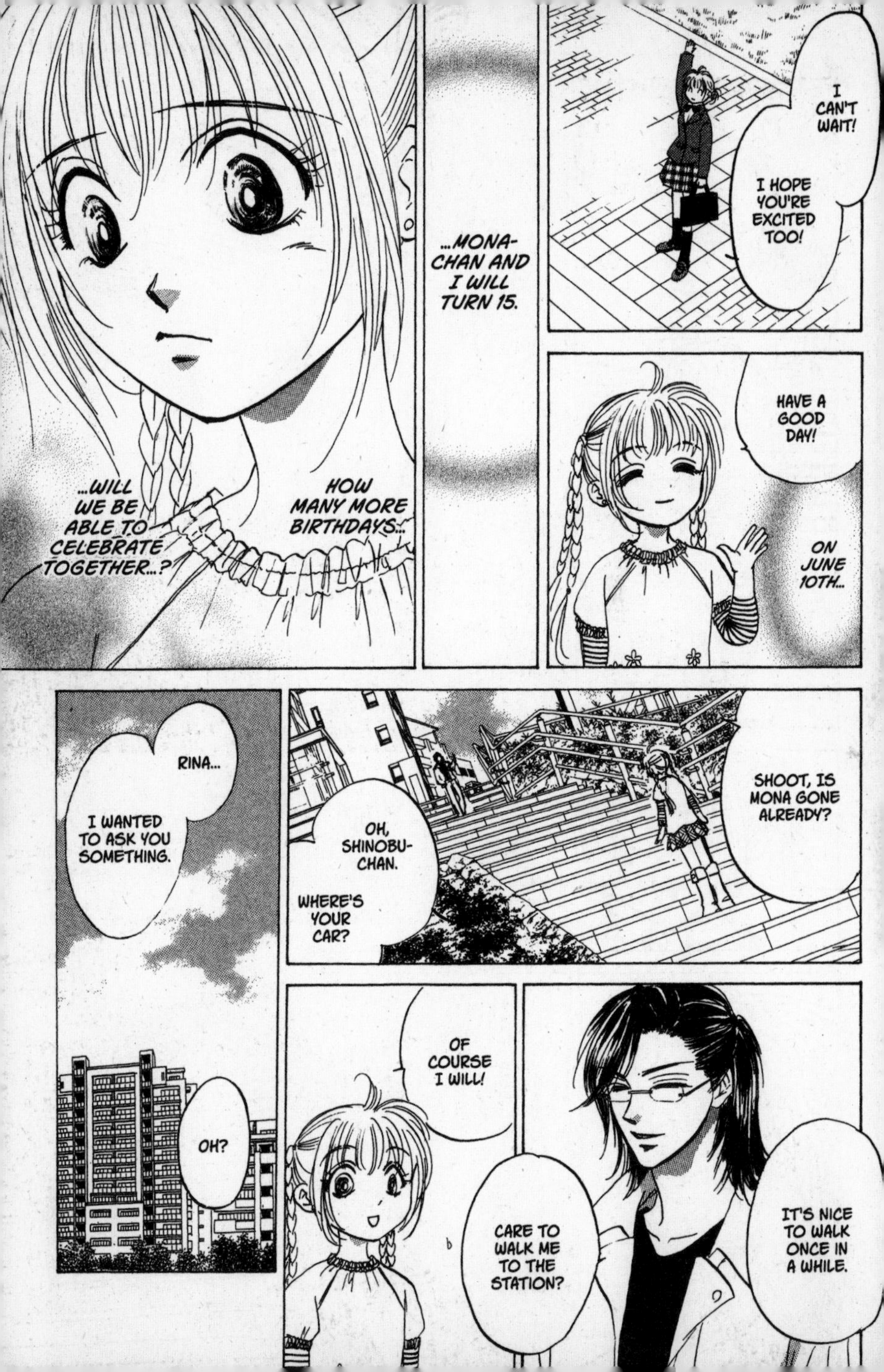
I CAN'T WAIT!
I HOPE YOU'RE EXCITED TOO!
HAVE A GOOD DAY!
ON JUNE 10TH...
...MONA-CHAN AND I WILL TURN 15.
HOW MANY MORE BIRTHDAYS...
...WILL WE BE ABLE TO CELEBRATE TOGETHER...?
SHOOT, IS MONA GONE ALREADY?
OH, SHINOBU-CHAN.
WHERE'S YOUR CAR?
IT'S NICE TO WALK ONCE IN A WHILE.
CARE TO WALK ME TO THE STATION?
OF COURSE I WILL!
RINA...
I WANTED TO ASK YOU SOMETHING.
OH?

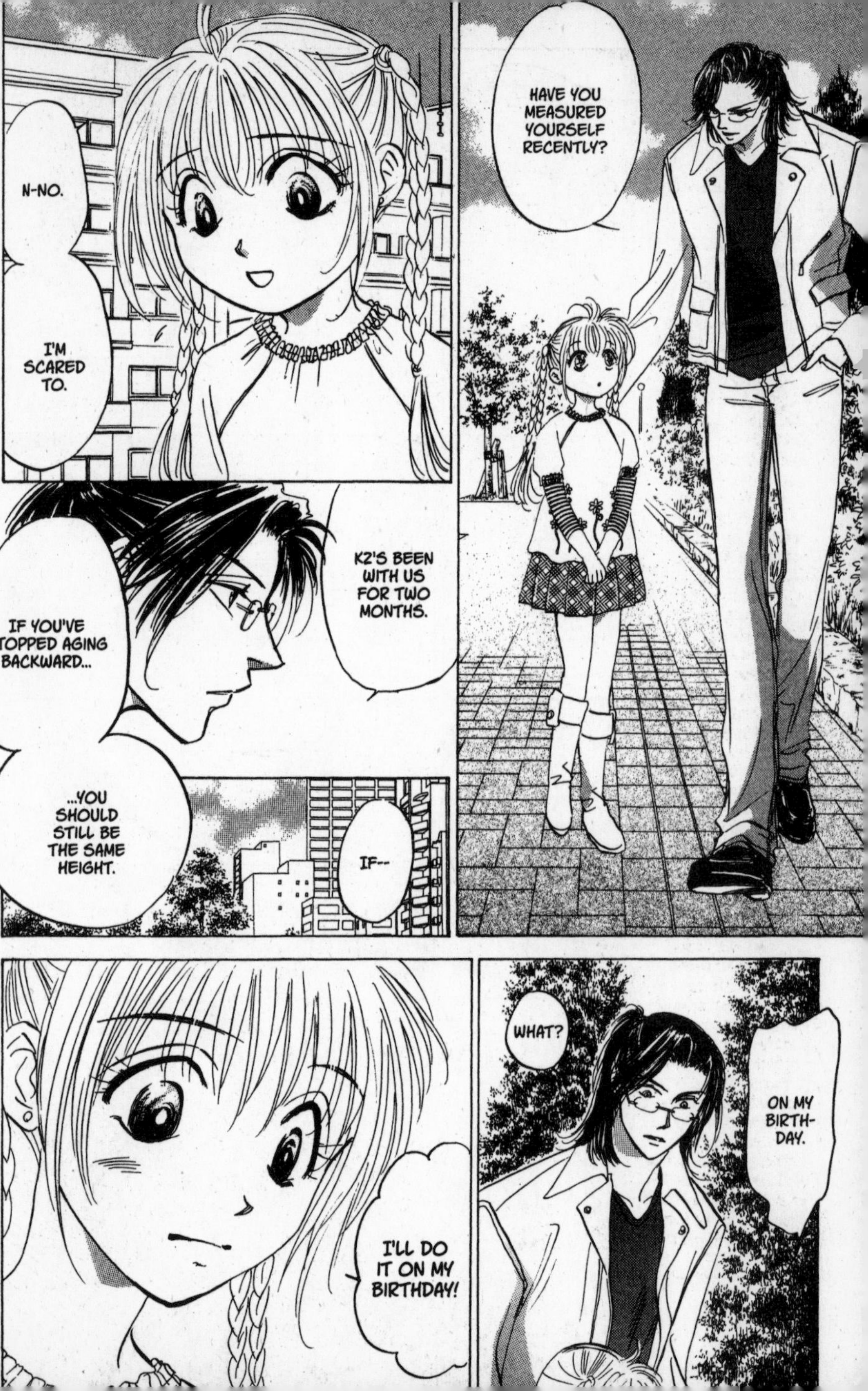
HAVE YOU MEASURED YOURSELF RECENTLY?
N-NO.
I'M SCARED TO.
KZ'S BEEN WITH US FOR TWO MONTHS.
IF YOU'VE STOPPED AGING BACKWARD...
...YOU SHOULD STILL BE THE SAME HEIGHT.
IF--
WHAT?
ON MY BIRTH-DAY.
I'LL DO IT ON MY BIRTHDAY!

FREE TALK
<1>

We've reached volume 4!

Right now it's the middle of July. This volume is scheduled to come out in September, so I'm busy making revisions and corrections. It got hot in June this year, so we've already had two full months of summer and there are still two hot months to go! Ugh...I'm making corrections despite the heat.

I'm also working on another job. I'm revising *OZ*, a project I worked on fourteen years ago. The book is scheduled for release in September, but starting two months after that (in November), the complete edition of *OZ* will be published every month for five months. Please take a look!

It's a fourteen-year-old story, so the drawings look different. I'm mostly working on the backgrounds--adding tone work, things like that. I had to write new chapters to meet the required page count. Since it's called the "Complete Edition" (published in Melody), I've worked hard to make it as complete as possible.

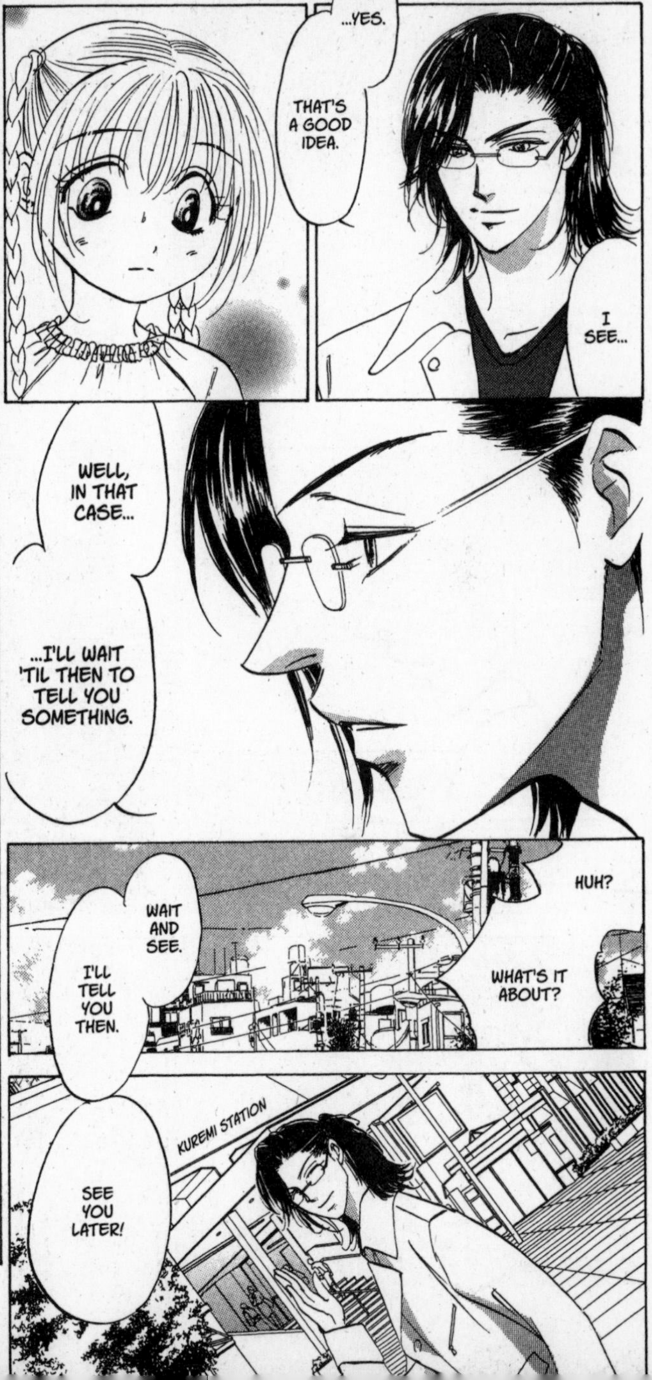
...YES.
THAT'S A GOOD IDEA.
I SEE...
WELL, IN THAT CASE...
...I'LL WAIT 'TIL THEN TO TELL YOU SOMETHING.
HUH?
WHAT'S IT ABOUT?
WAIT AND SEE.
I'LL TELL YOU THEN.
KUREMI STATION
SEE YOU LATER!

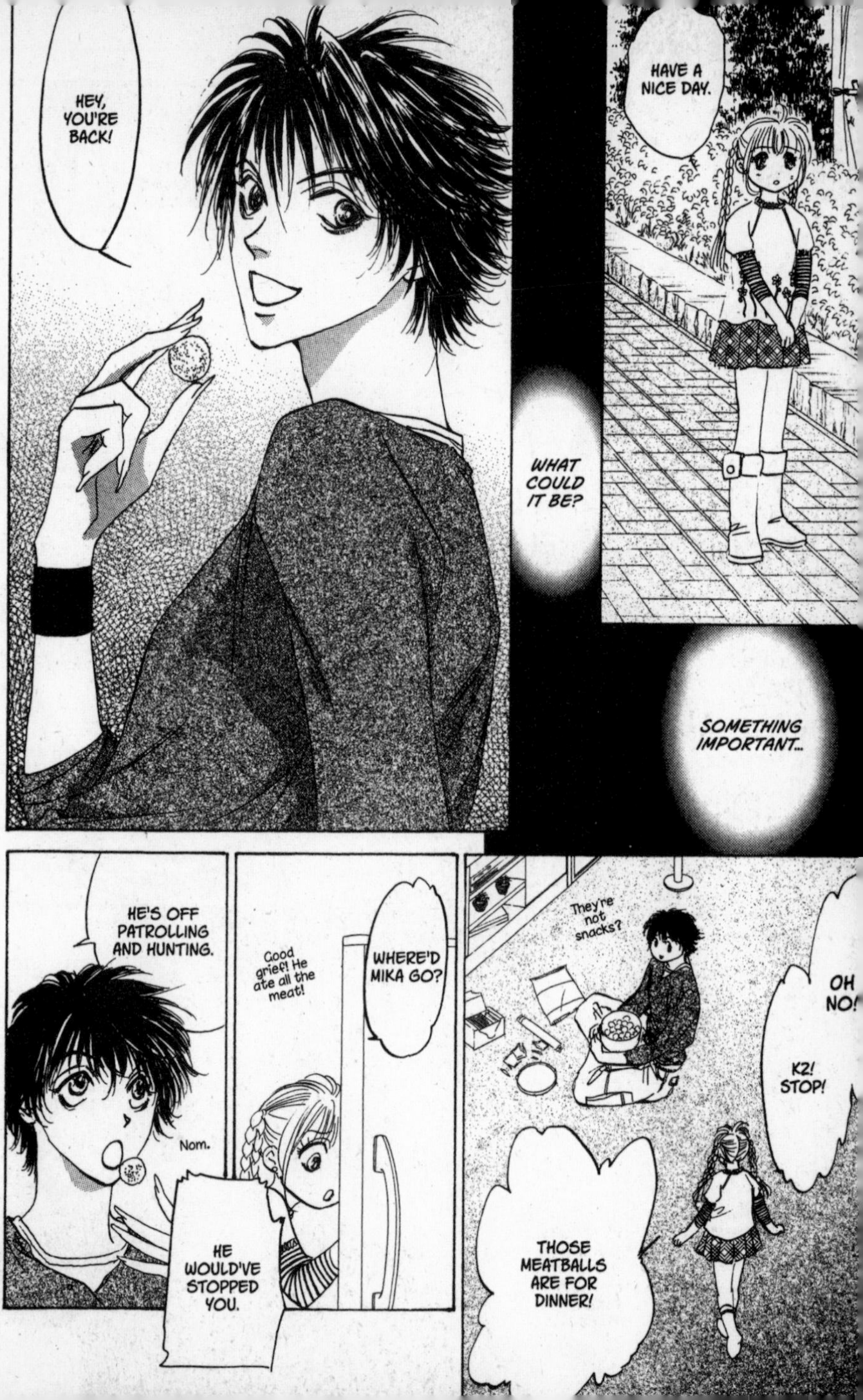

HAVE A NICE DAY.
WHAT COULD IT BE?
SOMETHING IMPORTANT...
HEY, YOU'RE BACK!
OH NO!
KZ! STOP!
They're not snacks?
THOSE MEATBALLS ARE FOR DINNER!
WHERE'D MIKA GO?
Good grief! He ate all the meat!
HE WOULD'VE STOPPED YOU.
HE'S OFF PATROLLING AND HUNTING.
Nom.

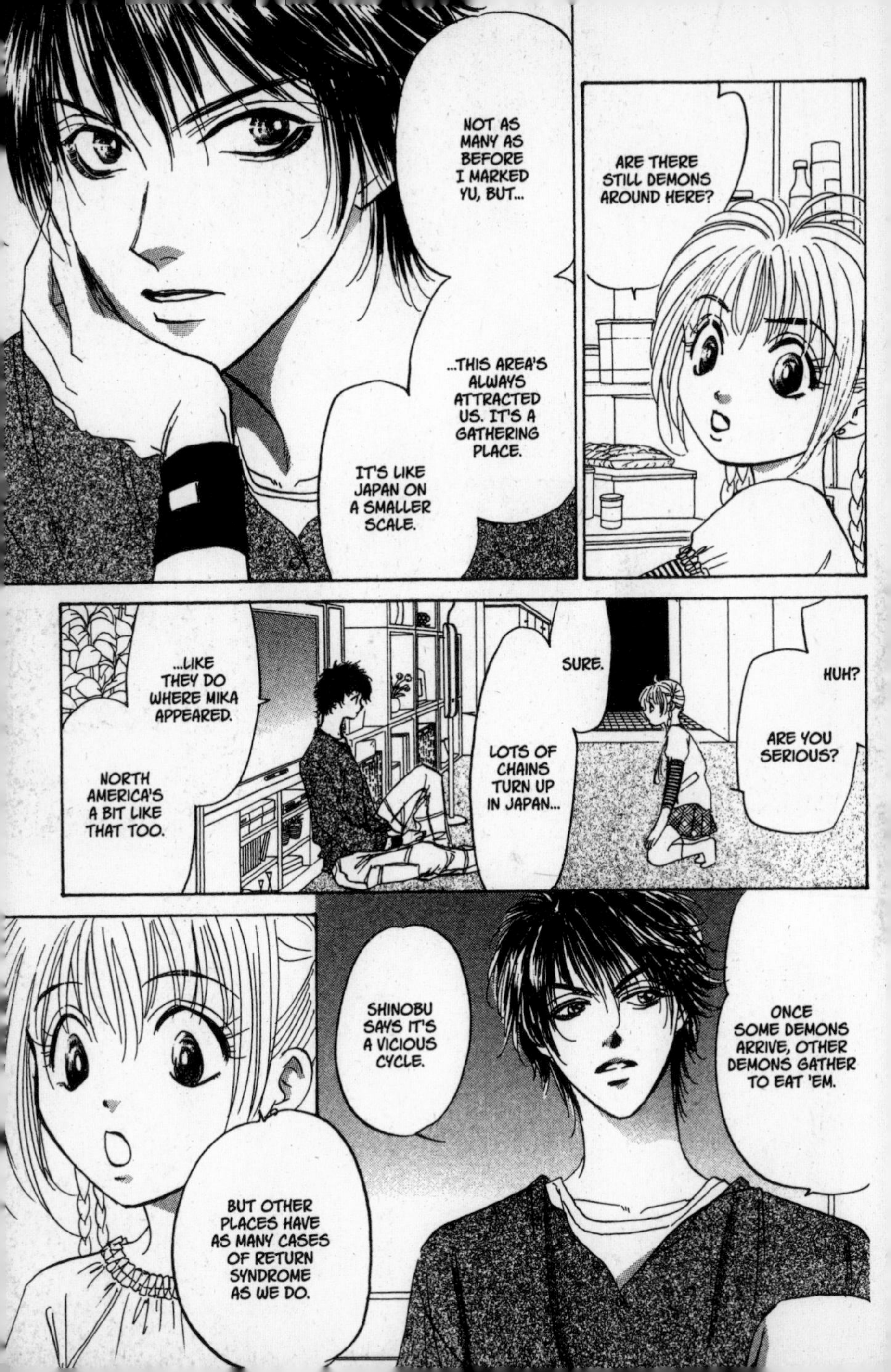
ARE THERE STILL DEMONS AROUND HERE?
NOT AS MANY AS BEFORE I MARKED YU, BUT...
...THIS AREA'S ALWAYS ATTRACTED US. IT'S A GATHERING PLACE.
IT'S LIKE JAPAN ON A SMALLER SCALE.
HUH?
ARE YOU SERIOUS?
SURE.
LOTS OF CHAINS TURN UP IN JAPAN...
...LIKE THEY DO WHERE MIKA APPEARED.
NORTH AMERICA'S A BIT LIKE THAT TOO.
ONCE SOME DEMONS ARRIVE, OTHER DEMONS GATHER TO EAT 'EM.
SHINOBU SAYS IT'S A VICIOUS CYCLE.
BUT OTHER PLACES HAVE AS MANY CASES OF RETURN SYNDROME AS WE DO.

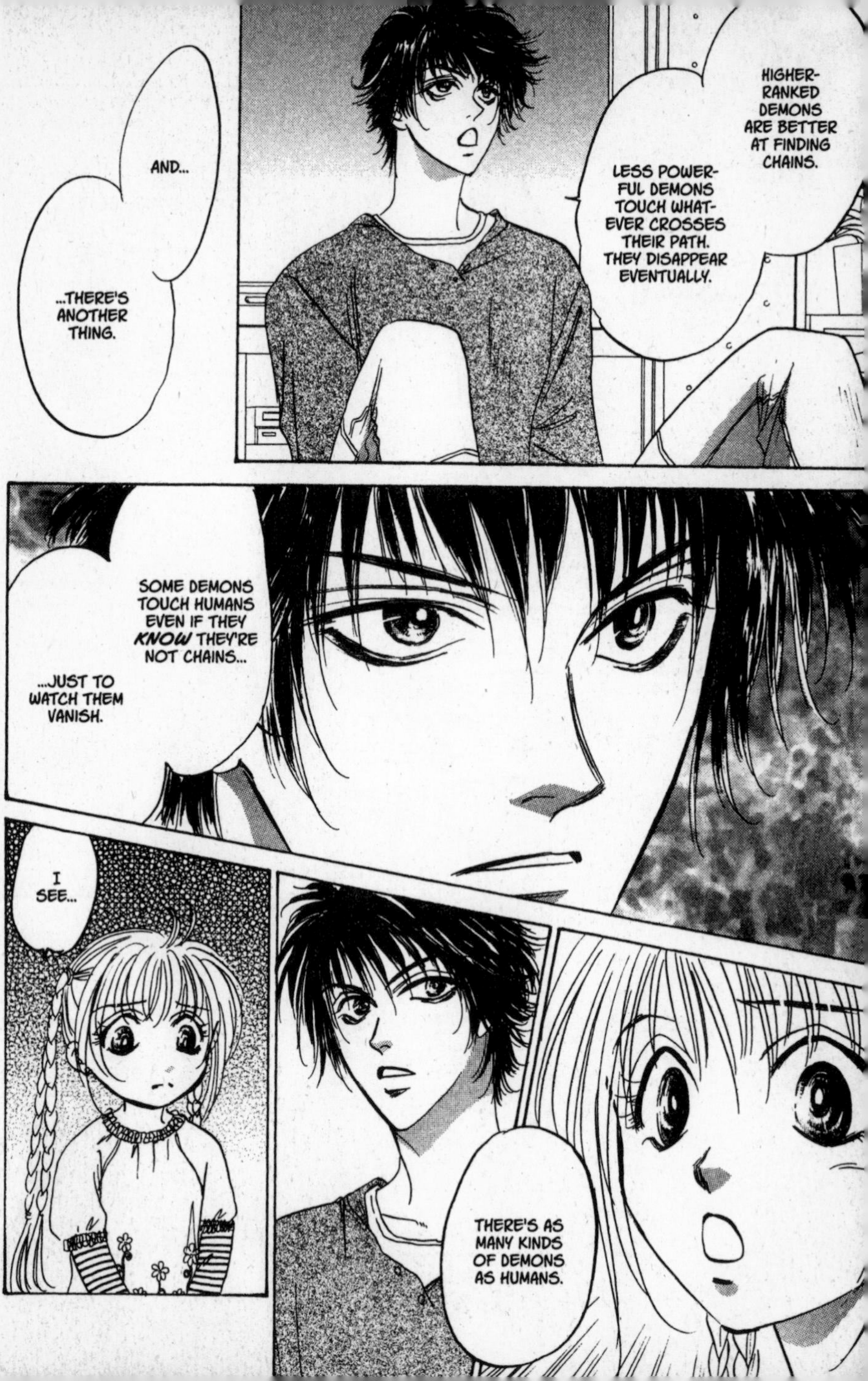
HIGHER-RANKED DEMONS ARE BETTER AT FINDING CHAINS.
LESS POWERFUL DEMONS TOUCH WHATEVER CROSSES THEIR PATH. THEY DISAPPEAR EVENTUALLY.
AND...
...THERE'S ANOTHER THING.
SOME DEMONS TOUCH HUMANS EVEN IF THEY *KNOW* THEY'RE NOT CHAINS...
...JUST TO WATCH THEM VANISH.
THERE'S AS MANY KINDS OF DEMONS AS HUMANS.
I SEE...

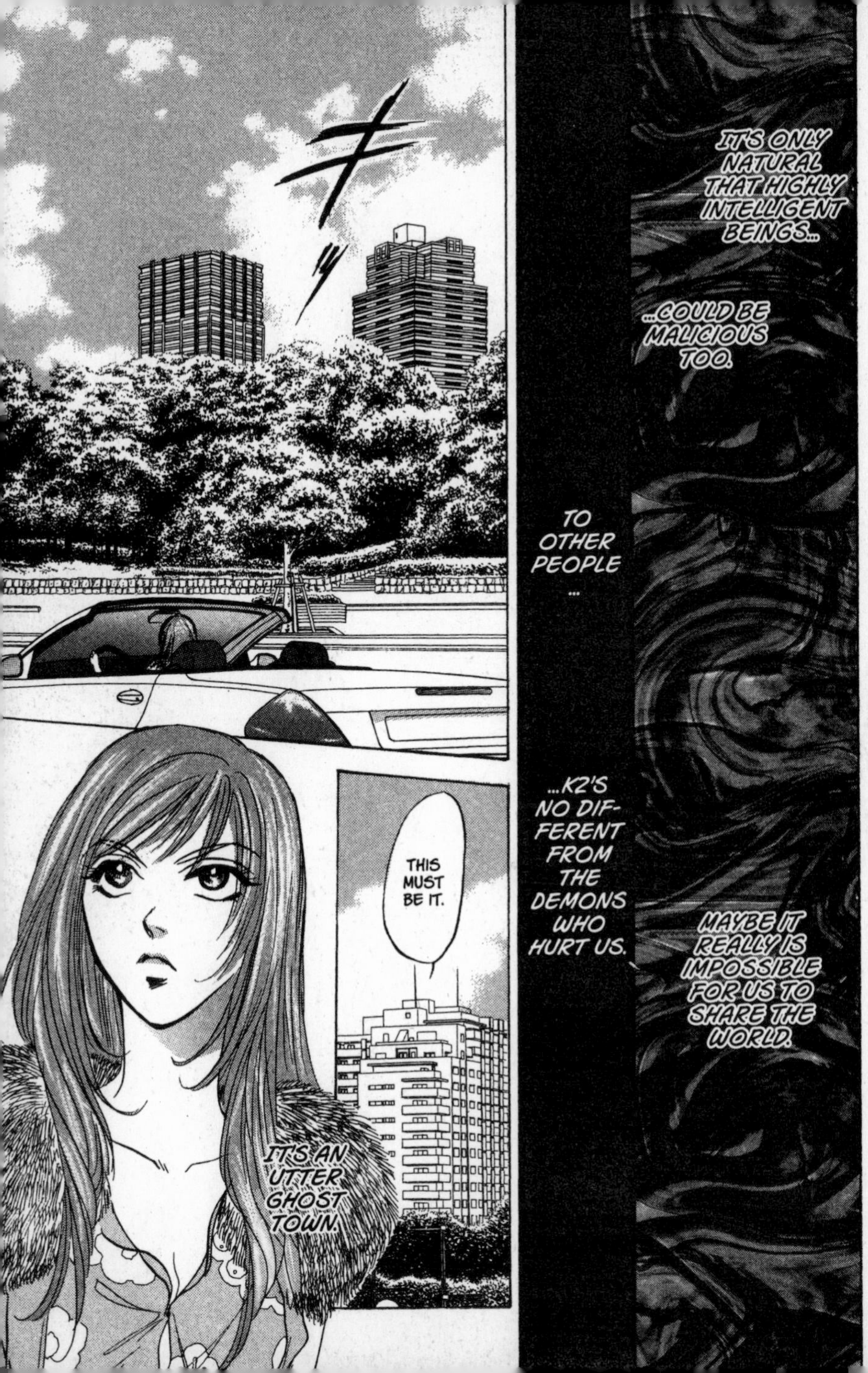
IT'S ONLY NATURAL THAT HIGHLY INTELLIGENT BEINGS...
...COULD BE MALICIOUS TOO.
TO OTHER PEOPLE...
...K2'S NO DIFFERENT FROM THE DEMONS WHO HURT US.
MAYBE IT REALLY IS IMPOSSIBLE FOR US TO SHARE THE WORLD.
THIS MUST BE IT.
IT'S AN UTTER GHOST TOWN.

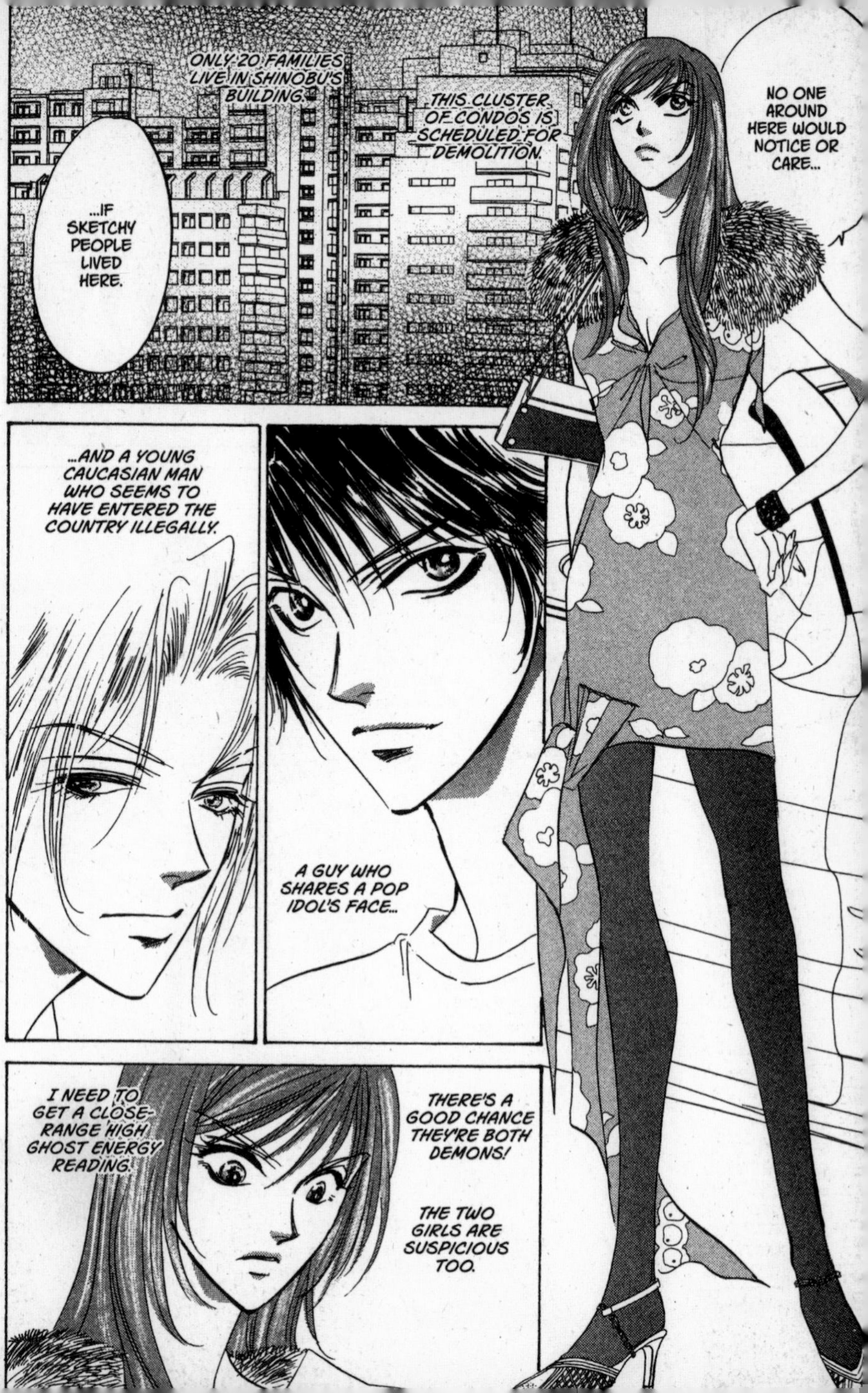
NO ONE AROUND HERE WOULD NOTICE OR CARE...
THIS CLUSTER OF CONDOS IS SCHEDULED FOR DEMOLITION.
ONLY 20 FAMILIES LIVE IN SHINOBU'S BUILDING.
...IF SKETCHY PEOPLE LIVED HERE.
A GUY WHO SHARES A POP IDOL'S FACE...
...AND A YOUNG CAUCASIAN MAN WHO SEEMS TO HAVE ENTERED THE COUNTRY ILLEGALLY.
THERE'S A GOOD CHANCE THEY'RE BOTH DEMONS!
THE TWO GIRLS ARE SUSPICIOUS TOO.
I NEED TO GET A CLOSE-RANGE HIGH GHOST ENERGY READING.

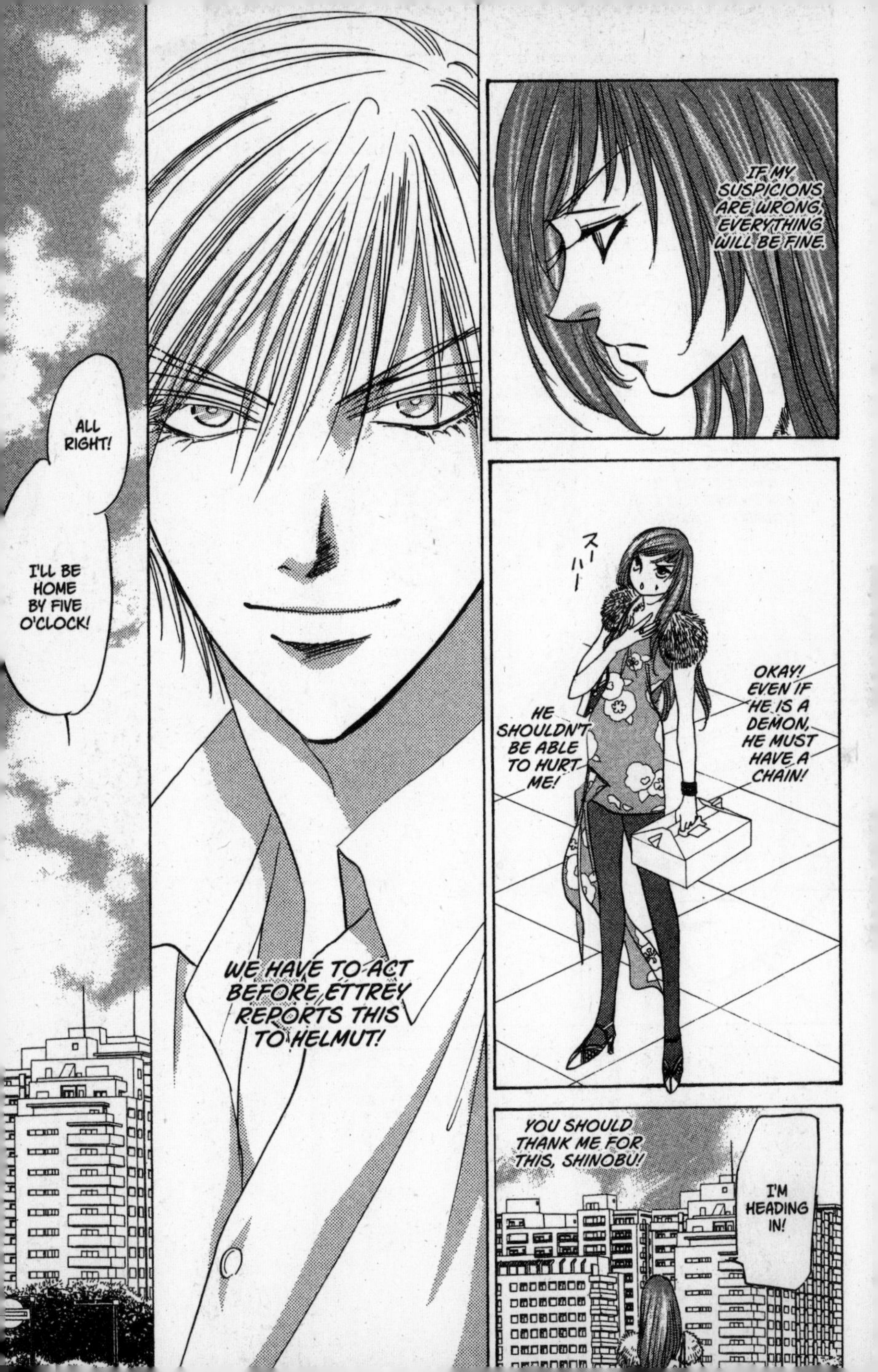
IF MY SUSPICIONS ARE WRONG, EVERYTHING WILL BE FINE.
スーハー
OKAY! EVEN IF HE IS A DEMON, HE MUST HAVE A CHAIN!
HE SHOULDN'T BE ABLE TO HURT ME!
I'M HEADING IN!
YOU SHOULD THANK ME FOR THIS, SHINOBU!
WE HAVE TO ACT BEFORE ETTREY REPORTS THIS TO HELMUT!
ALL RIGHT!
I'LL BE HOME BY FIVE O'CLOCK!

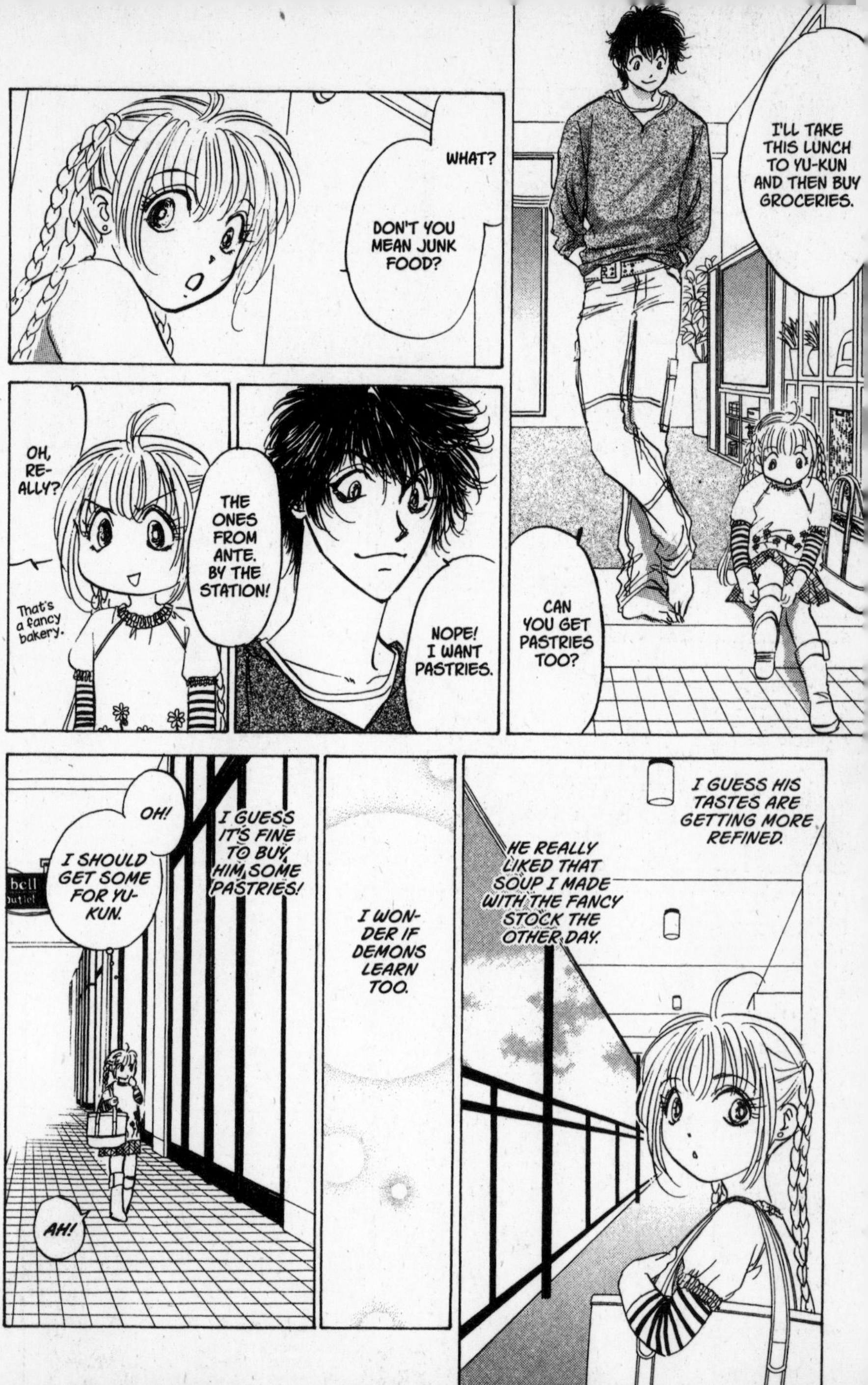
I'LL TAKE THIS LUNCH TO YU-KUN AND THEN BUY GROCERIES.
CAN YOU GET PASTRIES TOO?
WHAT?
DON'T YOU MEAN JUNK FOOD?
NOPE! I WANT PASTRIES.
THE ONES FROM ANTE. BY THE STATION!
OH, RE-ALLY?
That's a fancy bakery.
I GUESS HIS TASTES ARE GETTING MORE REFINED.
HE REALLY LIKED THAT SOUP I MADE WITH THE FANCY STOCK THE OTHER DAY.
I WONDER IF DEMONS LEARN TOO.
I GUESS IT'S FINE TO BUY HIM SOME PASTRIES!
OH!
I SHOULD GET SOME FOR YU-KUN.
bell
AH!

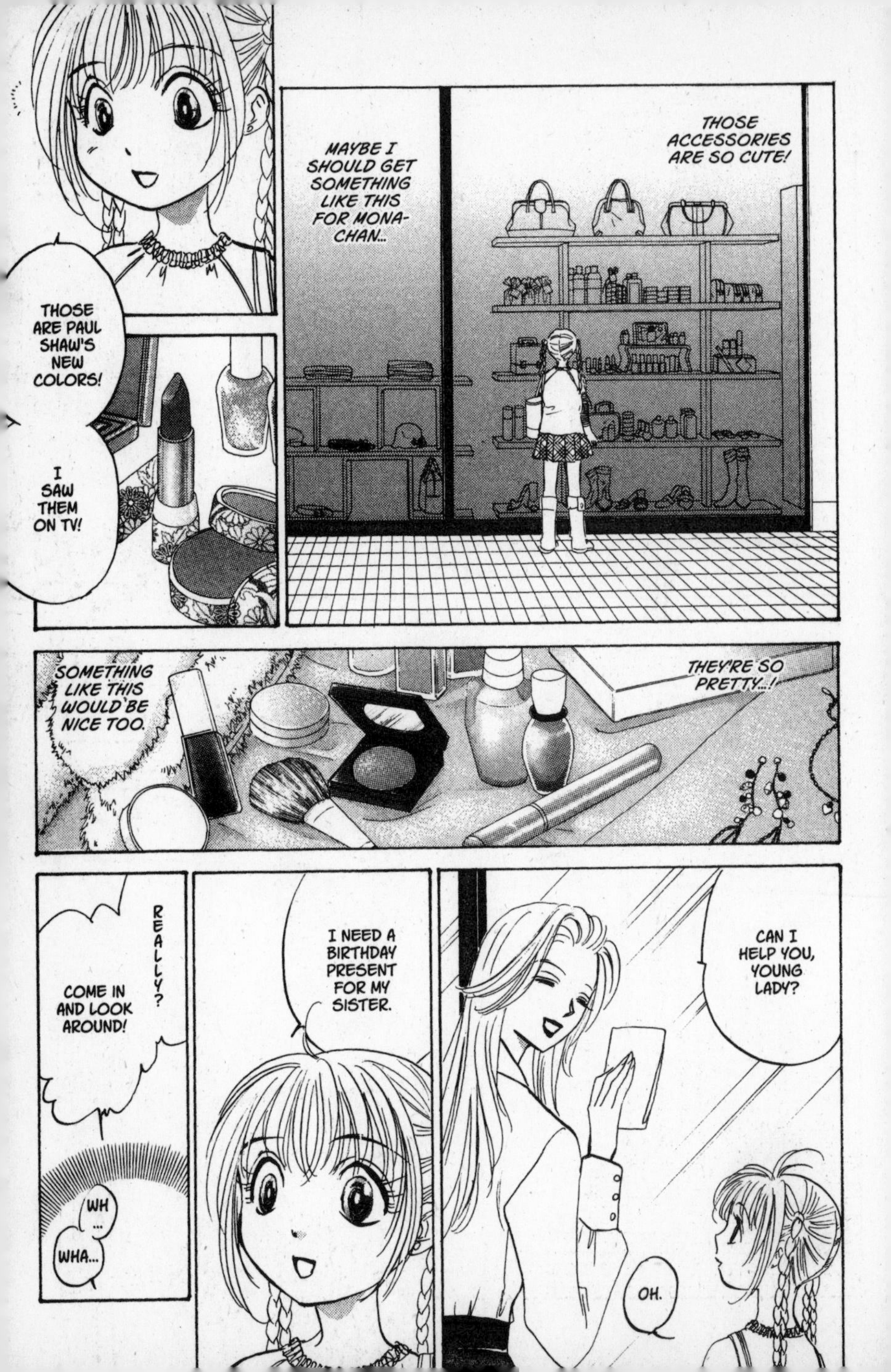
THOSE ACCESSORIES ARE SO CUTE!
MAYBE I SHOULD GET SOMETHING LIKE THIS FOR MONA-CHAN...
THOSE ARE PAUL SHAW'S NEW COLORS!
I SAW THEM ON TV!
THEY'RE SO PRETTY...!
SOMETHING LIKE THIS WOULD BE NICE TOO.
CAN I HELP YOU, YOUNG LADY?
OH.
I NEED A BIRTHDAY PRESENT FOR MY SISTER.
REALLY?
COME IN AND LOOK AROUND!
WH...
WHA...

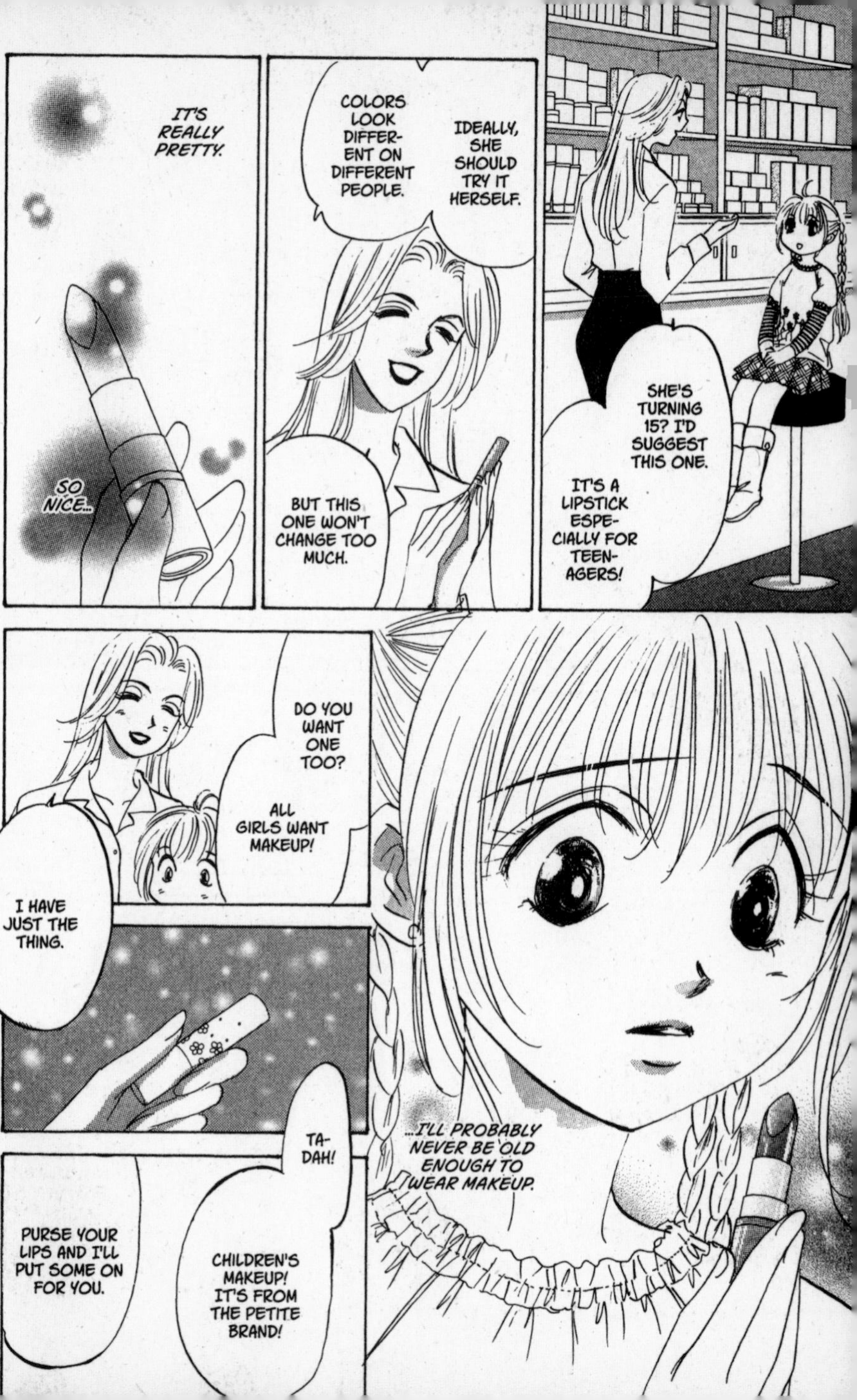

SHE'S TURNING 15? I'D SUGGEST THIS ONE.
IT'S A LIPSTICK ESPECIALLY FOR TEENAGERS!
IDEALLY, SHE SHOULD TRY IT HERSELF.
COLORS LOOK DIFFERENT ON DIFFERENT PEOPLE.
BUT THIS ONE WON'T CHANGE TOO MUCH.
IT'S REALLY PRETTY.
SO NICE...
...I'LL PROBABLY NEVER BE OLD ENOUGH TO WEAR MAKEUP.
DO YOU WANT ONE TOO?
ALL GIRLS WANT MAKEUP!
I HAVE JUST THE THING.
TA-DAH!
CHILDREN'S MAKEUP! IT'S FROM THE PETITE BRAND!
PURSE YOUR LIPS AND I'LL PUT SOME ON FOR YOU.

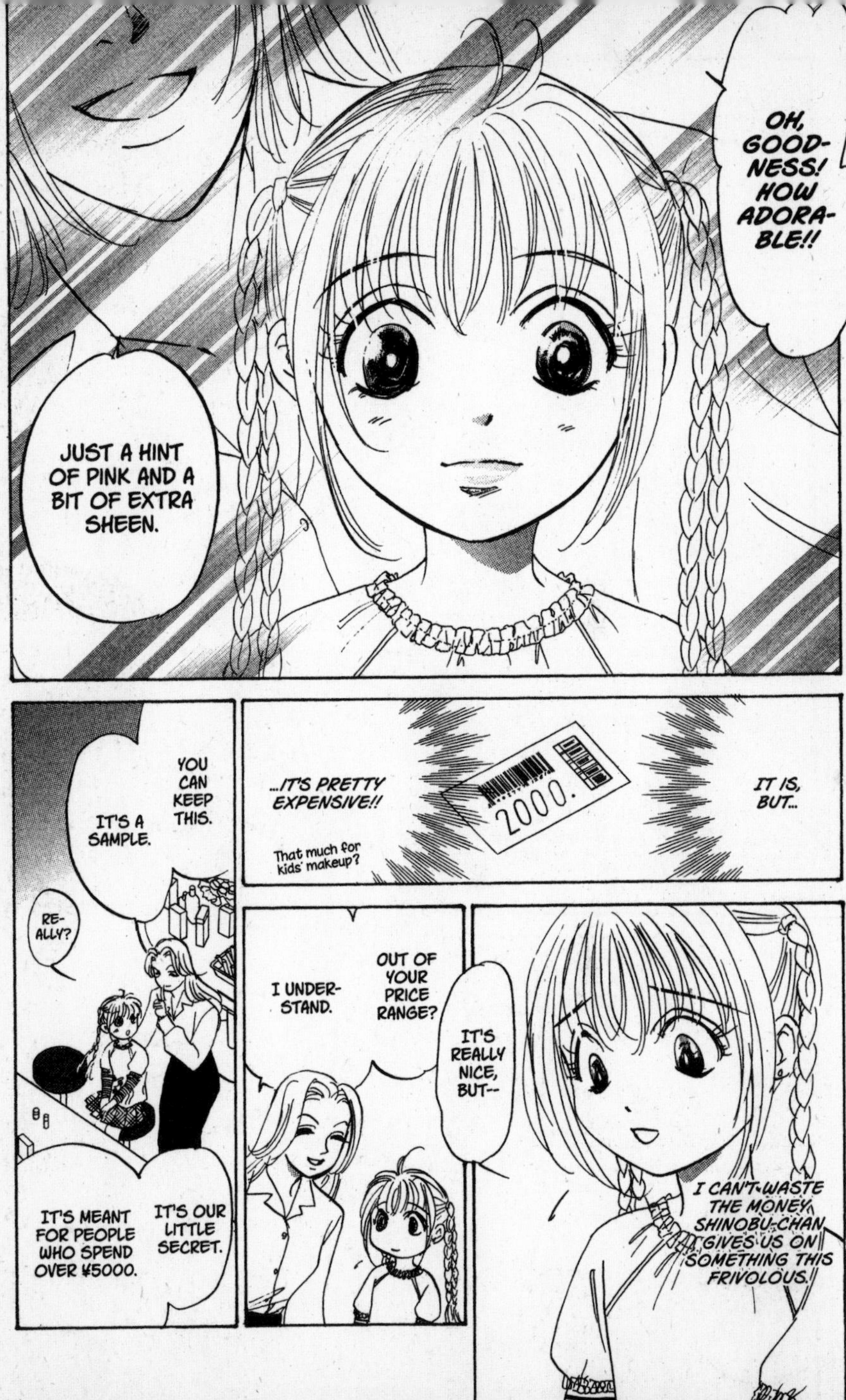
OH, GOODNESS! HOW ADORABLE!!
JUST A HINT OF PINK AND A BIT OF EXTRA SHEEN.
IT IS, BUT...
2000.
...IT'S PRETTY EXPENSIVE!!
That much for kids' makeup?
IT'S REALLY NICE, BUT--
I CAN'T WASTE THE MONEY SHINOBU-CHAN GIVES US ON SOMETHING THIS FRIVOLOUS.
OUT OF YOUR PRICE RANGE?
I UNDERSTAND.
YOU CAN KEEP THIS.
IT'S A SAMPLE.
REALLY?
IT'S OUR LITTLE SECRET.
IT'S MEANT FOR PEOPLE WHO SPEND OVER ¥5000.

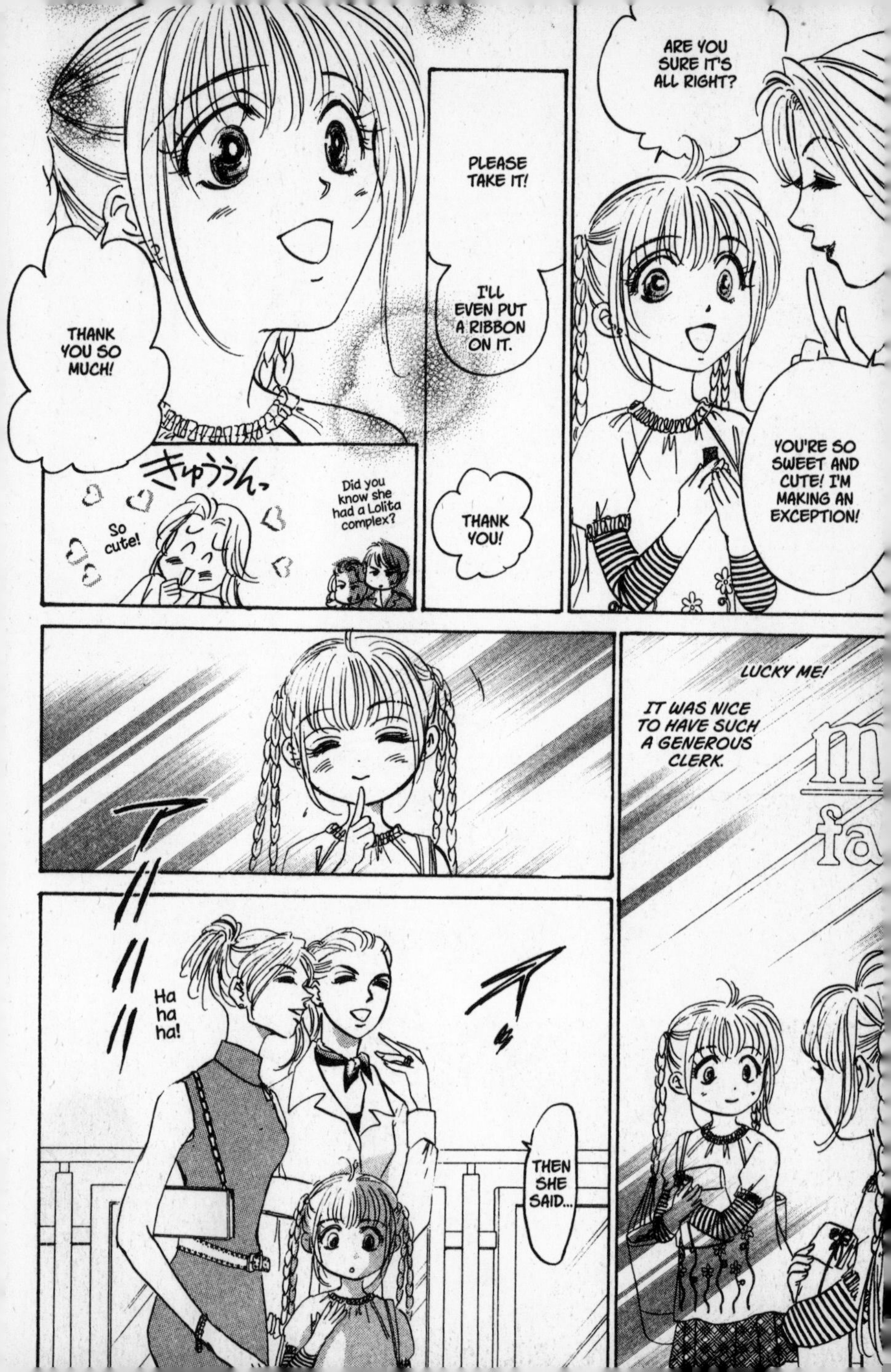
ARE YOU SURE IT'S ALL RIGHT?
YOU'RE SO SWEET AND CUTE! I'M MAKING AN EXCEPTION!
PLEASE TAKE IT!
I'LL EVEN PUT A RIBBON ON IT.
THANK YOU!
THANK YOU SO MUCH!
Did you know she had a Lolita complex?
きゅううん
So cute!
LUCKY ME!
IT WAS NICE TO HAVE SUCH A GENEROUS CLERK.
THEN SHE SAID...
Ha ha ha!

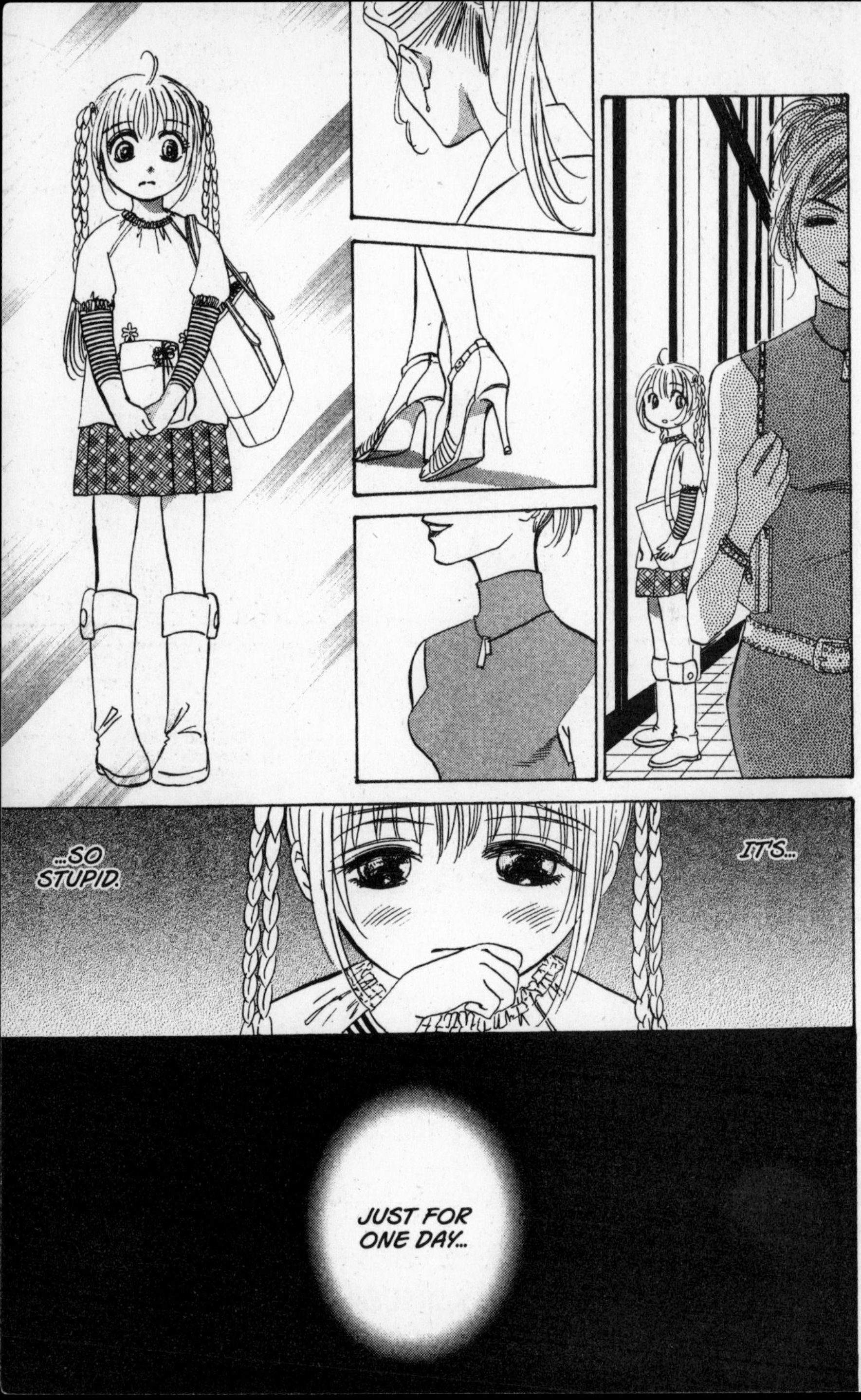
IT'S...
...SO STUPID.
JUST FOR ONE DAY...

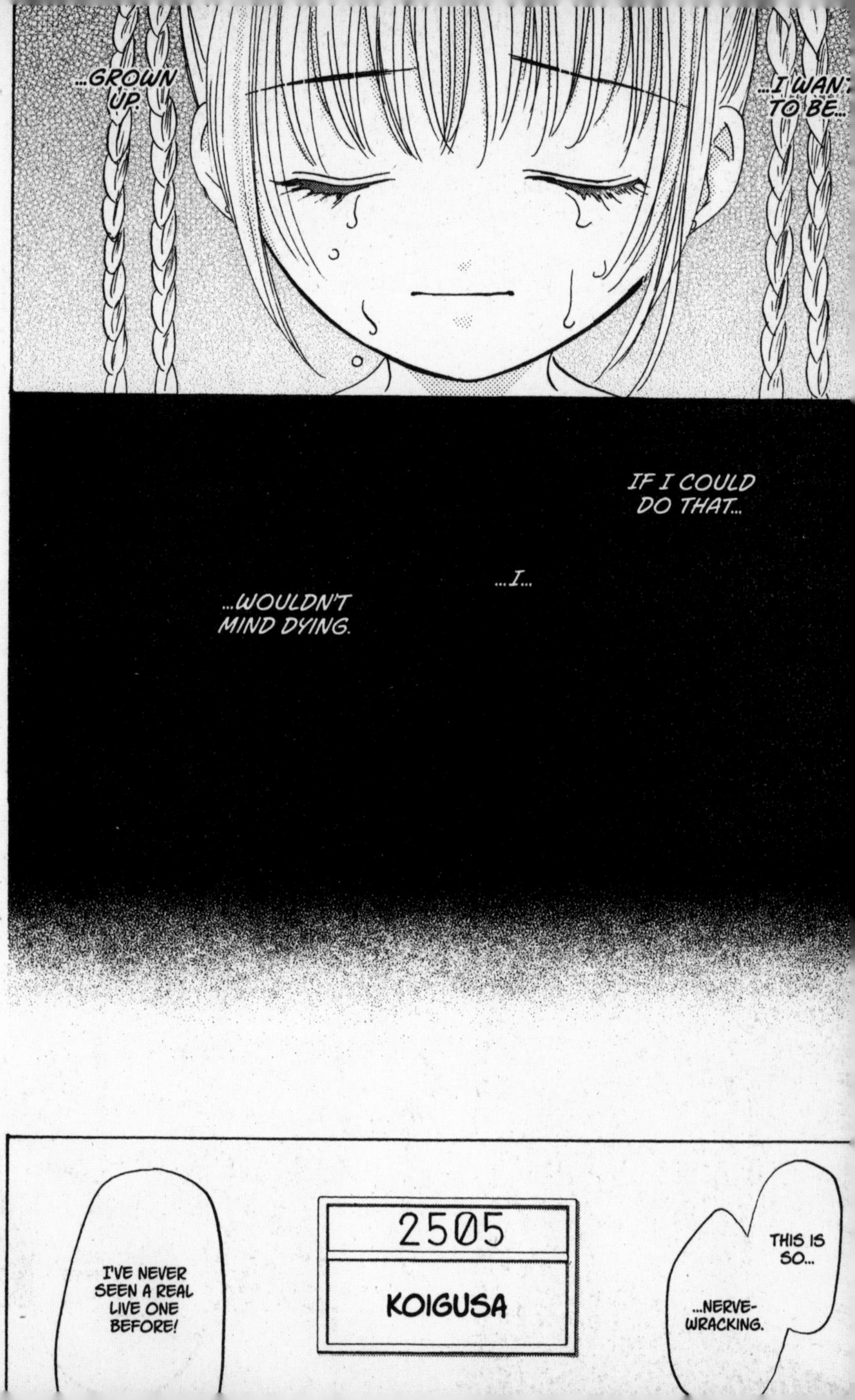

...I WAN
TO BE...
...GROWN UP.
IF I COULD DO THAT...
...I...
...WOULDN'T MIND DYING.
THIS IS SO...
...NERVE-WRACKING.
2505
KOIGUSA
I'VE NEVER SEEN A REAL LIVE ONE BEFORE!

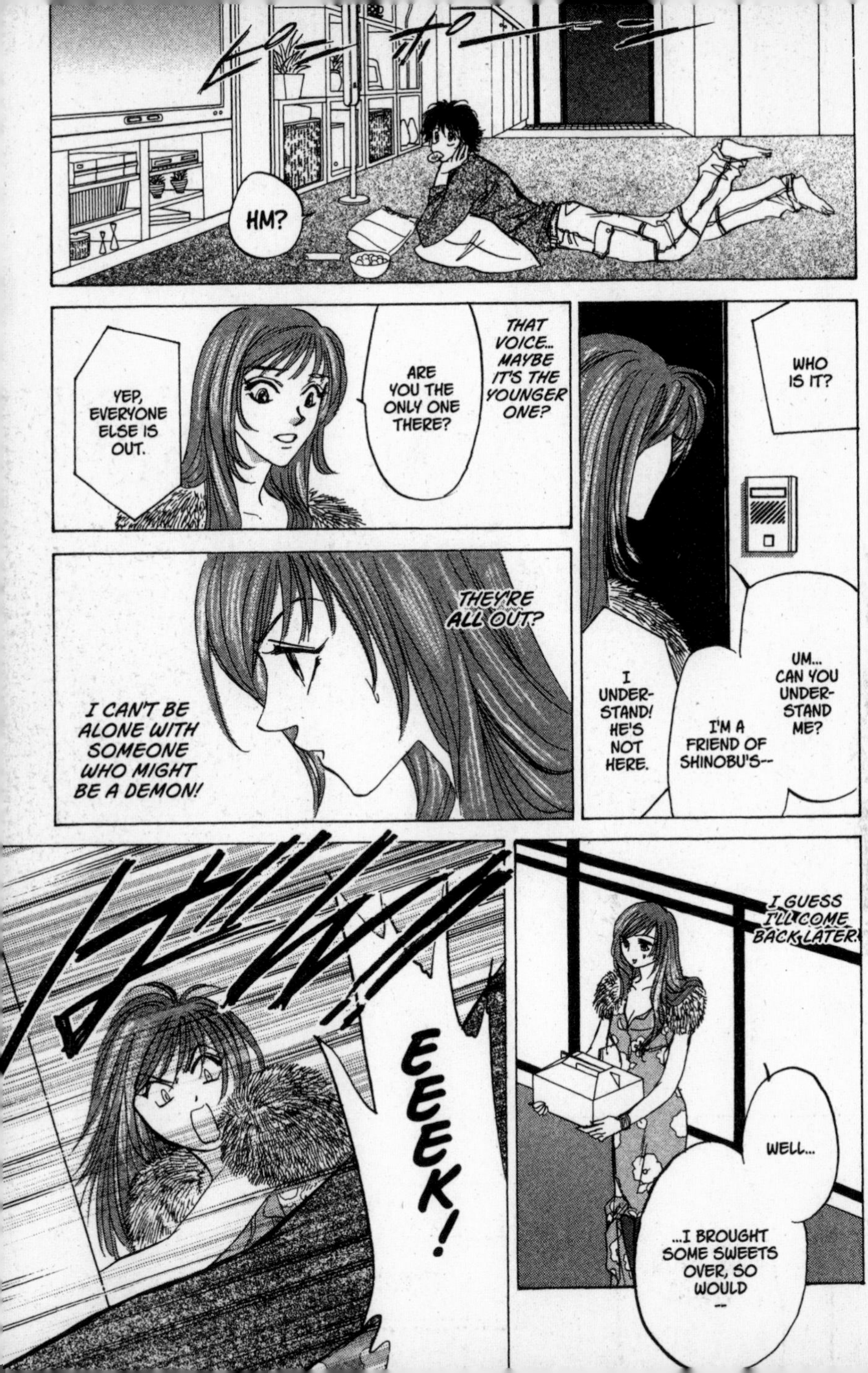
HM?
WHO IS IT?
UM... CAN YOU UNDERSTAND ME?
I'M A FRIEND OF SHINOBU'S--
I UNDERSTAND! HE'S NOT HERE.
THAT VOICE... MAYBE IT'S THE YOUNGER ONE?
ARE YOU THE ONLY ONE THERE?
YEP, EVERYONE ELSE IS OUT.
THEY'RE ALL OUT?
I CAN'T BE ALONE WITH SOMEONE WHO MIGHT BE A DEMON!
I GUESS I'LL COME BACK LATER!
WELL...
...I BROUGHT SOME SWEETS OVER, SO WOULD --
EEEEK!

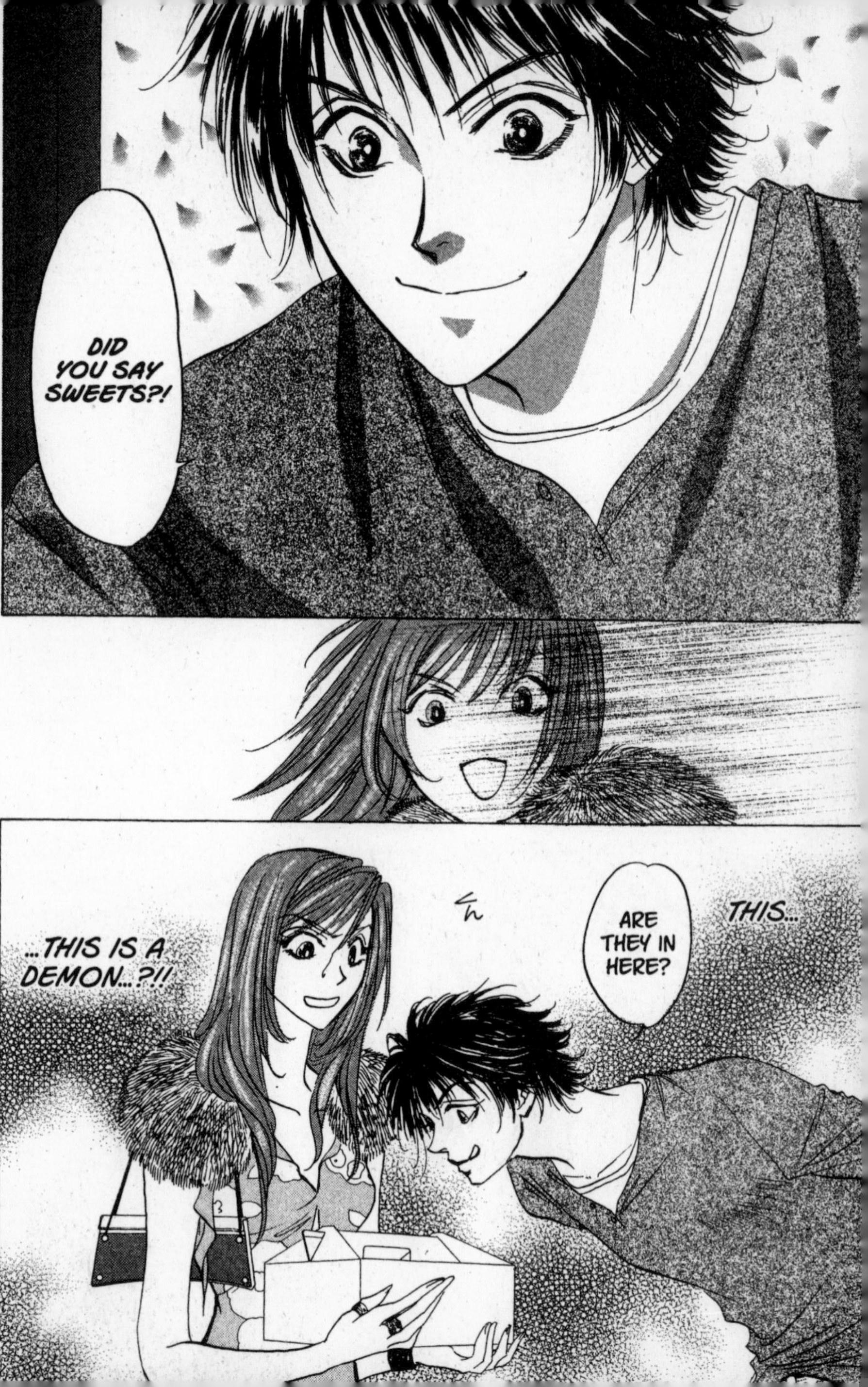
DID YOU SAY SWEETS?!
THIS...
ARE THEY IN HERE?
くん
...THIS IS A DEMON...?!!

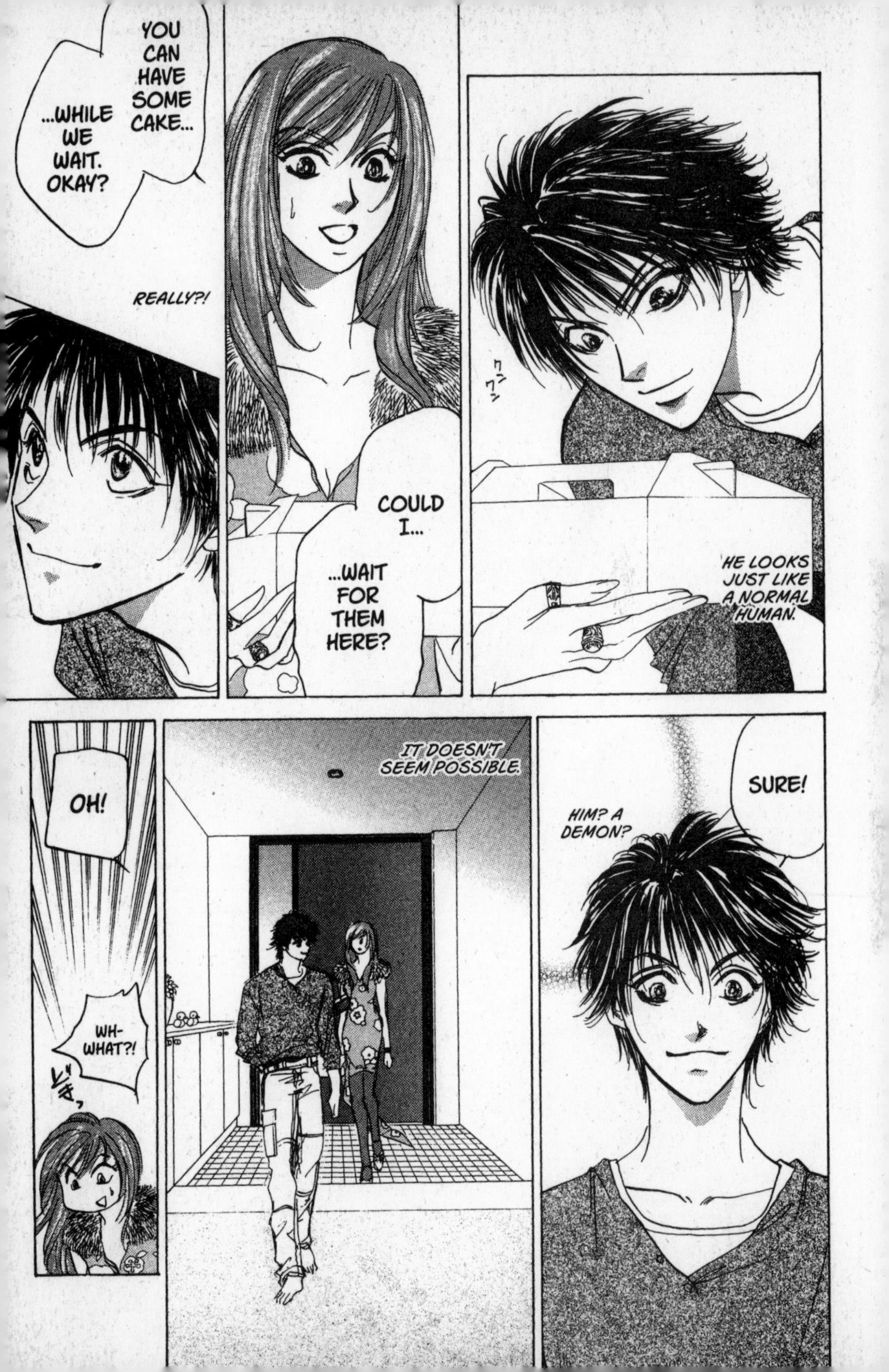
HE LOOKS JUST LIKE A NORMAL HUMAN.
COULD I...
...WAIT FOR THEM HERE?
YOU CAN HAVE SOME CAKE...
...WHILE WE WAIT. OKAY?
REALLY?!
SURE!
HIM? A DEMON?
IT DOESN'T SEEM POSSIBLE.
OH!
WH- WHAT?!

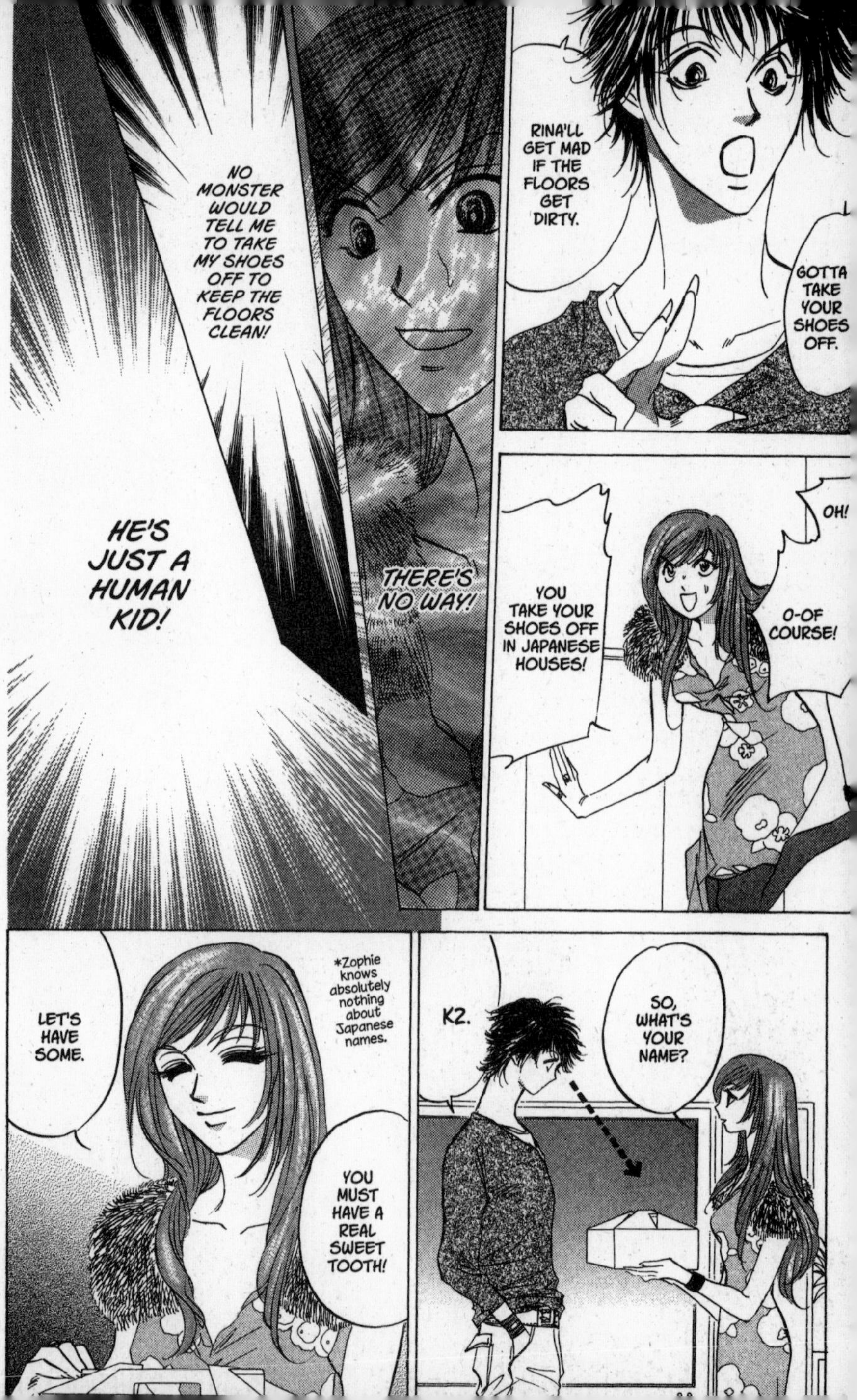
GOTTA TAKE YOUR SHOES OFF.
RINA'LL GET MAD IF THE FLOORS GET DIRTY.
OH!
O-OF COURSE!
YOU TAKE YOUR SHOES OFF IN JAPANESE HOUSES!
THERE'S NO WAY!
NO MONSTER WOULD TELL ME TO TAKE MY SHOES OFF TO KEEP THE FLOORS CLEAN!
HE'S JUST A HUMAN KID!
SO, WHAT'S YOUR NAME?
K2.
*Zophie knows absolutely nothing about Japanese names.
YOU MUST HAVE A REAL SWEET TOOTH!
LET'S HAVE SOME.

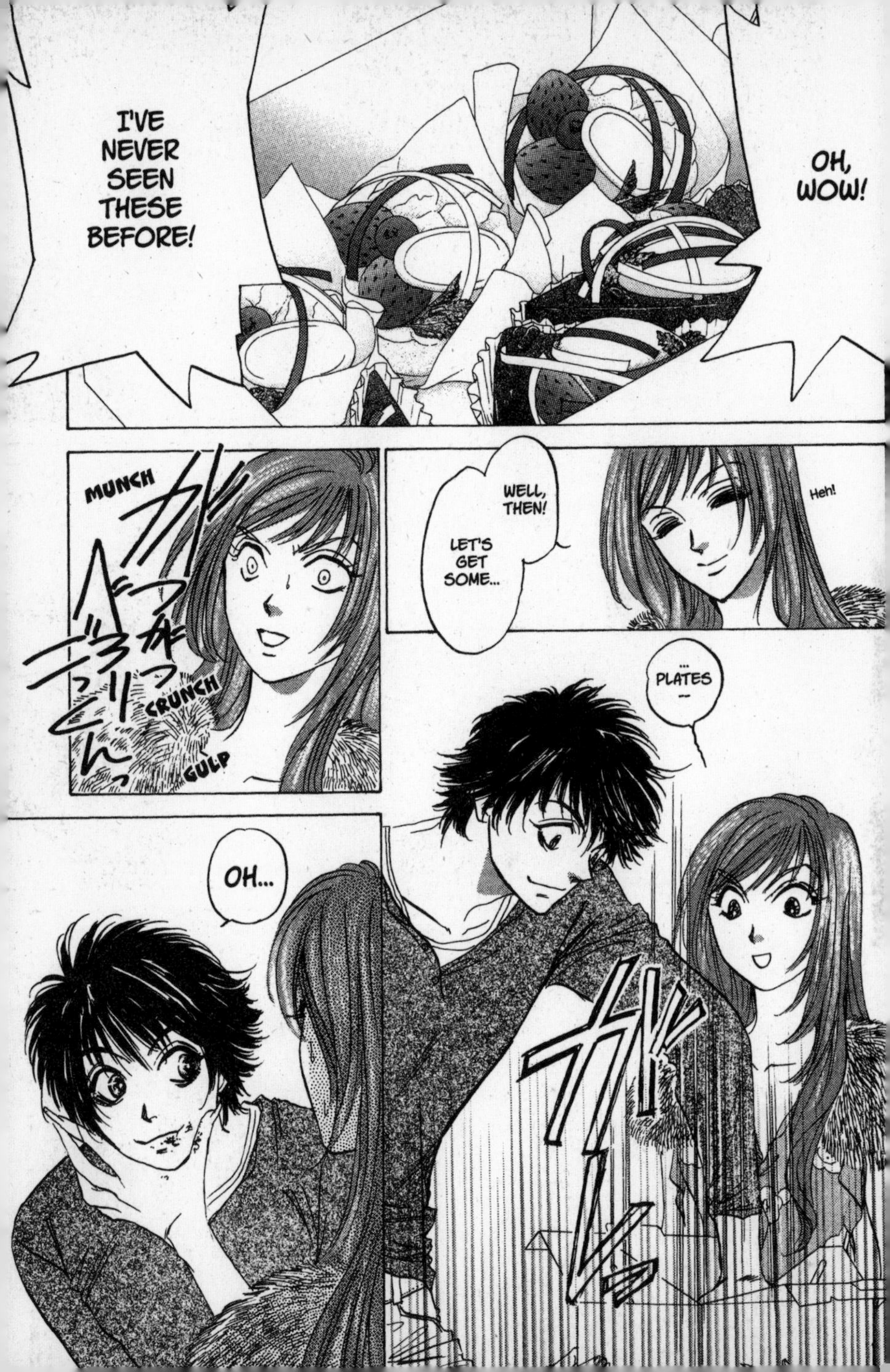
OH, WOW!
I'VE NEVER SEEN THESE BEFORE!
Heh!
WELL, THEN!
LET'S GET SOME...
MUNCH
CRUNCH
GULP
...PLATES—
OH...

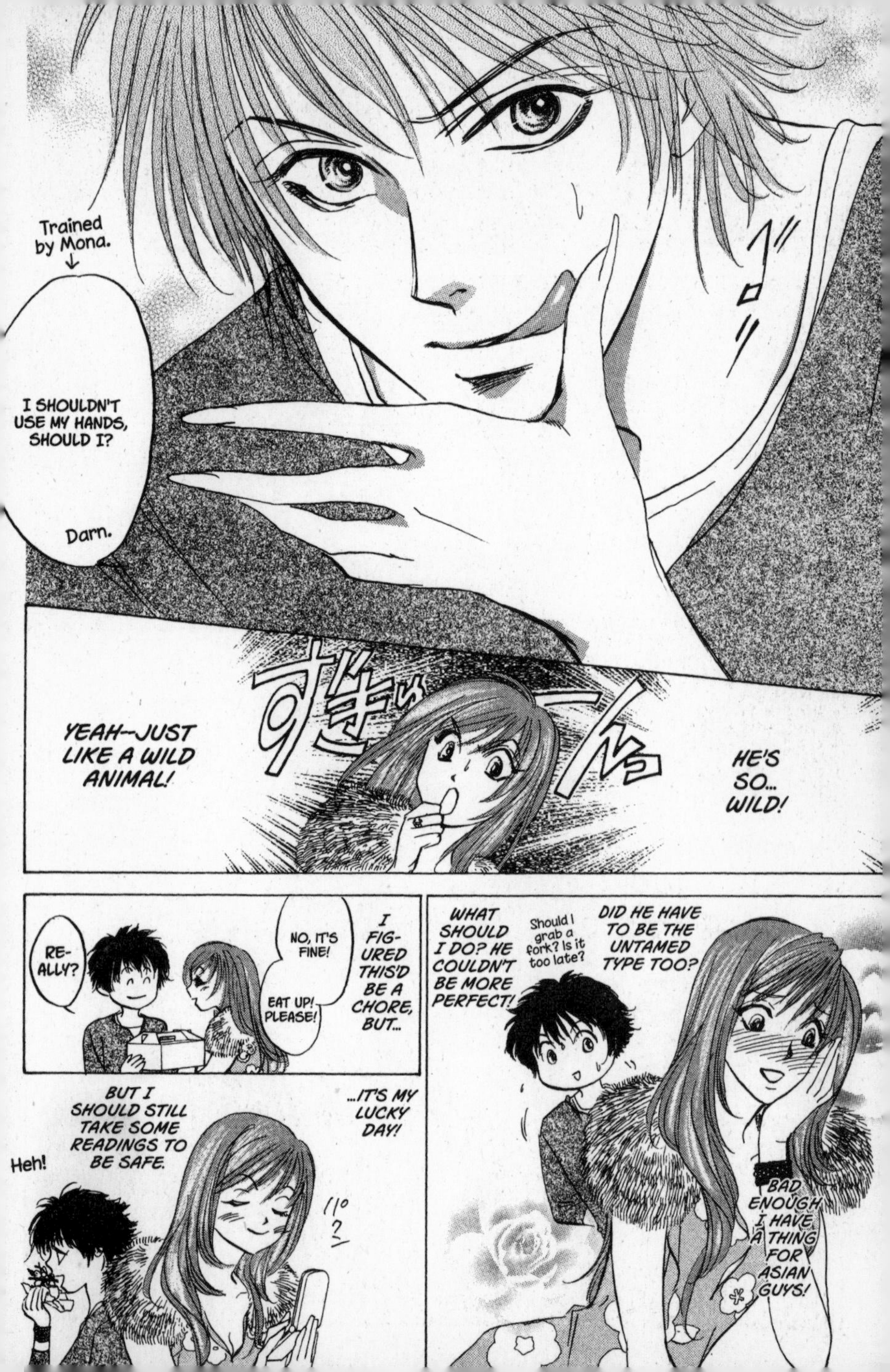
Trained by Mona. ↓
I SHOULDN'T USE MY HANDS, SHOULD I?
Darn.
HE'S SO... WILD!
YEAH--JUST LIKE A WILD ANIMAL!
DID HE HAVE TO BE THE UNTAMED TYPE TOO?
Should I grab a fork? Is it too late?
WHAT SHOULD I DO? HE COULDN'T BE MORE PERFECT!
BAD ENOUGH I HAVE A THING FOR ASIAN GUYS!
I FIG-URED THIS'D BE A CHORE, BUT...
NO, IT'S FINE!
EAT UP! PLEASE!
RE-ALLY?
...IT'S MY LUCKY DAY!
BUT I SHOULD STILL TAKE SOME READINGS TO BE SAFE.
Heh!

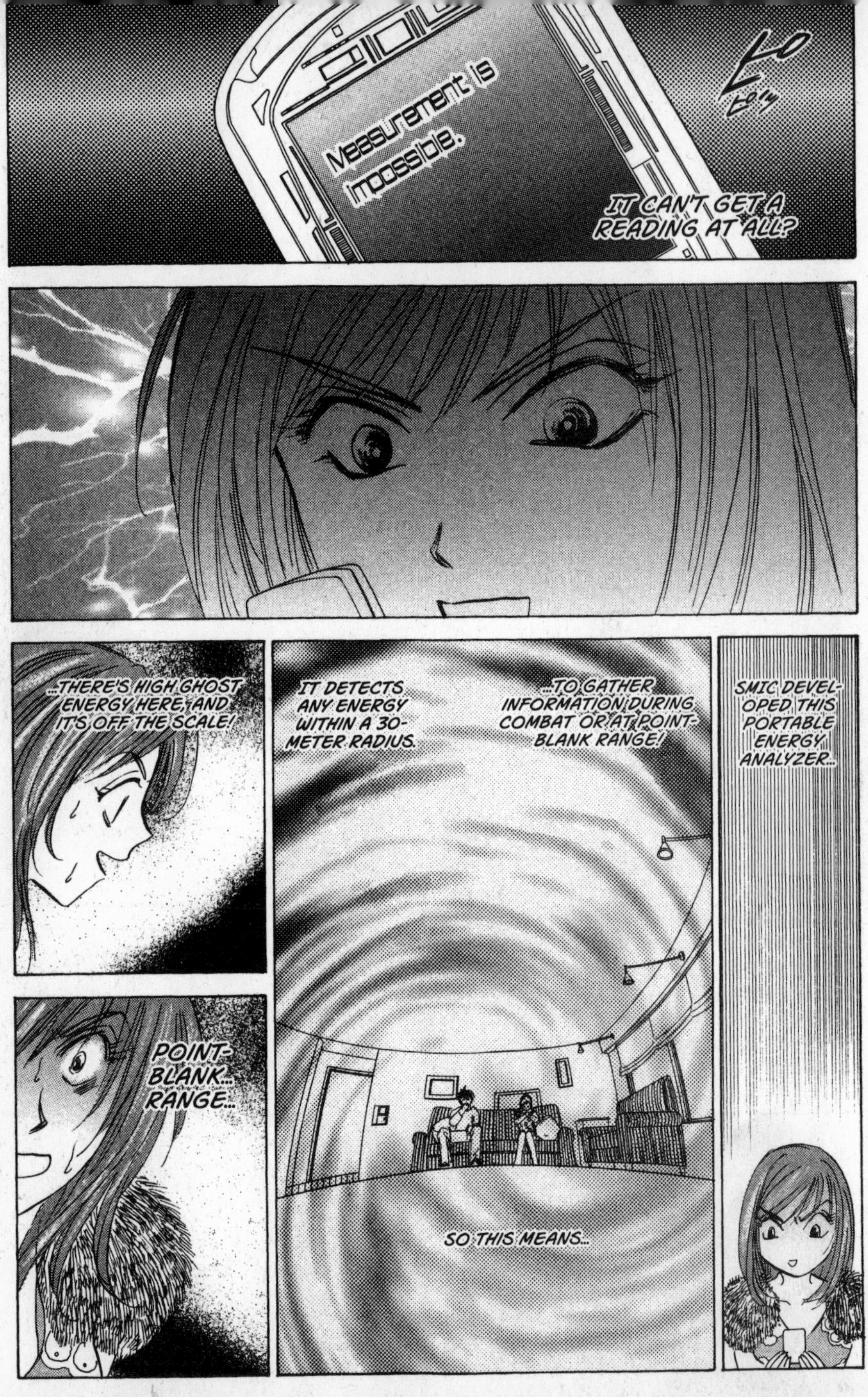
Measurement is impossible.
IT CAN'T GET A READING AT ALL?
SMIC DEVEL-OPED THIS PORTABLE ENERGY ANALYZER...
...TO GATHER INFORMATION DURING COMBAT OR AT POINT-BLANK RANGE!
IT DETECTS ANY ENERGY WITHIN A 30-METER RADIUS.
SO THIS MEANS...
...THERE'S HIGH GHOST ENERGY HERE, AND IT'S OFF THE SCALE!
POINT-BLANK... RANGE...

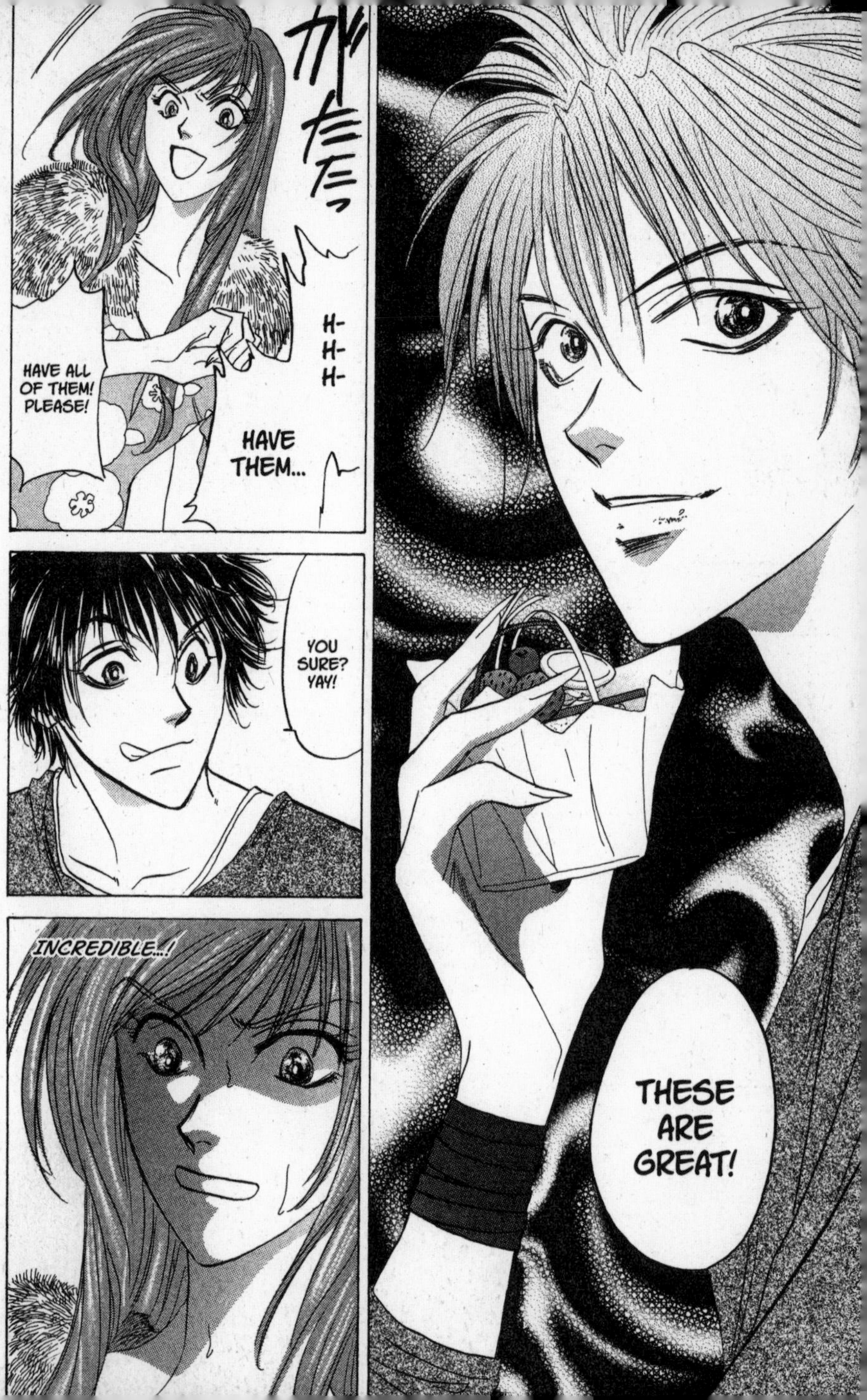
THESE ARE GREAT!
ガたたっ
H-H-H-
HAVE THEM...
HAVE ALL OF THEM! PLEASE!
YOU SURE? YAY!
INCREDIBLE...!

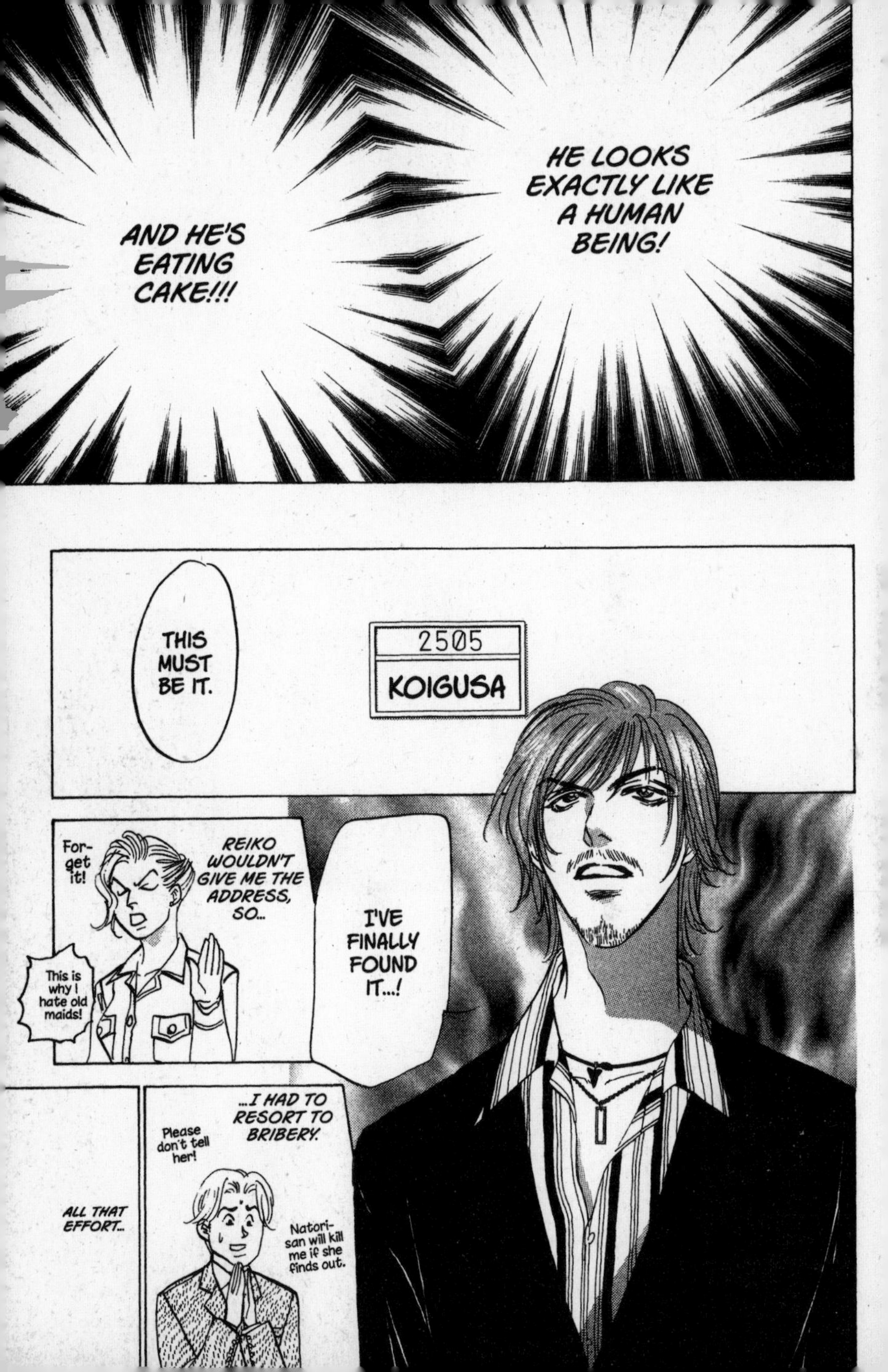
HE LOOKS EXACTLY LIKE A HUMAN BEING!
AND HE'S EATING CAKE!!!
2505
KOIGUSA
THIS MUST BE IT.
I'VE FINALLY FOUND IT...!
REIKO WOULDN'T GIVE ME THE ADDRESS, SO...
For-get it!
This is why I hate old maids!
...I HAD TO RESORT TO BRIBERY.
Please don't tell her!
Natori-san will kill me if she finds out.
ALL THAT EFFORT...

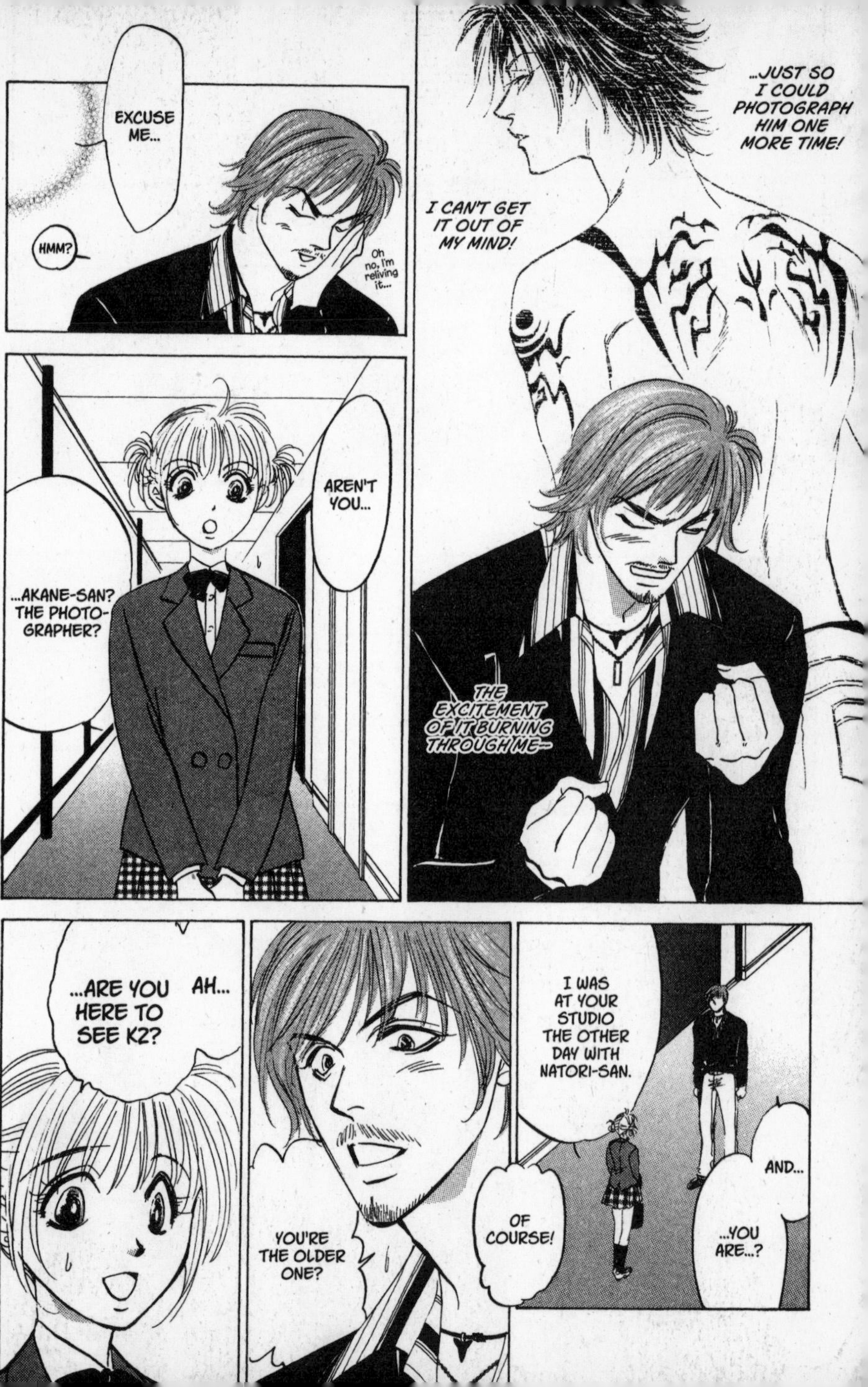
...JUST SO I COULD PHOTOGRAPH HIM ONE MORE TIME!
I CAN'T GET IT OUT OF MY MIND!
THE EXCITEMENT OF IT BURNING THROUGH ME—
EXCUSE ME...
Oh no, I'm reliving it...
HMM?
AREN'T YOU...
...AKANE-SAN? THE PHOTO-GRAPHER?
I WAS AT YOUR STUDIO THE OTHER DAY WITH NATORI-SAN.
AND...
...YOU ARE...?
OF COURSE!
YOU'RE THE OLDER ONE?
AH...
...ARE YOU HERE TO SEE K2?

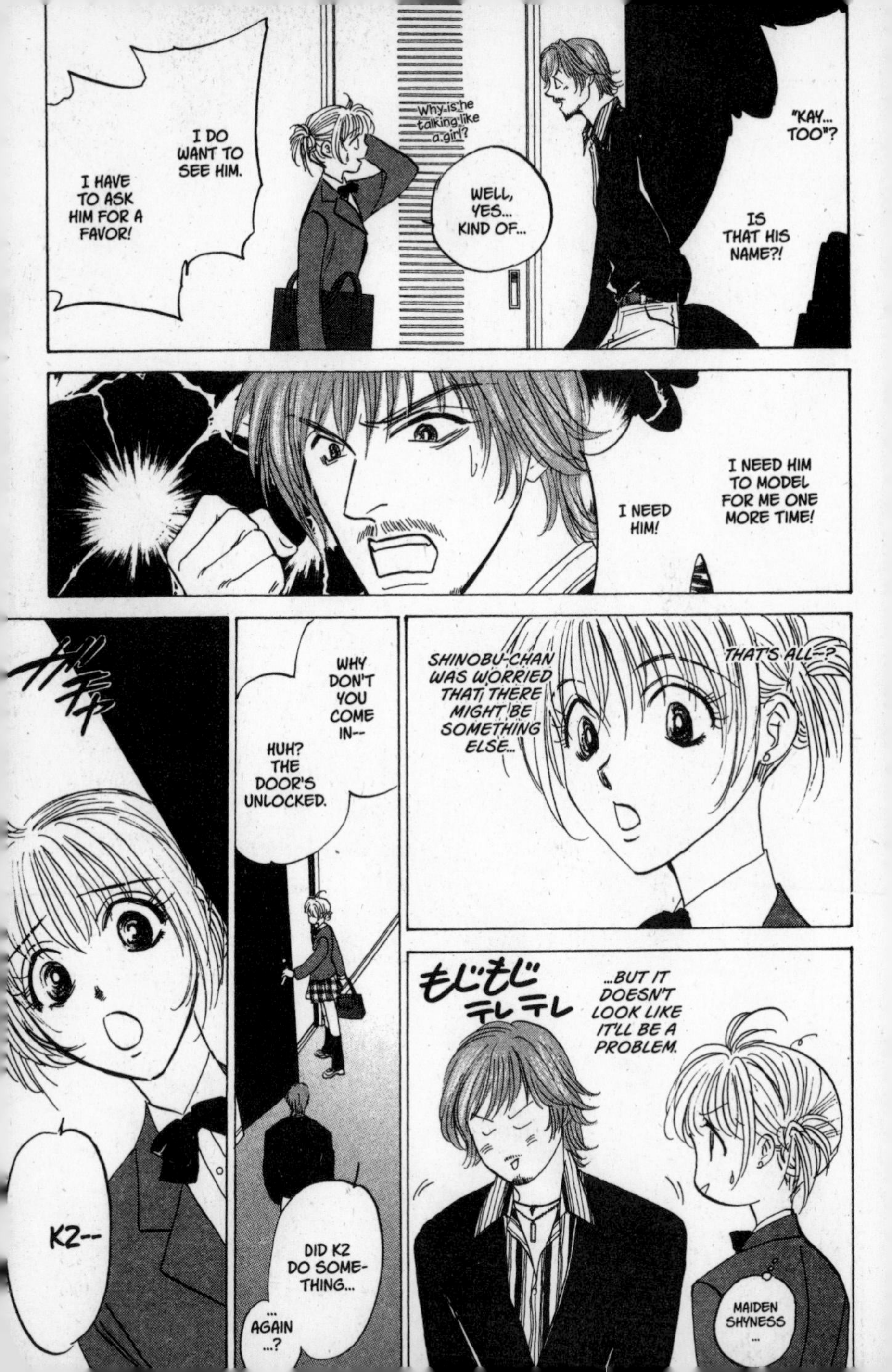
"KAY... TOO"?
Why is he talking like a girl?
IS THAT HIS NAME?!
WELL, YES... KIND OF...
I DO WANT TO SEE HIM.
I HAVE TO ASK HIM FOR A FAVOR!
I NEED HIM TO MODEL FOR ME ONE MORE TIME!
I NEED HIM!
THAT'S ALL--?
SHINOBU-CHAN WAS WORRIED THAT THERE MIGHT BE SOMETHING ELSE...
もじもじ
テレテレ
...BUT IT DOESN'T LOOK LIKE IT'LL BE A PROBLEM.
MAIDEN SHYNESS...
WHY DON'T YOU COME IN--
HUH? THE DOOR'S UNLOCKED.
DID K2 DO SOME-THING...
...AGAIN...?
K2--

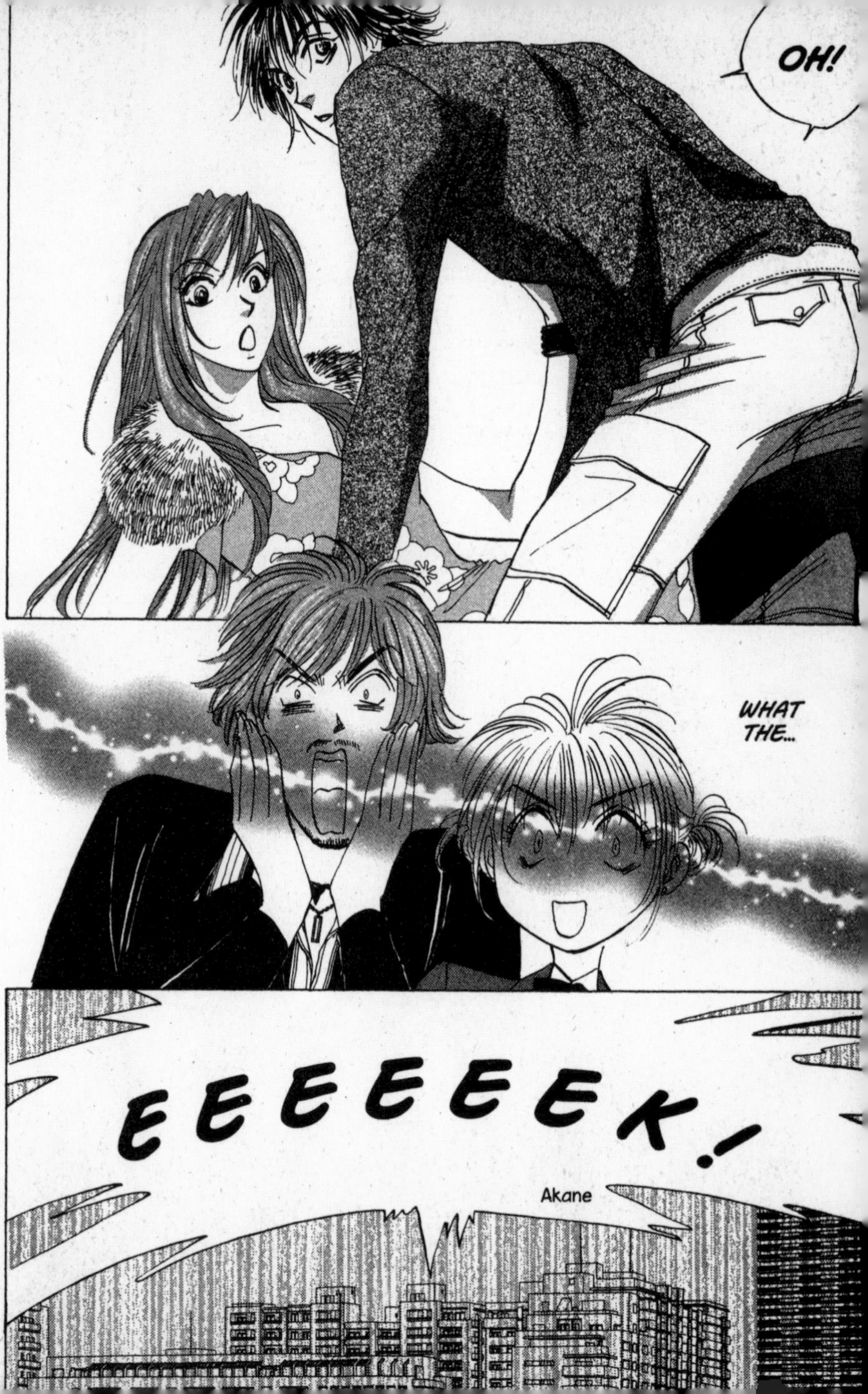
OH!
WHAT THE...
EEEEEEEK!
Akane

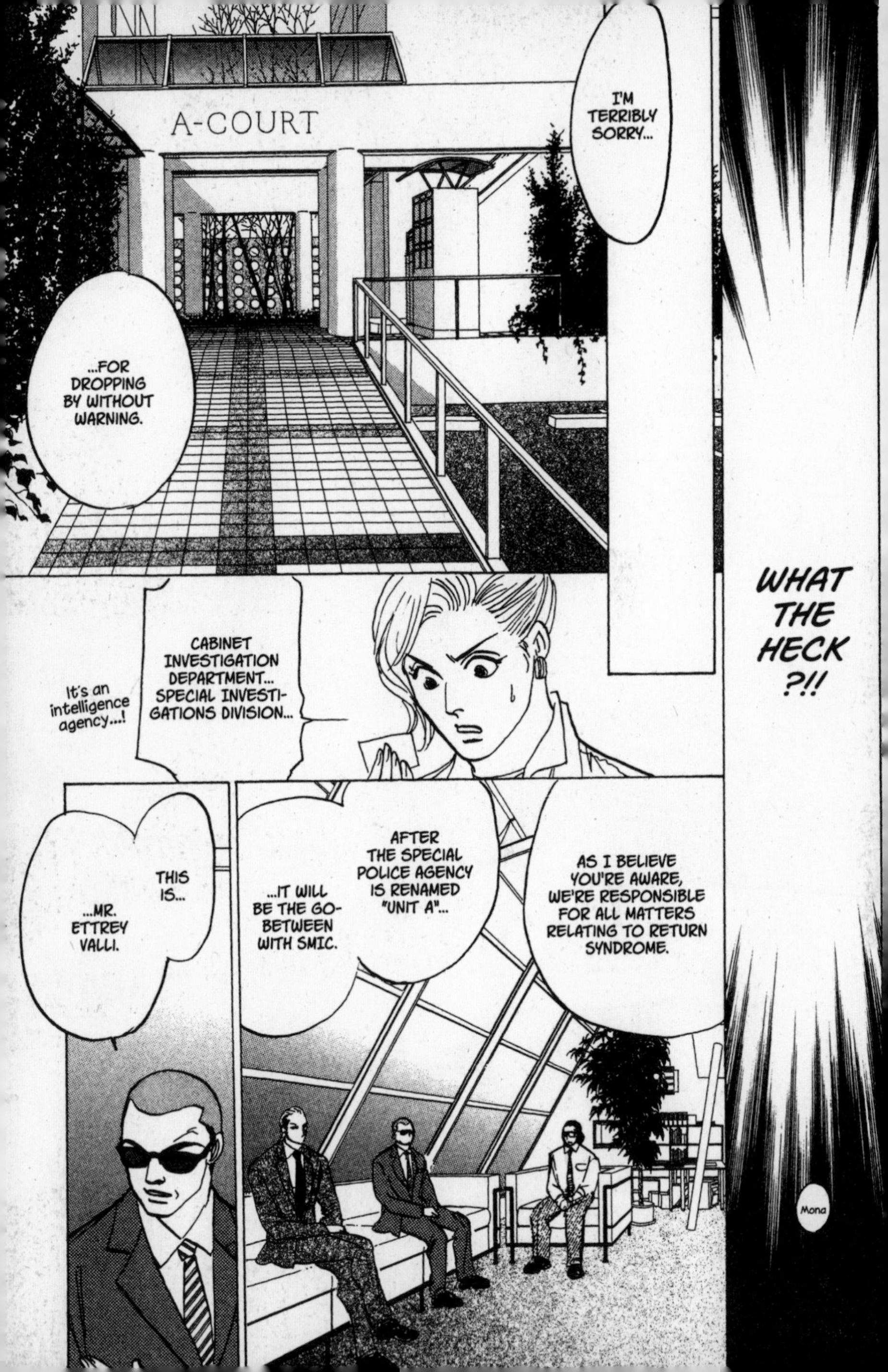
WHAT THE HECK ?!!
Mona
I'M TERRIBLY SORRY...
A-COURT
...FOR DROPPING BY WITHOUT WARNING.
CABINET INVESTIGATION DEPARTMENT... SPECIAL INVESTIGATIONS DIVISION...
It's an intelligence agency...!
AS I BELIEVE YOU'RE AWARE, WE'RE RESPONSIBLE FOR ALL MATTERS RELATING TO RETURN SYNDROME.
AFTER THE SPECIAL POLICE AGENCY IS RENAMED "UNIT A"...
...IT WILL BE THE GO-BETWEEN WITH SMIC.
THIS IS...
...MR. ETTREY VALLI.

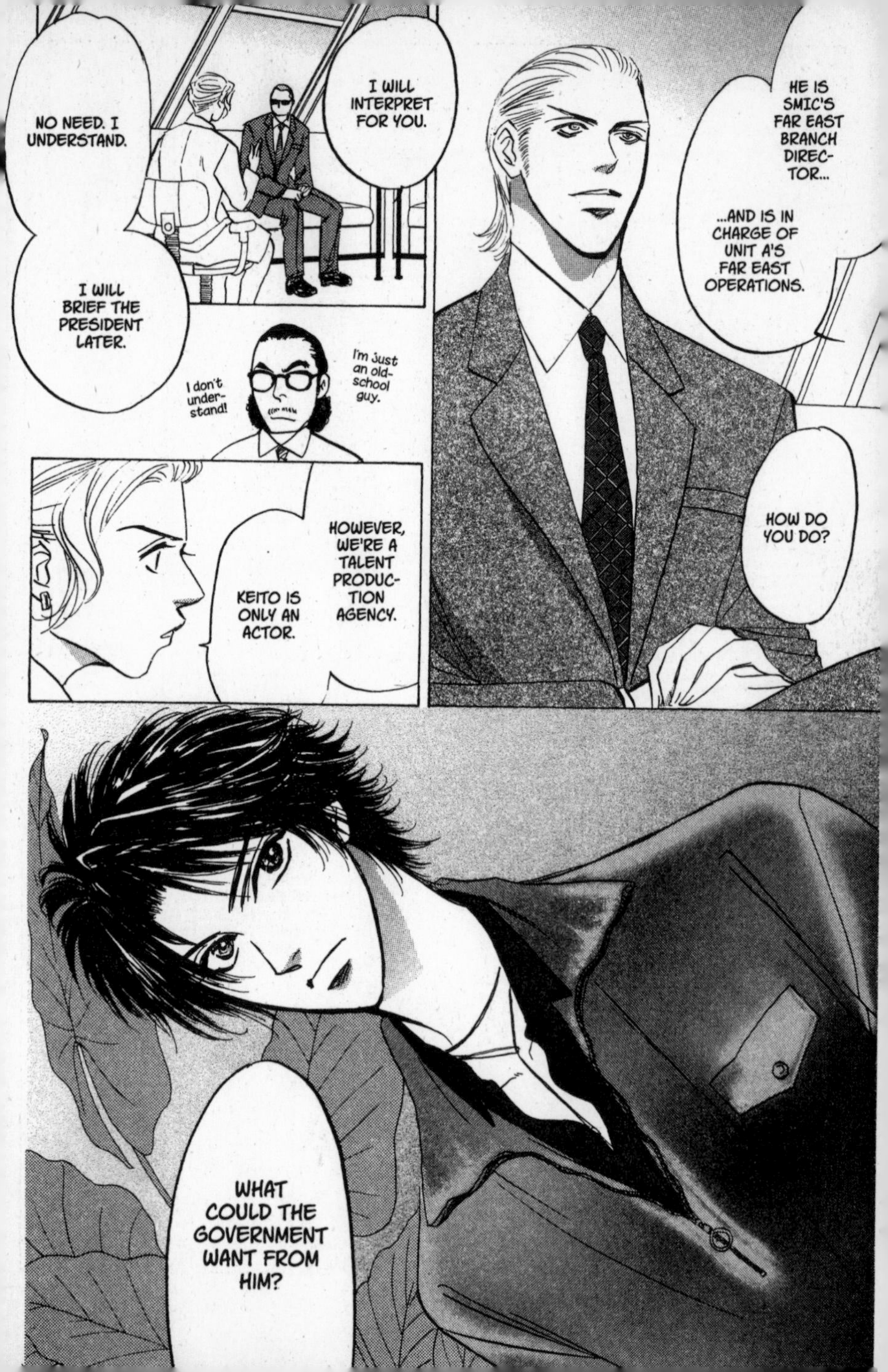
HE IS SMIC'S FAR EAST BRANCH DIRECTOR...
...AND IS IN CHARGE OF UNIT A'S FAR EAST OPERATIONS.
HOW DO YOU DO?
I WILL INTERPRET FOR YOU.
NO NEED. I UNDERSTAND.
I WILL BRIEF THE PRESIDENT LATER.
I'm just an old-school guy.
I don't understand!
HOWEVER, WE'RE A TALENT PRODUCTION AGENCY.
KEITO IS ONLY AN ACTOR.
WHAT COULD THE GOVERNMENT WANT FROM HIM?

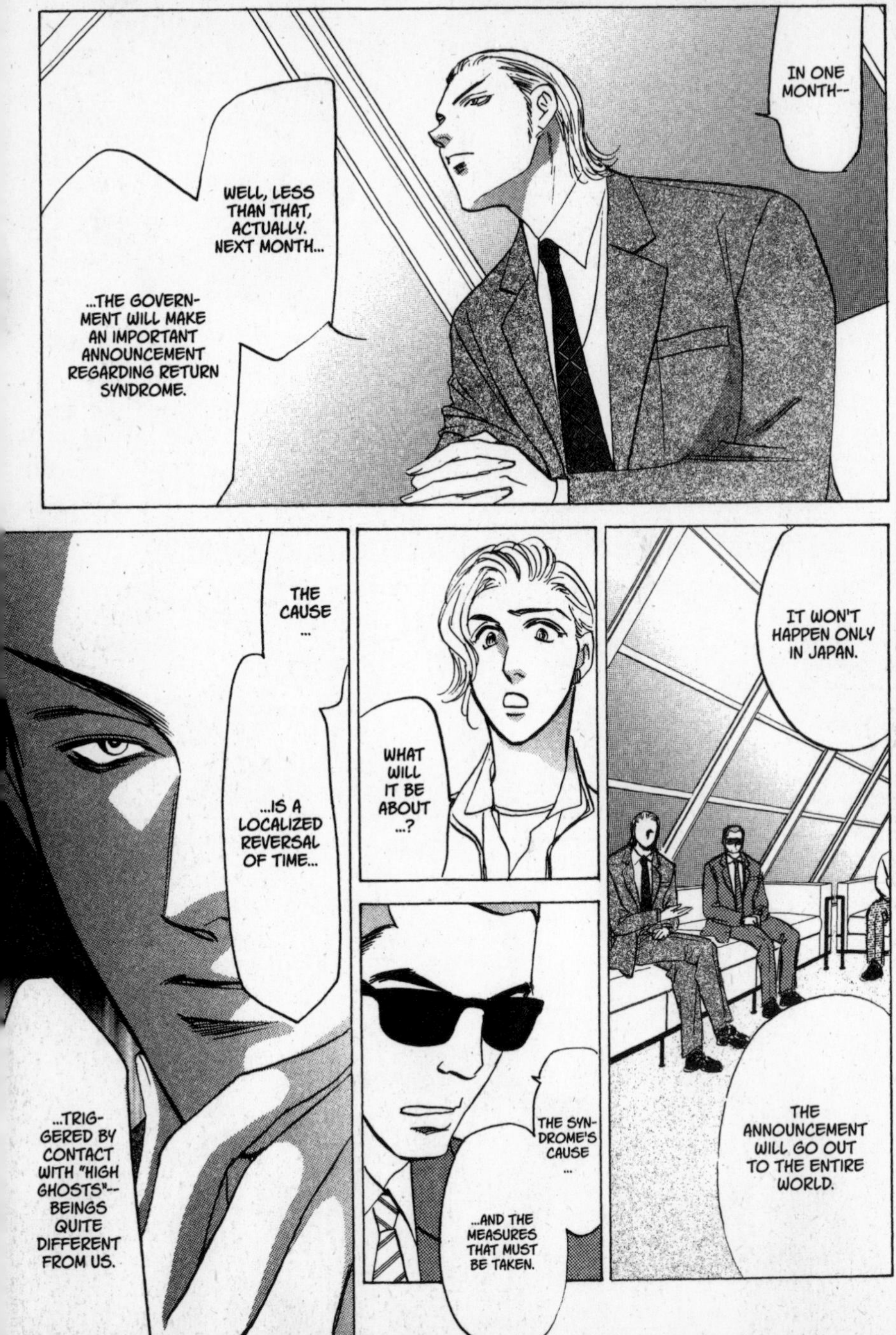
IN ONE MONTH--
WELL, LESS THAN THAT, ACTUALLY. NEXT MONTH...
...THE GOVERNMENT WILL MAKE AN IMPORTANT ANNOUNCEMENT REGARDING RETURN SYNDROME.
IT WON'T HAPPEN ONLY IN JAPAN.
THE ANNOUNCEMENT WILL GO OUT TO THE ENTIRE WORLD.
WHAT WILL IT BE ABOUT...?
THE SYNDROME'S CAUSE...
...AND THE MEASURES THAT MUST BE TAKEN.
THE CAUSE...
...IS A LOCALIZED REVERSAL OF TIME...
...TRIGGERED BY CONTACT WITH "HIGH GHOSTS"-- BEINGS QUITE DIFFERENT FROM US.

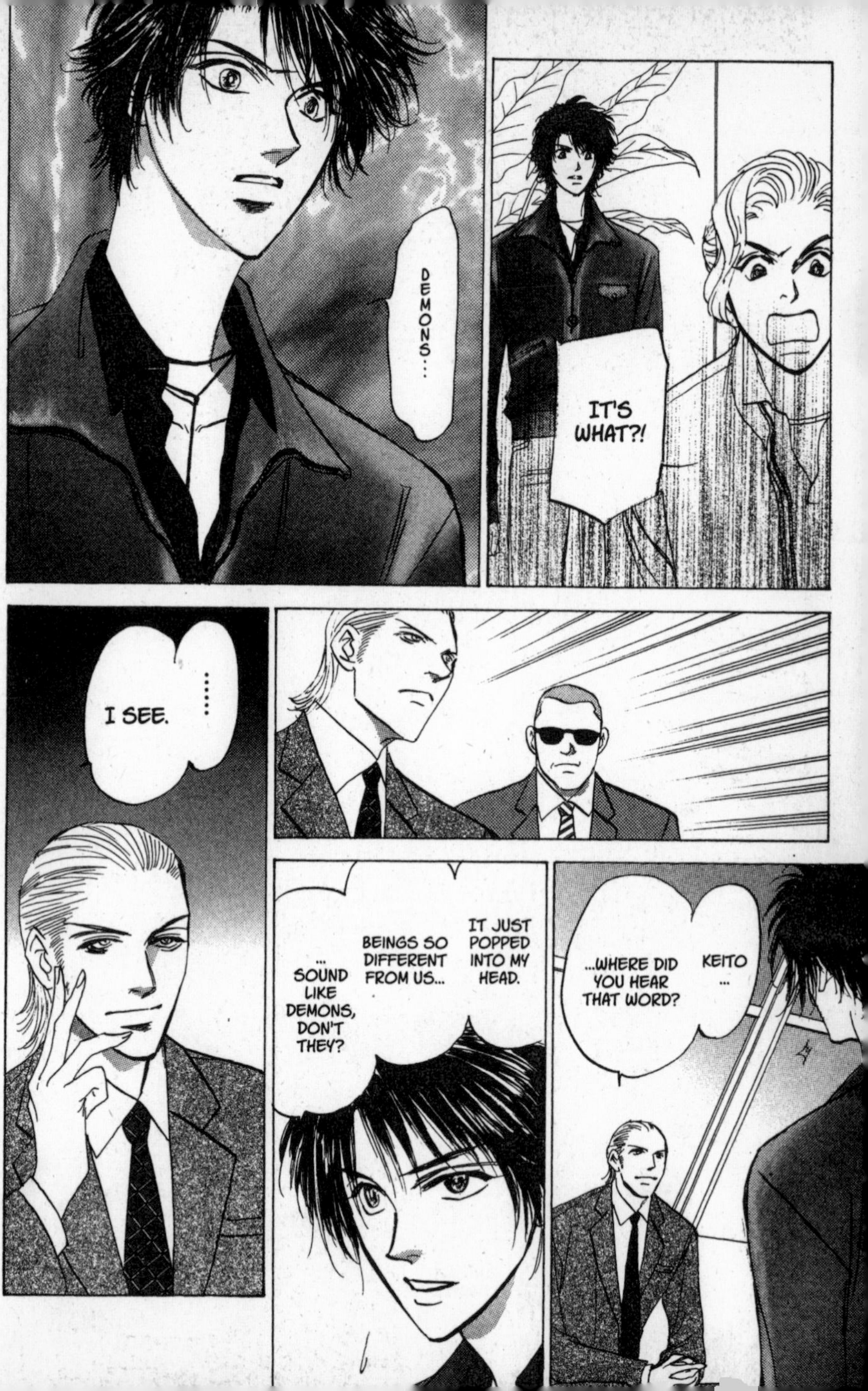
IT'S WHAT?!
DEMONS...
KEITO...
...WHERE DID YOU HEAR THAT WORD?
IT JUST POPPED INTO MY HEAD.
BEINGS SO DIFFERENT FROM US...
...SOUND LIKE DEMONS, DON'T THEY?
......
I SEE.

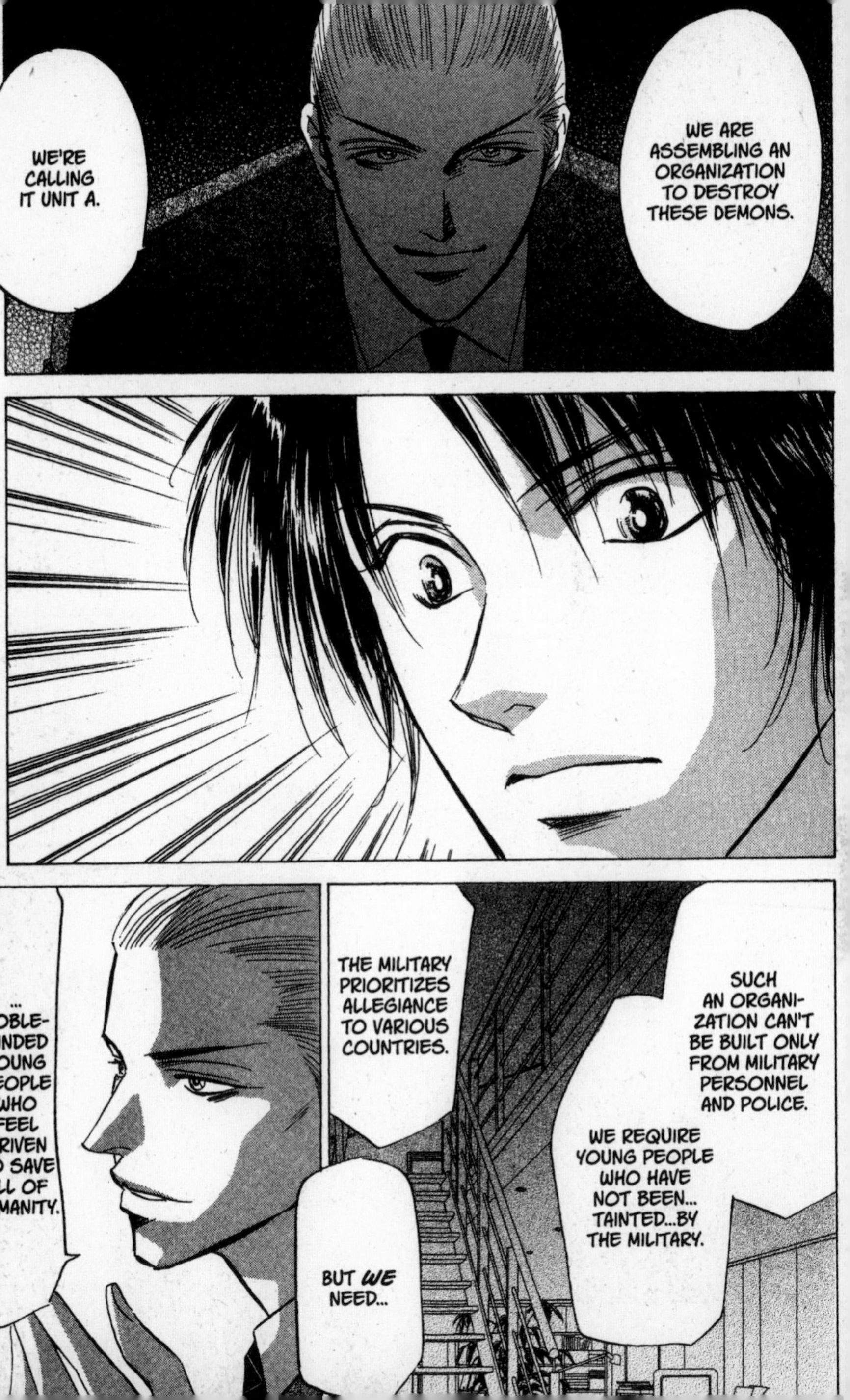
WE ARE ASSEMBLING AN ORGANIZATION TO DESTROY THESE DEMONS.
WE'RE CALLING IT UNIT A.
SUCH AN ORGANI-ZATION CAN'T BE BUILT ONLY FROM MILITARY PERSONNEL AND POLICE.
WE REQUIRE YOUNG PEOPLE WHO HAVE NOT BEEN... TAINTED...BY THE MILITARY.
THE MILITARY PRIORITIZES ALLEGIANCE TO VARIOUS COUNTRIES.
BUT *WE* NEED...
... NOBLE-MINDED YOUNG PEOPLE WHO FEEL DRIVEN TO SAVE ALL OF HUMANITY.

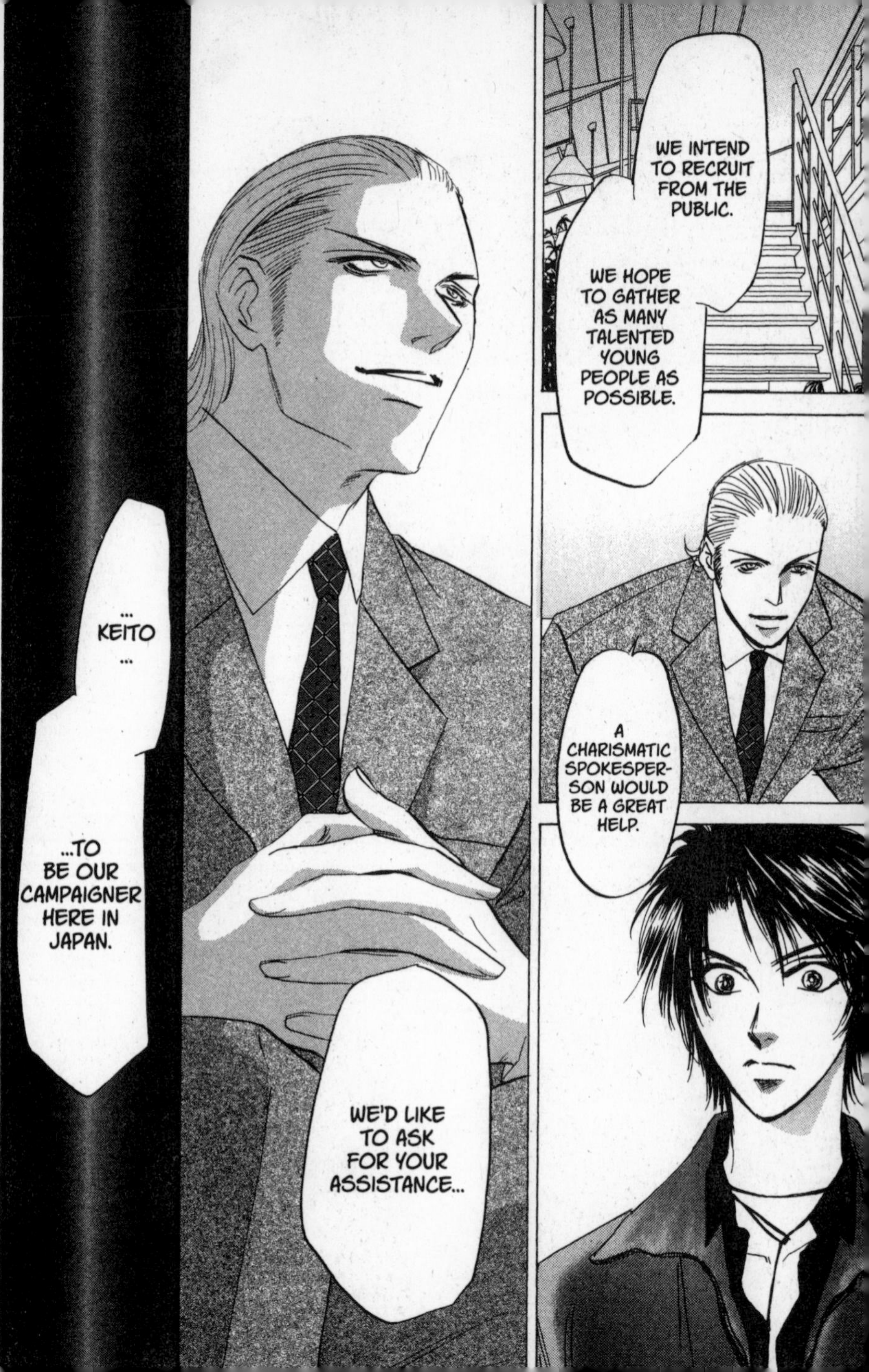
WE INTEND TO RECRUIT FROM THE PUBLIC.
WE HOPE TO GATHER AS MANY TALENTED YOUNG PEOPLE AS POSSIBLE.
A CHARISMATIC SPOKESPERSON WOULD BE A GREAT HELP.
WE'D LIKE TO ASK FOR YOUR ASSISTANCE...
...KEITO...
...TO BE OUR CAMPAIGNER HERE IN JAPAN.

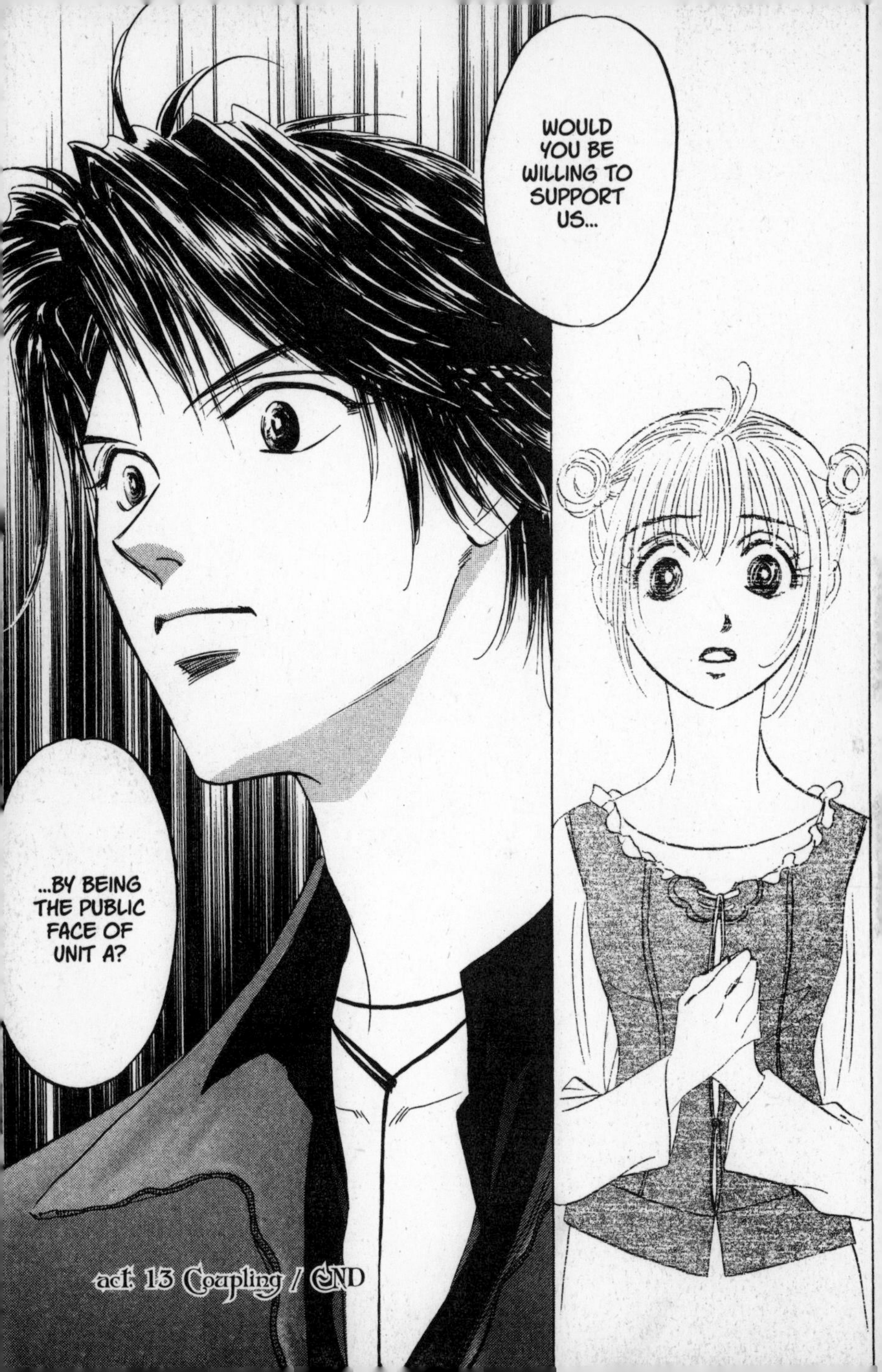
WOULD YOU BE WILLING TO SUPPORT US...
...BY BEING THE PUBLIC FACE OF UNIT A?
act. 13 Coupling / END

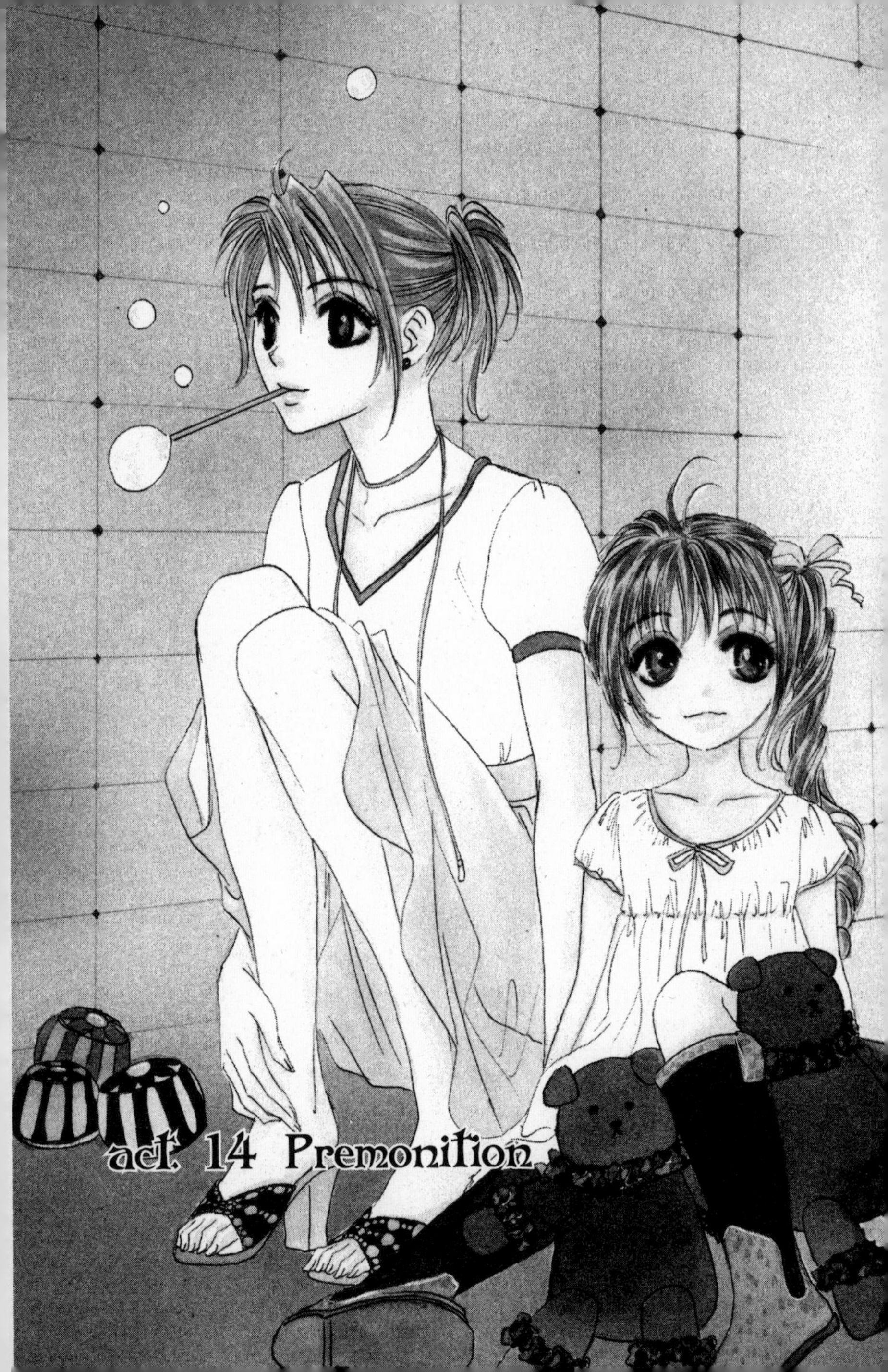
act. 14 Premonition

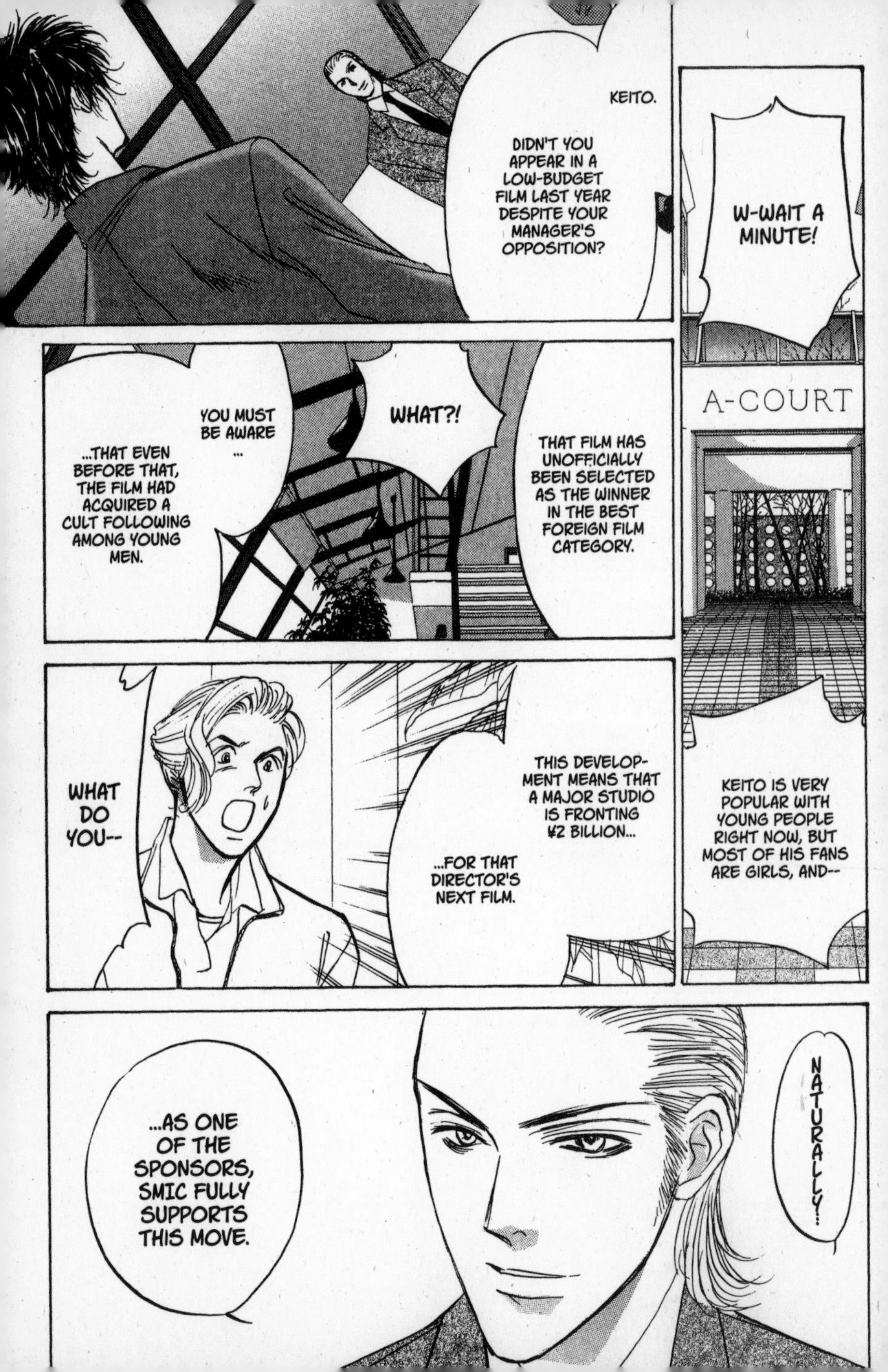
W-WAIT A MINUTE!
A-COURT
KEITO IS VERY POPULAR WITH YOUNG PEOPLE RIGHT NOW, BUT MOST OF HIS FANS ARE GIRLS, AND--
KEITO.
DIDN'T YOU APPEAR IN A LOW-BUDGET FILM LAST YEAR DESPITE YOUR MANAGER'S OPPOSITION?
THAT FILM HAS UNOFFICIALLY BEEN SELECTED AS THE WINNER IN THE BEST FOREIGN FILM CATEGORY.
WHAT?!
YOU MUST BE AWARE ...
...THAT EVEN BEFORE THAT, THE FILM HAD ACQUIRED A CULT FOLLOWING AMONG YOUNG MEN.
THIS DEVELOPMENT MEANS THAT A MAJOR STUDIO IS FRONTING ¥2 BILLION...
...FOR THAT DIRECTOR'S NEXT FILM.
WHAT DO YOU--
NATURALLY...
...AS ONE OF THE SPONSORS, SMIC FULLY SUPPORTS THIS MOVE.

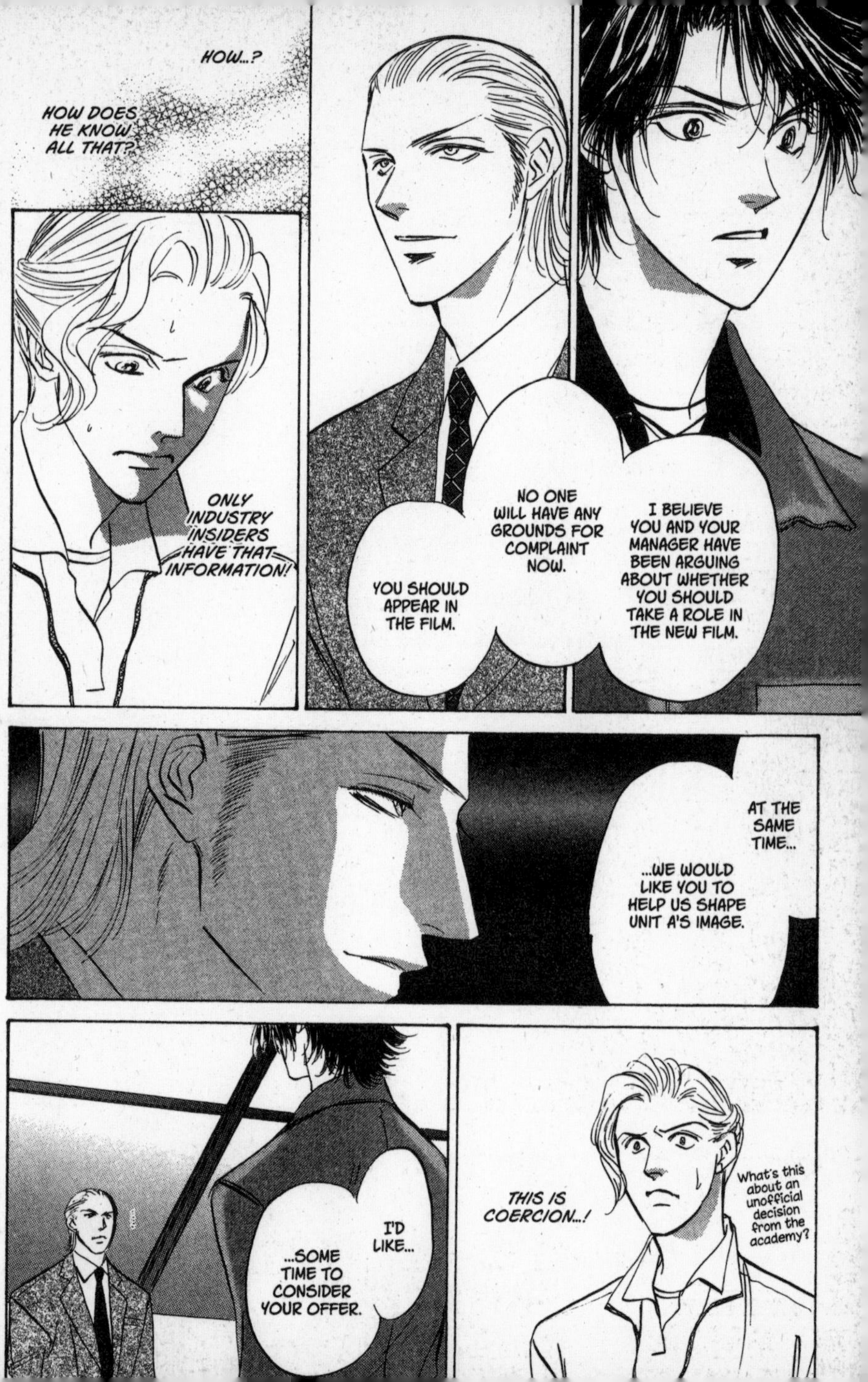
I BELIEVE YOU AND YOUR MANAGER HAVE BEEN ARGUING ABOUT WHETHER YOU SHOULD TAKE A ROLE IN THE NEW FILM.
NO ONE WILL HAVE ANY GROUNDS FOR COMPLAINT NOW.
YOU SHOULD APPEAR IN THE FILM.
HOW...?
HOW DOES HE KNOW ALL THAT?
ONLY INDUSTRY INSIDERS HAVE THAT INFORMATION!
AT THE SAME TIME...
...WE WOULD LIKE YOU TO HELP US SHAPE UNIT A'S IMAGE.
What's this about an unofficial decision from the academy?
THIS IS COERCION...!
I'D LIKE...
...SOME TIME TO CONSIDER YOUR OFFER.

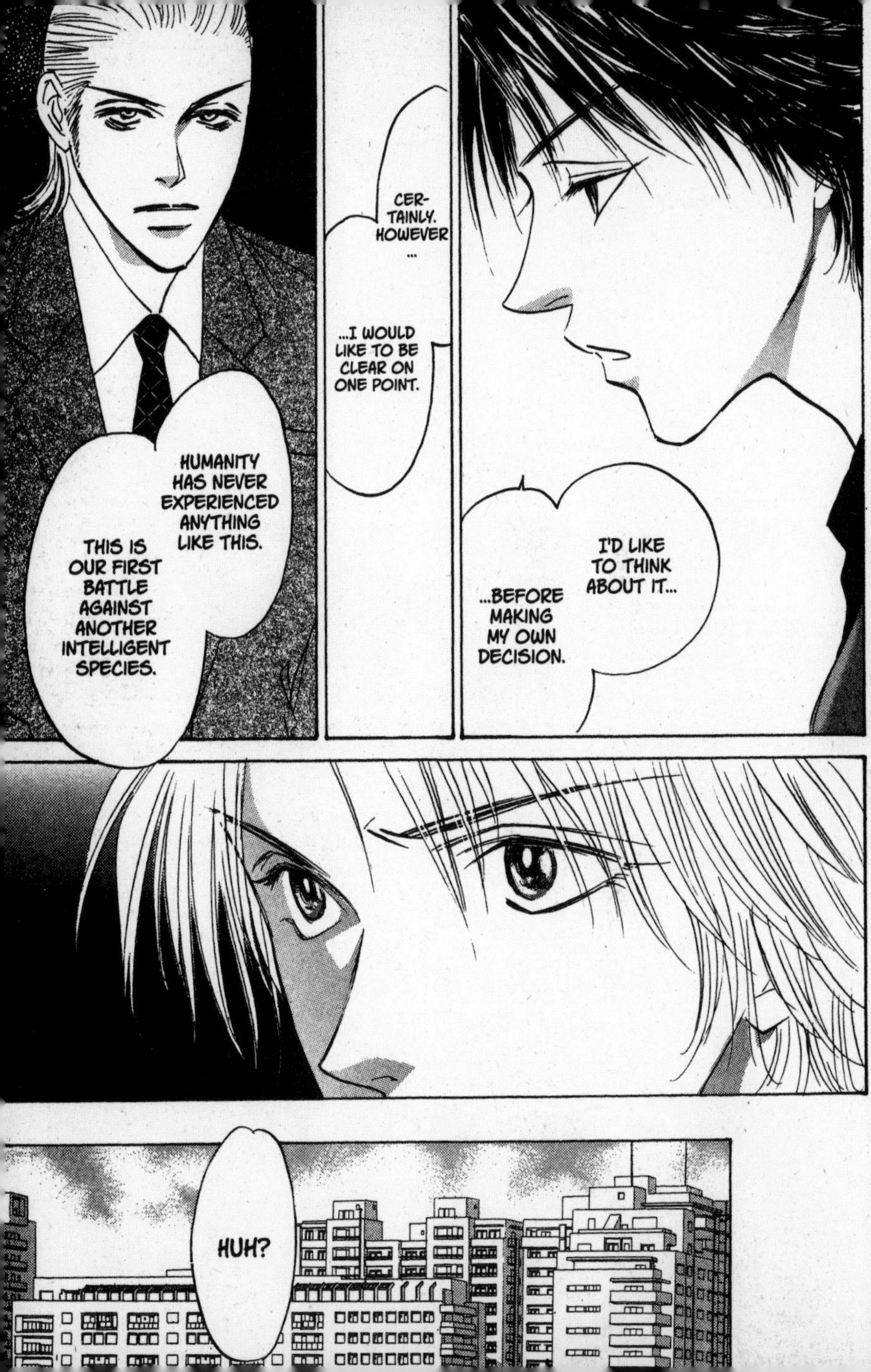
I'D LIKE TO THINK ABOUT IT...
...BEFORE MAKING MY OWN DECISION.
CER-TAINLY. HOWEVER ...
...I WOULD LIKE TO BE CLEAR ON ONE POINT.
HUMANITY HAS NEVER EXPERIENCED ANYTHING LIKE THIS.
THIS IS OUR FIRST BATTLE AGAINST ANOTHER INTELLIGENT SPECIES.
HUH?

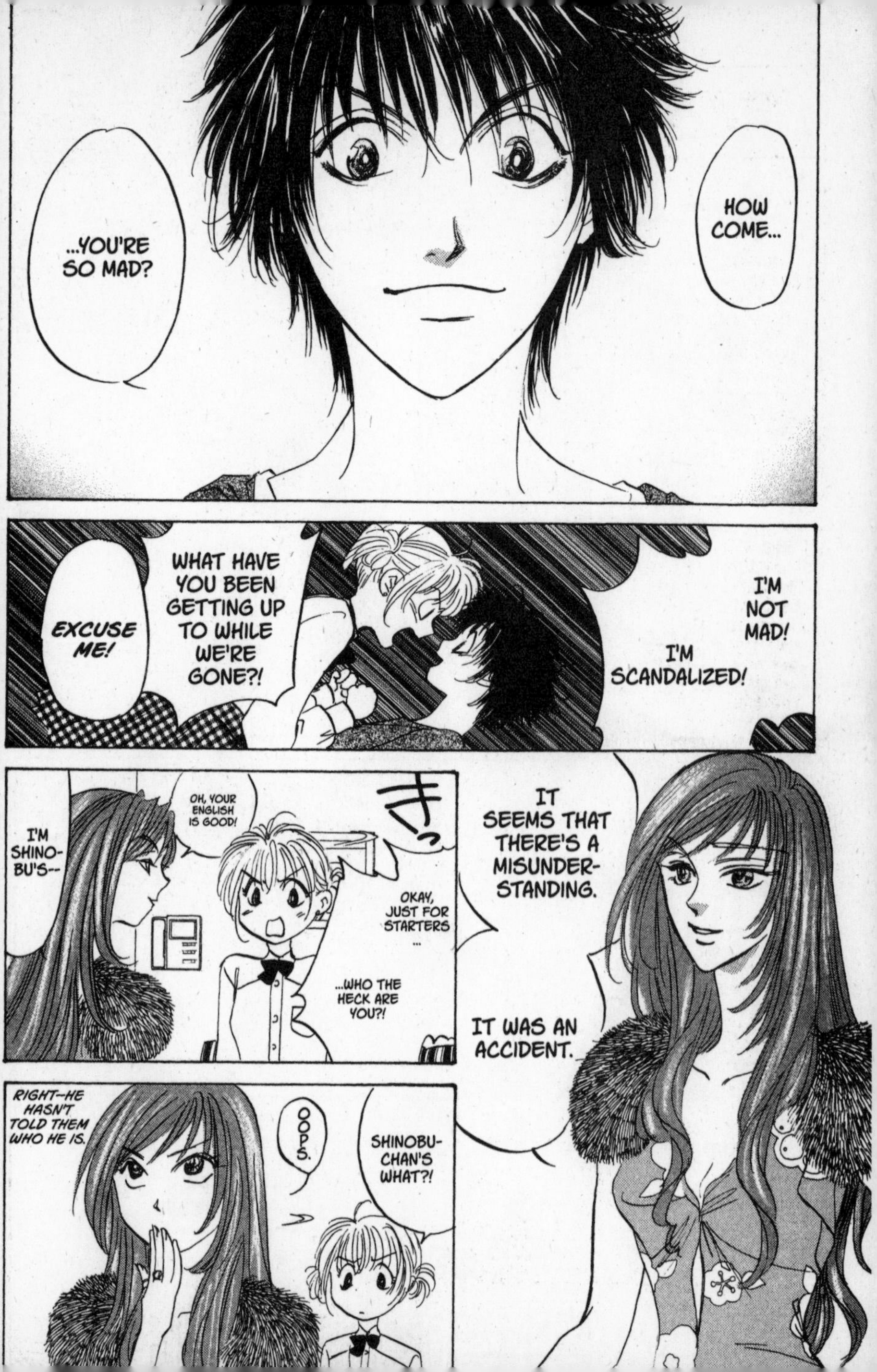
HOW COME...
...YOU'RE SO MAD?
I'M NOT MAD!
I'M SCANDALIZED!
WHAT HAVE YOU BEEN GETTING UP TO WHILE WE'RE GONE?!
EXCUSE ME!
IT SEEMS THAT THERE'S A MISUNDER-STANDING.
IT WAS AN ACCIDENT.
きっ
OH, YOUR ENGLISH IS GOOD!
OKAY, JUST FOR STARTERS ...
...WHO THE HECK ARE YOU?!
I'M SHINO-BU'S--
SHINOBU-CHAN'S WHAT?!
OOPS.
RIGHT--HE HASN'T TOLD THEM WHO HE IS.

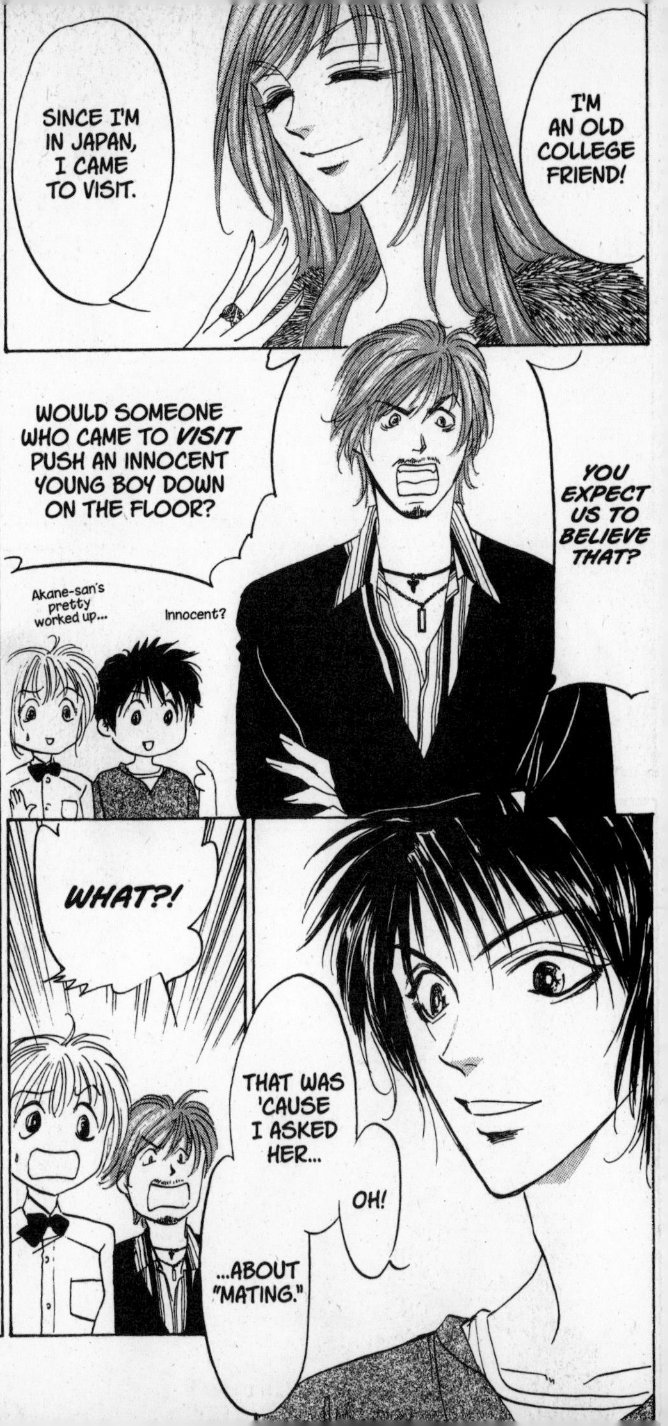
I'M AN OLD COLLEGE FRIEND!
SINCE I'M IN JAPAN, I CAME TO VISIT.
YOU EXPECT US TO BELIEVE THAT?
WOULD SOMEONE WHO CAME TO *VISIT* PUSH AN INNOCENT YOUNG BOY DOWN ON THE FLOOR?
Innocent?
Akane-san's pretty worked up...
THAT WAS 'CAUSE I ASKED HER...
OH!
...ABOUT "MATING."
WHAT?!

FREE TALK <2>

I have a little announcement to make about *OZ*. *OZ* was made into a play in 2003, and I just heard that the same group, Studio Life, would like to perform it again around March 2005.

When I first heard the idea of turning it into a play I was concerned about how it would work on stage, but when I saw it performed I was deeply moved. They did it so well! I'm looking forward to being in the audience for the next performance.

This time around they'll be staging it at a large theater, which will add another dimension to the play. (It was originally staged in a small theater.) The smaller space was nice, but being in a big theater might add something more dynamic to the show.

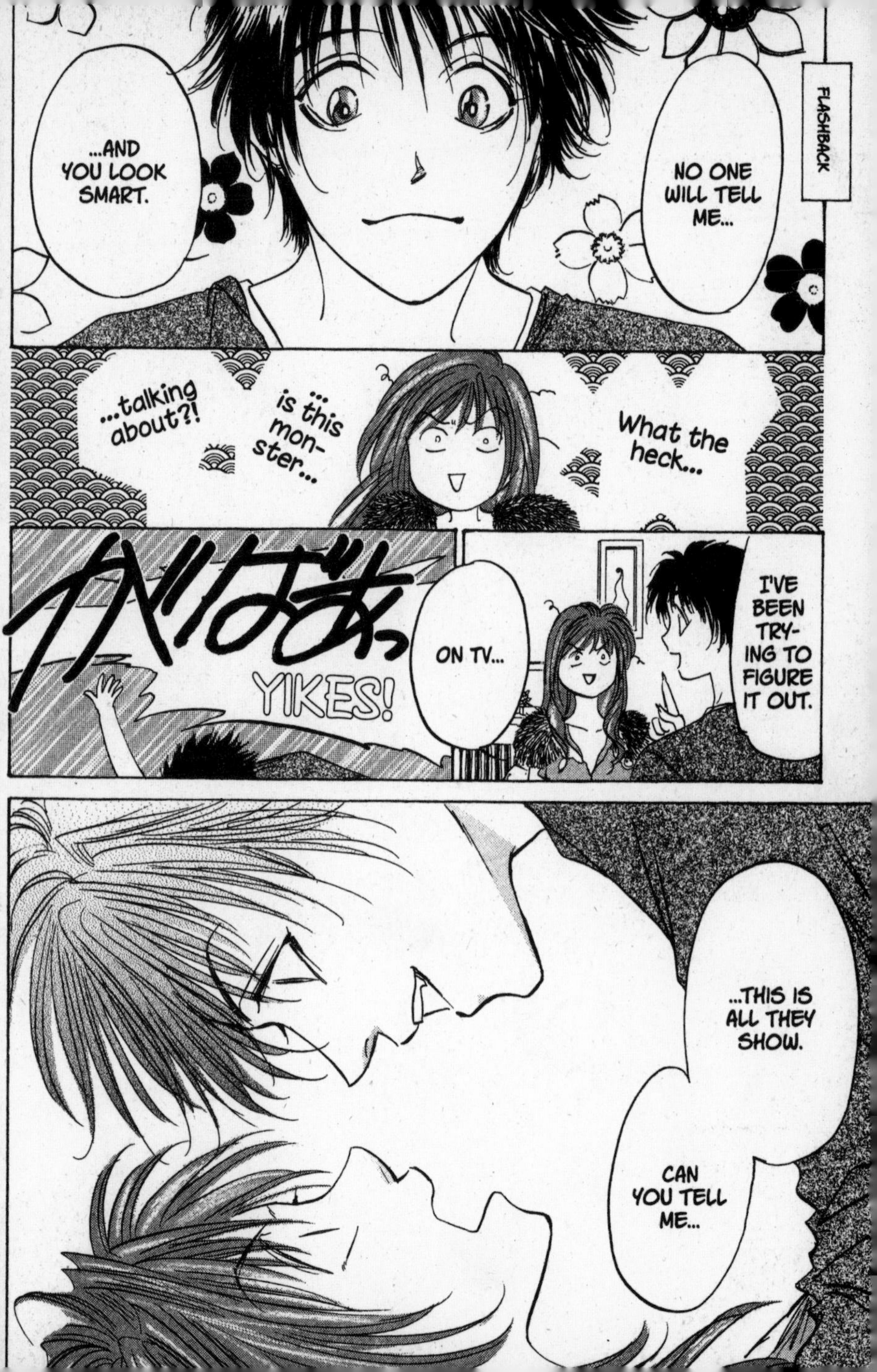
FLASHBACK
NO ONE WILL TELL ME...
...AND YOU LOOK SMART.
What the heck...
...is this monster...
...talking about?!
I'VE BEEN TRYING TO FIGURE IT OUT.
ON TV...
YIKES!
...THIS IS ALL THEY SHOW.
CAN YOU TELL ME...

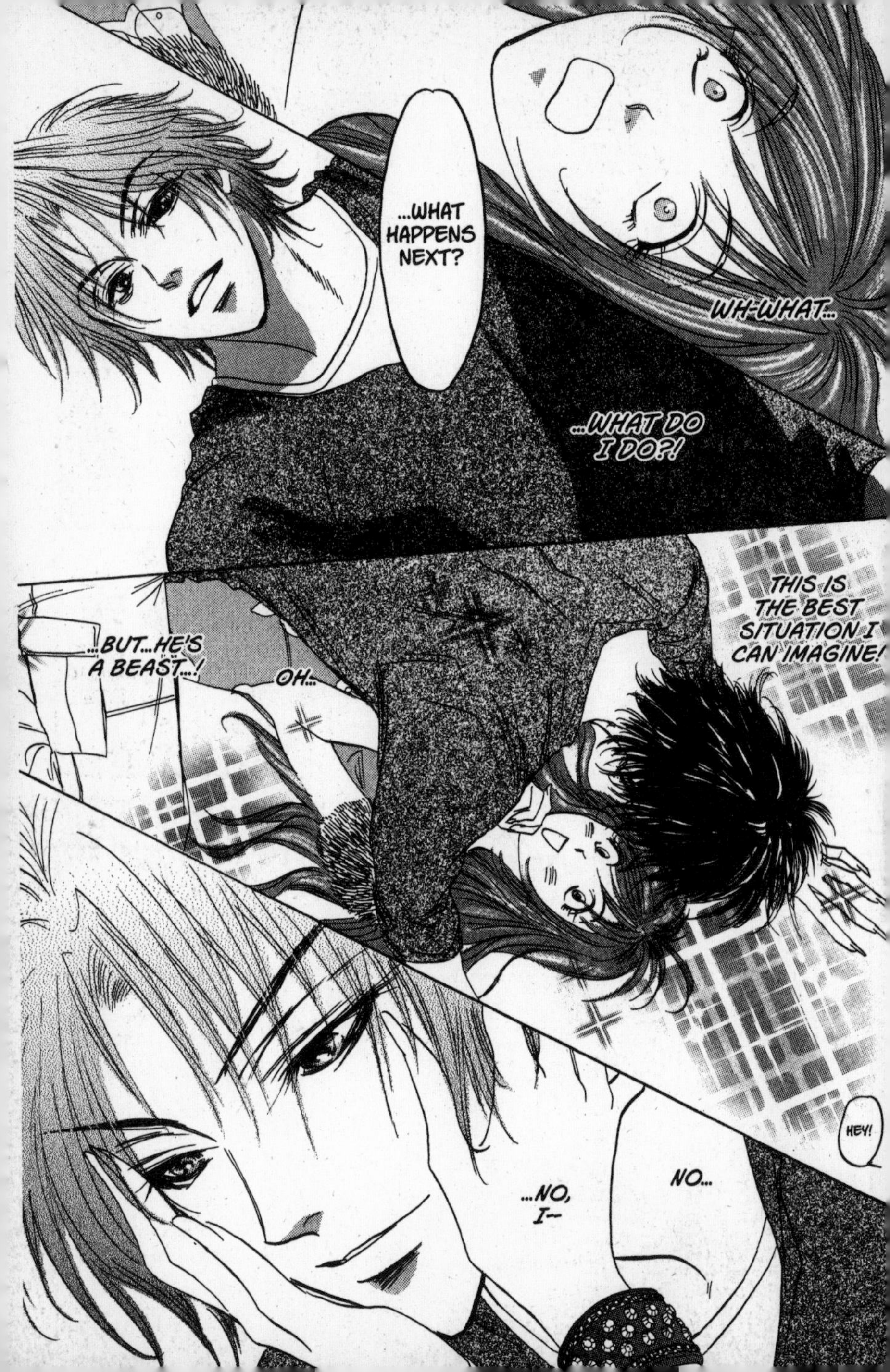
...WHAT HAPPENS NEXT?
WH-WHAT...
...WHAT DO I DO?!
THIS IS THE BEST SITUATION I CAN IMAGINE!
OH...
...BUT...HE'S A BEAST...!
HEY!
NO...
...NO, I--

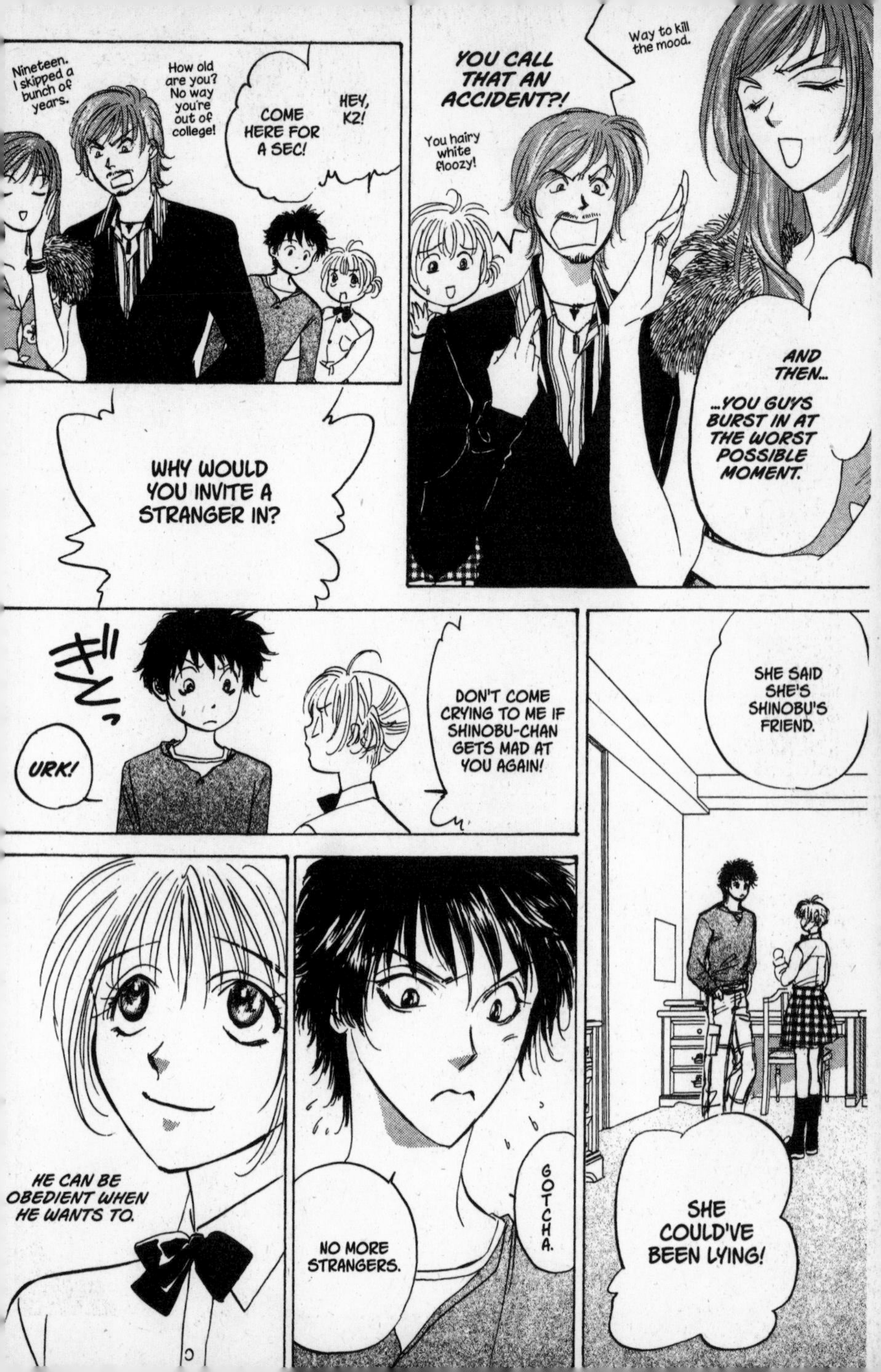
AND THEN...
...YOU GUYS BURST IN AT THE WORST POSSIBLE MOMENT.
YOU CALL THAT AN ACCIDENT?!
You hairy white floozy!
Way to kill the mood.
HEY, K2!
COME HERE FOR A SEC!
How old are you? No way you're out of college!
Nineteen. I skipped a bunch of years.
WHY WOULD YOU INVITE A STRANGER IN?
SHE SAID SHE'S SHINOBU'S FRIEND.
SHE COULD'VE BEEN LYING!
DON'T COME CRYING TO ME IF SHINOBU-CHAN GETS MAD AT YOU AGAIN!
ぎく
URK!
GOTCHA.
NO MORE STRANGERS.
HE CAN BE OBEDIENT WHEN HE WANTS TO.

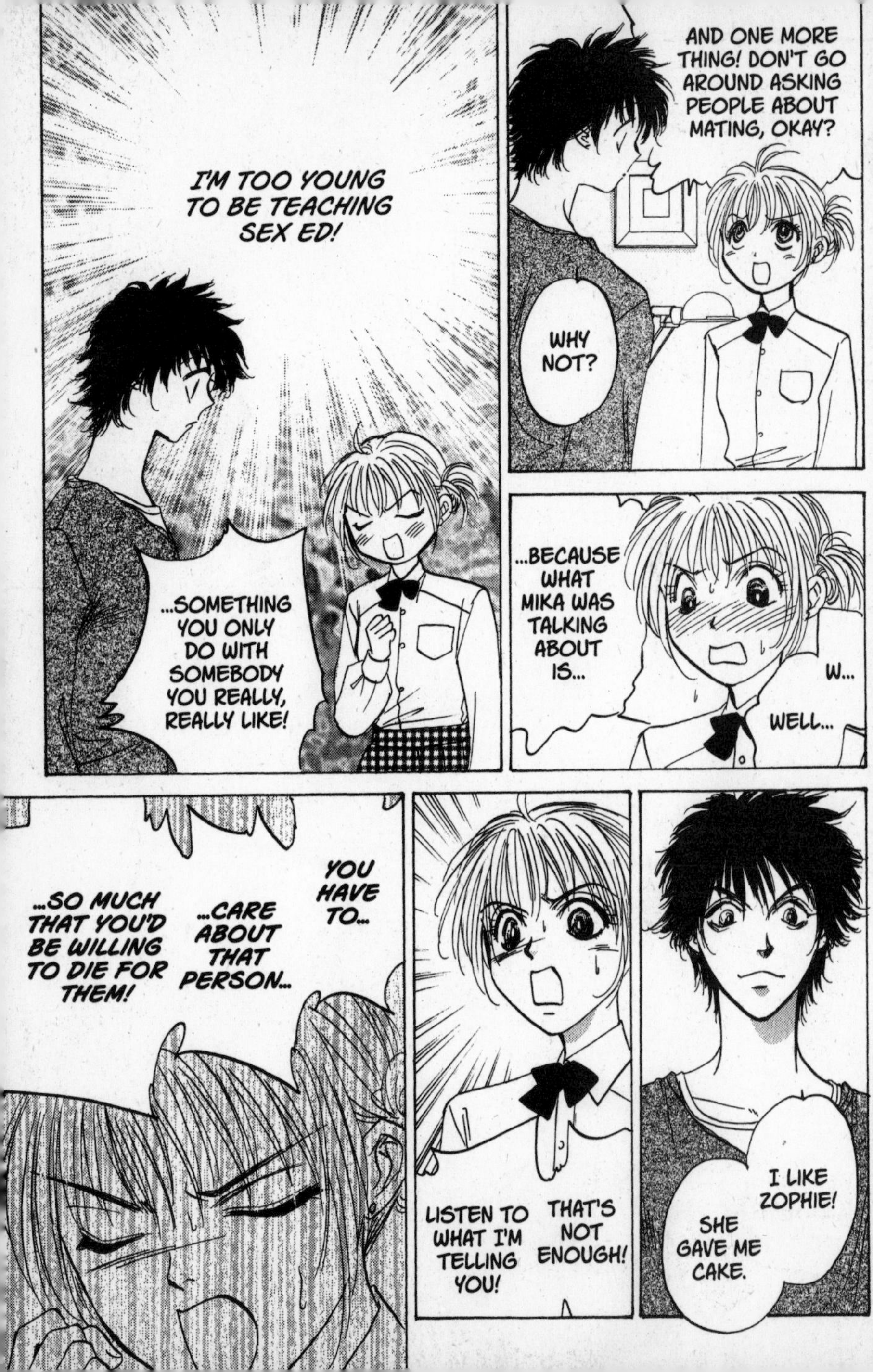
AND ONE MORE THING! DON'T GO AROUND ASKING PEOPLE ABOUT MATING, OKAY?
WHY NOT?
W... WELL...
...BECAUSE WHAT MIKA WAS TALKING ABOUT IS...
I'M TOO YOUNG TO BE TEACHING SEX ED!
...SOMETHING YOU ONLY DO WITH SOMEBODY YOU REALLY, REALLY LIKE!
I LIKE ZOPHIE! SHE GAVE ME CAKE.
THAT'S NOT ENOUGH!
LISTEN TO WHAT I'M TELLING YOU!
YOU HAVE TO...
...CARE ABOUT THAT PERSON...
...SO MUCH THAT YOU'D BE WILLING TO DIE FOR THEM!

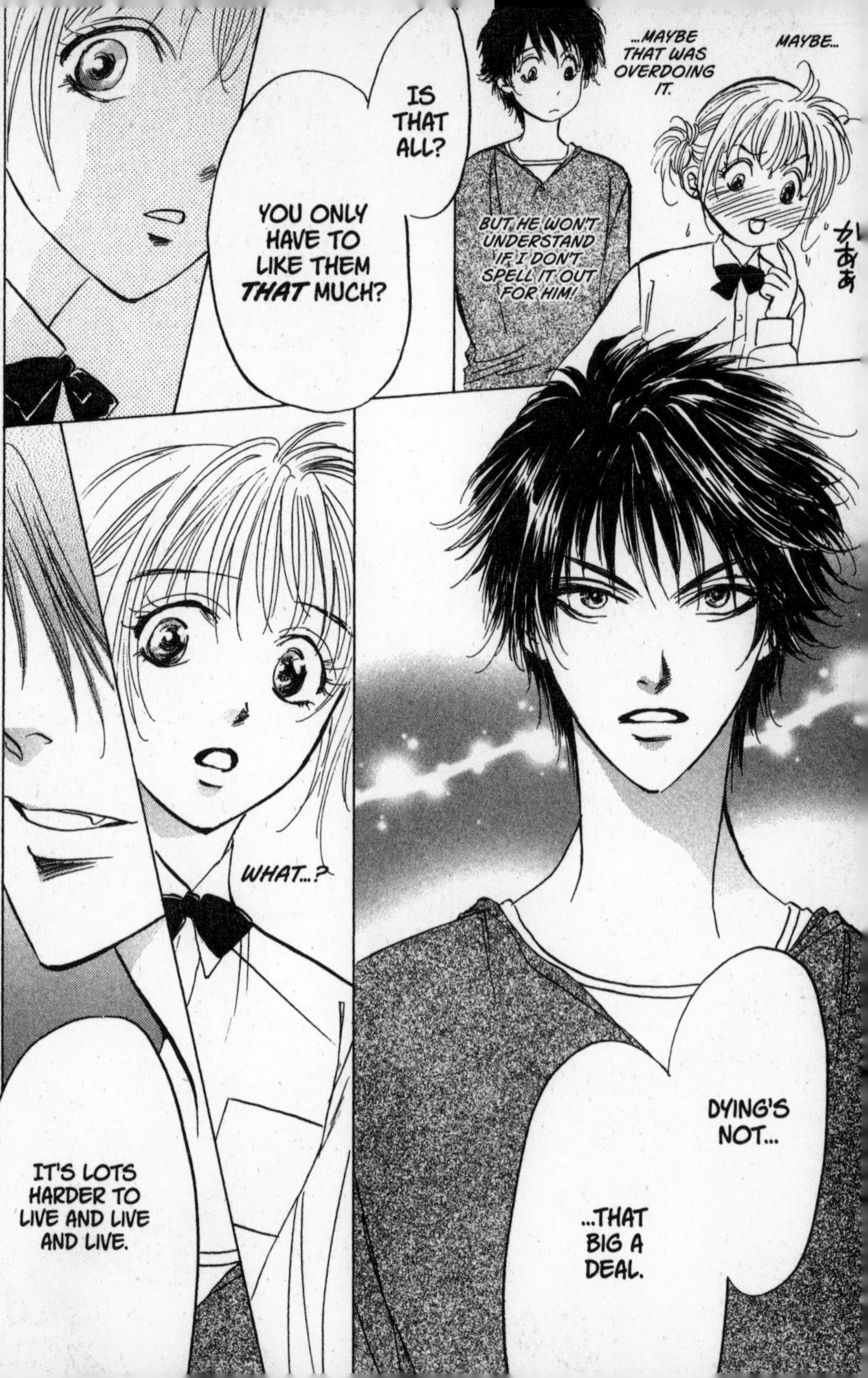
MAYBE...
...MAYBE THAT WAS OVERDOING IT.
かああ
BUT HE WON'T UNDERSTAND IF I DON'T SPELL IT OUT FOR HIM!
IS THAT ALL?
YOU ONLY HAVE TO LIKE THEM THAT MUCH?
DYING'S NOT...
...THAT BIG A DEAL.
WHAT...?
IT'S LOTS HARDER TO LIVE AND LIVE AND LIVE.

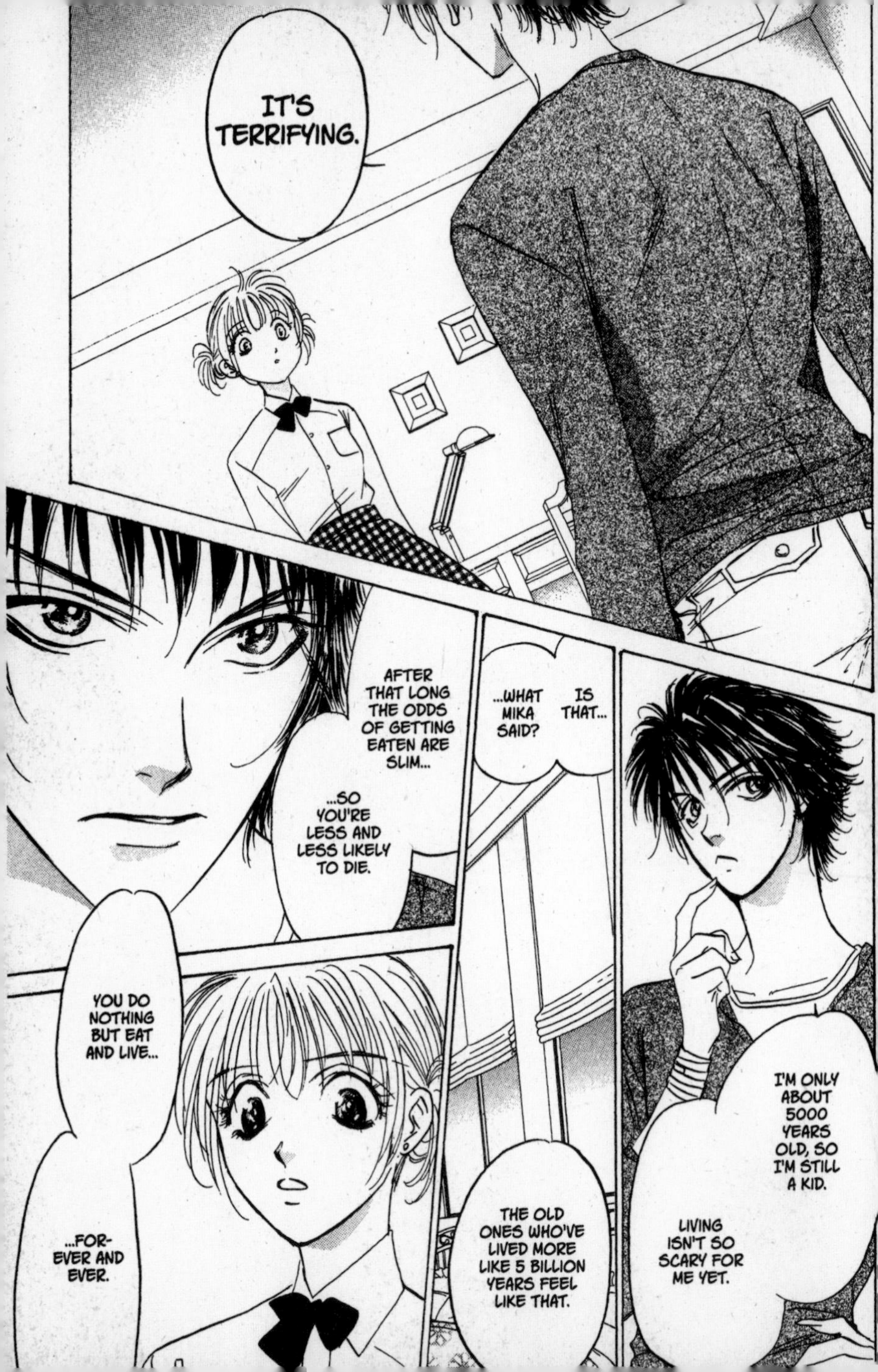
IT'S TERRIFYING.
IS THAT...
...WHAT MIKA SAID?
I'M ONLY ABOUT 5000 YEARS OLD, SO I'M STILL A KID.
LIVING ISN'T SO SCARY FOR ME YET.
THE OLD ONES WHO'VE LIVED MORE LIKE 5 BILLION YEARS FEEL LIKE THAT.
AFTER THAT LONG THE ODDS OF GETTING EATEN ARE SLIM...
...SO YOU'RE LESS AND LESS LIKELY TO DIE.
YOU DO NOTHING BUT EAT AND LIVE...
...FOR-EVER AND EVER.

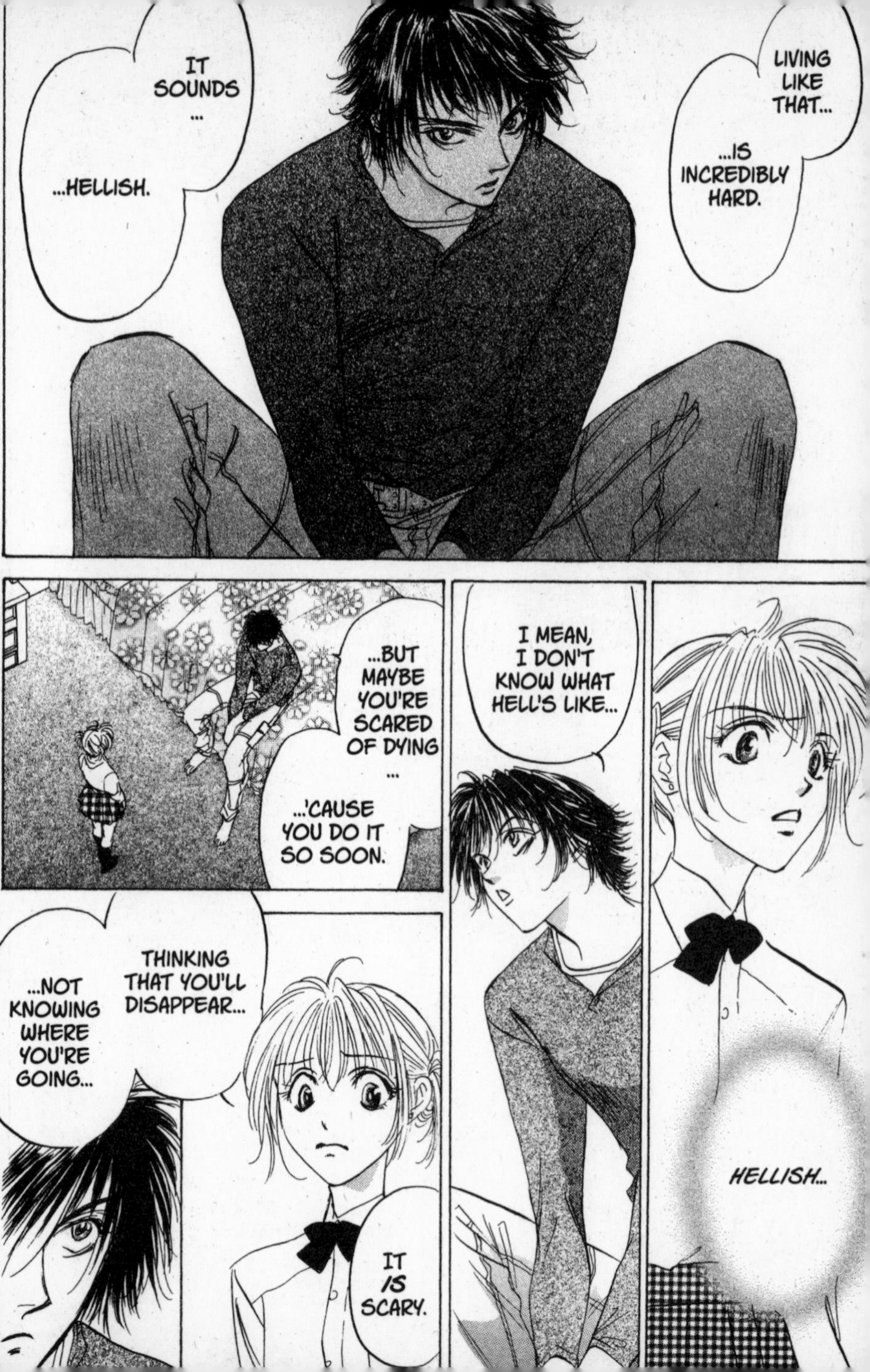
LIVING LIKE THAT...
...IS INCREDIBLY HARD.
IT SOUNDS ...
...HELLISH.
HELLISH...
I MEAN, I DON'T KNOW WHAT HELL'S LIKE...
...BUT MAYBE YOU'RE SCARED OF DYING ...
...'CAUSE YOU DO IT SO SOON.
THINKING THAT YOU'LL DISAPPEAR...
...NOT KNOWING WHERE YOU'RE GOING...
IT *IS* SCARY.

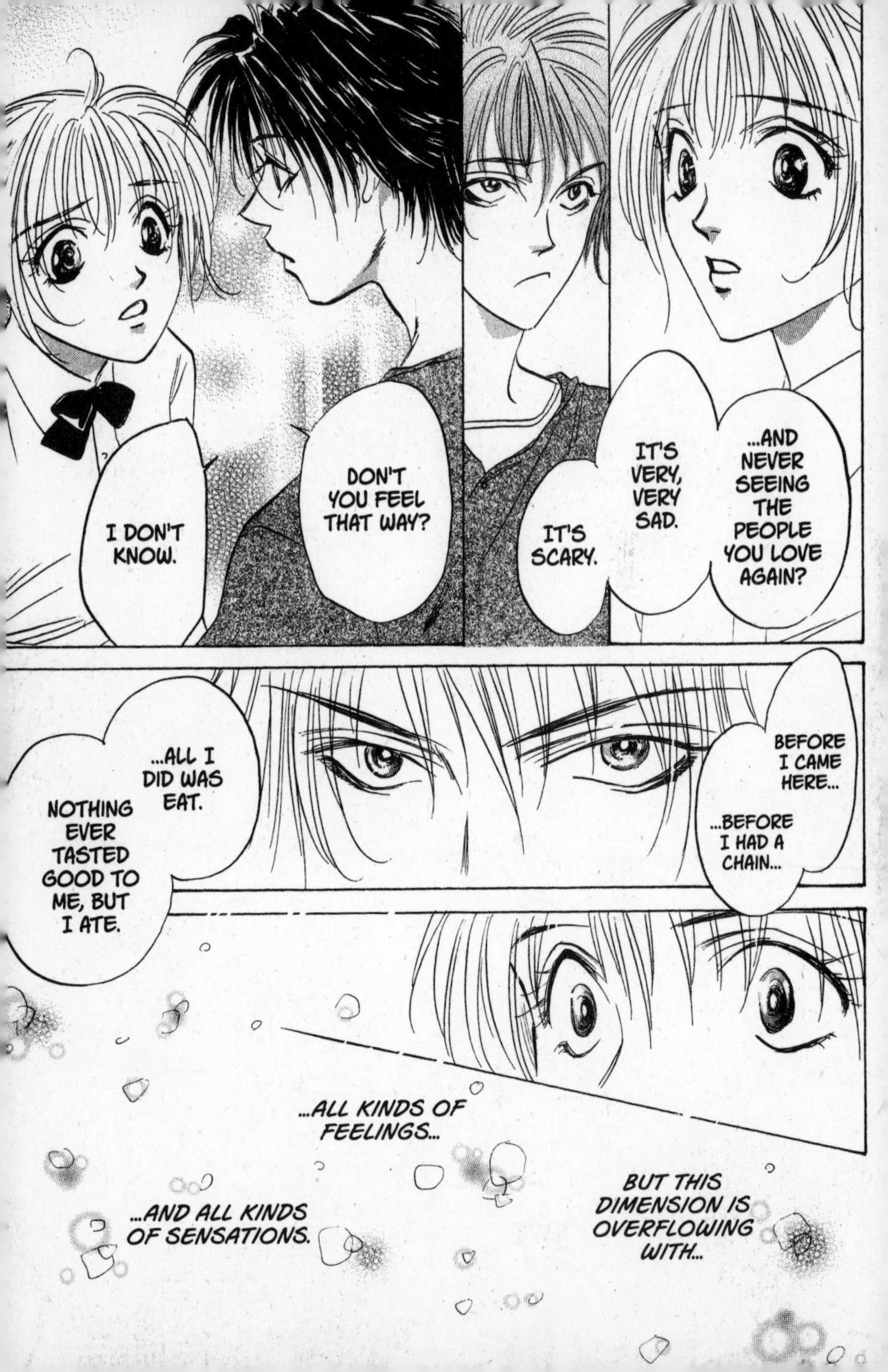
...AND NEVER SEEING THE PEOPLE YOU LOVE AGAIN?
IT'S VERY, VERY SAD.
IT'S SCARY.
DON'T YOU FEEL THAT WAY?
I DON'T KNOW.
BEFORE I CAME HERE...
...BEFORE I HAD A CHAIN...
...ALL I DID WAS EAT.
NOTHING EVER TASTED GOOD TO ME, BUT I ATE.
BUT THIS DIMENSION IS OVERFLOWING WITH...
...ALL KINDS OF FEELINGS...
...AND ALL KINDS OF SENSATIONS.

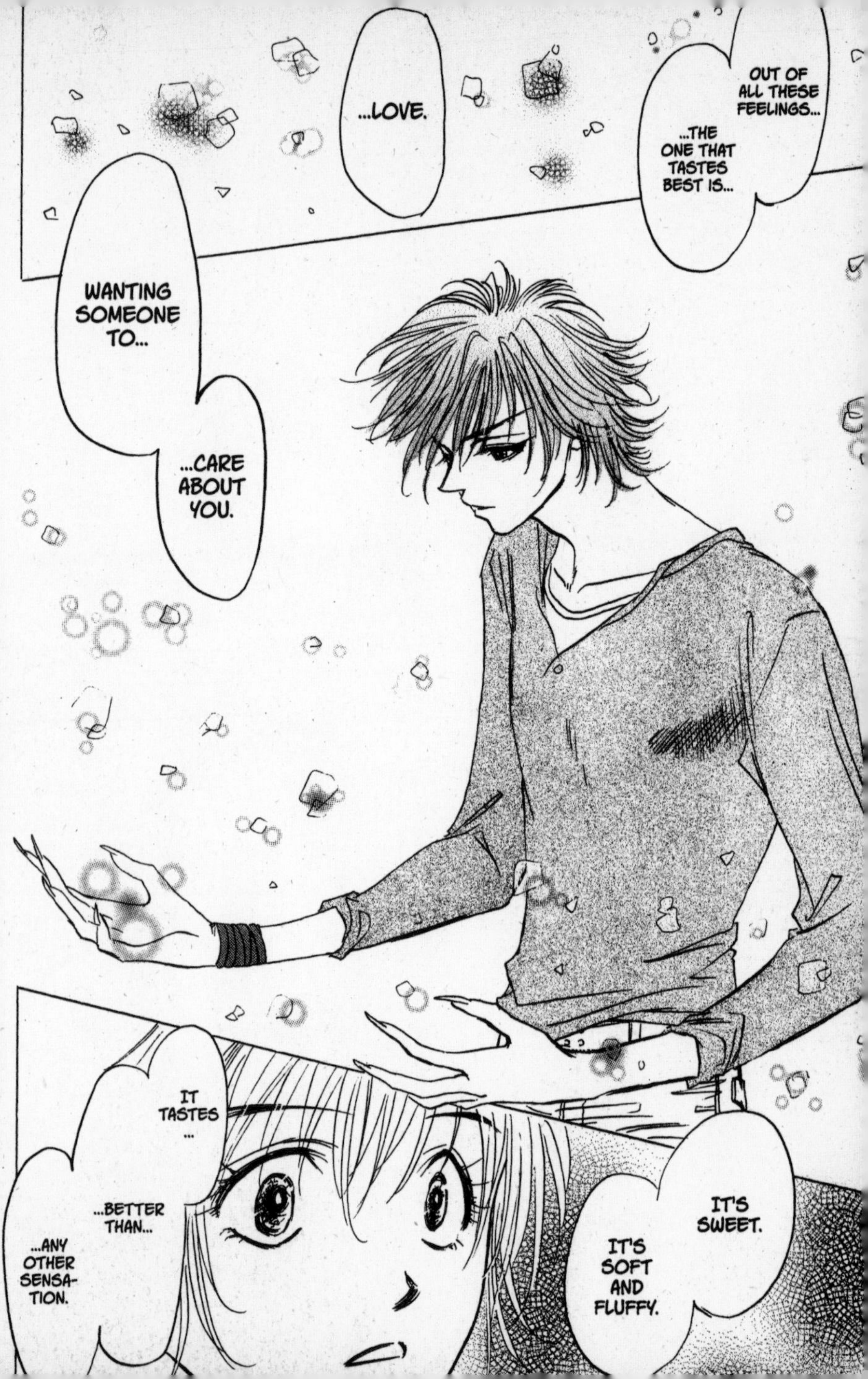
OUT OF ALL THESE FEELINGS...
...THE ONE THAT TASTES BEST IS...
...LOVE.
WANTING SOMEONE TO...
...CARE ABOUT YOU.
IT'S SWEET.
IT'S SOFT AND FLUFFY.
IT TASTES...
...BETTER THAN...
...ANY OTHER SENSATION.

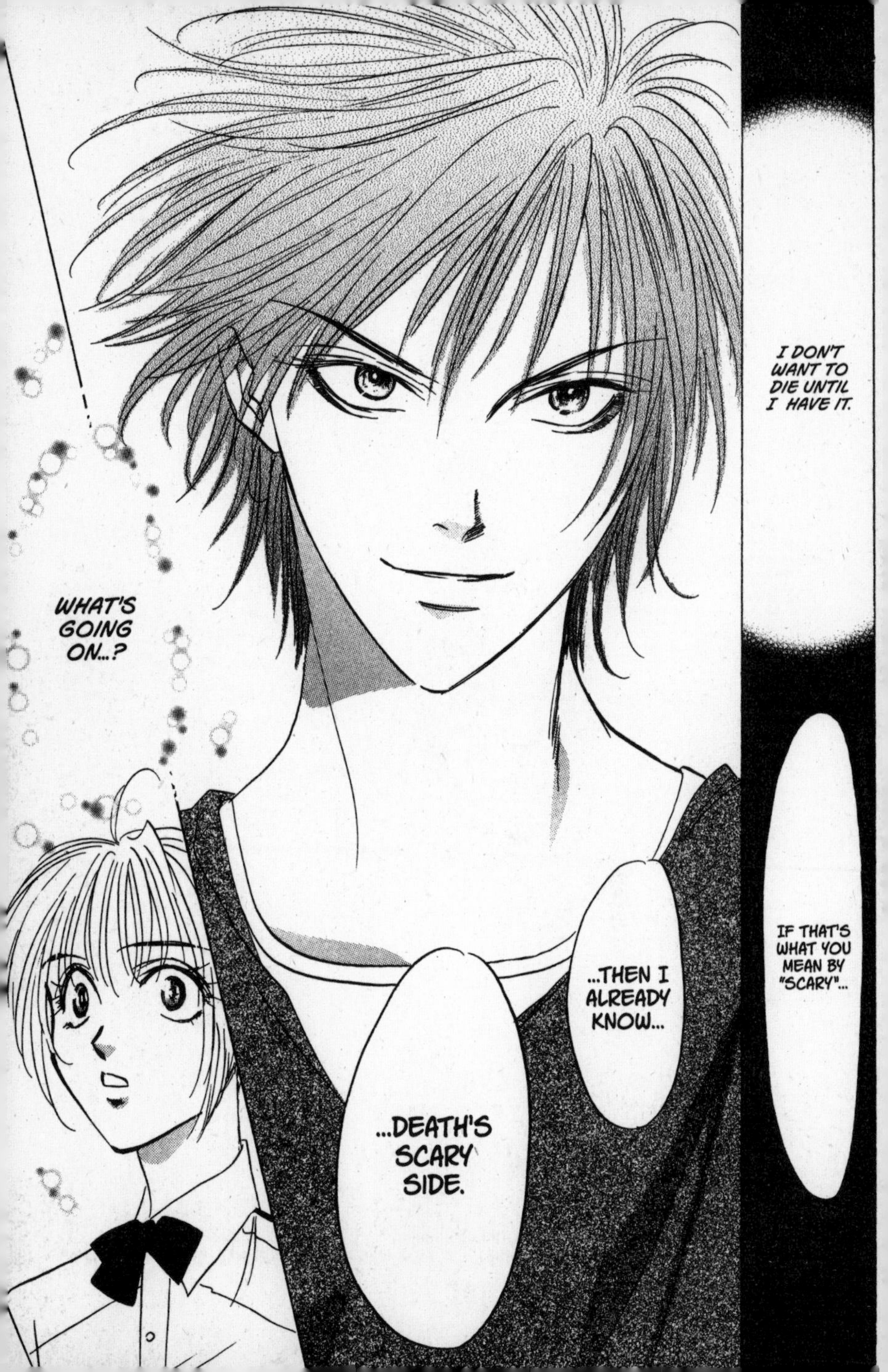
I DON'T WANT TO DIE UNTIL I HAVE IT.
IF THAT'S WHAT YOU MEAN BY "SCARY"...
...THEN I ALREADY KNOW...
...DEATH'S SCARY SIDE.
WHAT'S GOING ON...?

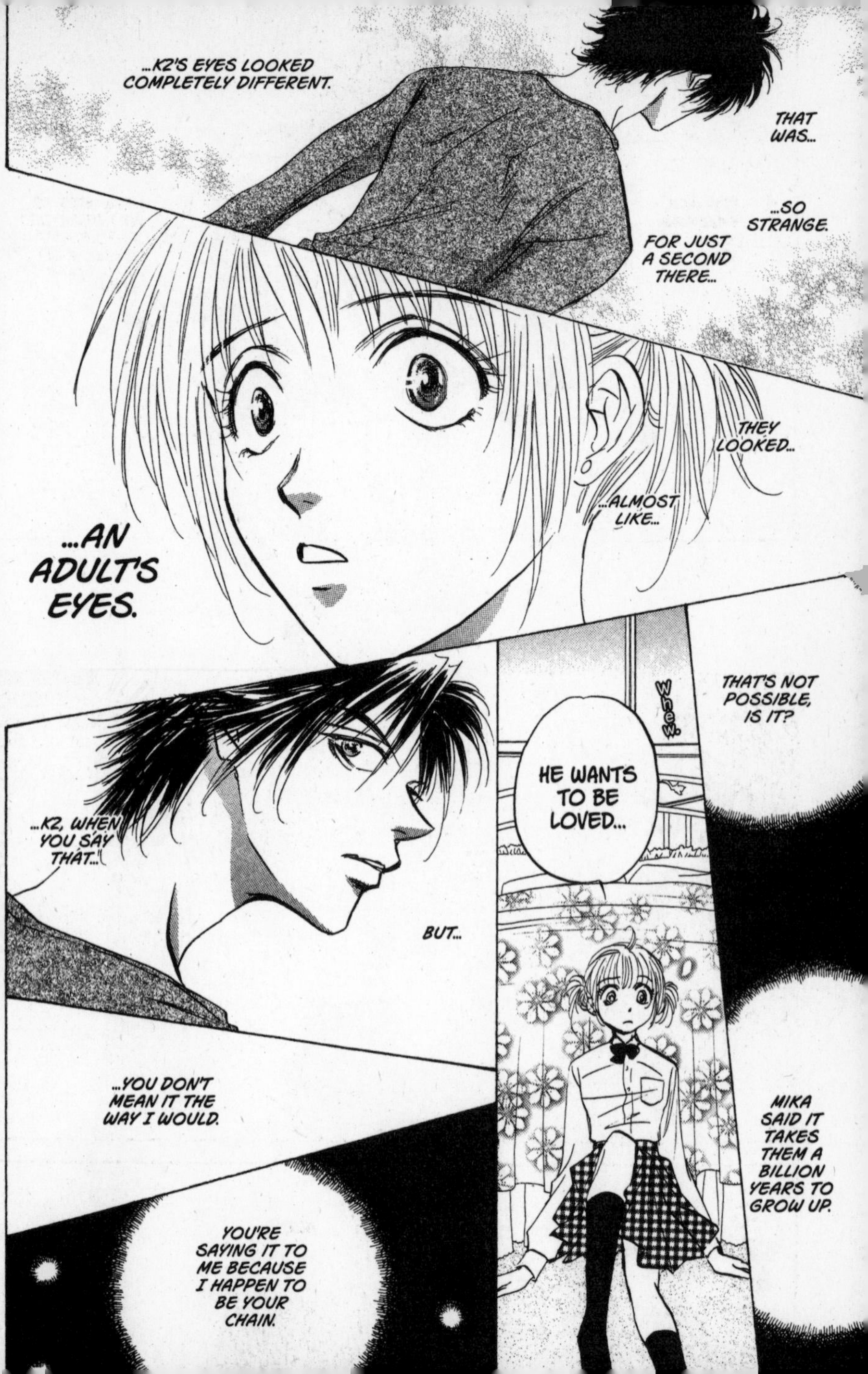
THAT WAS...
...SO STRANGE.
FOR JUST A SECOND THERE...
...K2'S EYES LOOKED COMPLETELY DIFFERENT.
THEY LOOKED...
...ALMOST LIKE...
...AN ADULT'S EYES.
THAT'S NOT POSSIBLE, IS IT?
Whew.
HE WANTS TO BE LOVED...
MIKA SAID IT TAKES THEM A BILLION YEARS TO GROW UP.
...K2, WHEN YOU SAY THAT...
BUT...
...YOU DON'T MEAN IT THE WAY I WOULD.
YOU'RE SAYING IT TO ME BECAUSE I HAPPEN TO BE YOUR CHAIN.

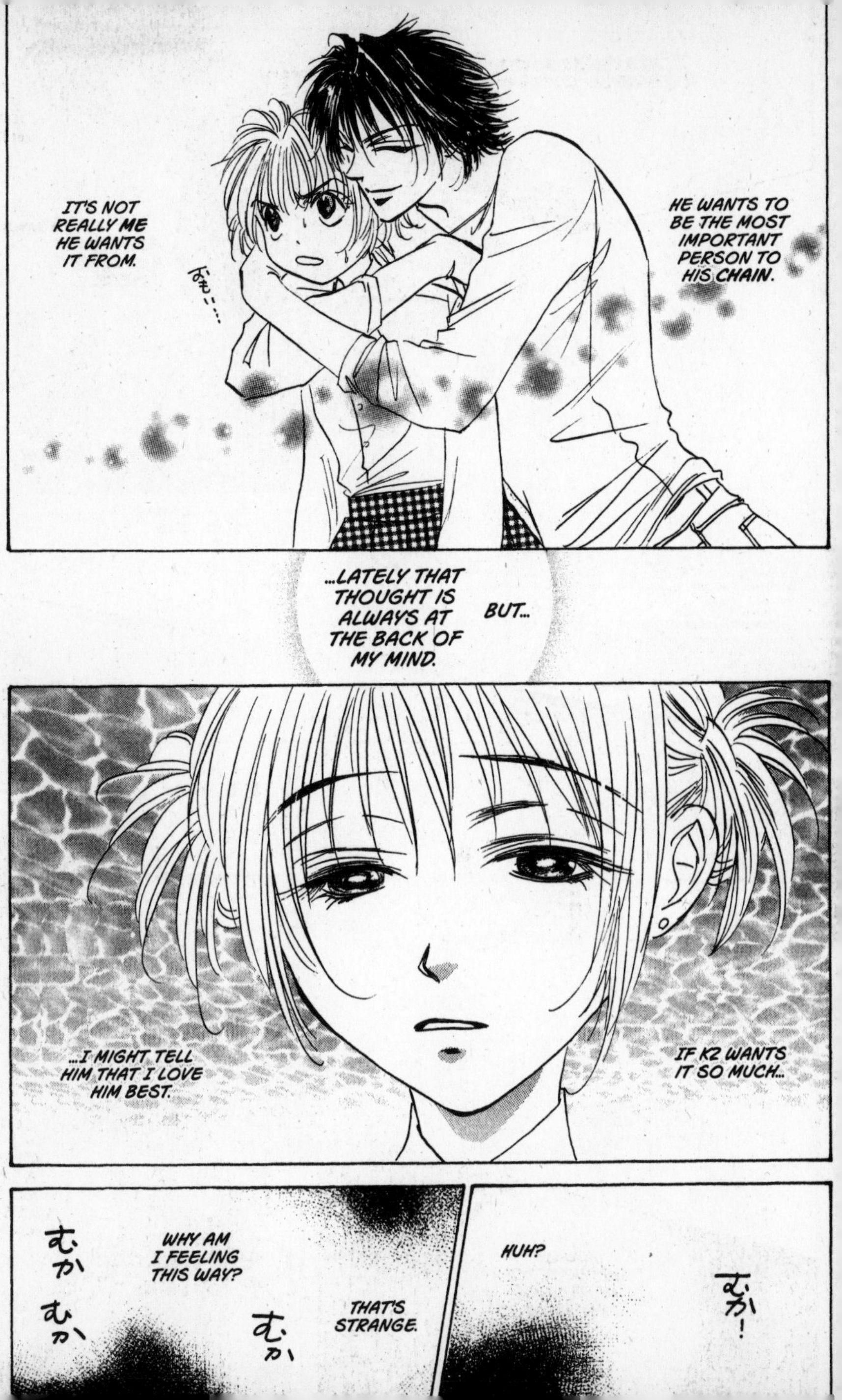
HE WANTS TO BE THE MOST IMPORTANT PERSON TO HIS CHAIN.
IT'S NOT REALLY ME HE WANTS IT FROM.
おもい…
BUT...
...LATELY THAT THOUGHT IS ALWAYS AT THE BACK OF MY MIND.
IF K2 WANTS IT SO MUCH...
...I MIGHT TELL HIM THAT I LOVE HIM BEST.
むかっ!
HUH?
WHY AM I FEELING THIS WAY?
THAT'S STRANGE.
むか
むか むか

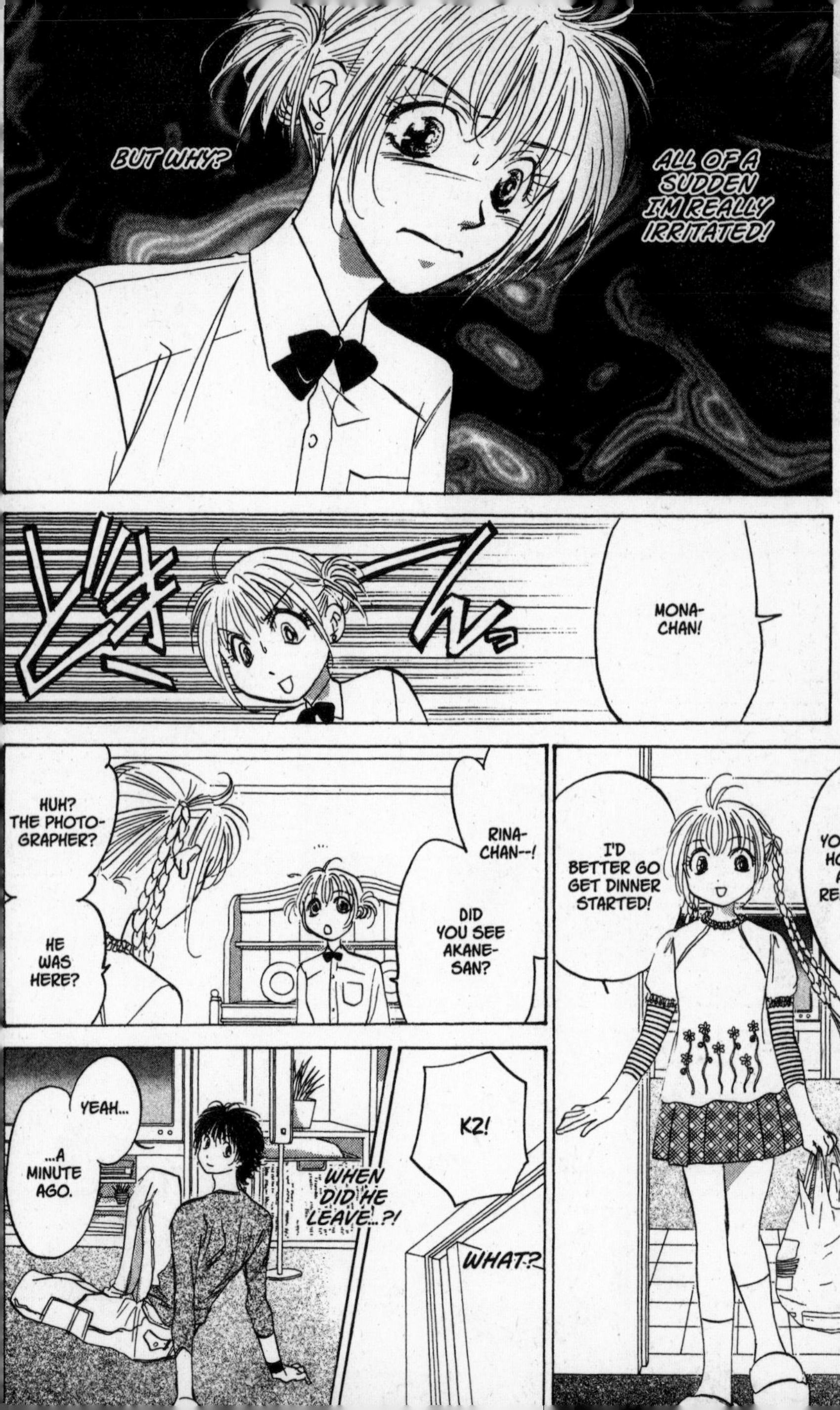
ALL OF A SUDDEN I'M REALLY IRRITATED!
BUT WHY?
MONA-CHAN!
YOU'RE HOME AL-READY?
I'D BETTER GO GET DINNER STARTED!
RINA-CHAN--!
DID YOU SEE AKANE-SAN?
HUH? THE PHOTOG-RAPHER?
HE WAS HERE?
KZ!
WHAT?
WHEN DID HE LEAVE...?!
YEAH...
...A MINUTE AGO.

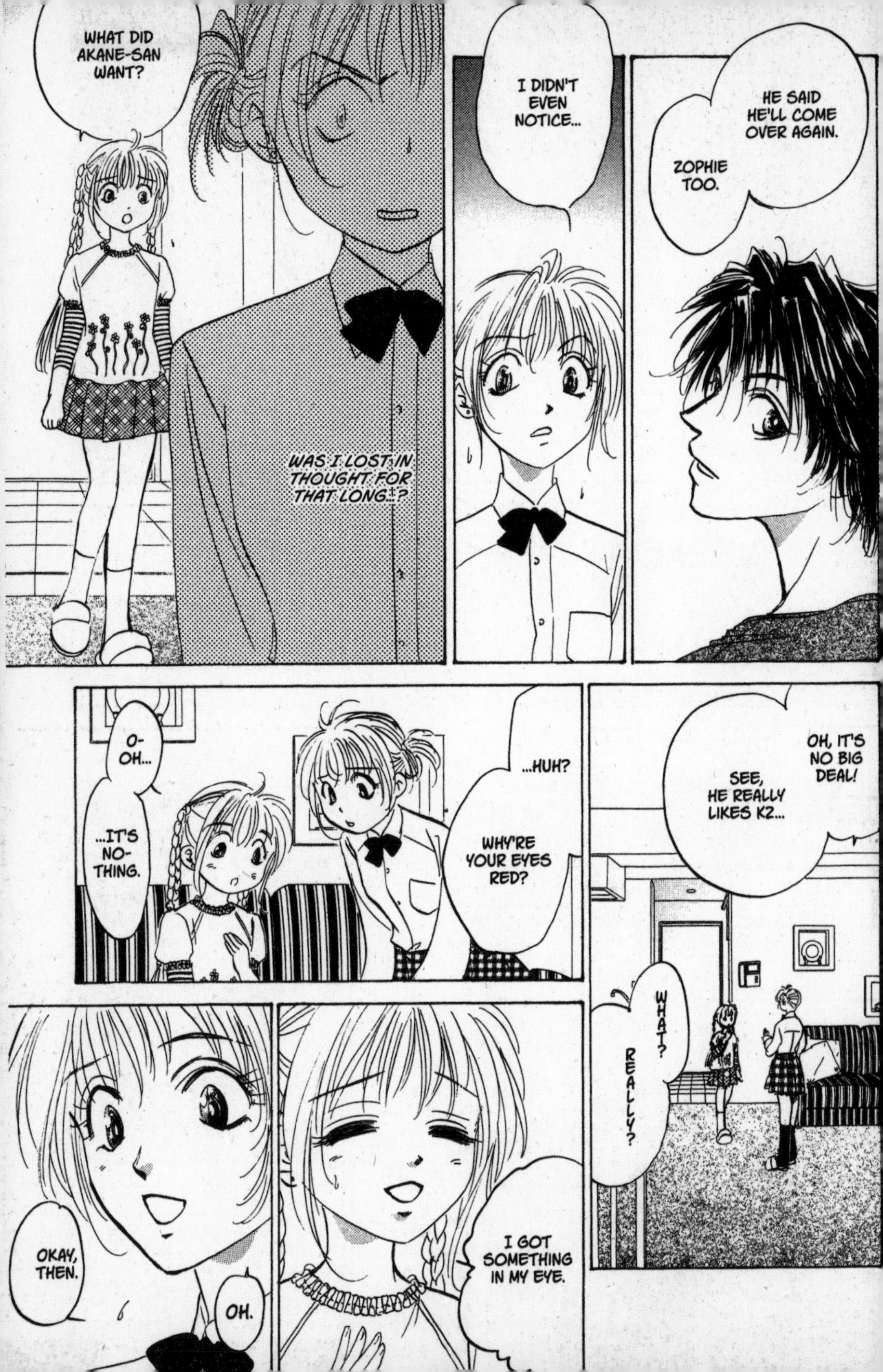
HE SAID HE'LL COME OVER AGAIN.
ZOPHIE TOO.
I DIDN'T EVEN NOTICE...
WHAT DID AKANE-SAN WANT?
WAS I LOST IN THOUGHT FOR THAT LONG!?
OH, IT'S NO BIG DEAL!
SEE, HE REALLY LIKES K2...
WHAT? REALLY?
...HUH?
WHY'RE YOUR EYES RED?
O-OH...
...IT'S NO-THING.
I GOT SOMETHING IN MY EYE.
OH.
OKAY, THEN.

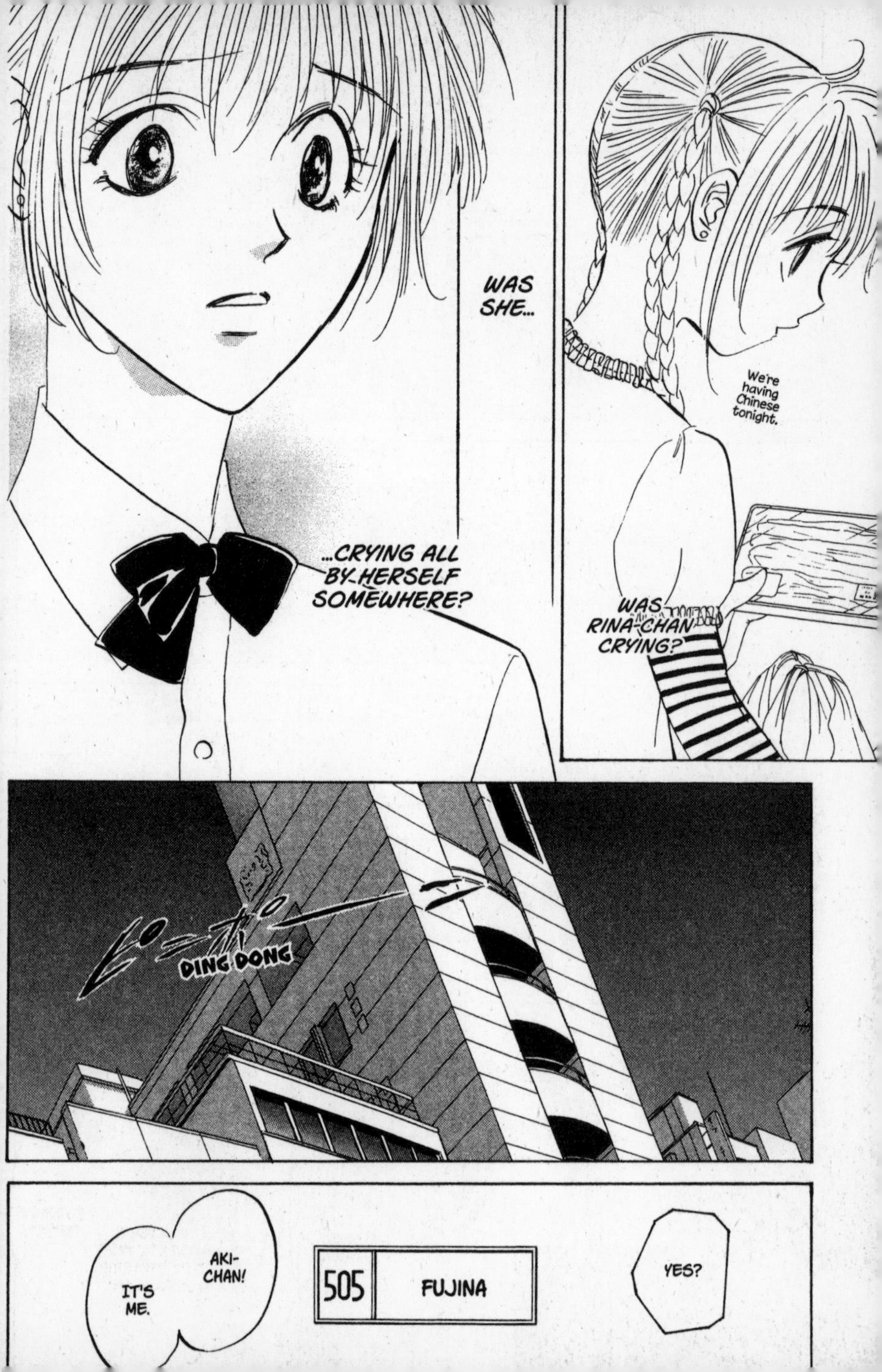
We're having Chinese tonight.
WAS RINA-CHAN CRYING?
WAS SHE...
...CRYING ALL BY-HERSELF SOMEWHERE?
DING DONG
YES?
505 FUJINA
AKI-CHAN!
IT'S ME.

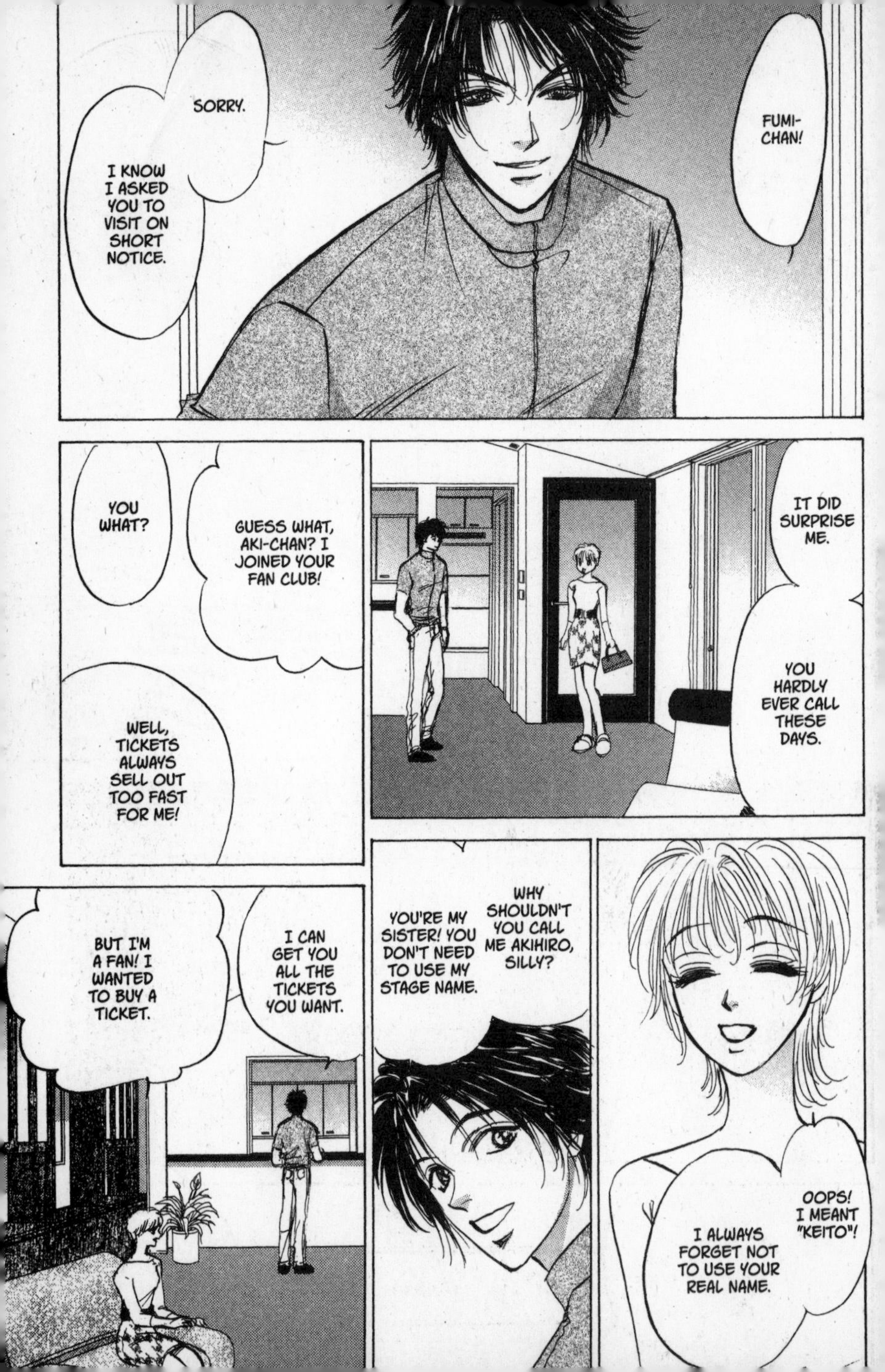
FUMI-CHAN!
SORRY.
I KNOW I ASKED YOU TO VISIT ON SHORT NOTICE.
IT DID SURPRISE ME.
YOU HARDLY EVER CALL THESE DAYS.
GUESS WHAT, AKI-CHAN? I JOINED YOUR FAN CLUB!
YOU WHAT?
WELL, TICKETS ALWAYS SELL OUT TOO FAST FOR ME!
OOPS! I MEANT "KEITO"!
I ALWAYS FORGET NOT TO USE YOUR REAL NAME.
WHY SHOULDN'T YOU CALL ME AKIHIRO, SILLY?
YOU'RE MY SISTER! YOU DON'T NEED TO USE MY STAGE NAME.
I CAN GET YOU ALL THE TICKETS YOU WANT.
BUT I'M A FAN! I WANTED TO BUY A TICKET.

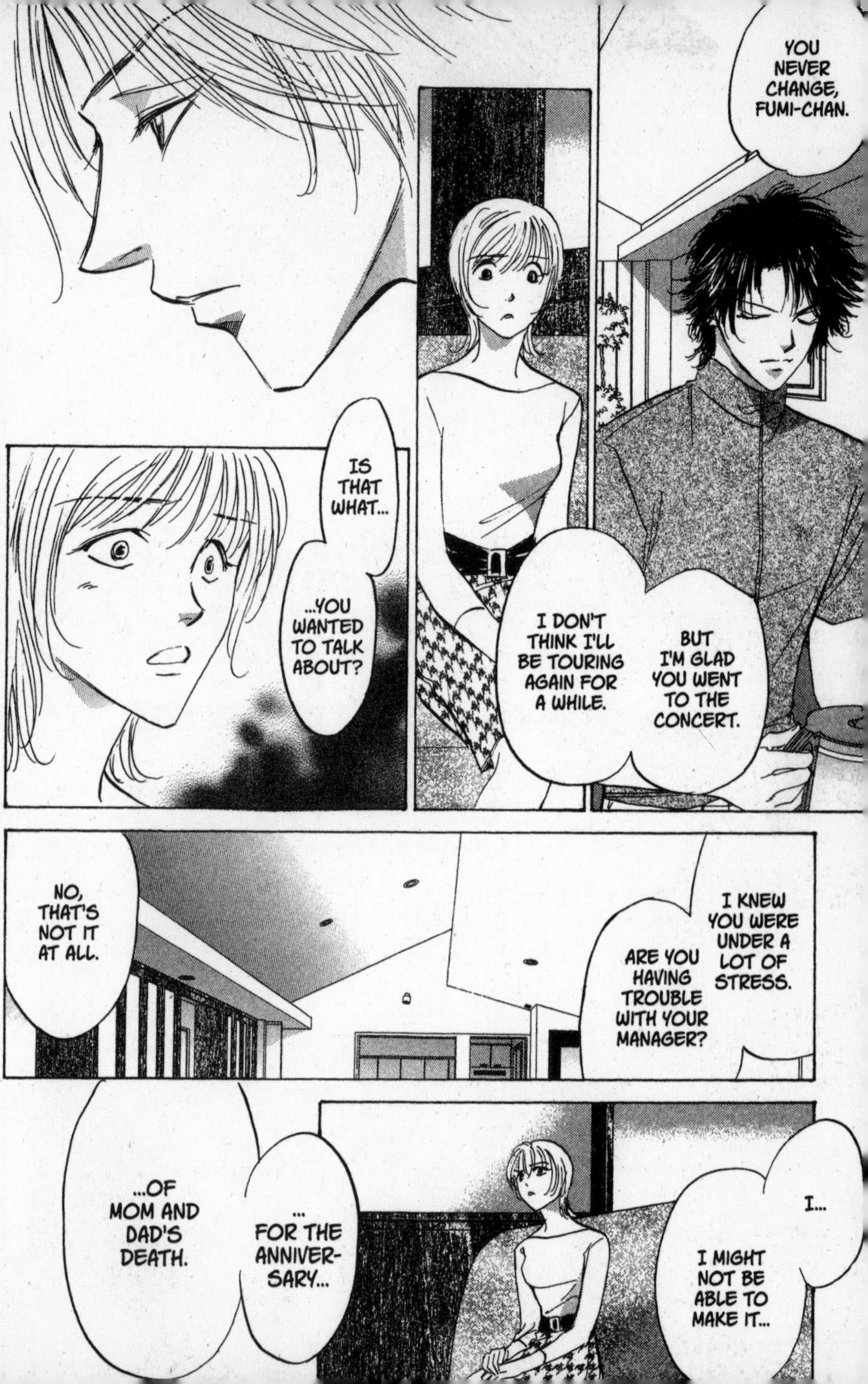
YOU NEVER CHANGE, FUMI-CHAN.
BUT I'M GLAD YOU WENT TO THE CONCERT.
I DON'T THINK I'LL BE TOURING AGAIN FOR A WHILE.
IS THAT WHAT...
...YOU WANTED TO TALK ABOUT?
I KNEW YOU WERE UNDER A LOT OF STRESS.
ARE YOU HAVING TROUBLE WITH YOUR MANAGER?
NO, THAT'S NOT IT AT ALL.
I...
I MIGHT NOT BE ABLE TO MAKE IT...
... FOR THE ANNIVER-SARY...
...OF MOM AND DAD'S DEATH.

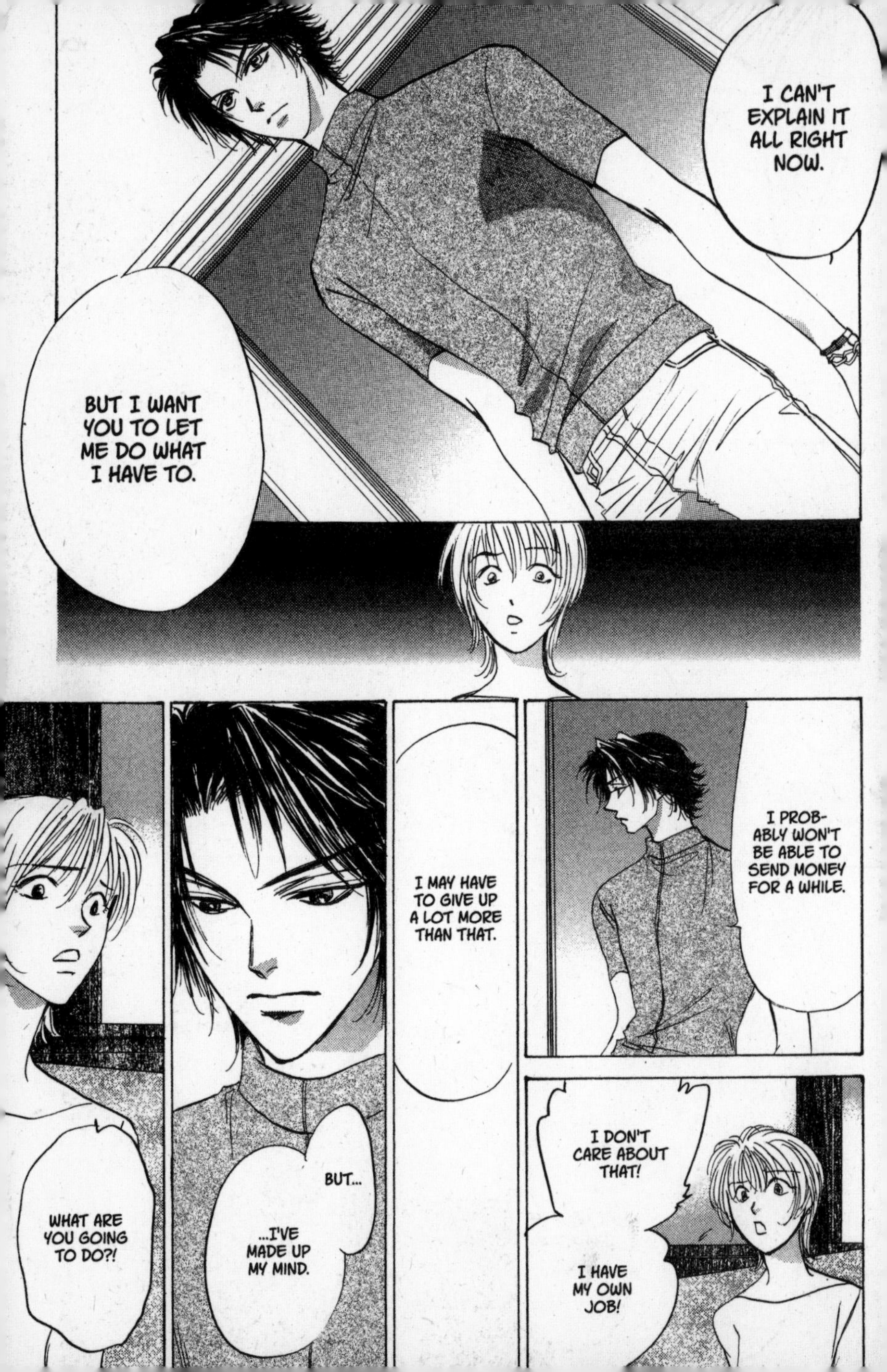
I CAN'T EXPLAIN IT ALL RIGHT NOW.
BUT I WANT YOU TO LET ME DO WHAT I HAVE TO.
I PROB-ABLY WON'T BE ABLE TO SEND MONEY FOR A WHILE.
I DON'T CARE ABOUT THAT!
I HAVE MY OWN JOB!
I MAY HAVE TO GIVE UP A LOT MORE THAN THAT.
BUT...
...I'VE MADE UP MY MIND.
WHAT ARE YOU GOING TO DO?!

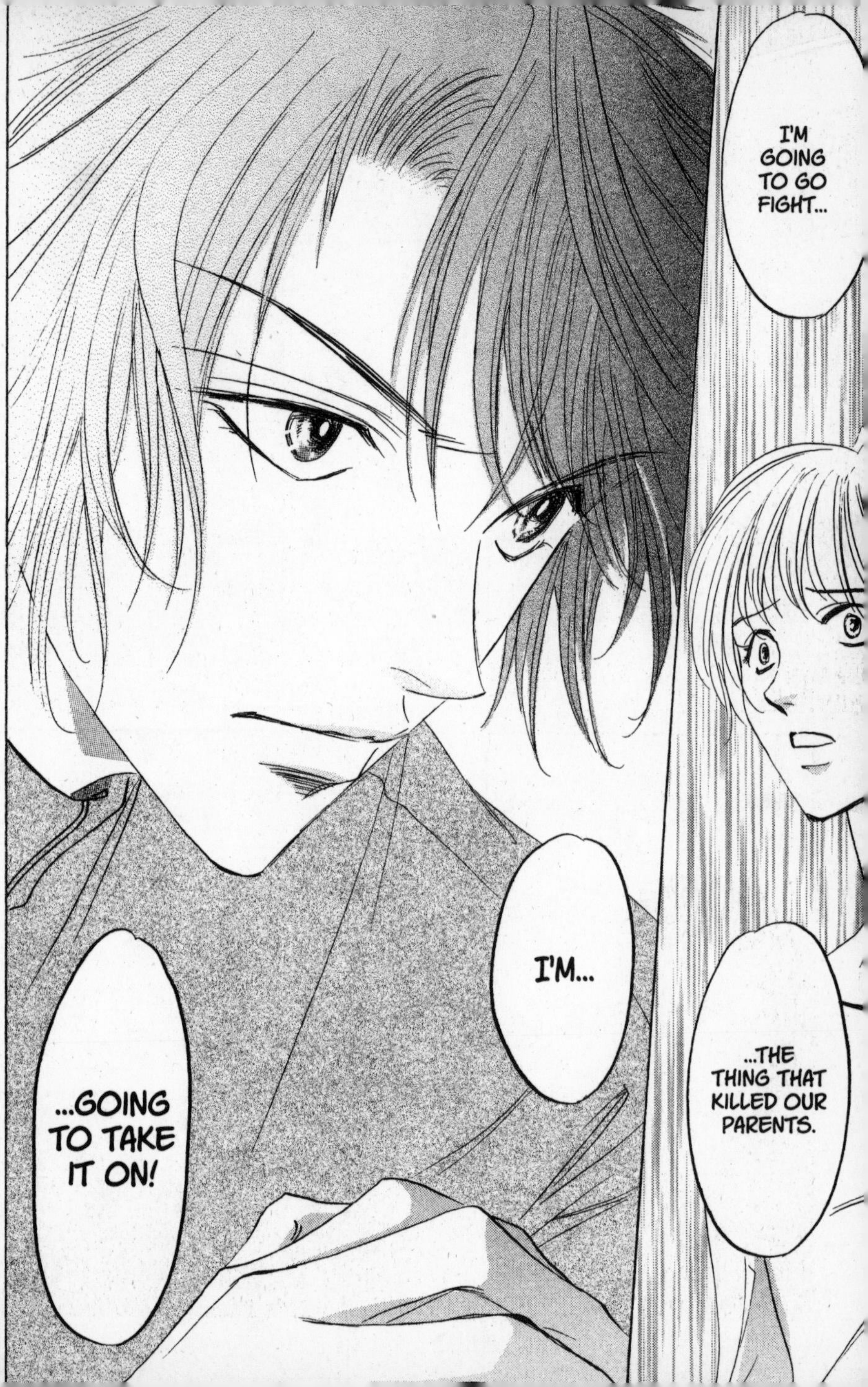
I'M GOING TO GO FIGHT...
...THE THING THAT KILLED OUR PARENTS.
I'M...
...GOING TO TAKE IT ON!

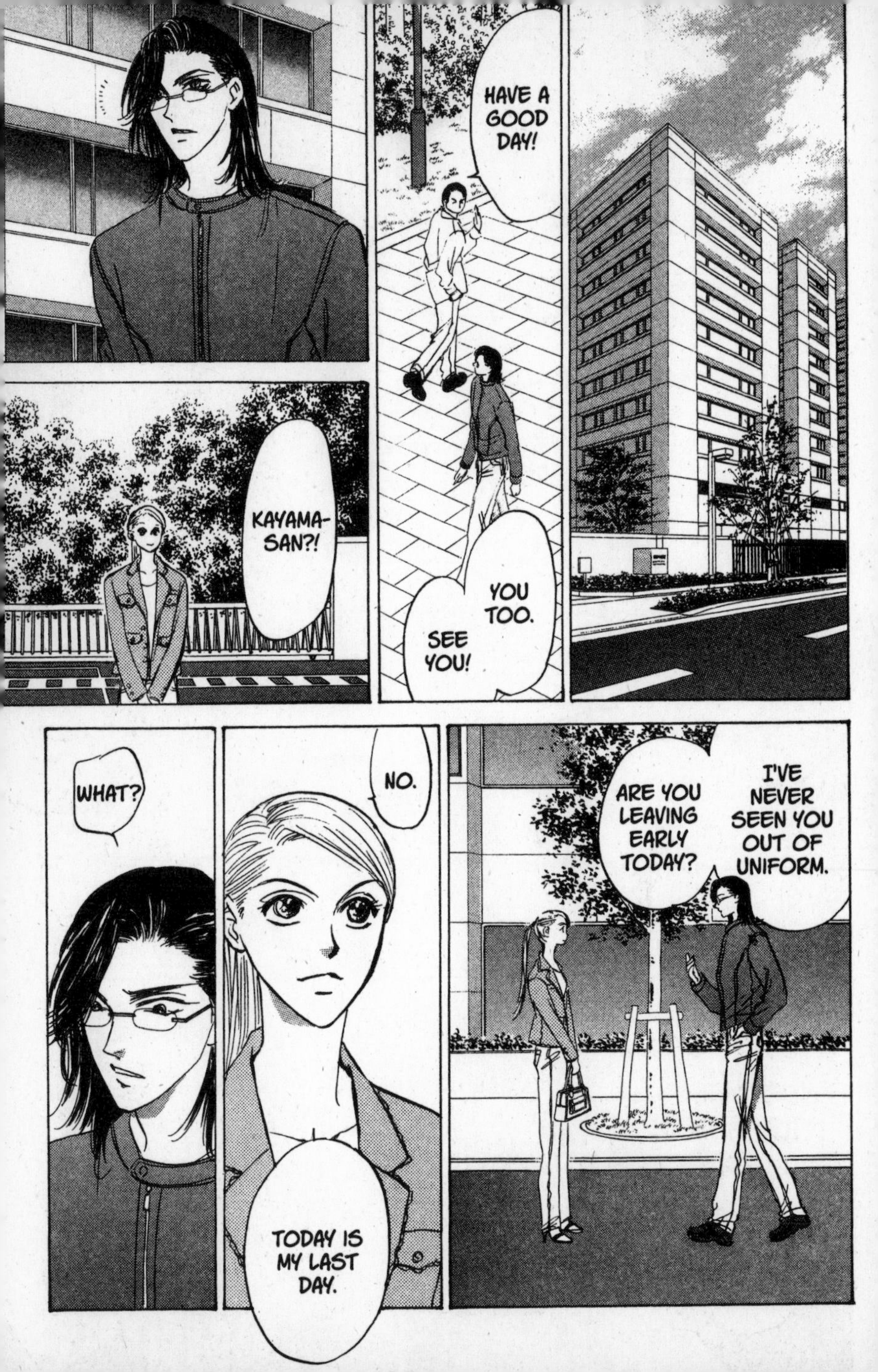
HAVE A GOOD DAY!
YOU TOO.
SEE YOU!
KAYAMA-SAN?!
I'VE NEVER SEEN YOU OUT OF UNIFORM.
ARE YOU LEAVING EARLY TODAY?
NO.
TODAY IS MY LAST DAY.
WHAT?

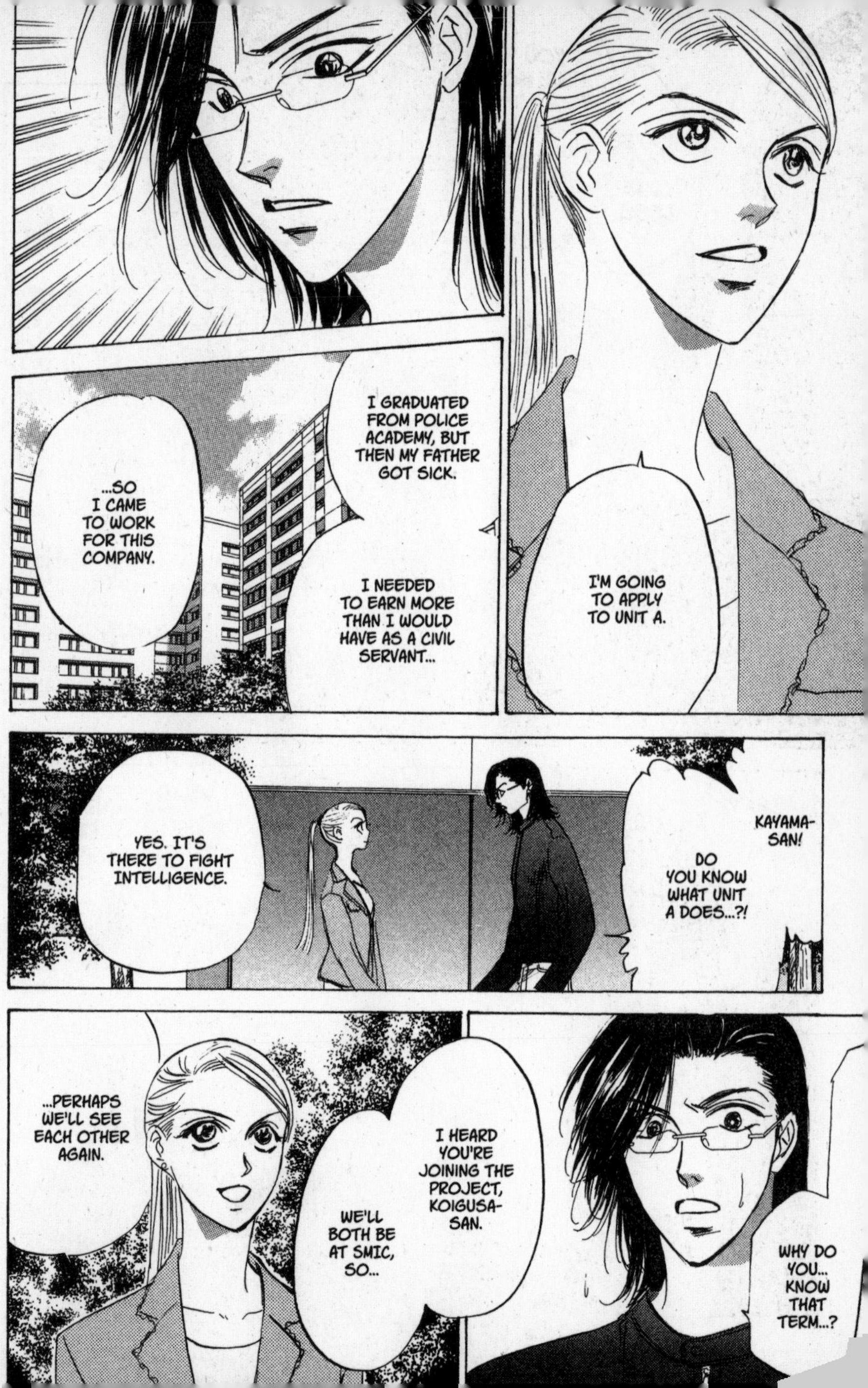
I'M GOING TO APPLY TO UNIT A.
I GRADUATED FROM POLICE ACADEMY, BUT THEN MY FATHER GOT SICK.
I NEEDED TO EARN MORE THAN I WOULD HAVE AS A CIVIL SERVANT...
...SO I CAME TO WORK FOR THIS COMPANY.
KAYAMA-SAN!
DO YOU KNOW WHAT UNIT A DOES...?!
YES. IT'S THERE TO FIGHT INTELLIGENCE.
WHY DO YOU... KNOW THAT TERM...?
I HEARD YOU'RE JOINING THE PROJECT, KOIGUSA-SAN.
WE'LL BOTH BE AT SMIC, SO...
...PERHAPS WE'LL SEE EACH OTHER AGAIN.

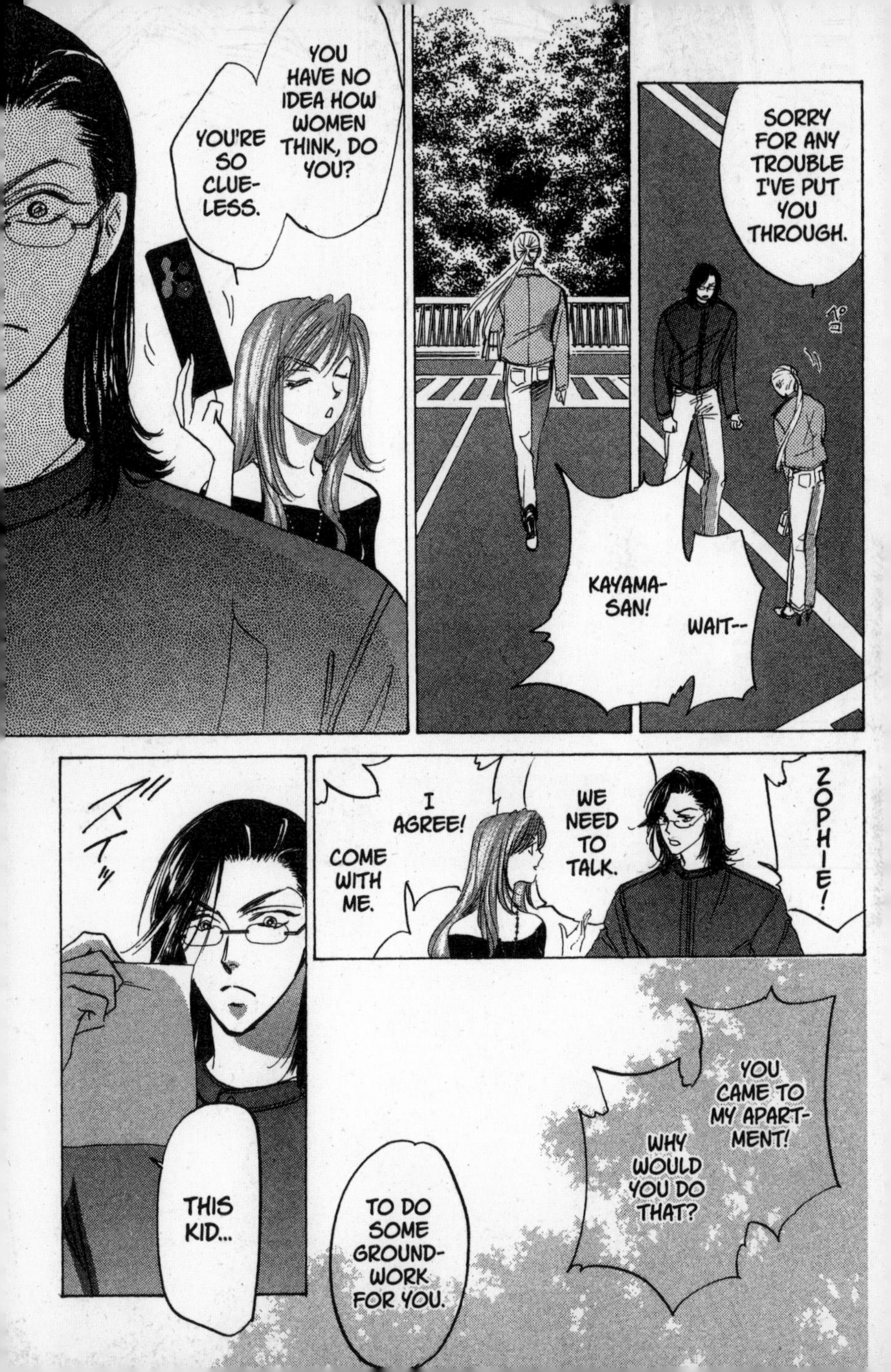
SORRY FOR ANY TROUBLE I'VE PUT YOU THROUGH.
WAIT--
KAYAMA-SAN!
YOU HAVE NO IDEA HOW WOMEN THINK, DO YOU?
YOU'RE SO CLUE-LESS.
ZOPHIE!
WE NEED TO TALK.
I AGREE!
COME WITH ME.
YOU CAME TO MY APART-MENT!
WHY WOULD YOU DO THAT?
TO DO SOME GROUND-WORK FOR YOU.
THIS KID...

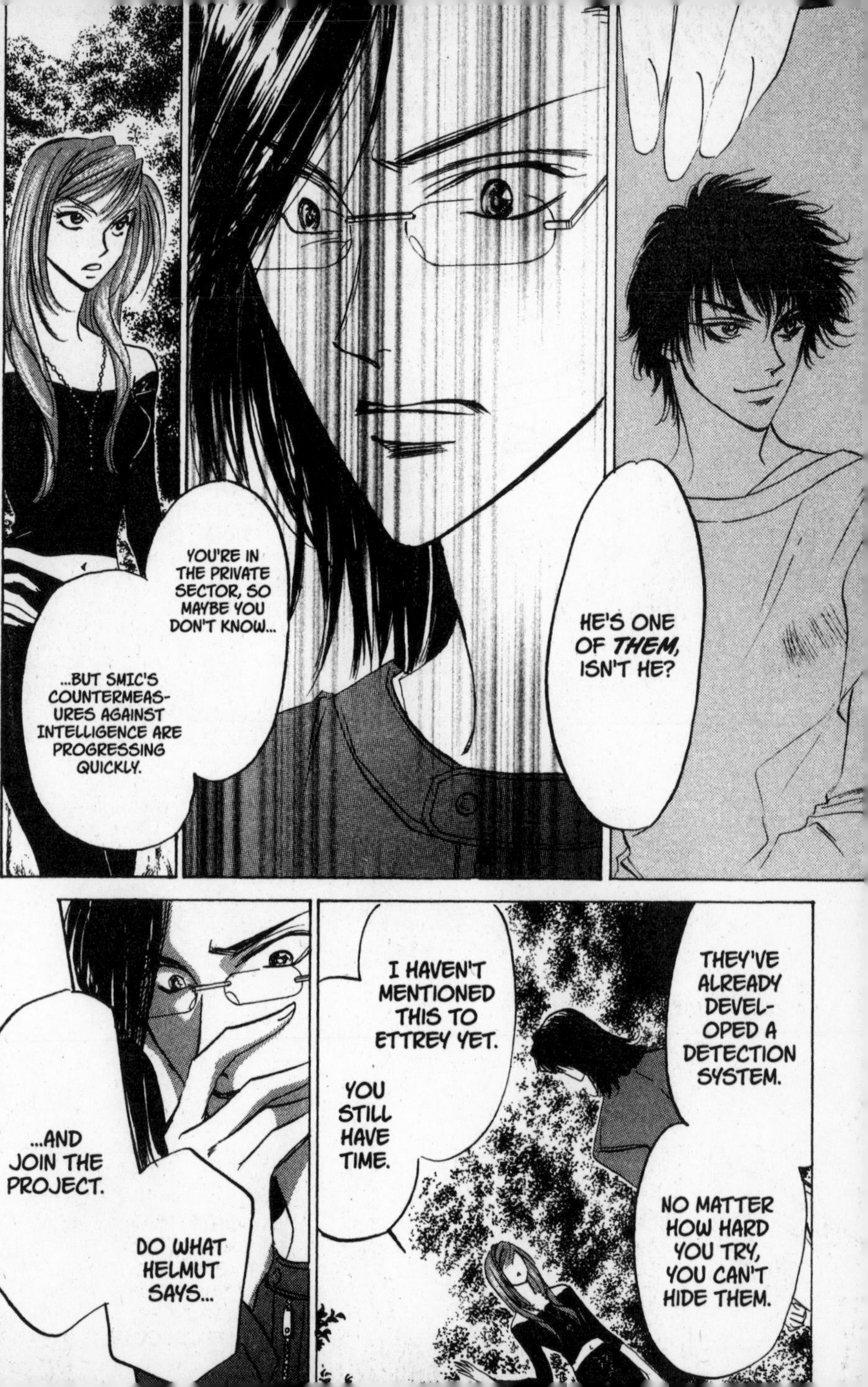
HE'S ONE OF *THEM*, ISN'T HE?
YOU'RE IN THE PRIVATE SECTOR, SO MAYBE YOU DON'T KNOW...
...BUT SMIC'S COUNTERMEAS-URES AGAINST INTELLIGENCE ARE PROGRESSING QUICKLY.
THEY'VE ALREADY DEVEL-OPED A DETECTION SYSTEM.
NO MATTER HOW HARD YOU TRY, YOU CAN'T HIDE THEM.
I HAVEN'T MENTIONED THIS TO ETTREY YET.
YOU STILL HAVE TIME.
DO WHAT HELMUT SAYS...
...AND JOIN THE PROJECT.

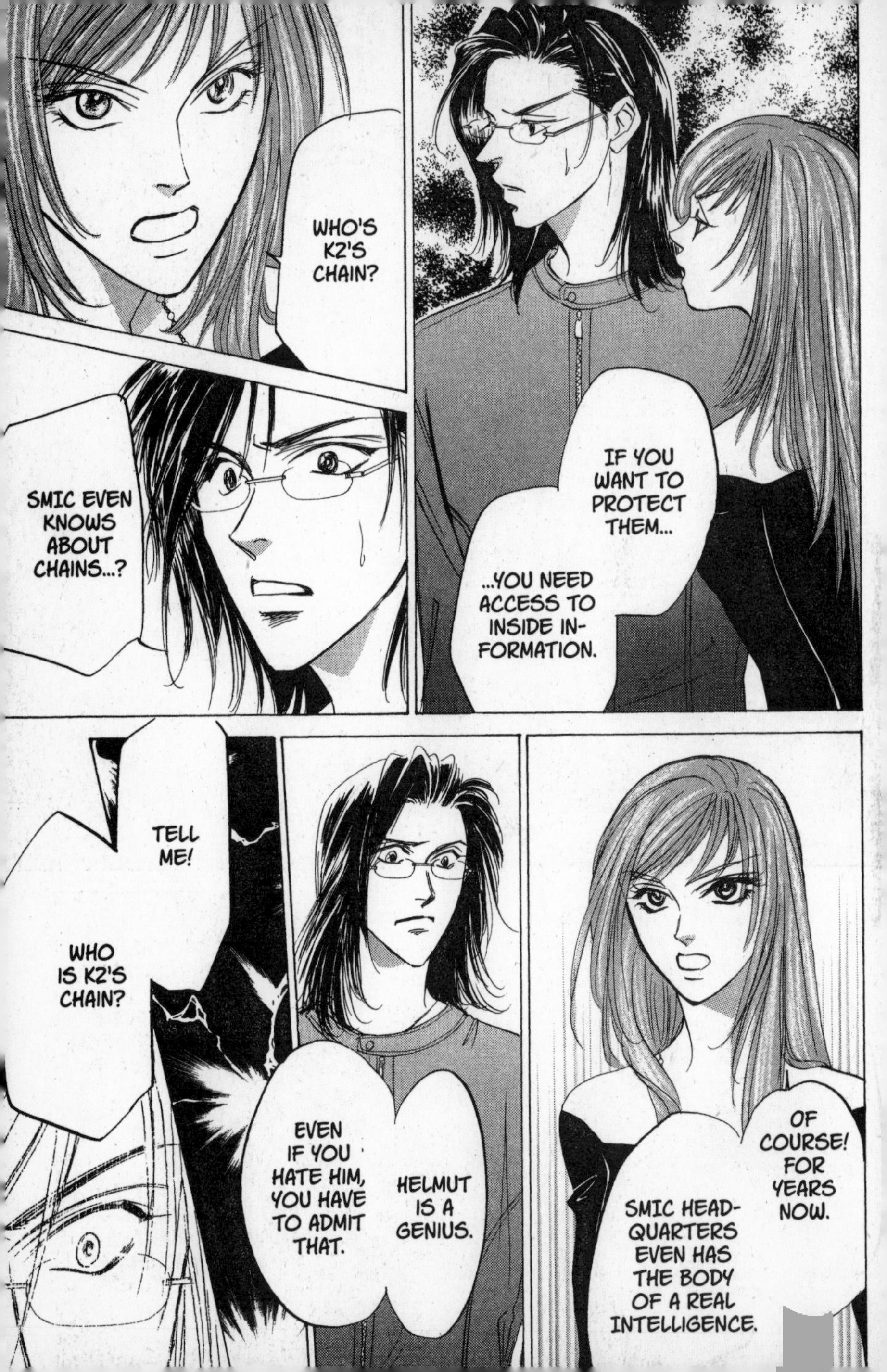
IF YOU WANT TO PROTECT THEM...
...YOU NEED ACCESS TO INSIDE IN-FORMATION.
WHO'S K2'S CHAIN?
SMIC EVEN KNOWS ABOUT CHAINS...?
OF COURSE! FOR YEARS NOW.
SMIC HEAD-QUARTERS EVEN HAS THE BODY OF A REAL INTELLIGENCE.
HELMUT IS A GENIUS.
EVEN IF YOU HATE HIM, YOU HAVE TO ADMIT THAT.
TELL ME!
WHO IS K2'S CHAIN?

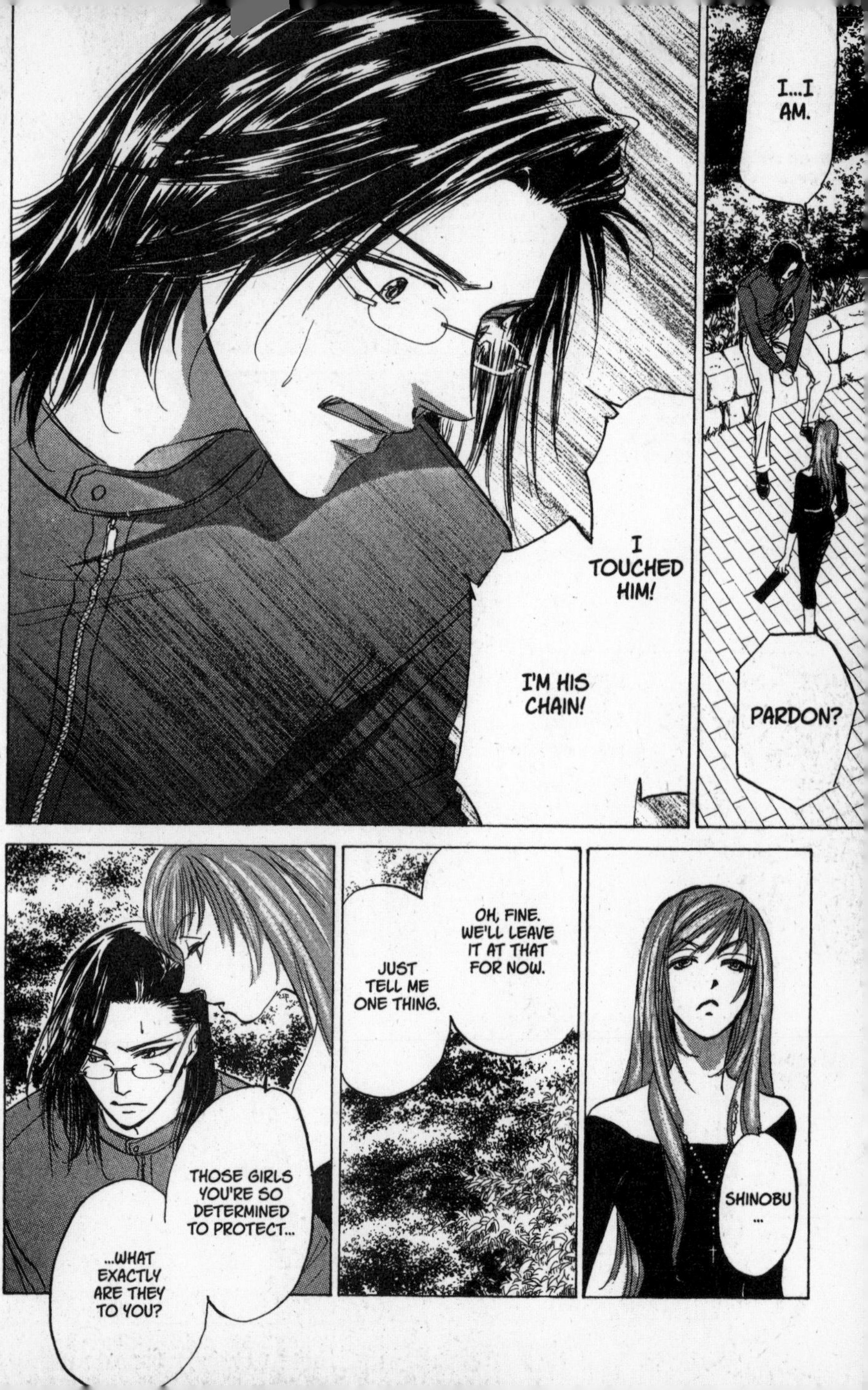
I...I AM.
PARDON?
I TOUCHED HIM!
I'M HIS CHAIN!
SHINOBU ...
OH, FINE. WE'LL LEAVE IT AT THAT FOR NOW.
JUST TELL ME ONE THING.
THOSE GIRLS YOU'RE SO DETERMINED TO PROTECT...
...WHAT EXACTLY ARE THEY TO YOU?

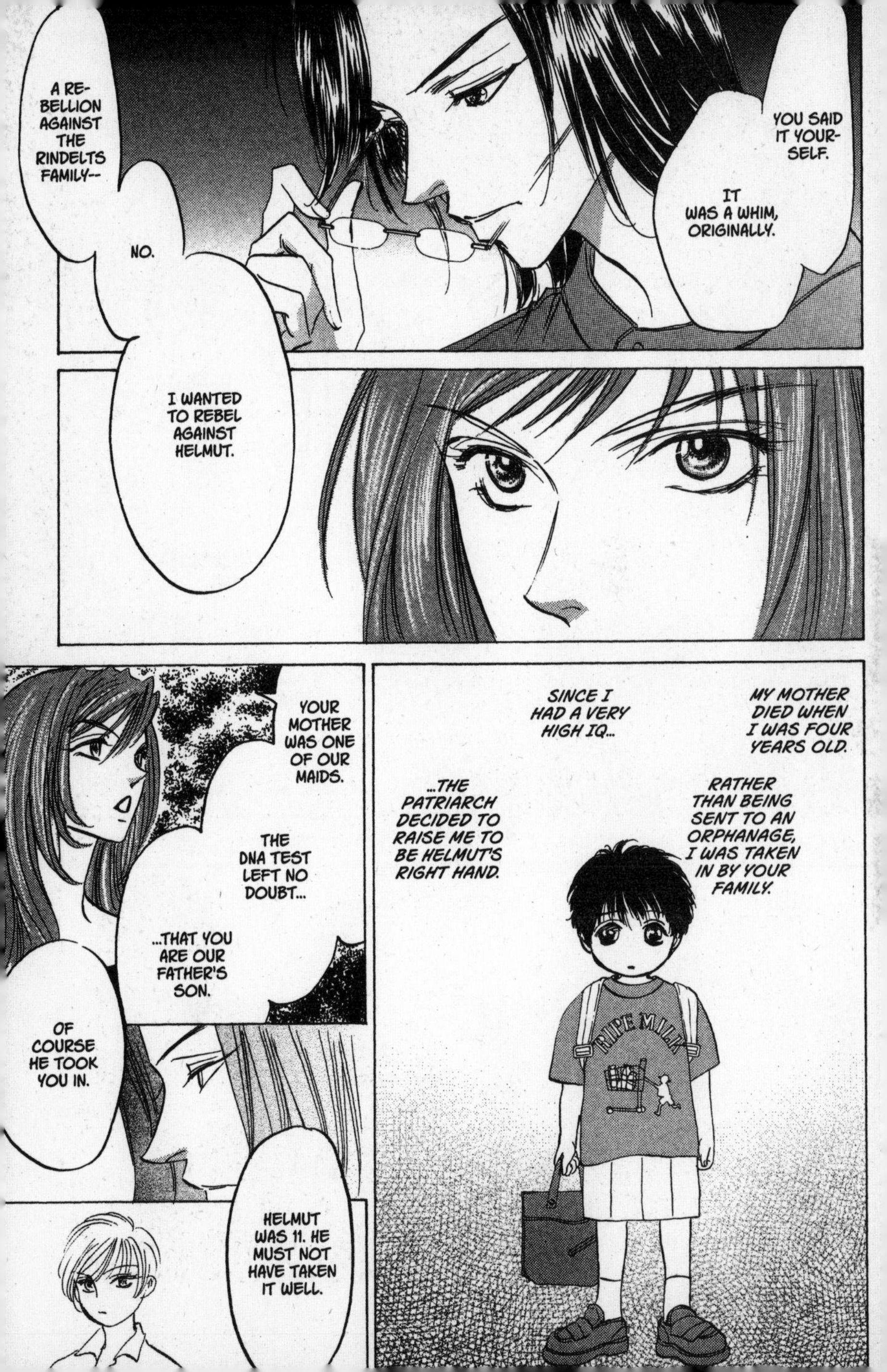
YOU SAID IT YOURSELF.
IT WAS A WHIM, ORIGINALLY.
A REBELLION AGAINST THE RINDELTS FAMILY--
NO.
I WANTED TO REBEL AGAINST HELMUT.
MY MOTHER DIED WHEN I WAS FOUR YEARS OLD.
RATHER THAN BEING SENT TO AN ORPHANAGE, I WAS TAKEN IN BY YOUR FAMILY.
SINCE I HAD A VERY HIGH IQ...
...THE PATRIARCH DECIDED TO RAISE ME TO BE HELMUT'S RIGHT HAND.
RIPE MILK
YOUR MOTHER WAS ONE OF OUR MAIDS.
THE DNA TEST LEFT NO DOUBT...
...THAT YOU ARE OUR FATHER'S SON.
OF COURSE HE TOOK YOU IN.
HELMUT WAS 11. HE MUST NOT HAVE TAKEN IT WELL.

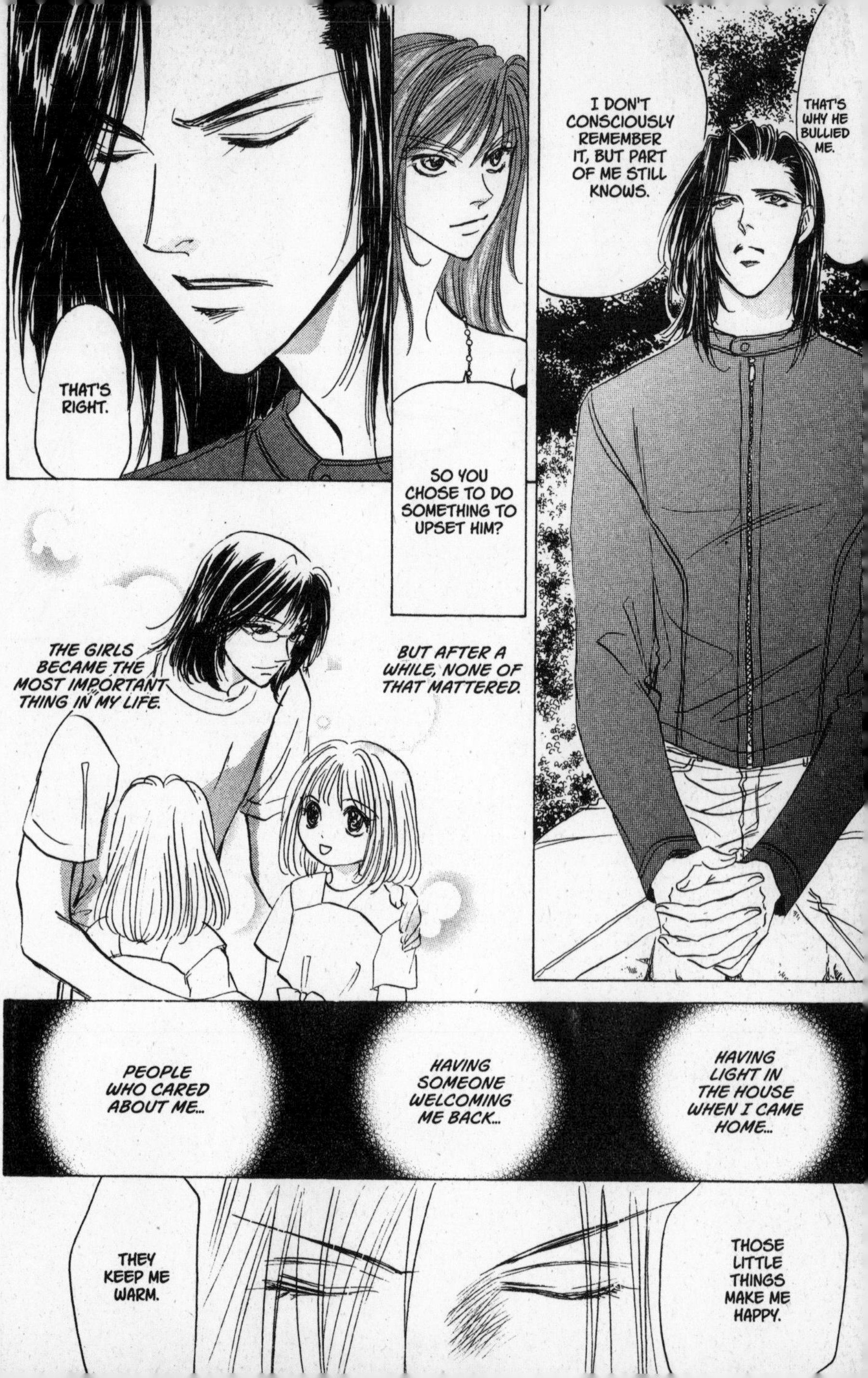
THAT'S WHY HE BULLIED ME.
I DON'T CONSCIOUSLY REMEMBER IT, BUT PART OF ME STILL KNOWS.
SO YOU CHOSE TO DO SOMETHING TO UPSET HIM?
THAT'S RIGHT.
BUT AFTER A WHILE, NONE OF THAT MATTERED.
THE GIRLS BECAME THE MOST IMPORTANT THING IN MY LIFE.
HAVING LIGHT IN THE HOUSE WHEN I CAME HOME...
HAVING SOMEONE WELCOMING ME BACK...
PEOPLE WHO CARED ABOUT ME...
THOSE LITTLE THINGS MAKE ME HAPPY.
THEY KEEP ME WARM.

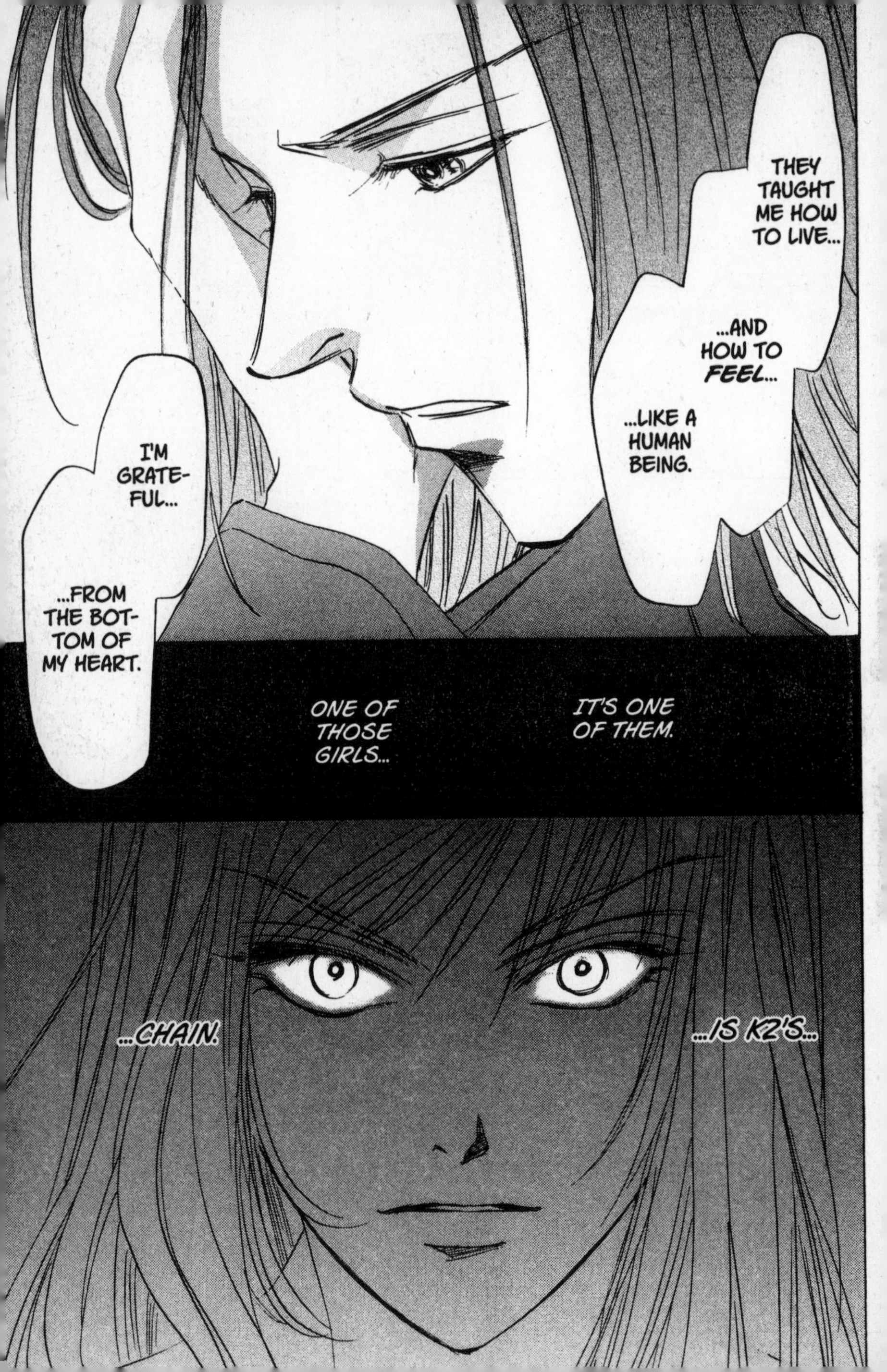
THEY TAUGHT ME HOW TO LIVE...
...AND HOW TO *FEEL*...
...LIKE A HUMAN BEING.
I'M GRATE-FUL...
...FROM THE BOT-TOM OF MY HEART.
IT'S ONE OF THEM.
ONE OF THOSE GIRLS...
...IS K2'S...
...CHAIN.

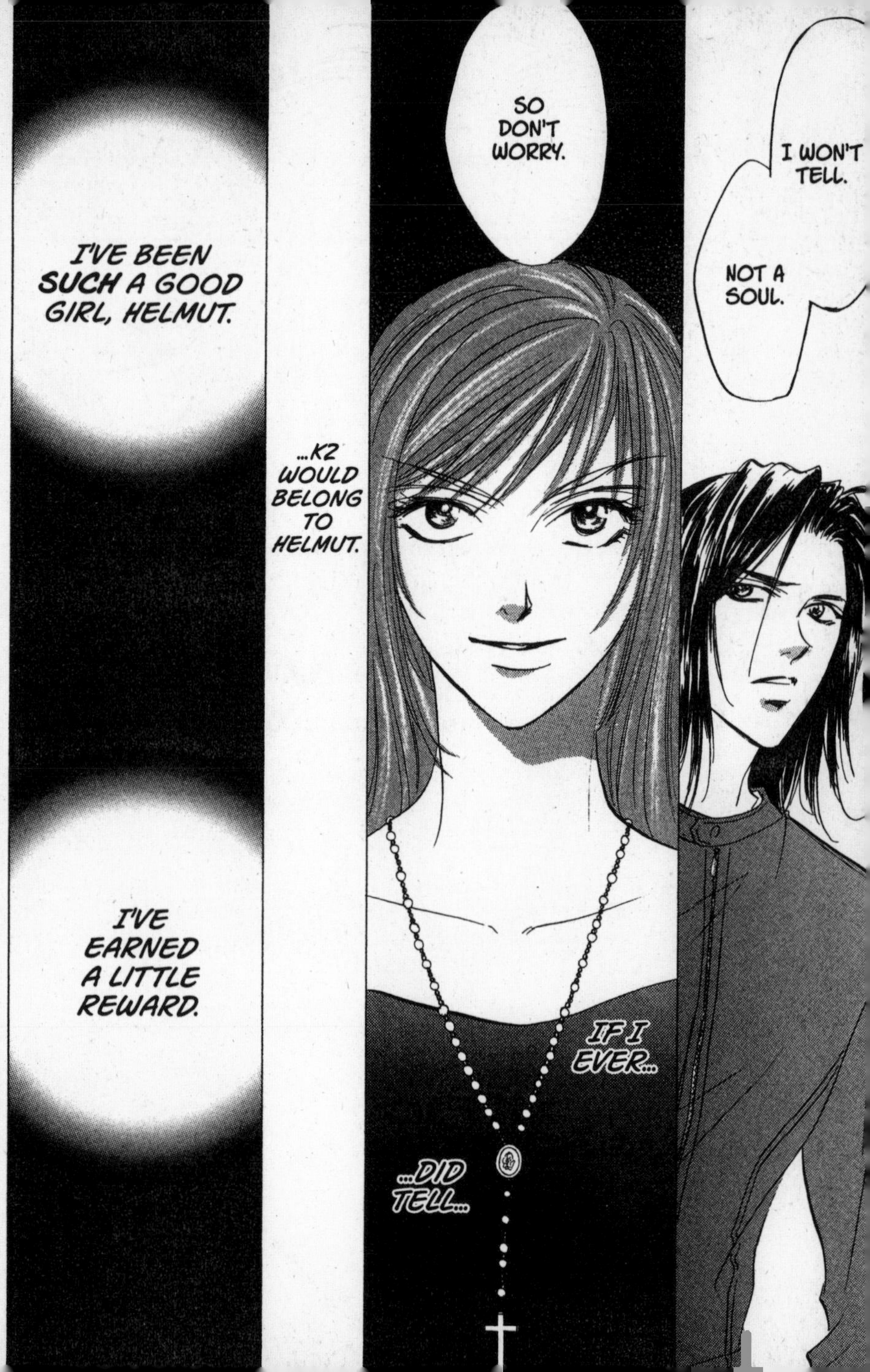
I WON'T TELL.
NOT A SOUL.
SO DON'T WORRY.
IF I EVER...
...DID TELL...
...K2 WOULD BELONG TO HELMUT.
I'VE BEEN SUCH A GOOD GIRL, HELMUT.
I'VE EARNED A LITTLE REWARD.

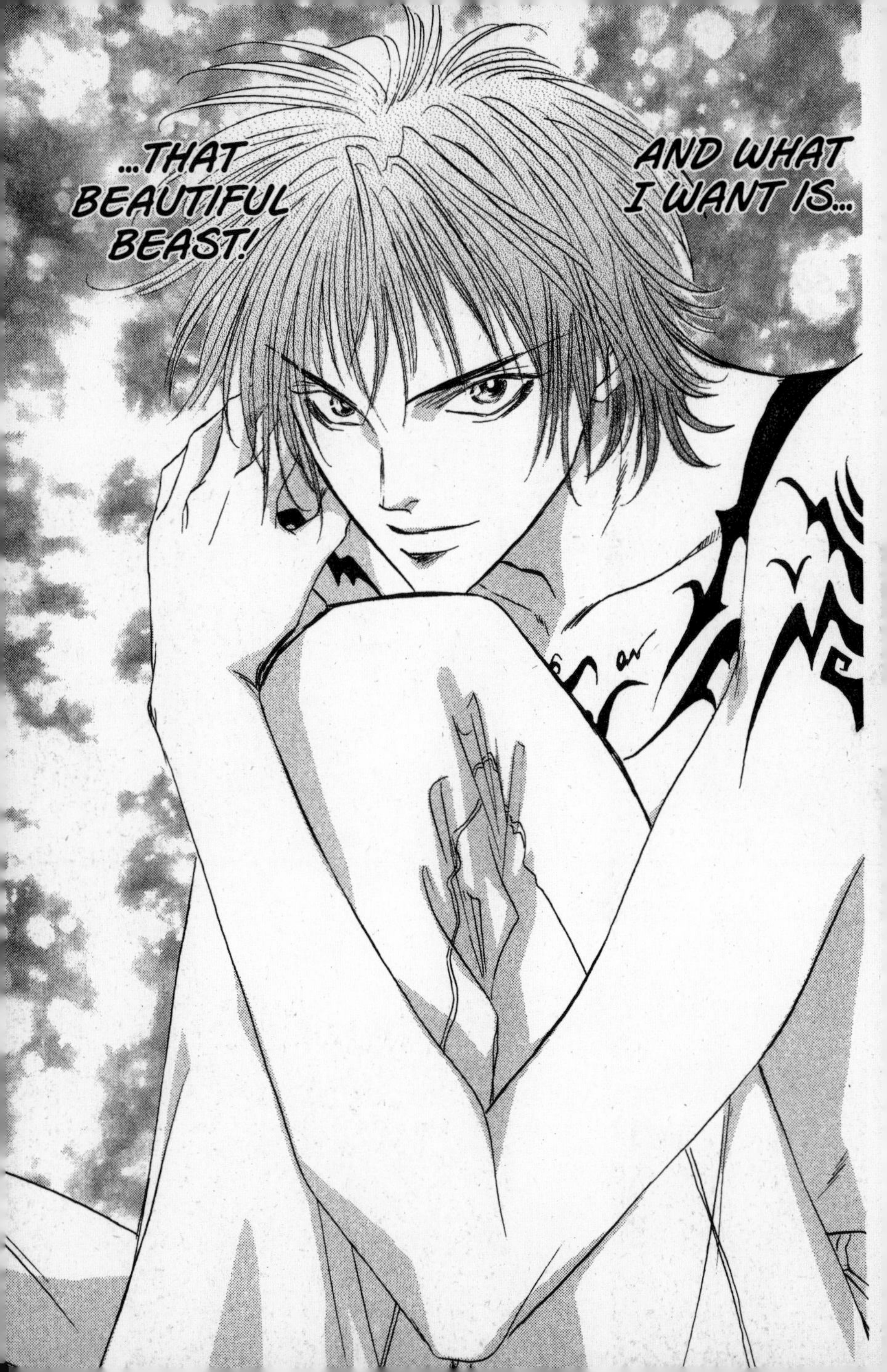
AND WHAT I WANT IS...
...THAT BEAUTIFUL BEAST!

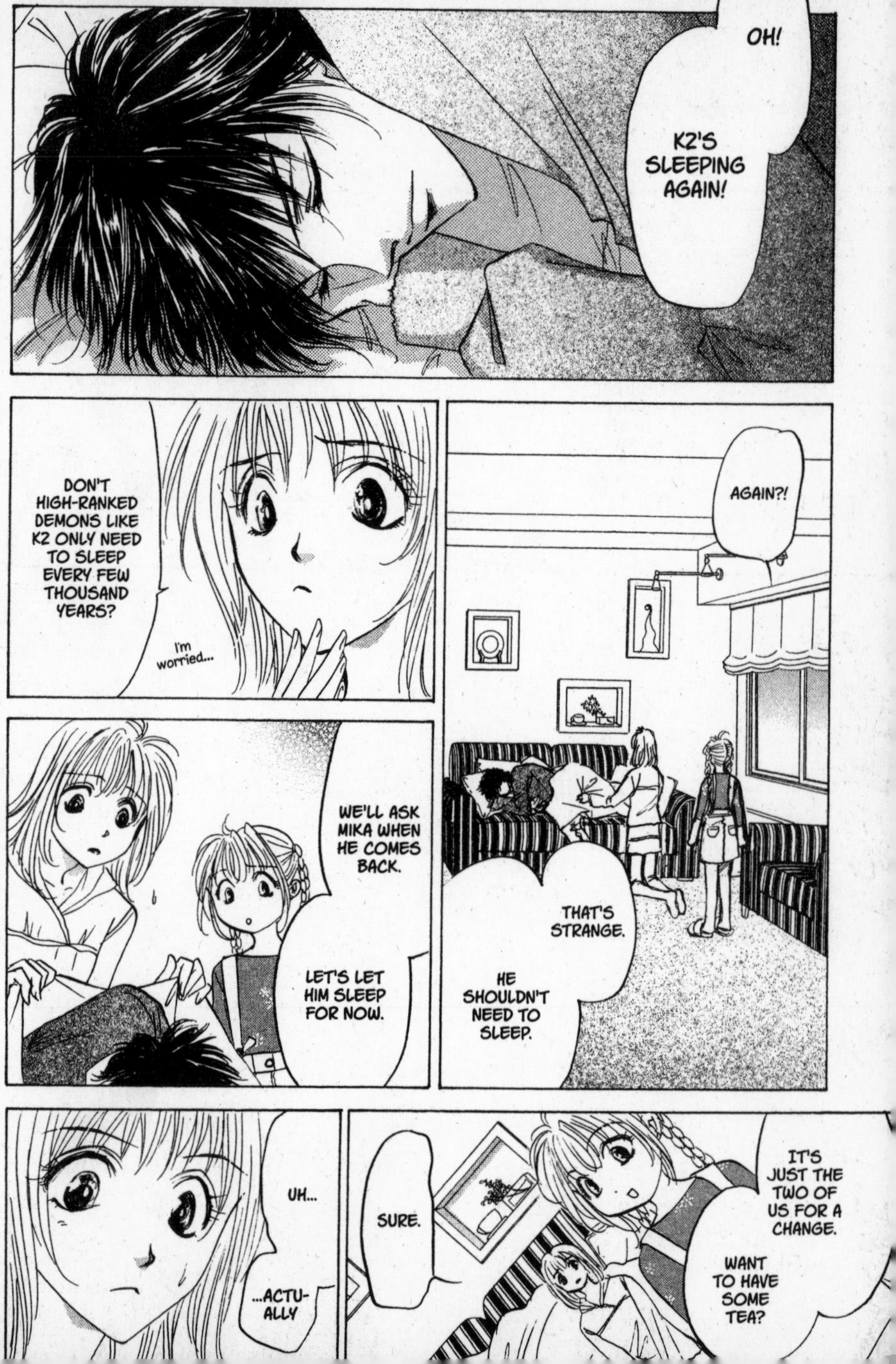
OH!
K2'S SLEEPING AGAIN!
AGAIN?!
THAT'S STRANGE.
HE SHOULDN'T NEED TO SLEEP.
DON'T HIGH-RANKED DEMONS LIKE K2 ONLY NEED TO SLEEP EVERY FEW THOUSAND YEARS?
I'm worried...
WE'LL ASK MIKA WHEN HE COMES BACK.
LET'S LET HIM SLEEP FOR NOW.
IT'S JUST THE TWO OF US FOR A CHANGE.
WANT TO HAVE SOME TEA?
SURE.
UH...
...ACTU-ALLY

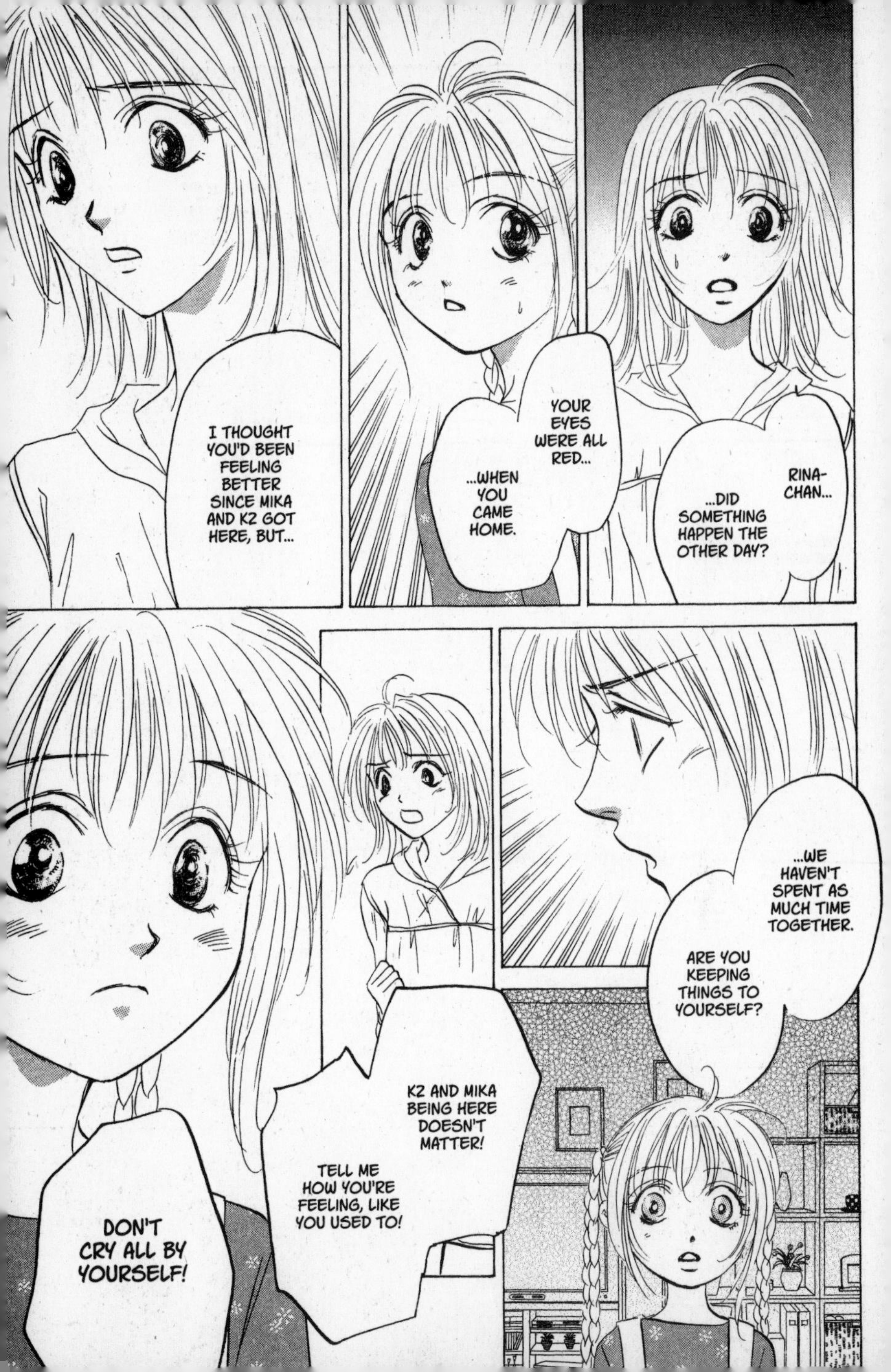
RINA-CHAN...
...DID SOMETHING HAPPEN THE OTHER DAY?
YOUR EYES WERE ALL RED...
...WHEN YOU CAME HOME.
I THOUGHT YOU'D BEEN FEELING BETTER SINCE MIKA AND K2 GOT HERE, BUT...
...WE HAVEN'T SPENT AS MUCH TIME TOGETHER.
ARE YOU KEEPING THINGS TO YOURSELF?
K2 AND MIKA BEING HERE DOESN'T MATTER!
TELL ME HOW YOU'RE FEELING, LIKE YOU USED TO!
DON'T CRY ALL BY YOURSELF!

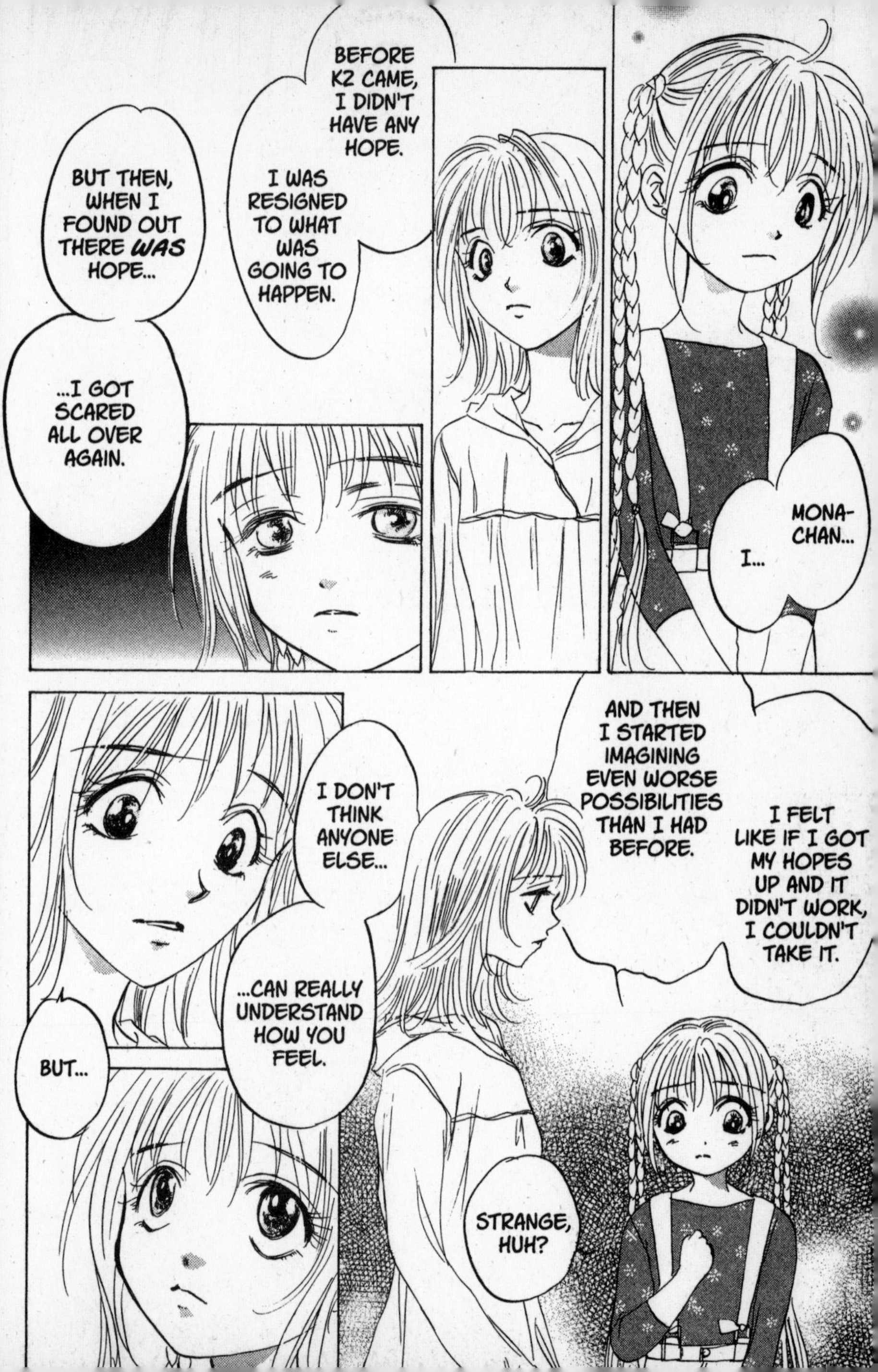
MONA-CHAN...
I...
BEFORE K2 CAME, I DIDN'T HAVE ANY HOPE.
I WAS RESIGNED TO WHAT WAS GOING TO HAPPEN.
BUT THEN, WHEN I FOUND OUT THERE *WAS* HOPE...
...I GOT SCARED ALL OVER AGAIN.
I FELT LIKE IF I GOT MY HOPES UP AND IT DIDN'T WORK, I COULDN'T TAKE IT.
AND THEN I STARTED IMAGINING EVEN WORSE POSSIBILITIES THAN I HAD BEFORE.
STRANGE, HUH?
I DON'T THINK ANYONE ELSE...
...CAN REALLY UNDERSTAND HOW YOU FEEL.
BUT...

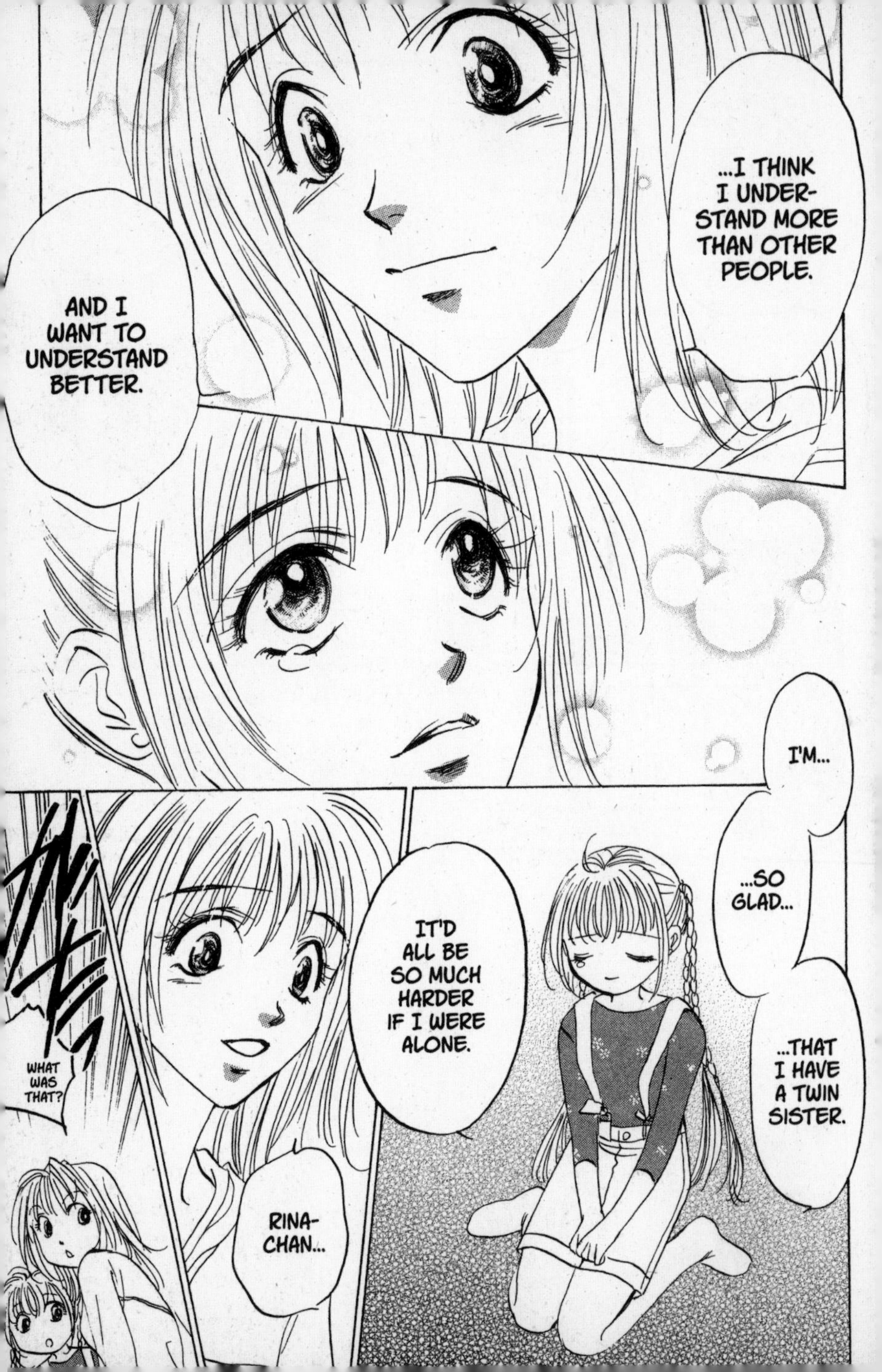
...I THINK I UNDER-STAND MORE THAN OTHER PEOPLE.
AND I WANT TO UNDERSTAND BETTER.
I'M...
...SO GLAD...
...THAT I HAVE A TWIN SISTER.
IT'D ALL BE SO MUCH HARDER IF I WERE ALONE.
RINA-CHAN...
WHAT WAS THAT?

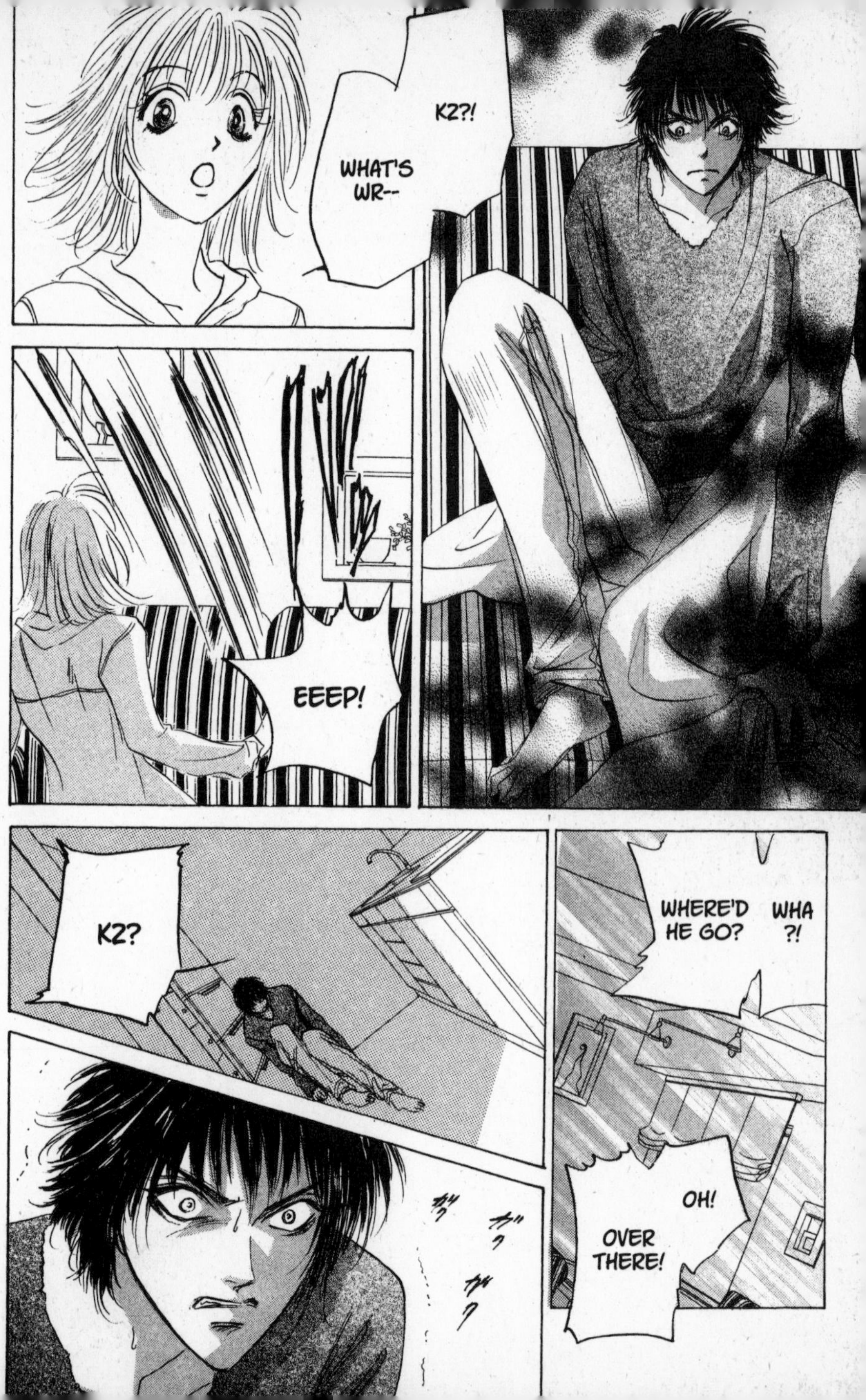
KZ?! WHAT'S WR--
EEEP!
WHA ?!
WHERE'D HE GO?
OH! OVER THERE!
KZ?

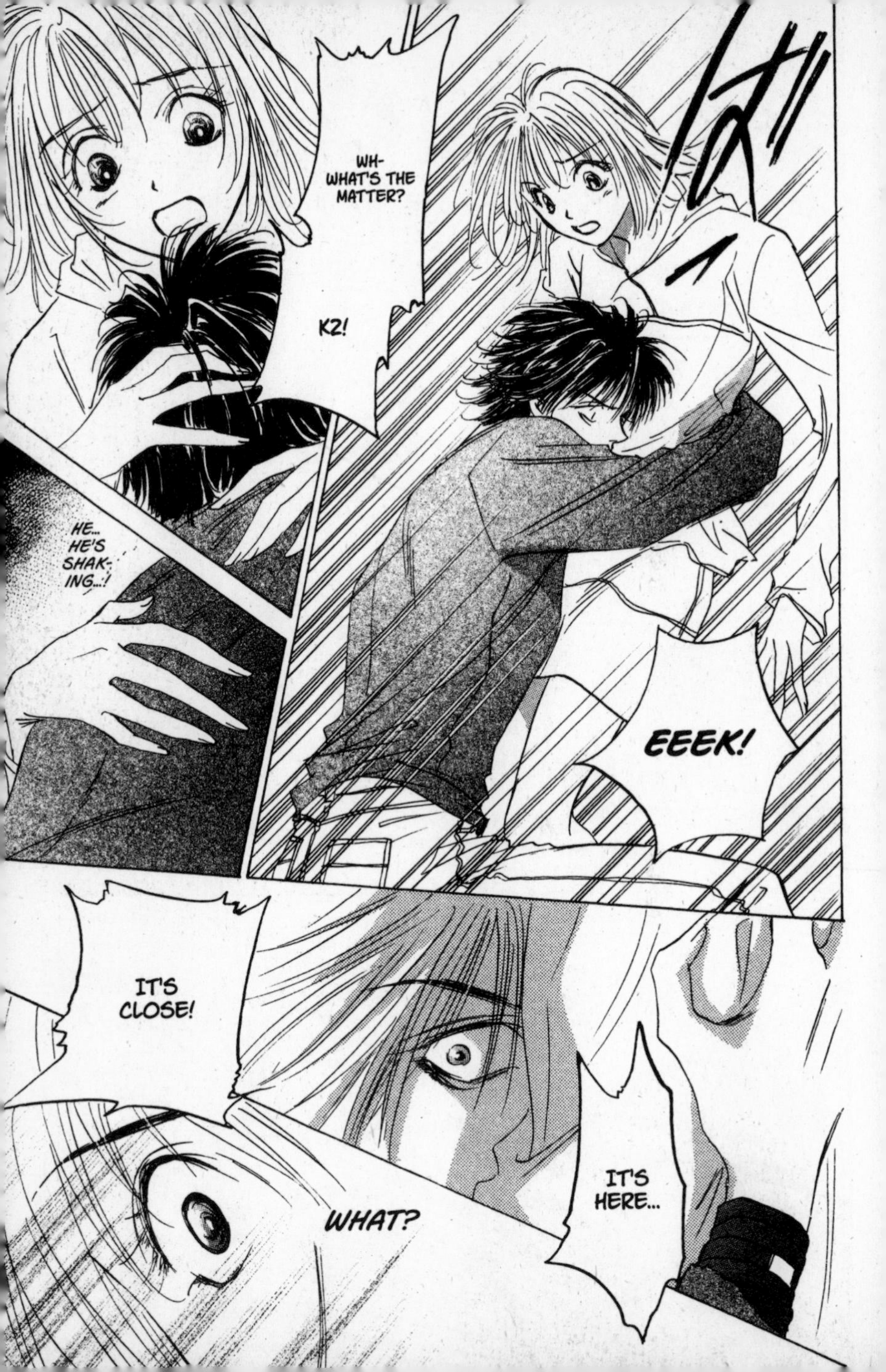
EEEK!
WH- WHAT'S THE MATTER?
K2!
HE... HE'S SHAKING...!
IT'S CLOSE!
IT'S HERE...
WHAT?

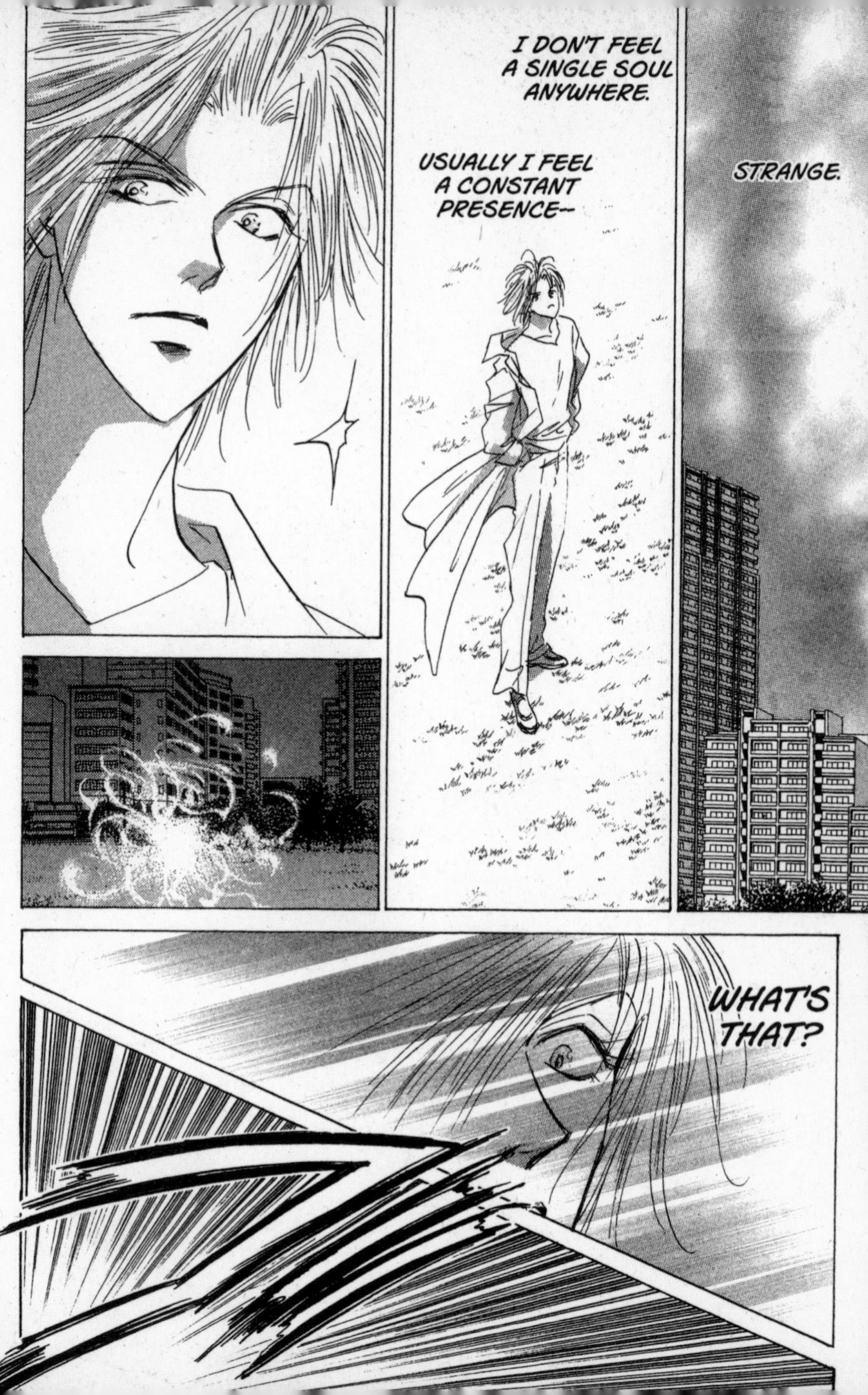
STRANGE.
I DON'T FEEL A SINGLE SOUL ANYWHERE.
USUALLY I FEEL A CONSTANT PRESENCE--
WHAT'S THAT?

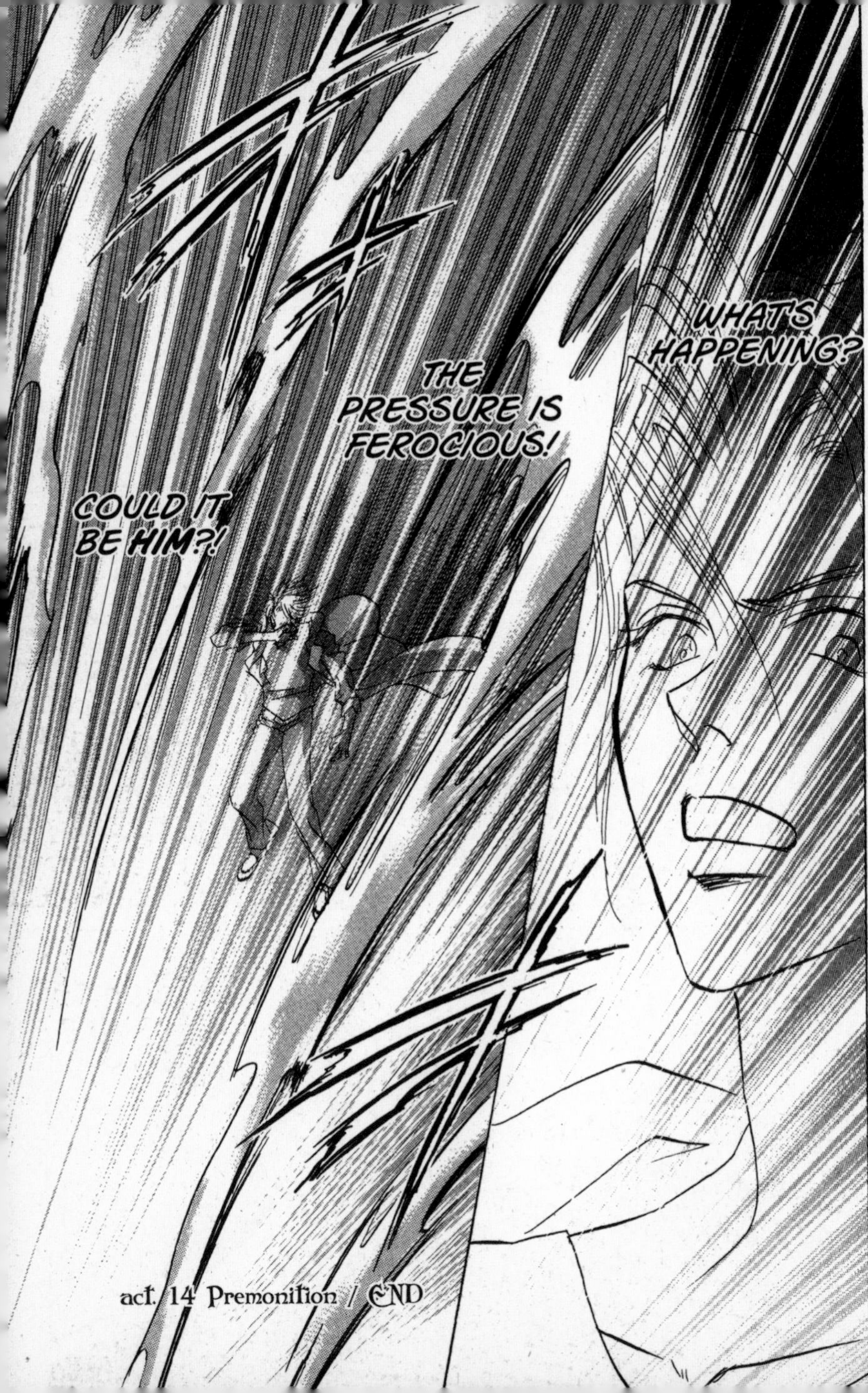
WHAT'S HAPPENING?
THE PRESSURE IS FEROCIOUS!
COULD IT BE HIM?!
act. 14 Premonition / END

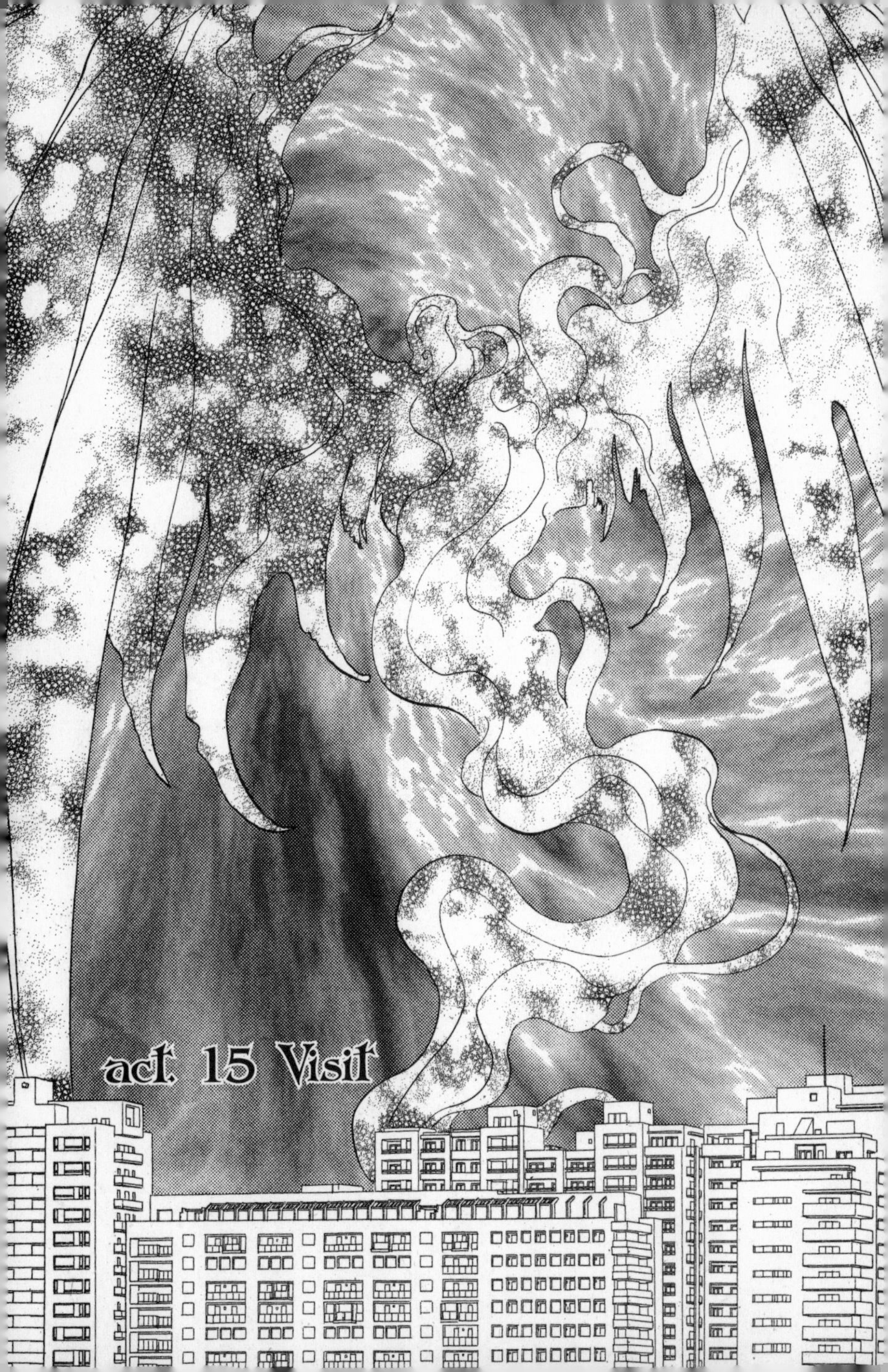
act. 15 Visit

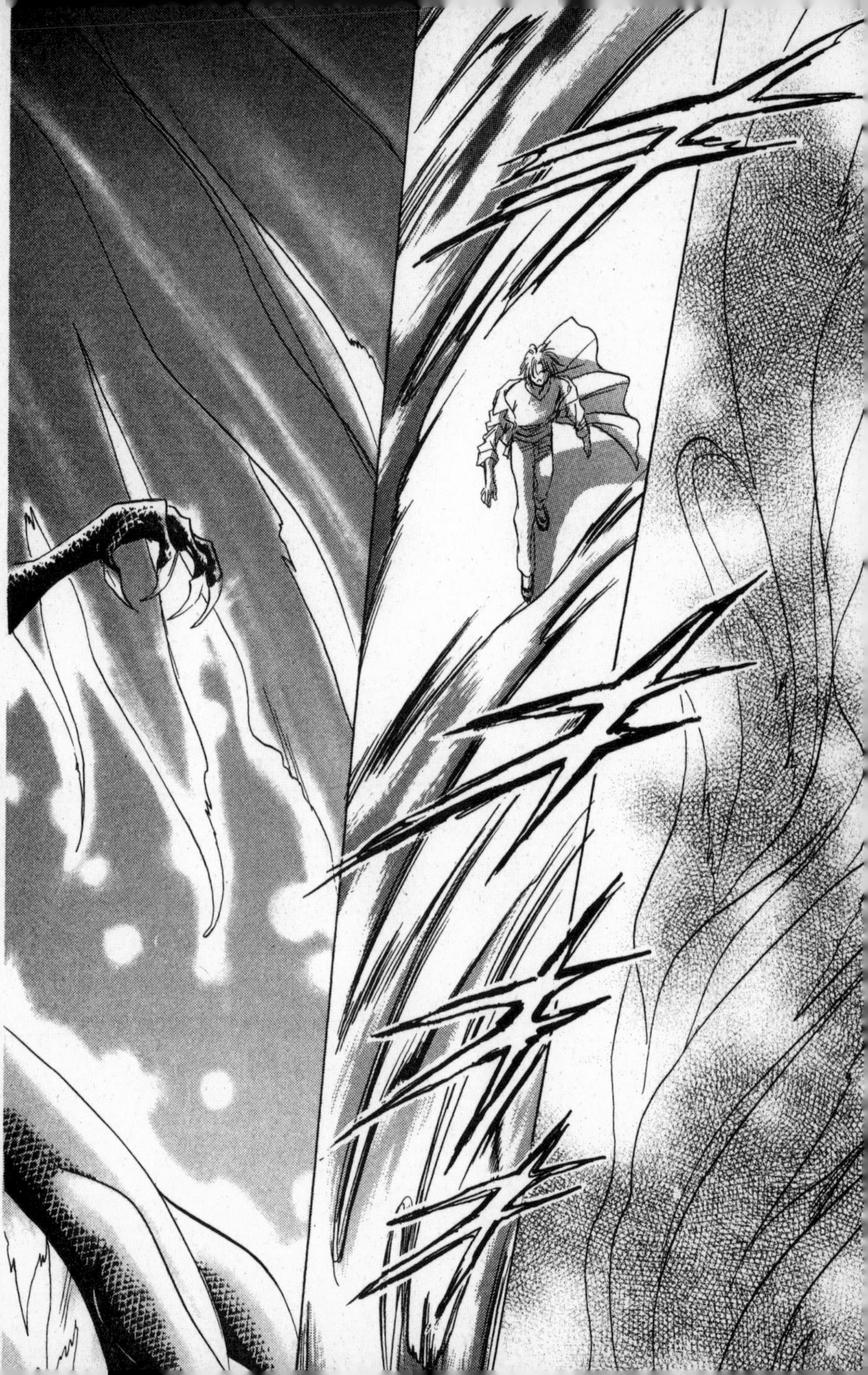

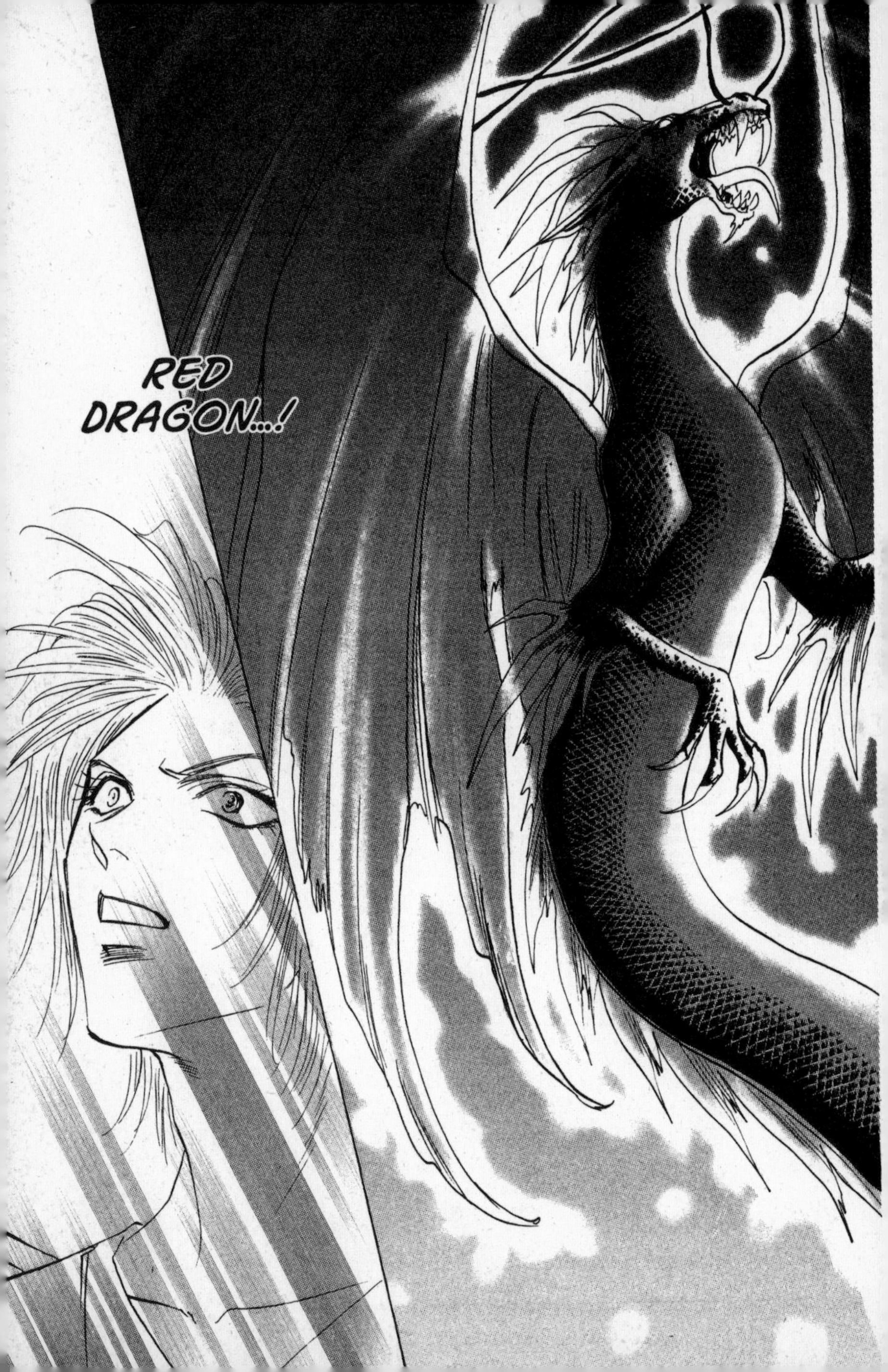
RED DRAGON...!

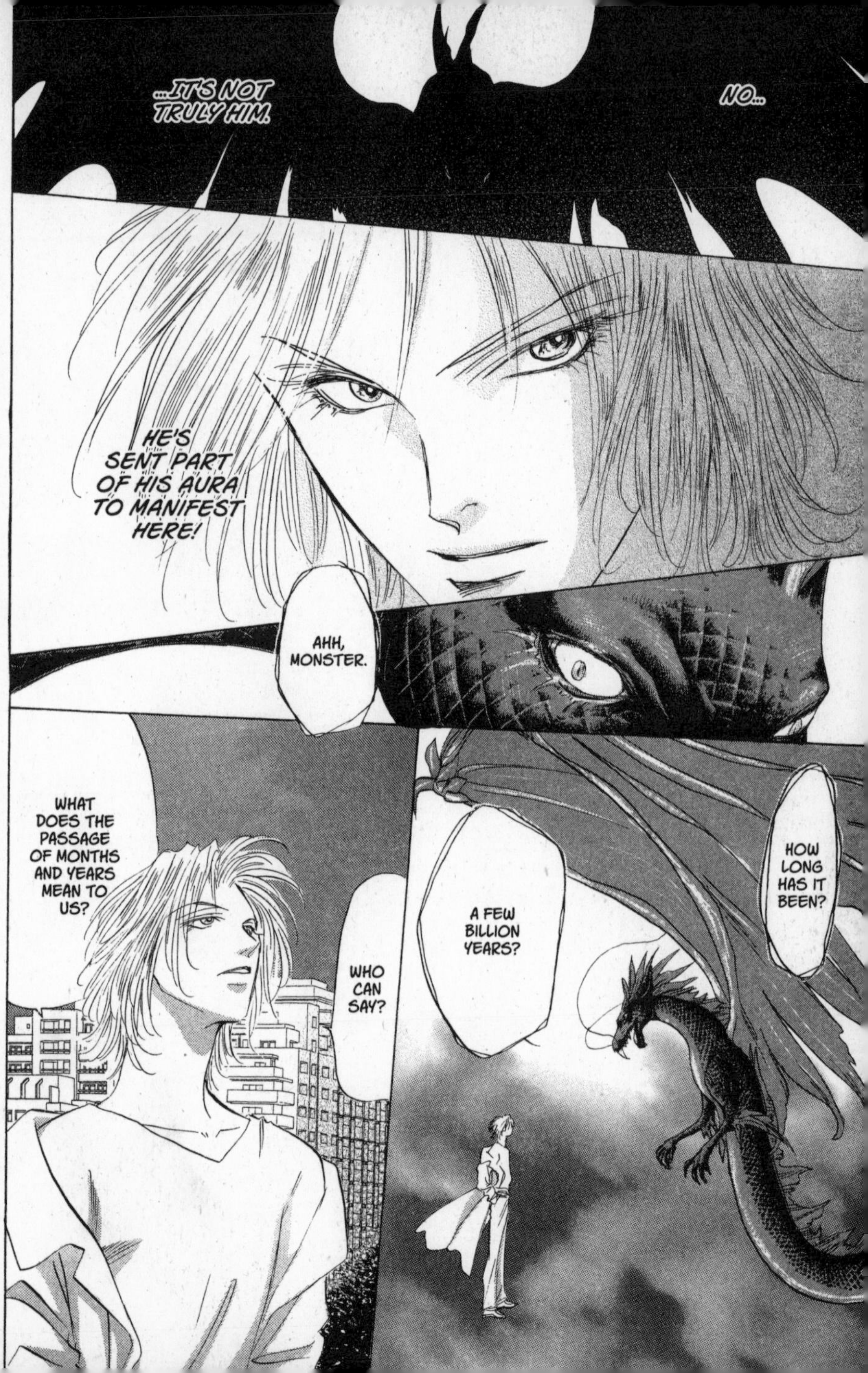

NO...
...IT'S NOT TRULY HIM.
HE'S SENT PART OF HIS AURA TO MANIFEST HERE!
AHH, MONSTER.
HOW LONG HAS IT BEEN?
A FEW BILLION YEARS?
WHO CAN SAY?
WHAT DOES THE PASSAGE OF MONTHS AND YEARS MEAN TO US?

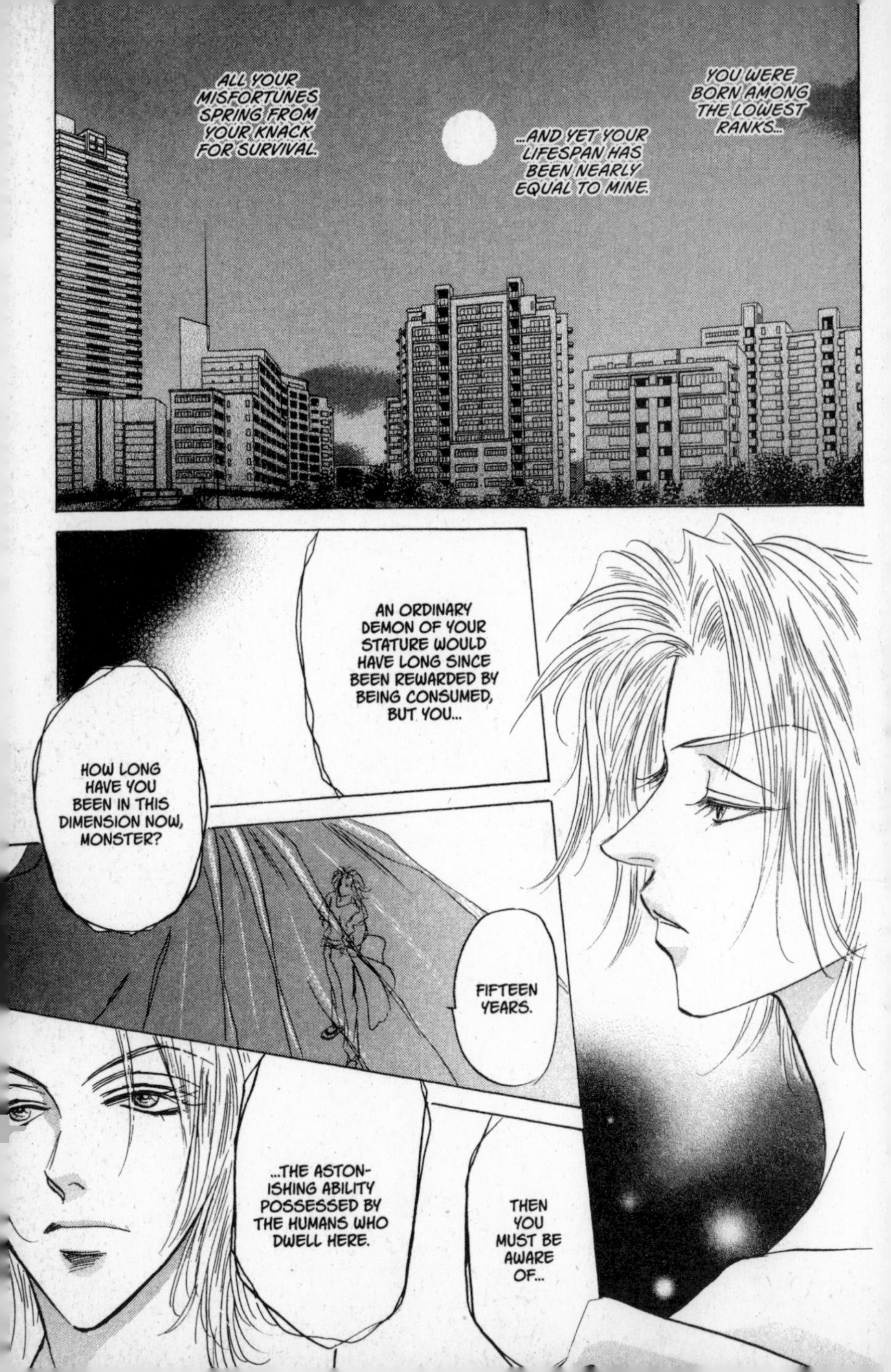
YOU WERE BORN AMONG THE LOWEST RANKS...
...AND YET YOUR LIFESPAN HAS BEEN NEARLY EQUAL TO MINE.
ALL YOUR MISFORTUNES SPRING FROM YOUR KNACK FOR SURVIVAL.
AN ORDINARY DEMON OF YOUR STATURE WOULD HAVE LONG SINCE BEEN REWARDED BY BEING CONSUMED, BUT YOU...
HOW LONG HAVE YOU BEEN IN THIS DIMENSION NOW, MONSTER?
FIFTEEN YEARS.
THEN YOU MUST BE AWARE OF...
...THE ASTON-ISHING ABILITY POSSESSED BY THE HUMANS WHO DWELL HERE.

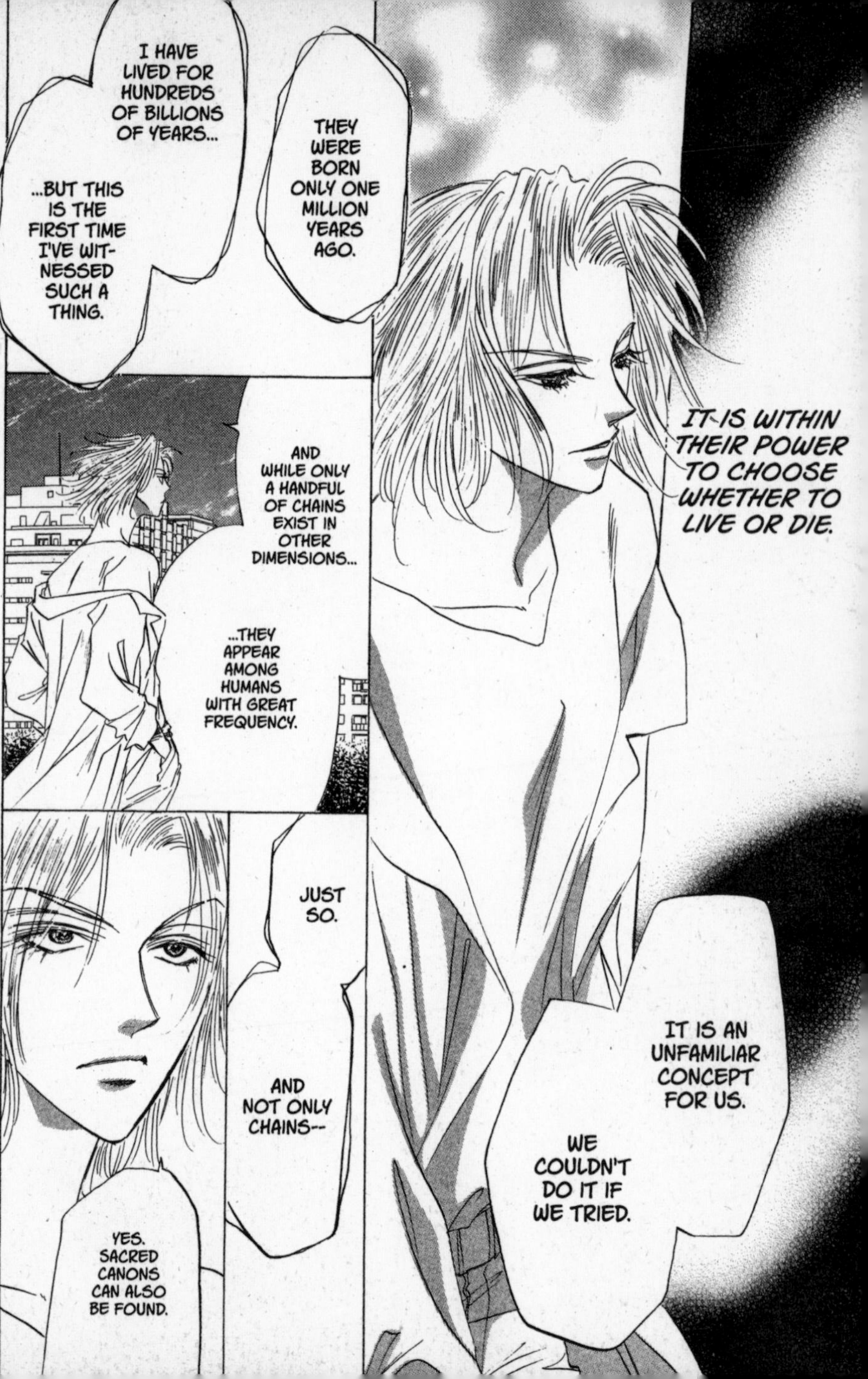

THEY WERE BORN ONLY ONE MILLION YEARS AGO.
IT IS WITHIN THEIR POWER TO CHOOSE WHETHER TO LIVE OR DIE.
IT IS AN UNFAMILIAR CONCEPT FOR US.
WE COULDN'T DO IT IF WE TRIED.
I HAVE LIVED FOR HUNDREDS OF BILLIONS OF YEARS...
...BUT THIS IS THE FIRST TIME I'VE WIT-NESSED SUCH A THING.
AND WHILE ONLY A HANDFUL OF CHAINS EXIST IN OTHER DIMENSIONS...
...THEY APPEAR AMONG HUMANS WITH GREAT FREQUENCY.
JUST SO.
AND NOT ONLY CHAINS--
YES. SACRED CANONS CAN ALSO BE FOUND.

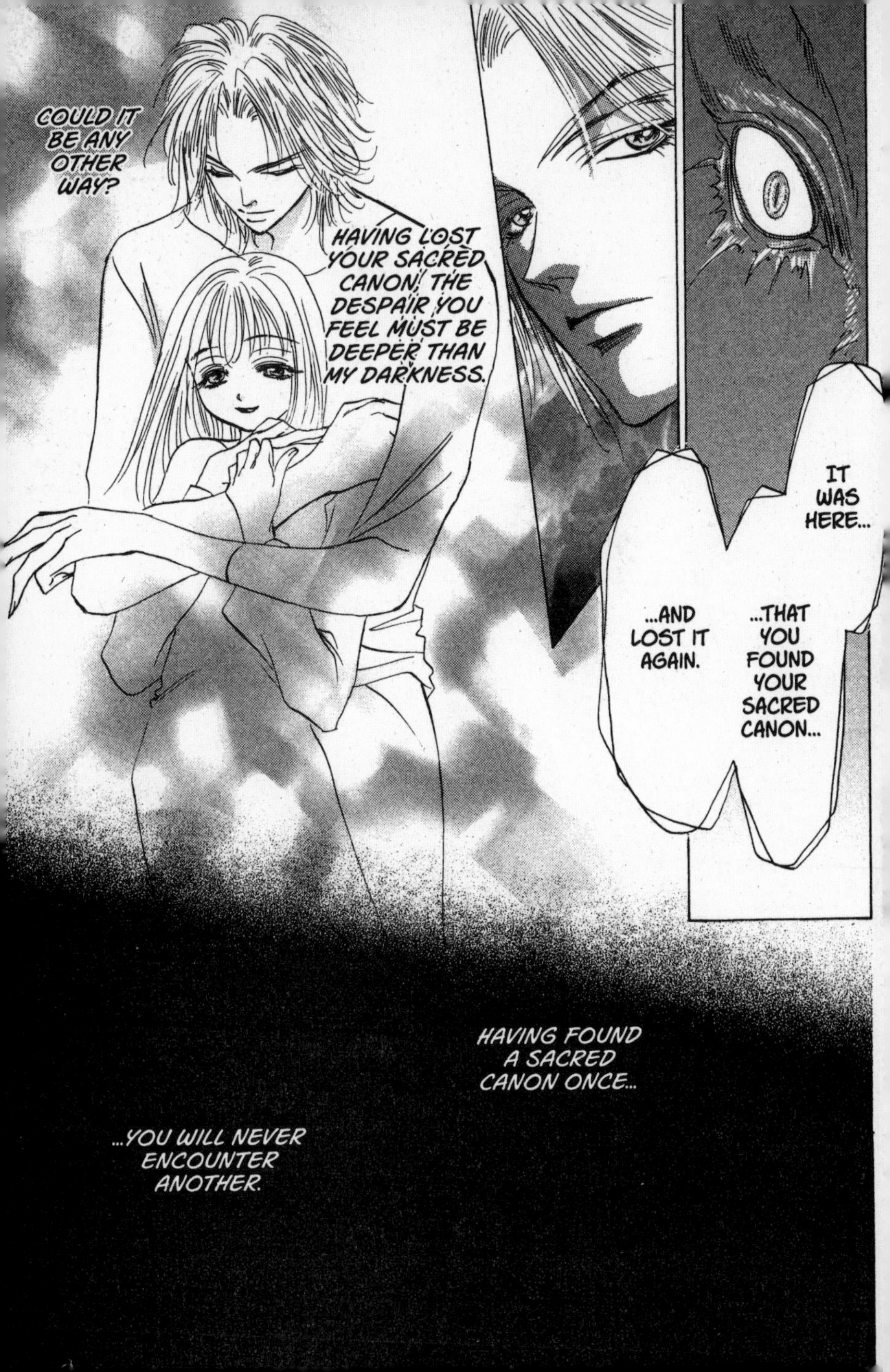
IT WAS HERE...
...THAT YOU FOUND YOUR SACRED CANON...
...AND LOST IT AGAIN.
HAVING LOST YOUR SACRED CANON, THE DESPAIR YOU FEEL MUST BE DEEPER THAN MY DARKNESS.
COULD IT BE ANY OTHER WAY?
HAVING FOUND A SACRED CANON ONCE...
...YOU WILL NEVER ENCOUNTER ANOTHER.

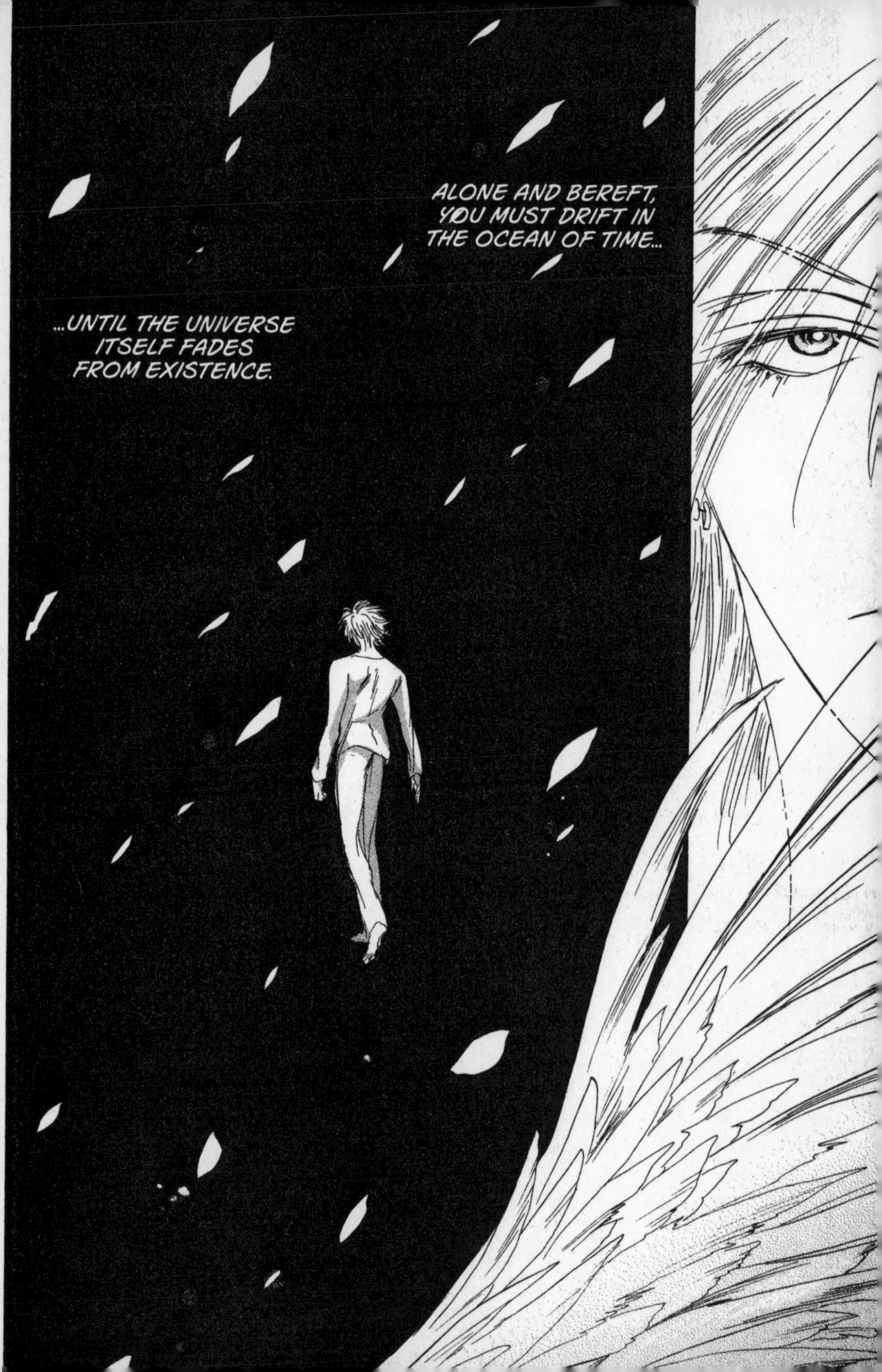

ALONE AND BEREFT, YOU MUST DRIFT IN THE OCEAN OF TIME...
...UNTIL THE UNIVERSE ITSELF FADES FROM EXISTENCE.

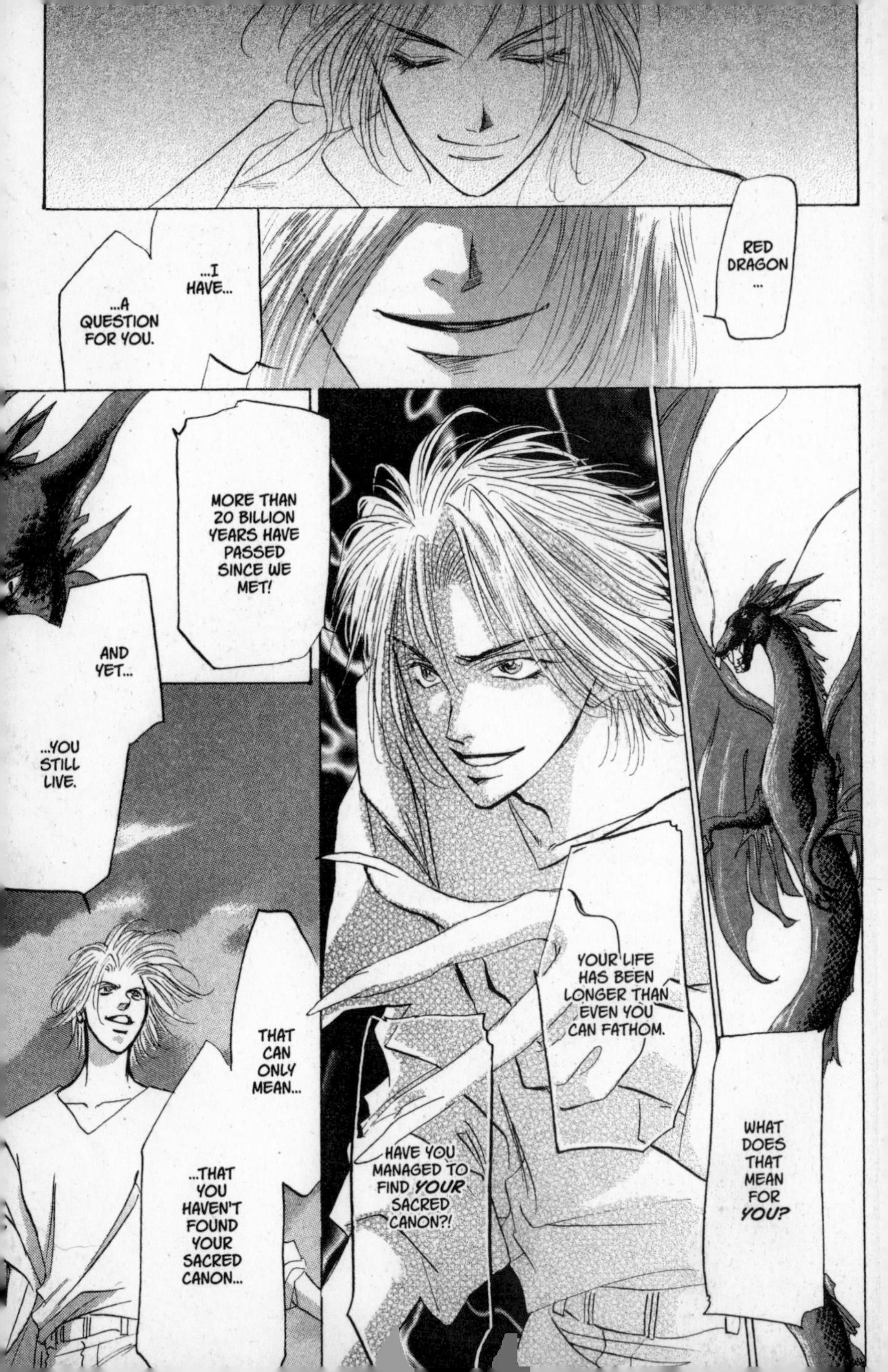
RED DRAGON ...
...I HAVE...
...A QUESTION FOR YOU.
WHAT DOES THAT MEAN FOR *YOU?*
YOUR LIFE HAS BEEN LONGER THAN EVEN YOU CAN FATHOM.
HAVE YOU MANAGED TO FIND *YOUR* SACRED CANON?!
MORE THAN 20 BILLION YEARS HAVE PASSED SINCE WE MET!
AND YET...
...YOU STILL LIVE.
THAT CAN ONLY MEAN...
...THAT YOU HAVEN'T FOUND YOUR SACRED CANON...

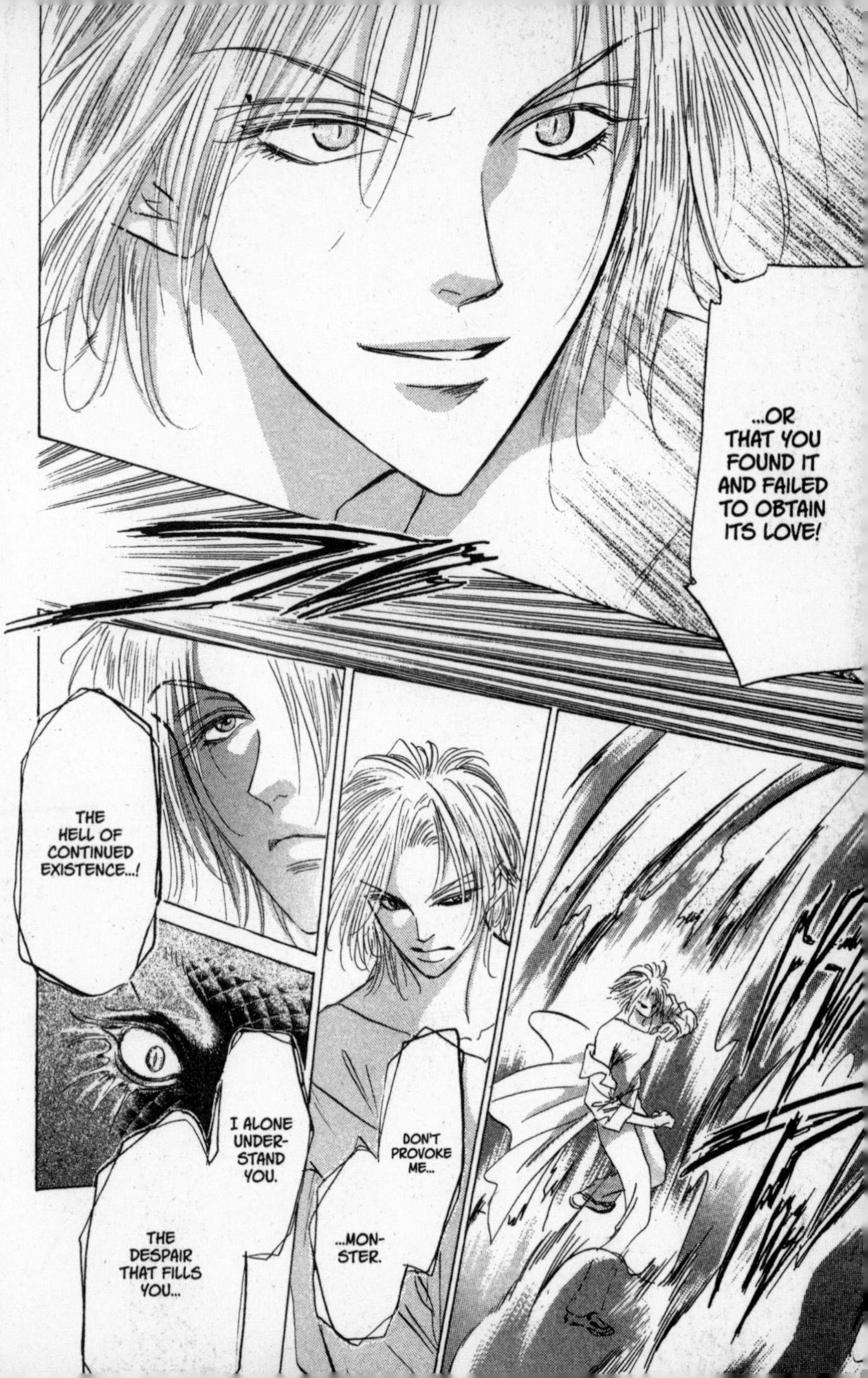
...OR THAT YOU FOUND IT AND FAILED TO OBTAIN ITS LOVE!
DON'T PROVOKE ME...
...MON-STER.
THE HELL OF CONTINUED EXISTENCE...!
I ALONE UNDER-STAND YOU.
THE DESPAIR THAT FILLS YOU...

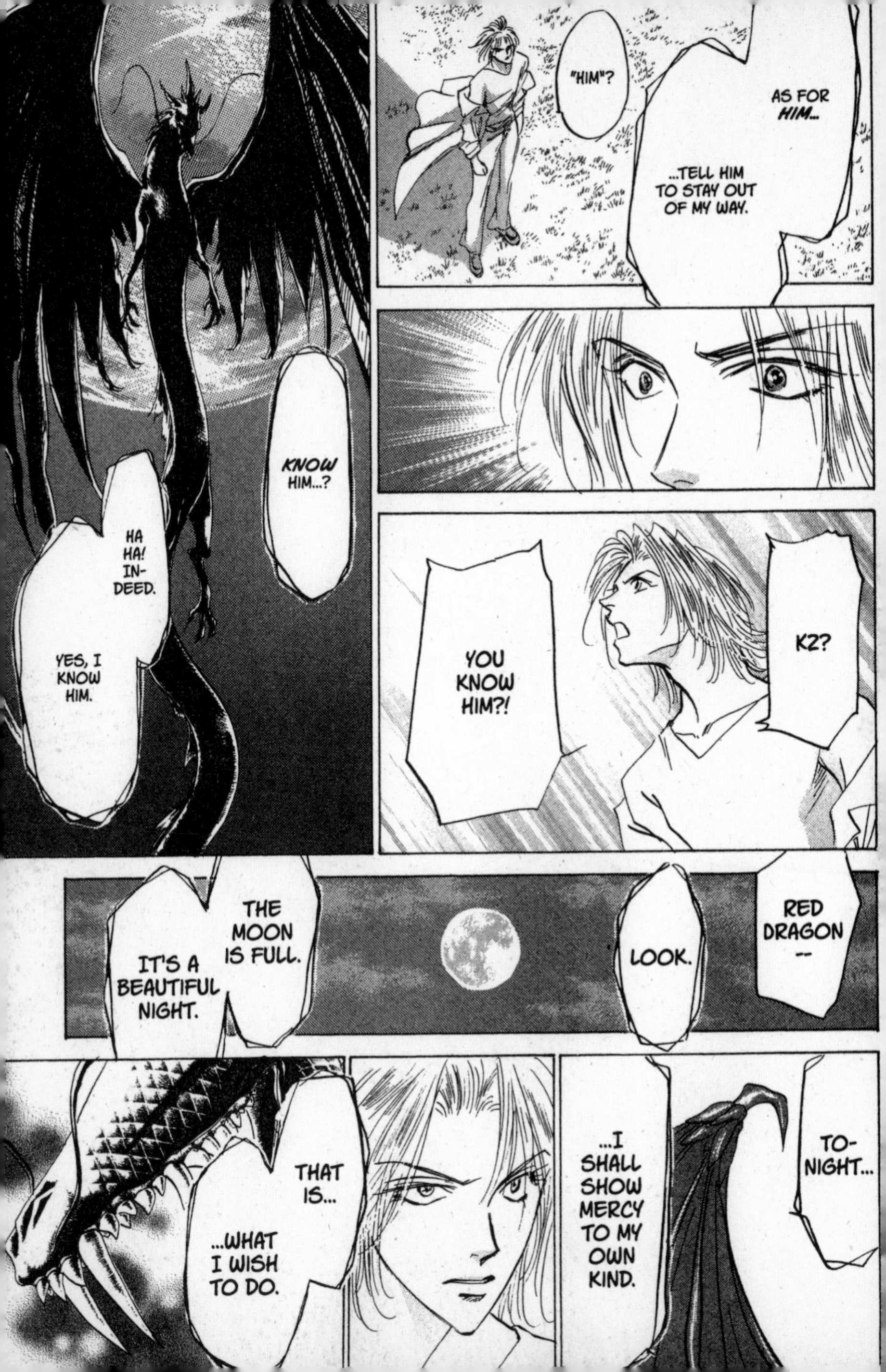
AS FOR HIM...
...TELL HIM TO STAY OUT OF MY WAY.
"HIM"?
KZ?
YOU KNOW HIM?!
KNOW HIM...?
HA HA! INDEED.
YES, I KNOW HIM.
RED DRAGON --
LOOK.
THE MOON IS FULL.
IT'S A BEAUTIFUL NIGHT.
TO-NIGHT...
...I SHALL SHOW MERCY TO MY OWN KIND.
THAT IS...
...WHAT I WISH TO DO.

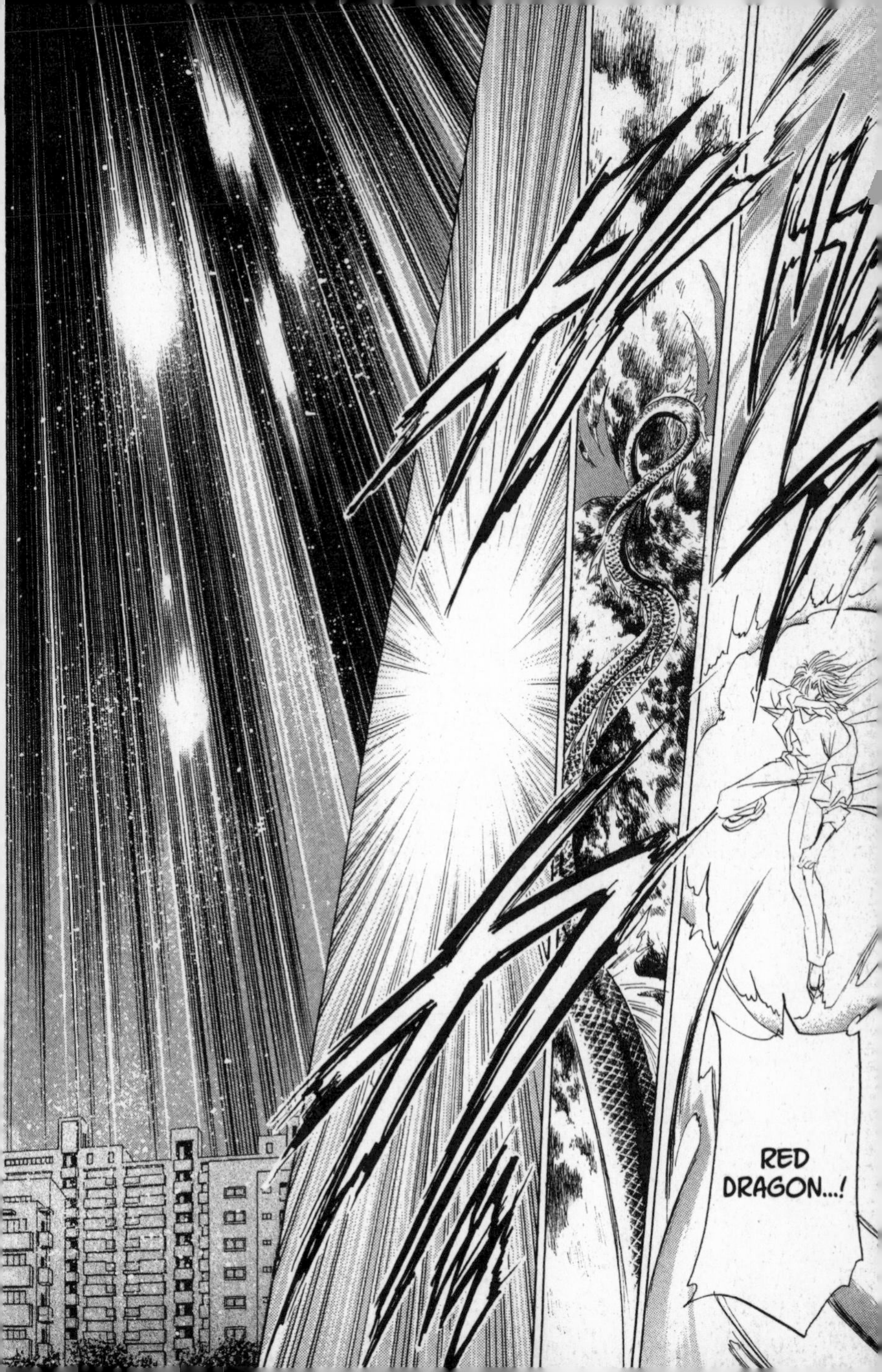
RED DRAGON...!

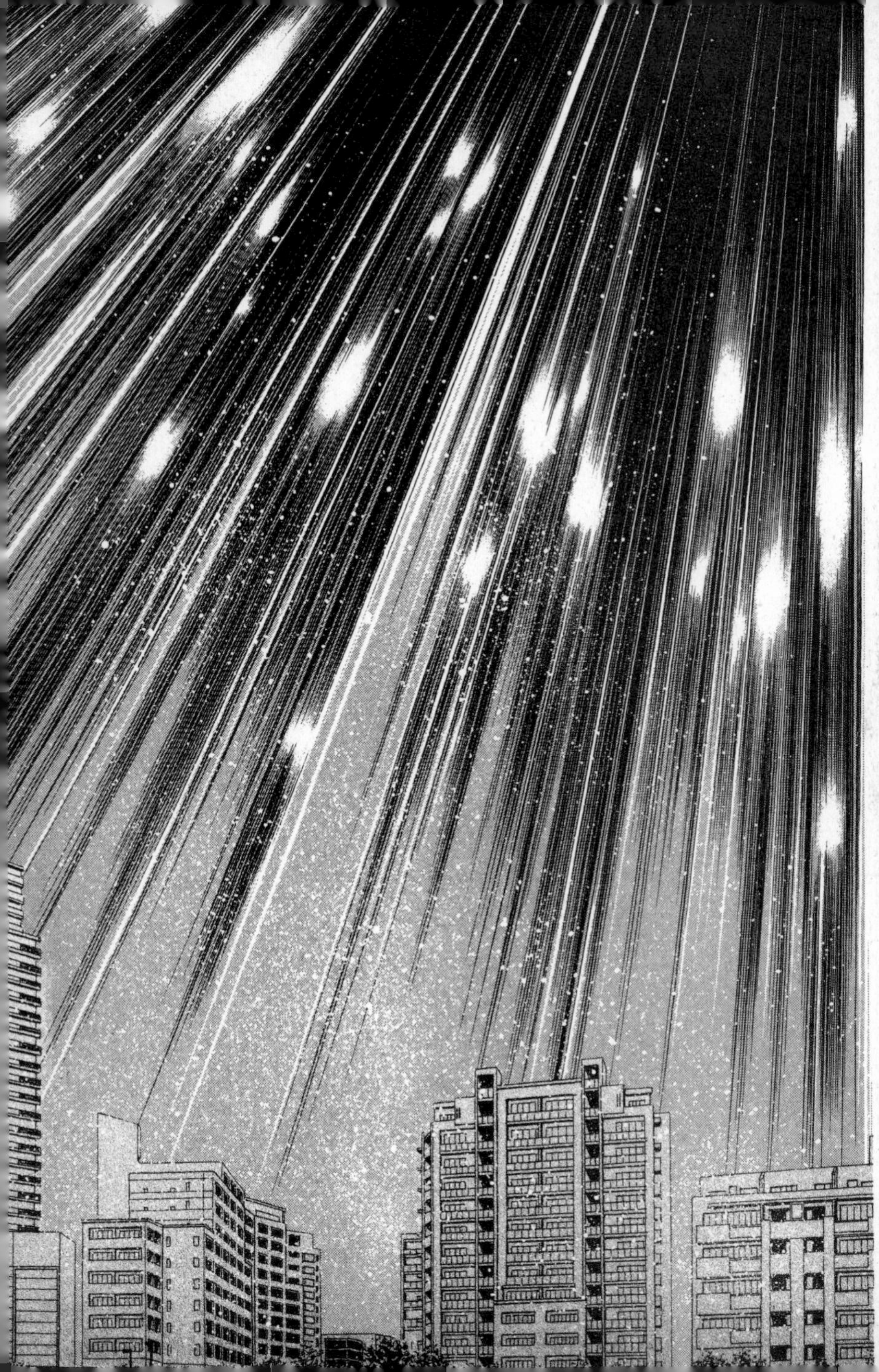

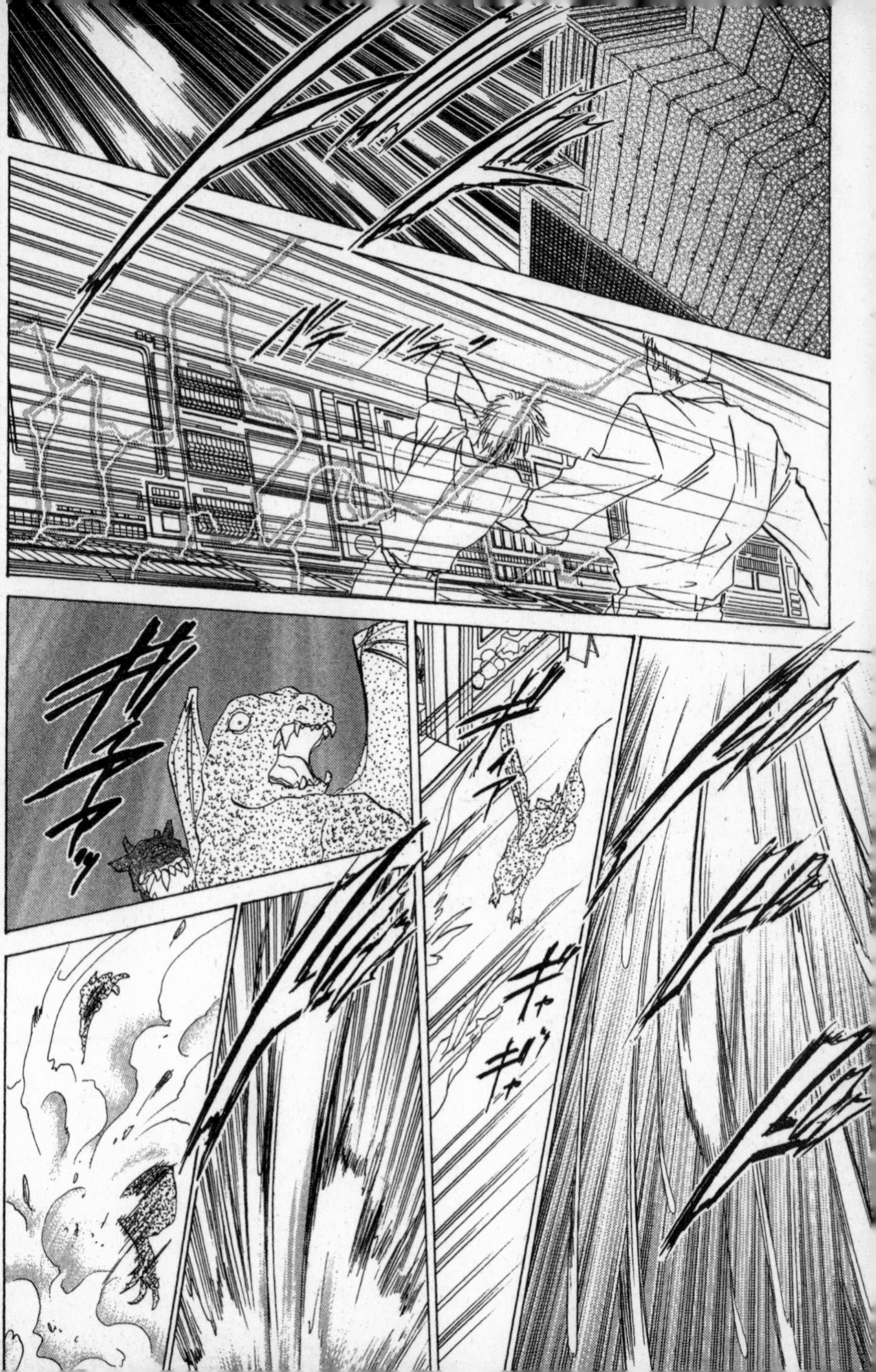
バチ バチッ
ギャギャ

FREE TALK
<3>

Back to Demon Sacred! Beginning in this volume we'll be seeing a lot more of the Rindelts kids, especially Zophie. Since she's a tall, redheaded Germanic girl, I've been dressing her in styles that wouldn't look good on Japanese. Also, she doesn't often wear a bra. (Foreigners don't wear bras much, do they? Especially Americans.)

Caucasian and Asian bodies are very different. It seems like their energy levels and body temperatures are nothing alike.

That became clear to me when I went to Germany. There was the man who took off his shirt to change in front of the train station in the middle of winter... The cute young woman who was a maid at my hotel, who opened the door to my room without noticing that the chain was on... They're just made differently.

In my imagination, Zophie is one of those Germanic people who's superhumanly strong.

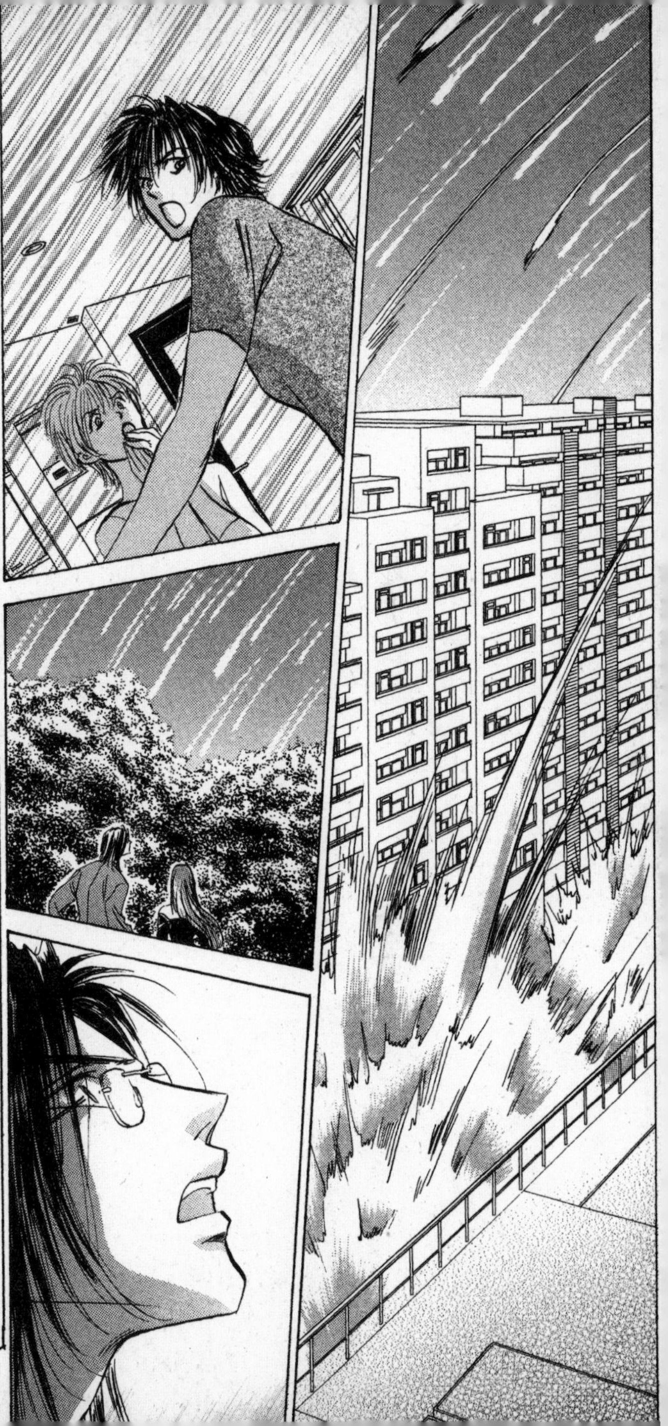

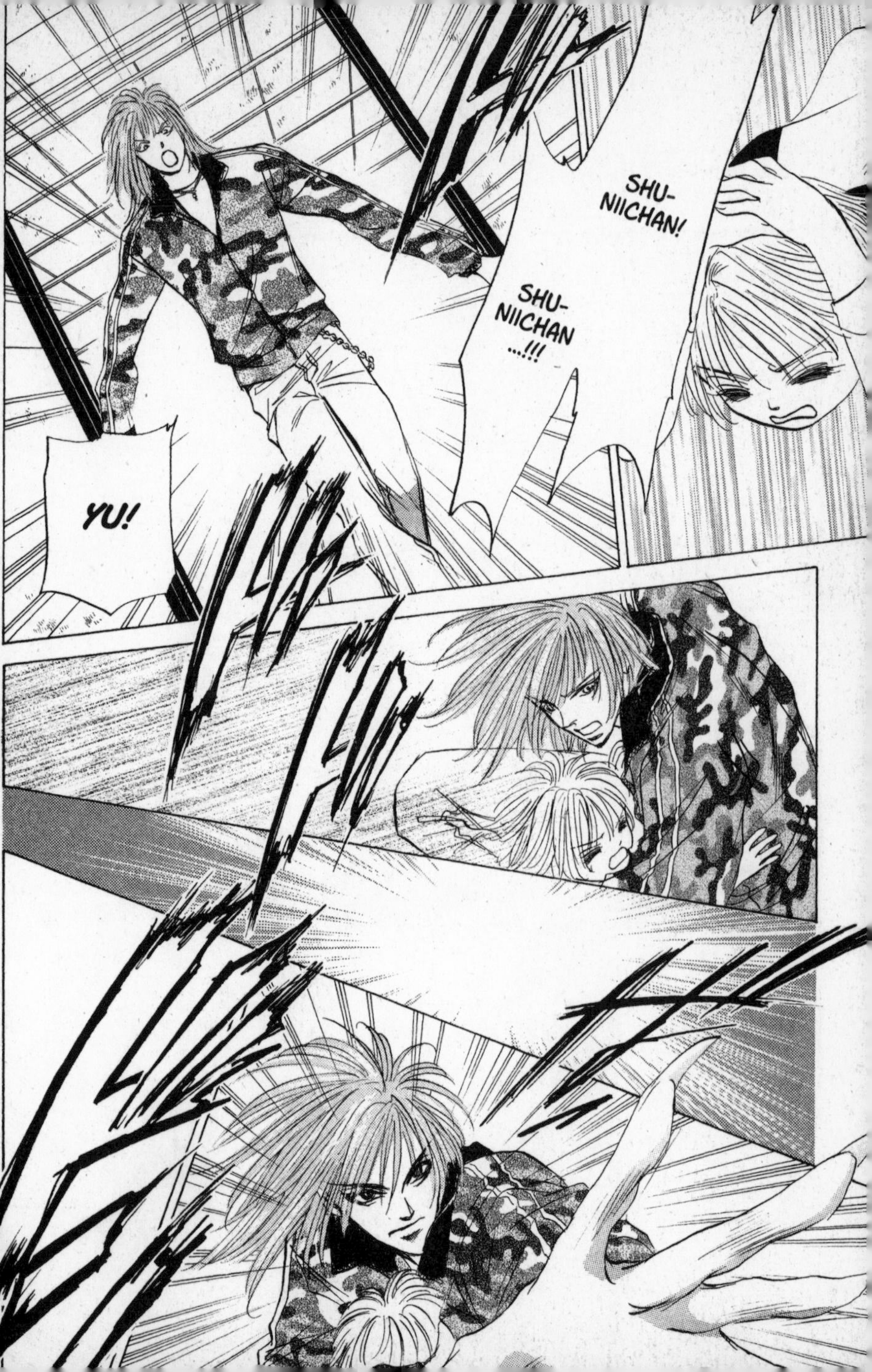
SHU-NIICHAN!
SHU-NIICHAN ...!!!
YU!

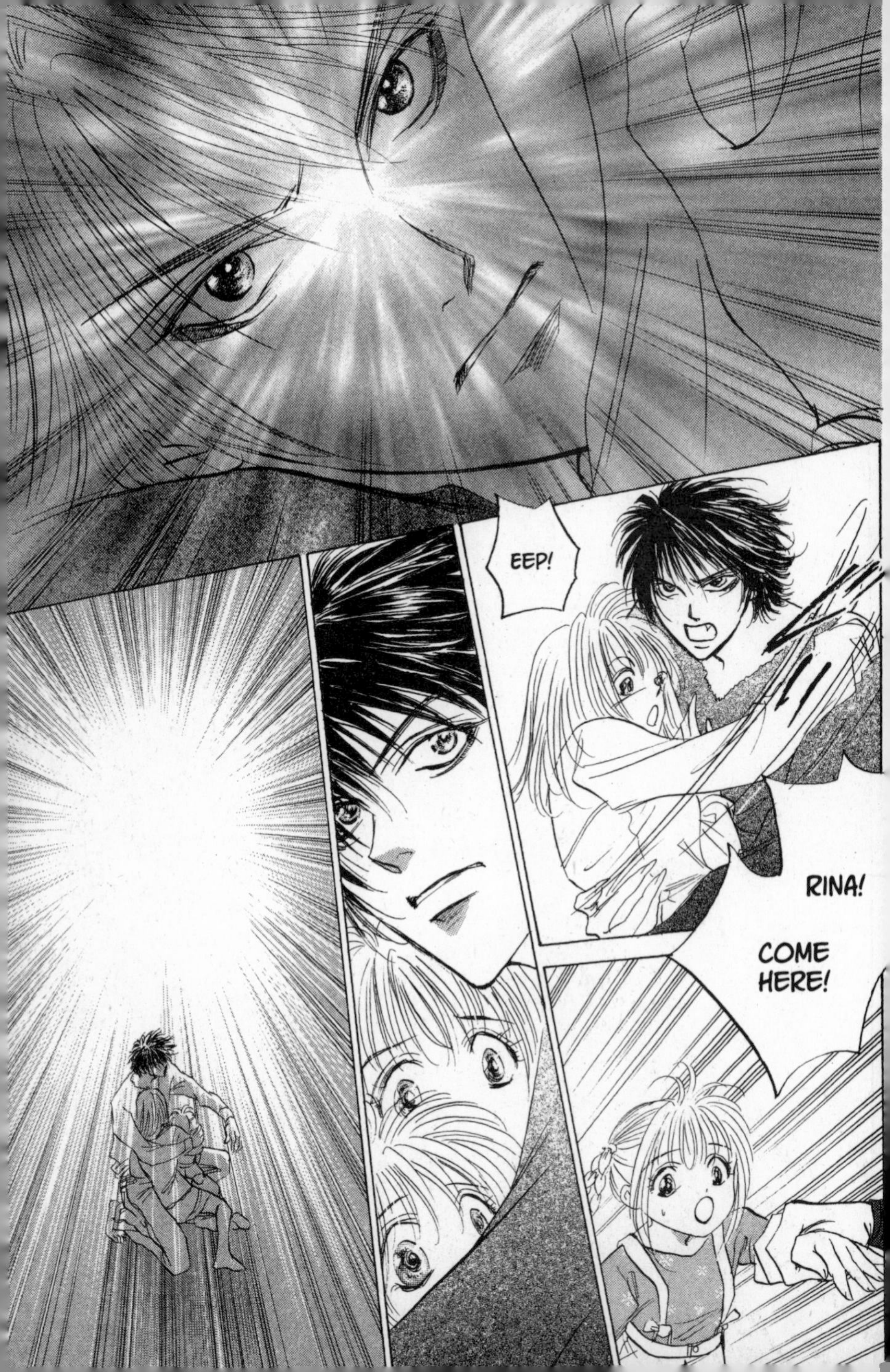
EEP!
RINA!
COME HERE!

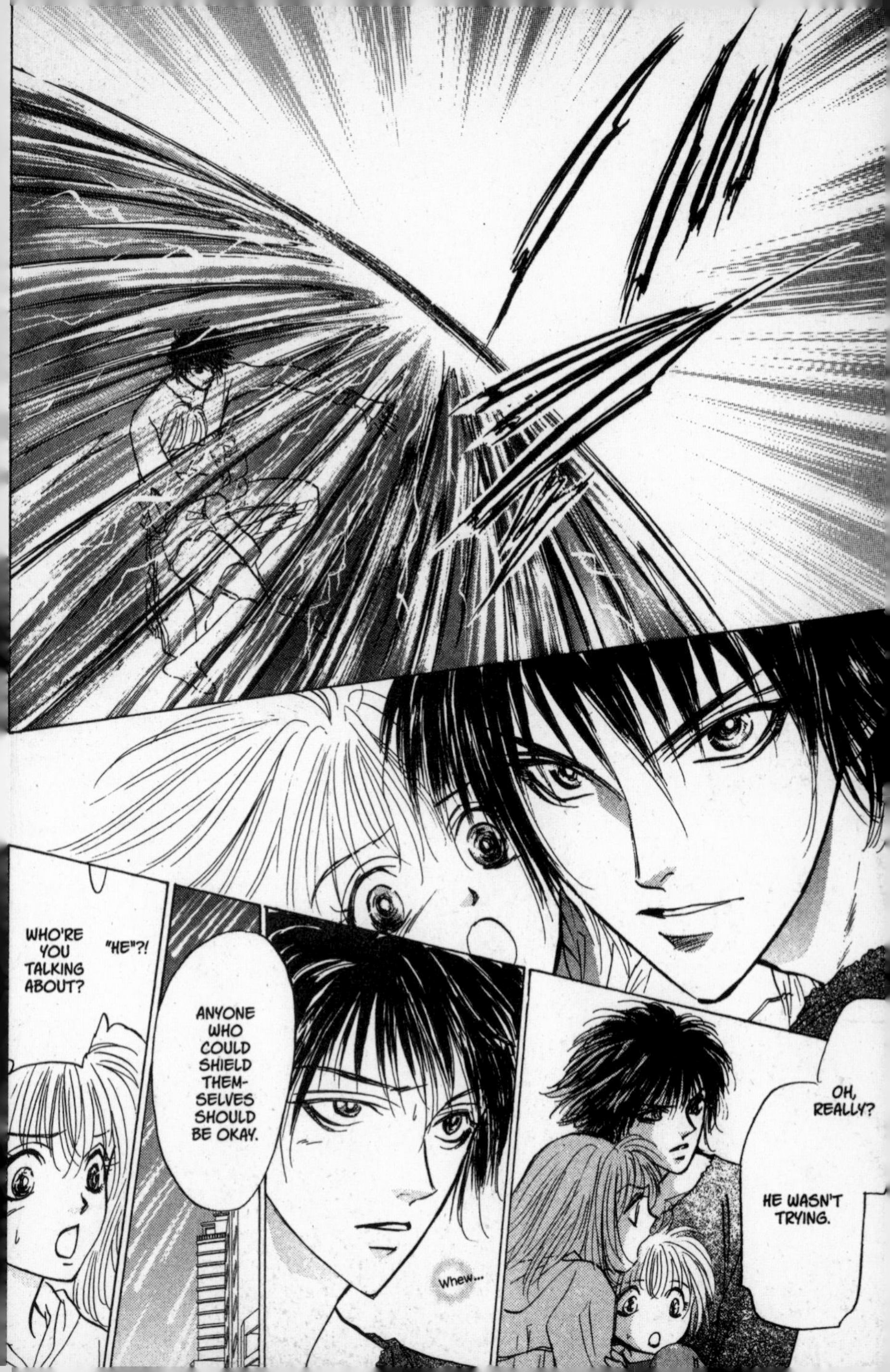
OH, REALLY?
HE WASN'T TRYING.
Whew...
ANYONE WHO COULD SHIELD THEM-SELVES SHOULD BE OKAY.
"HE"?!
WHO'RE YOU TALKING ABOUT?

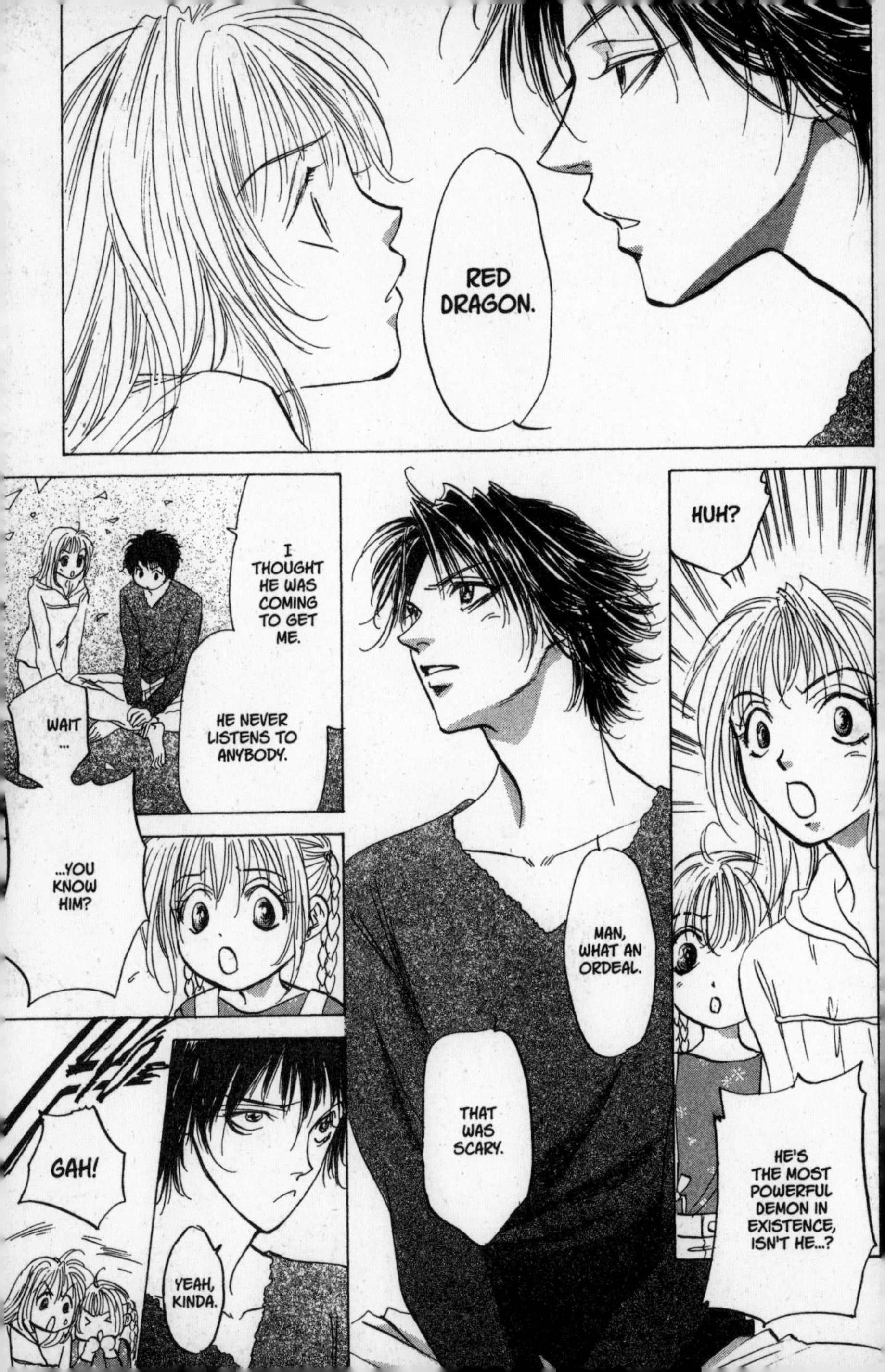
RED DRAGON.
HUH?
HE'S THE MOST POWERFUL DEMON IN EXISTENCE, ISN'T HE...?
MAN, WHAT AN ORDEAL.
THAT WAS SCARY.
I THOUGHT HE WAS COMING TO GET ME.
HE NEVER LISTENS TO ANYBODY.
WAIT ...
...YOU KNOW HIM?
GAH!
YEAH, KINDA.

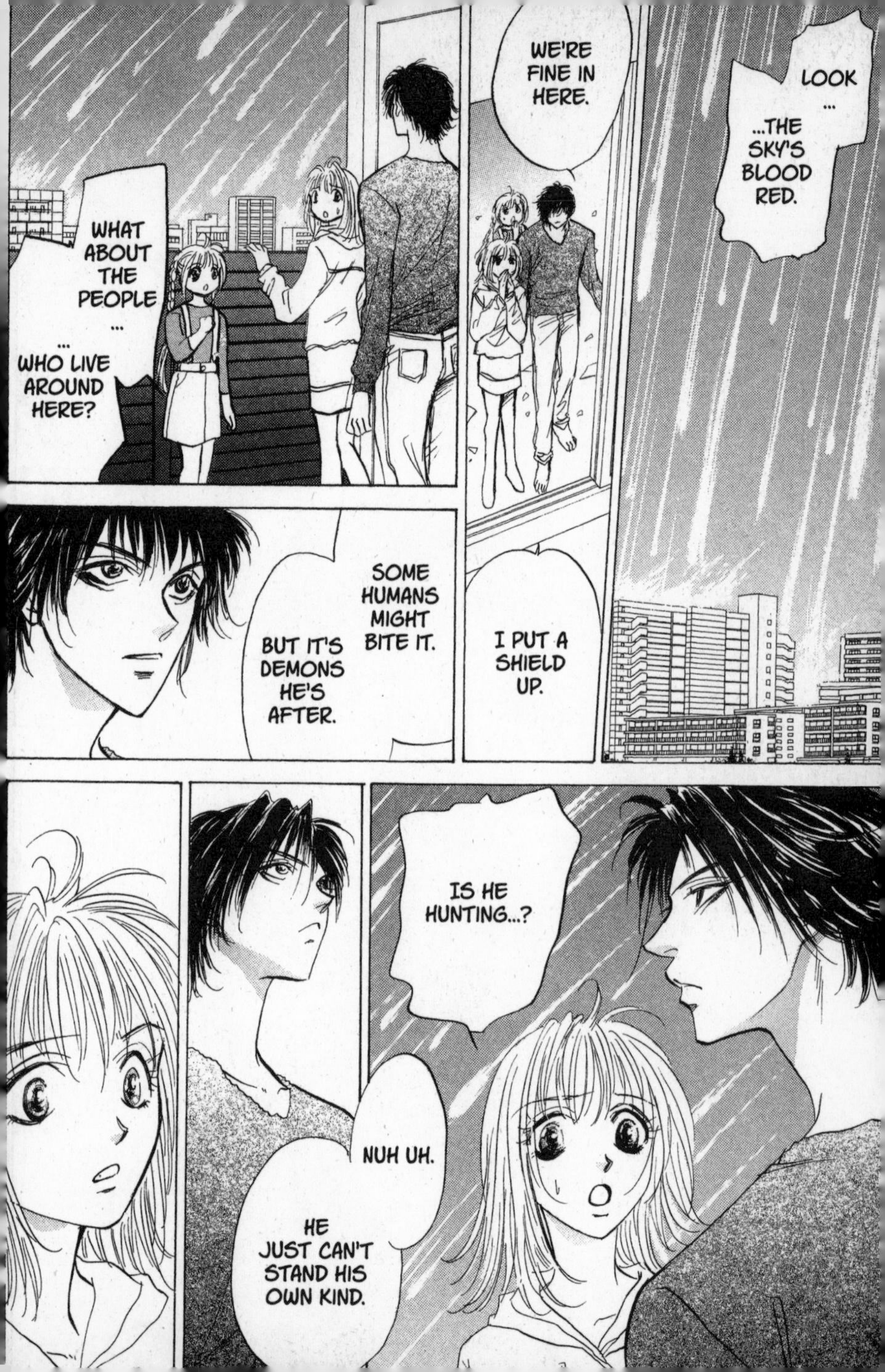
LOOK ...
...THE SKY'S BLOOD RED.
WE'RE FINE IN HERE.
I PUT A SHIELD UP.
WHAT ABOUT THE PEOPLE ...
... WHO LIVE AROUND HERE?
SOME HUMANS MIGHT BITE IT.
BUT IT'S DEMONS HE'S AFTER.
IS HE HUNTING...?
NUH UH.
HE JUST CAN'T STAND HIS OWN KIND.

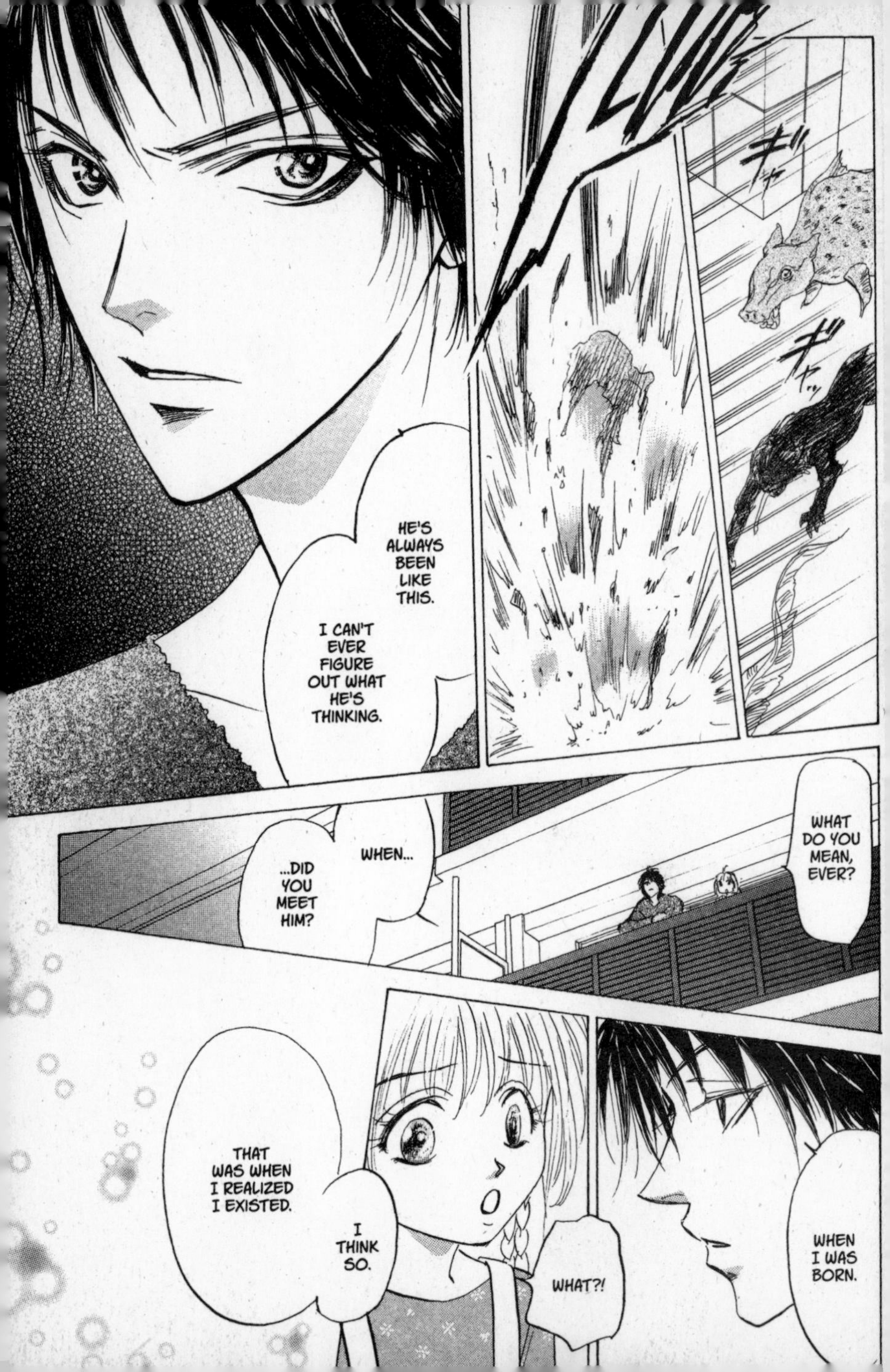

ギャ
ギャッ
HE'S ALWAYS BEEN LIKE THIS.
I CAN'T EVER FIGURE OUT WHAT HE'S THINKING.
WHAT DO YOU MEAN, EVER?
WHEN...
...DID YOU MEET HIM?
WHEN I WAS BORN.
WHAT?!
I THINK SO.
THAT WAS WHEN I REALIZED I EXISTED.

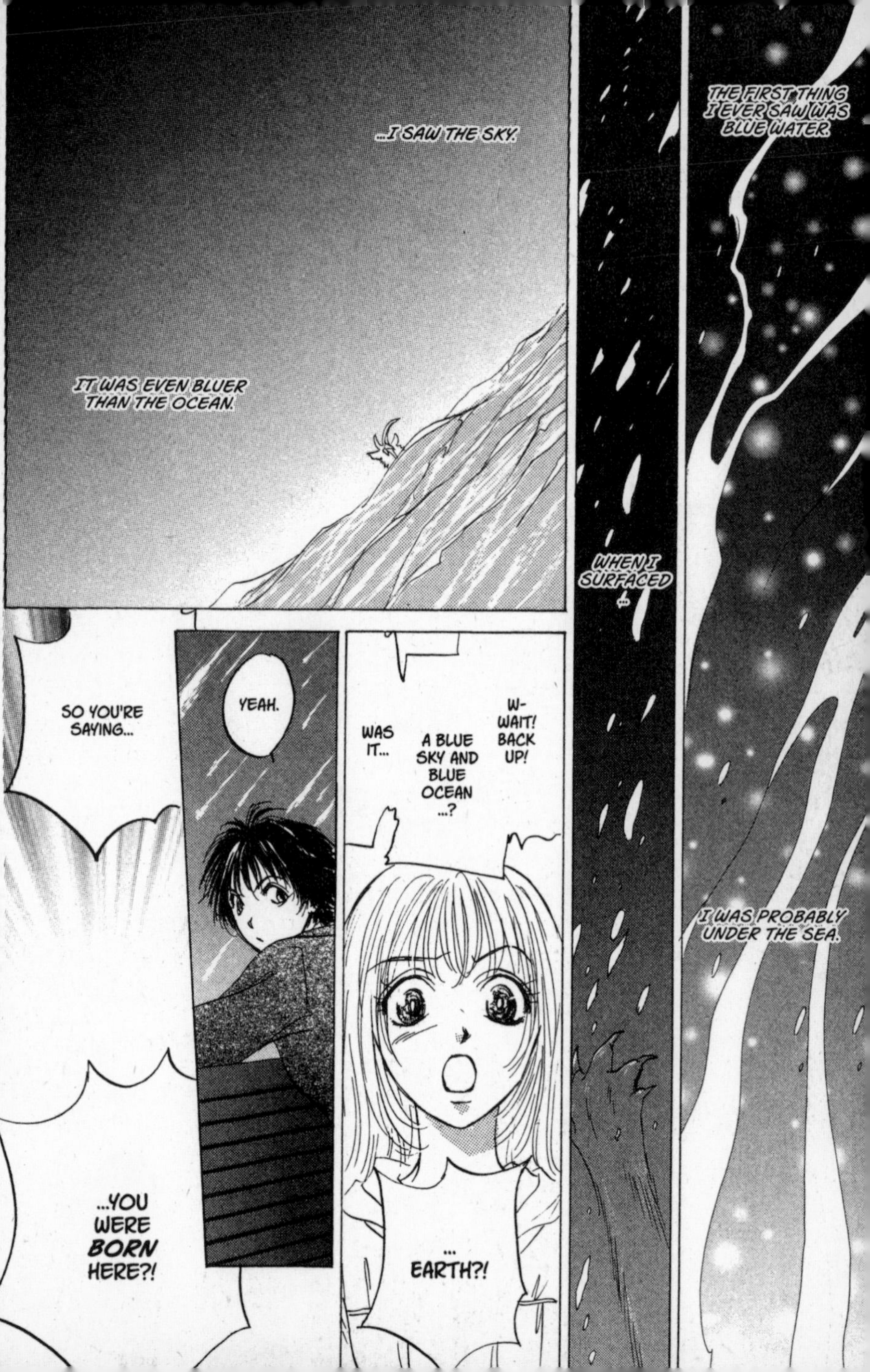
THE FIRST THING I EVER SAW WAS BLUE WATER.
I WAS PROBABLY UNDER THE SEA.
WHEN I SURFACED...
...I SAW THE SKY.
IT WAS EVEN BLUER THAN THE OCEAN.
W-WAIT! BACK UP!
A BLUE SKY AND BLUE OCEAN...?
WAS IT...
...EARTH?!
YEAH.
SO YOU'RE SAYING...
...YOU WERE **BORN** HERE?!

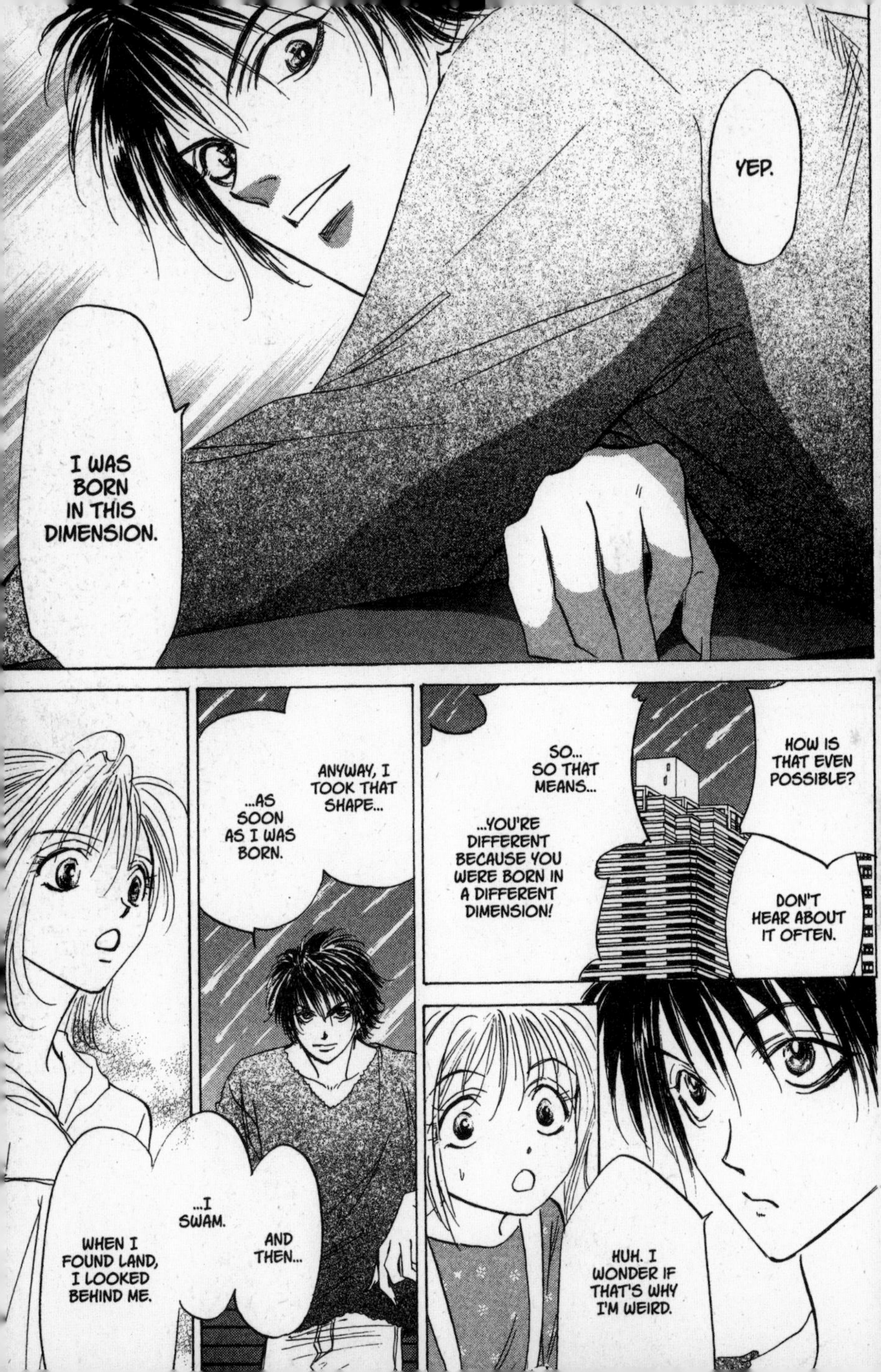
YEP.
I WAS BORN IN THIS DIMENSION.
HOW IS THAT EVEN POSSIBLE?
SO... SO THAT MEANS...
...YOU'RE DIFFERENT BECAUSE YOU WERE BORN IN A DIFFERENT DIMENSION!
DON'T HEAR ABOUT IT OFTEN.
HUH. I WONDER IF THAT'S WHY I'M WEIRD.
ANYWAY, I TOOK THAT SHAPE...
...AS SOON AS I WAS BORN.
AND THEN...
...I SWAM.
WHEN I FOUND LAND, I LOOKED BEHIND ME.

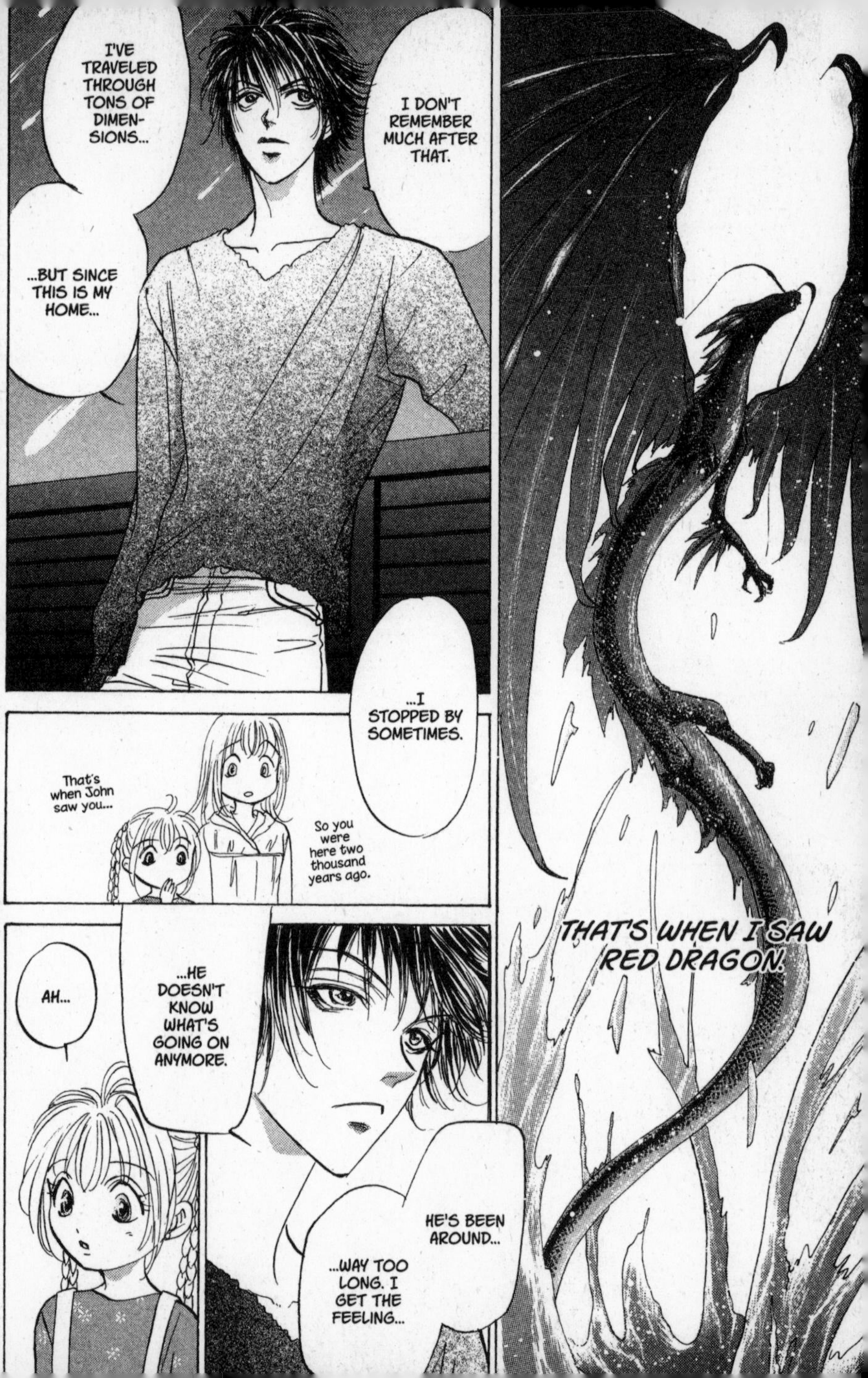
THAT'S WHEN I SAW RED DRAGON.
I DON'T REMEMBER MUCH AFTER THAT.
I'VE TRAVELED THROUGH TONS OF DIMENSIONS...
...BUT SINCE THIS IS MY HOME...
...I STOPPED BY SOMETIMES.
So you were here two thousand years ago.
That's when John saw you...
...HE DOESN'T KNOW WHAT'S GOING ON ANYMORE.
AH...
HE'S BEEN AROUND...
...WAY TOO LONG. I GET THE FEELING...

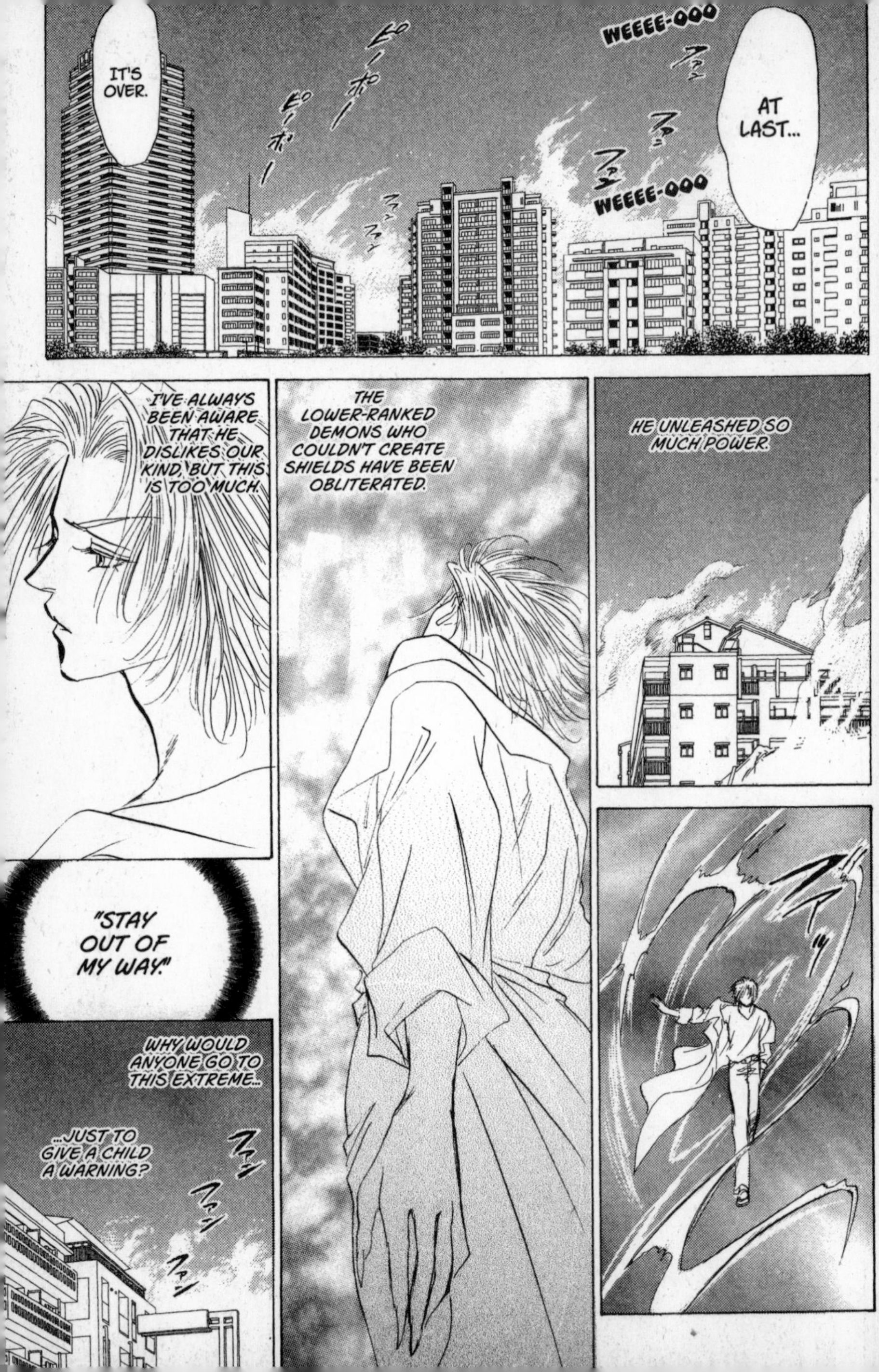
AT LAST...
WEEEE-OOO
WEEEE-OOO
IT'S OVER.
HE UNLEASHED SO MUCH POWER.
THE LOWER-RANKED DEMONS WHO COULDN'T CREATE SHIELDS HAVE BEEN OBLITERATED.
I'VE ALWAYS BEEN AWARE THAT HE DISLIKES OUR KIND, BUT THIS IS TOO MUCH.
"STAY OUT OF MY WAY."
WHY WOULD ANYONE GO TO THIS EXTREME...
...JUST TO GIVE A CHILD A WARNING?

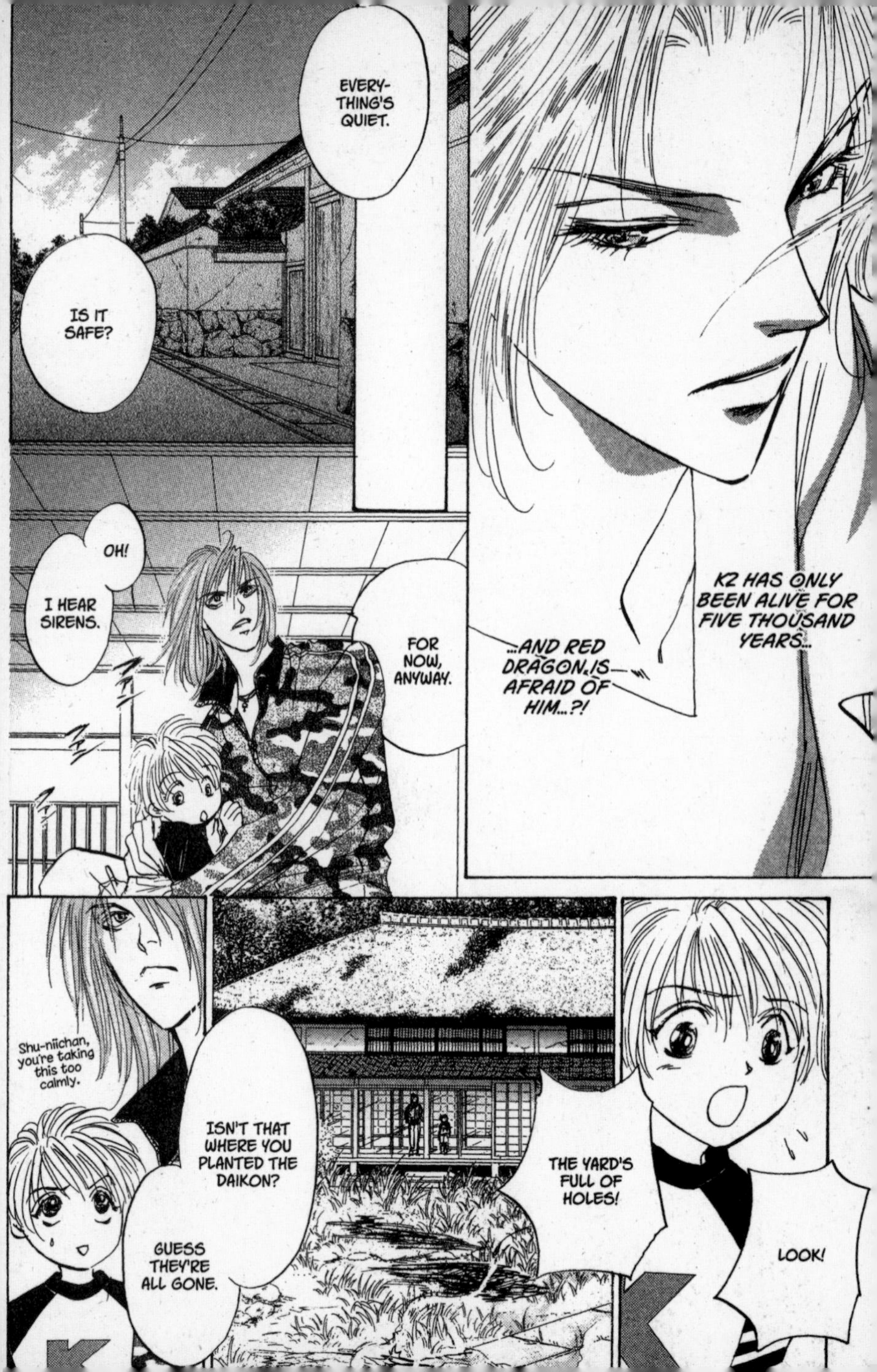
K2 HAS ONLY BEEN ALIVE FOR FIVE THOUSAND YEARS...
...AND RED DRAGON IS AFRAID OF HIM...?!
EVERY-THING'S QUIET.
IS IT SAFE?
FOR NOW, ANYWAY.
OH!
I HEAR SIRENS.
LOOK!
THE YARD'S FULL OF HOLES!
ISN'T THAT WHERE YOU PLANTED THE DAIKON?
GUESS THEY'RE ALL GONE.
Shu-niichan, you're taking this too calmly.

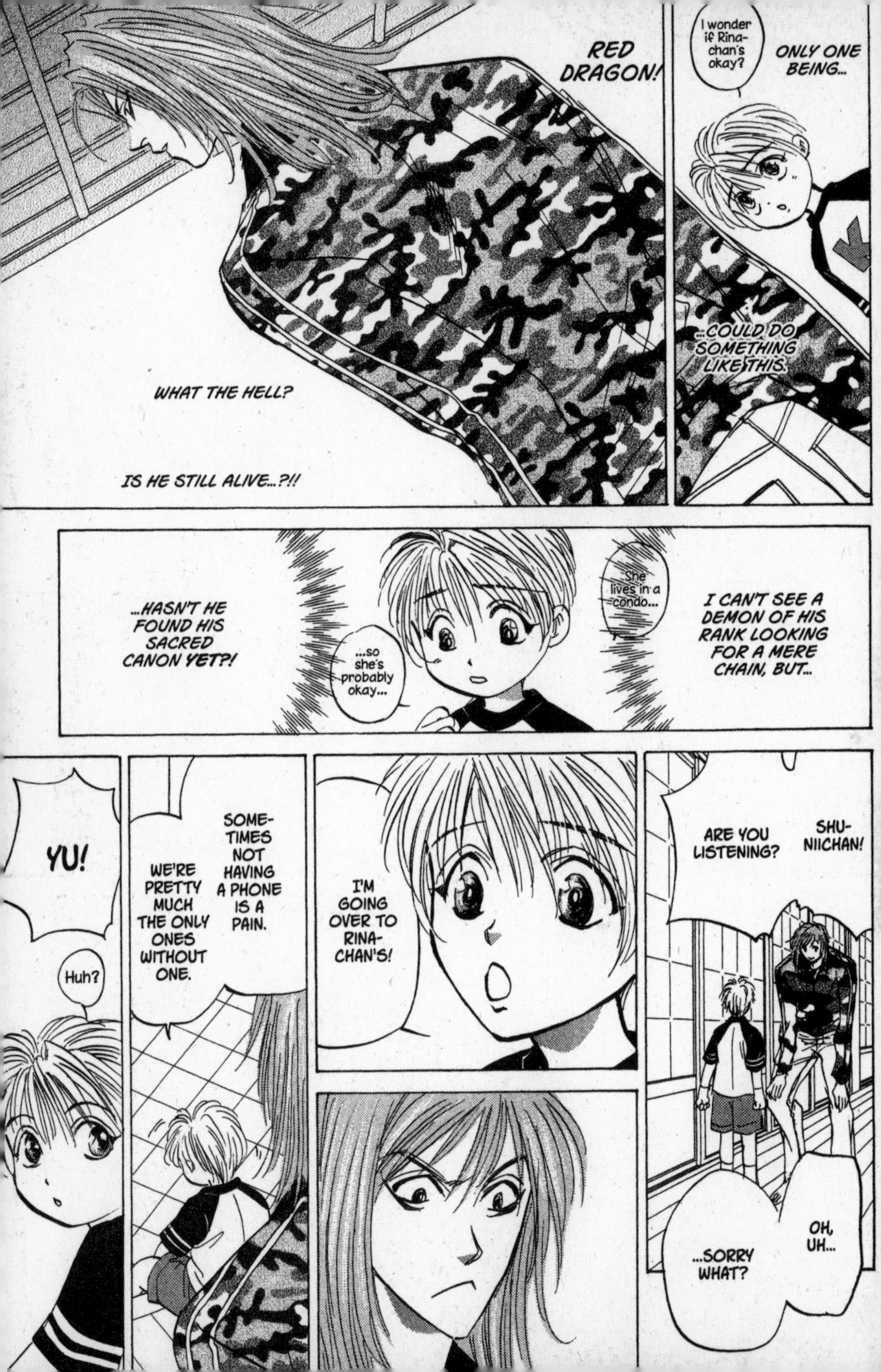
ONLY ONE BEING...
I wonder if Rina-chan's okay?
...COULD DO SOMETHING LIKE THIS.
RED DRAGON!
WHAT THE HELL?
IS HE STILL ALIVE...?!!
I CAN'T SEE A DEMON OF HIS RANK LOOKING FOR A MERE CHAIN, BUT...
She lives in a condo...
...so she's probably okay...
...HASN'T HE FOUND HIS SACRED CANON YET?!
SHU-NIICHAN!
ARE YOU LISTENING?
OH, UH...
...SORRY WHAT?
I'M GOING OVER TO RINA-CHAN'S!
SOME-TIMES NOT HAVING A PHONE IS A PAIN.
WE'RE PRETTY MUCH THE ONLY ONES WITHOUT ONE.
YU!
Huh?

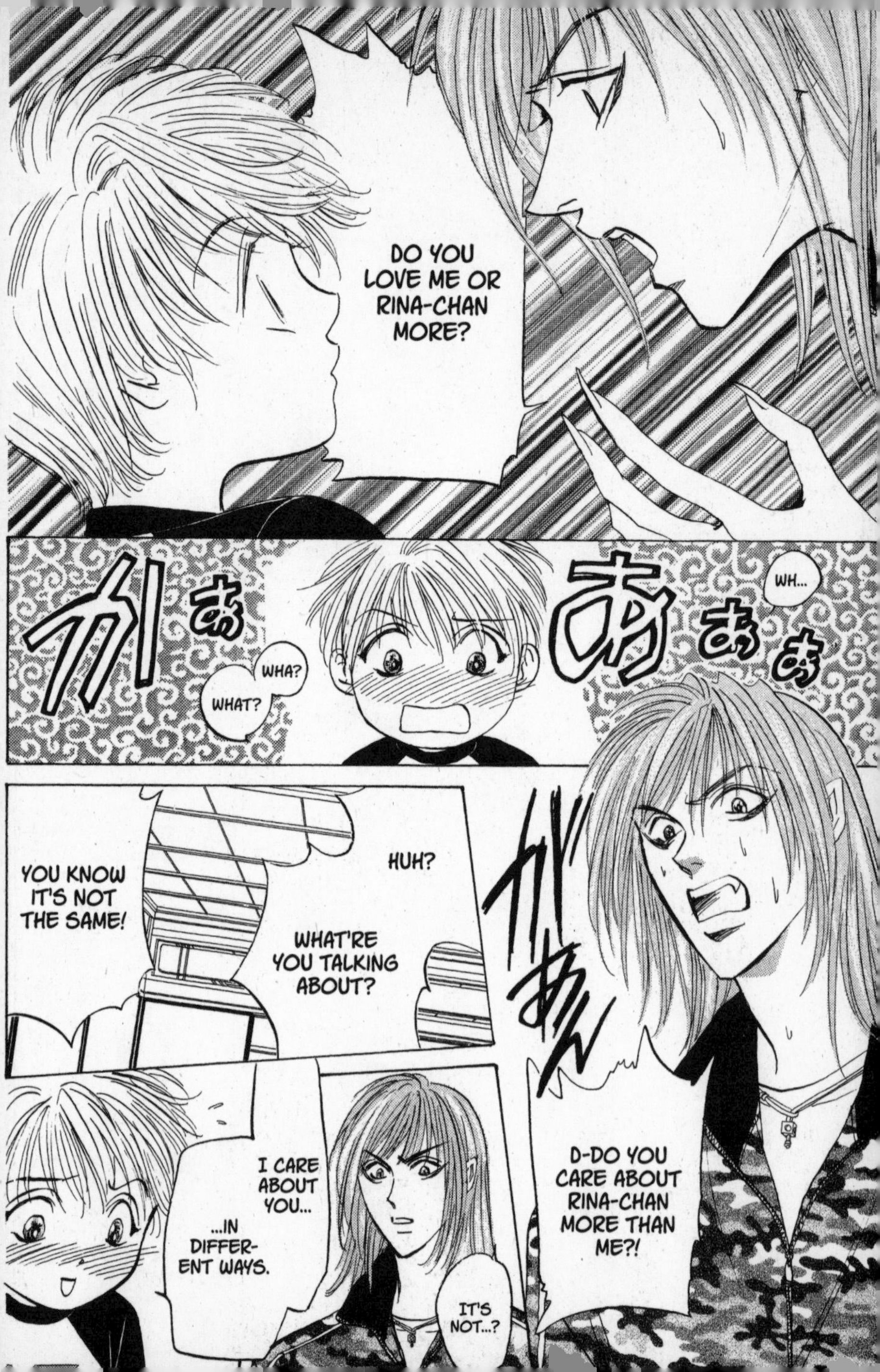
DO YOU LOVE ME OR RINA-CHAN MORE?
WH...
WHA?
WHAT?
D-DO YOU CARE ABOUT RINA-CHAN MORE THAN ME?!
HUH?
WHAT'RE YOU TALKING ABOUT?
YOU KNOW IT'S NOT THE SAME!
I CARE ABOUT YOU...
...IN DIFFER-ENT WAYS.
IT'S NOT...?

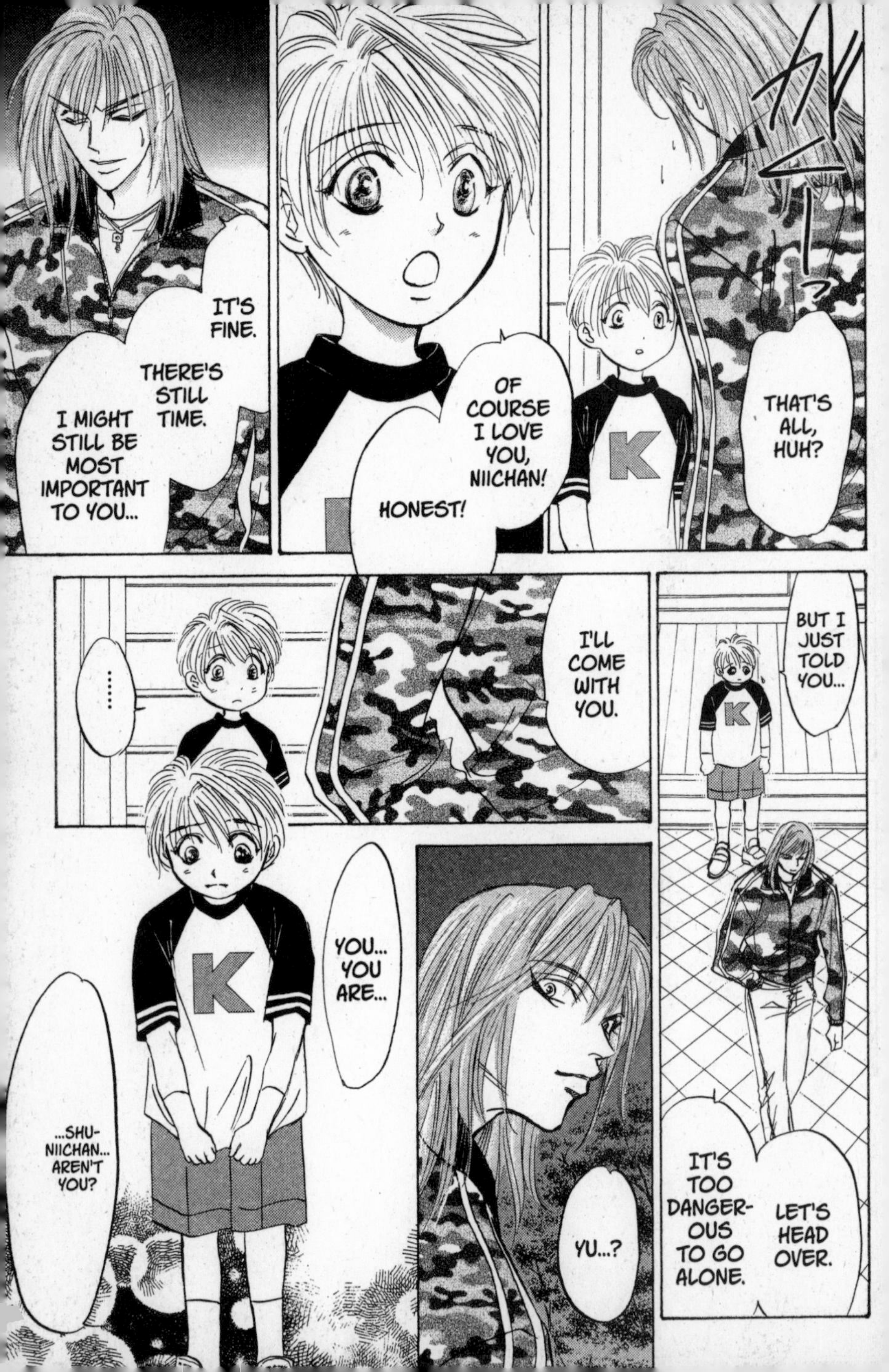
THAT'S ALL, HUH?
OF COURSE I LOVE YOU, NIICHAN!
HONEST!
IT'S FINE.
THERE'S STILL TIME.
I MIGHT STILL BE MOST IMPORTANT TO YOU...
BUT I JUST TOLD YOU...
LET'S HEAD OVER.
IT'S TOO DANGER-OUS TO GO ALONE.
I'LL COME WITH YOU.
......
YU...?
YOU... YOU ARE...
...SHU-NIICHAN... AREN'T YOU?

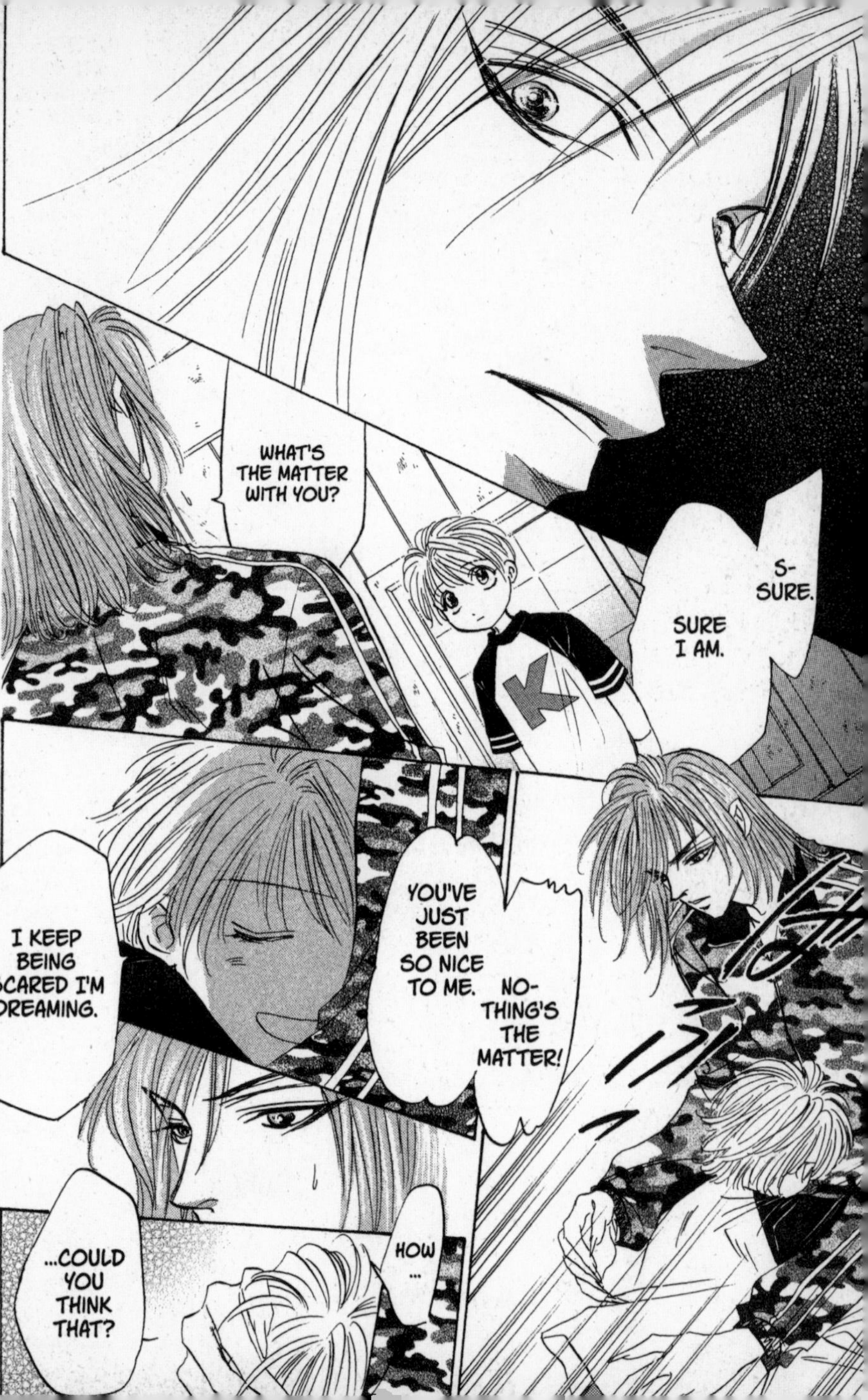
WHAT'S THE MATTER WITH YOU?
S-SURE.
SURE I AM.
NO-THING'S THE MATTER!
YOU'VE JUST BEEN SO NICE TO ME.
I KEEP BEING SCARED I'M DREAMING.
HOW ...
...COULD YOU THINK THAT?

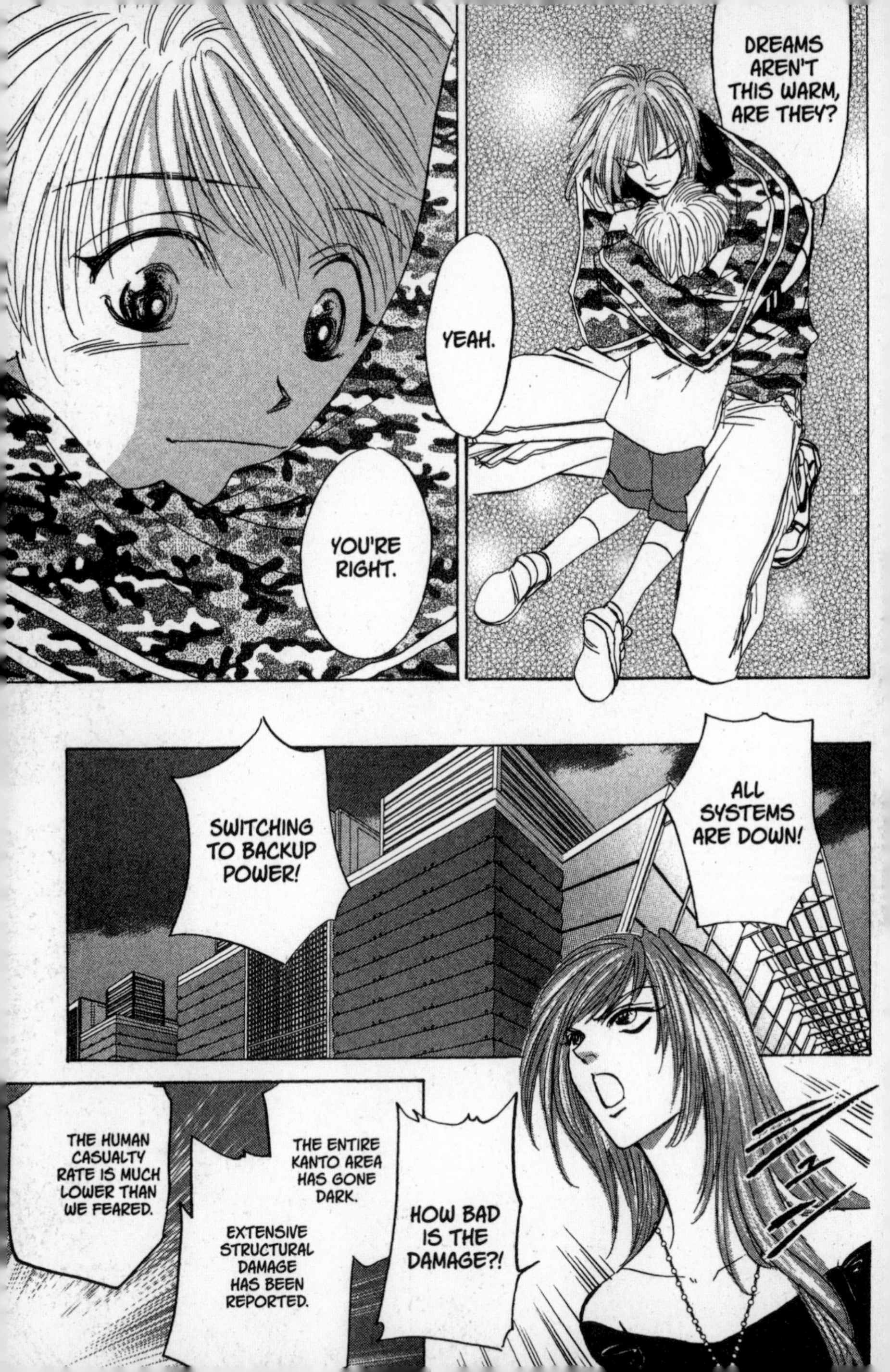
DREAMS AREN'T THIS WARM, ARE THEY?
YEAH.
YOU'RE RIGHT.
ALL SYSTEMS ARE DOWN!
SWITCHING TO BACKUP POWER!
HOW BAD IS THE DAMAGE?!
THE ENTIRE KANTO AREA HAS GONE DARK.
EXTENSIVE STRUCTURAL DAMAGE HAS BEEN REPORTED.
THE HUMAN CASUALTY RATE IS MUCH LOWER THAN WE FEARED.

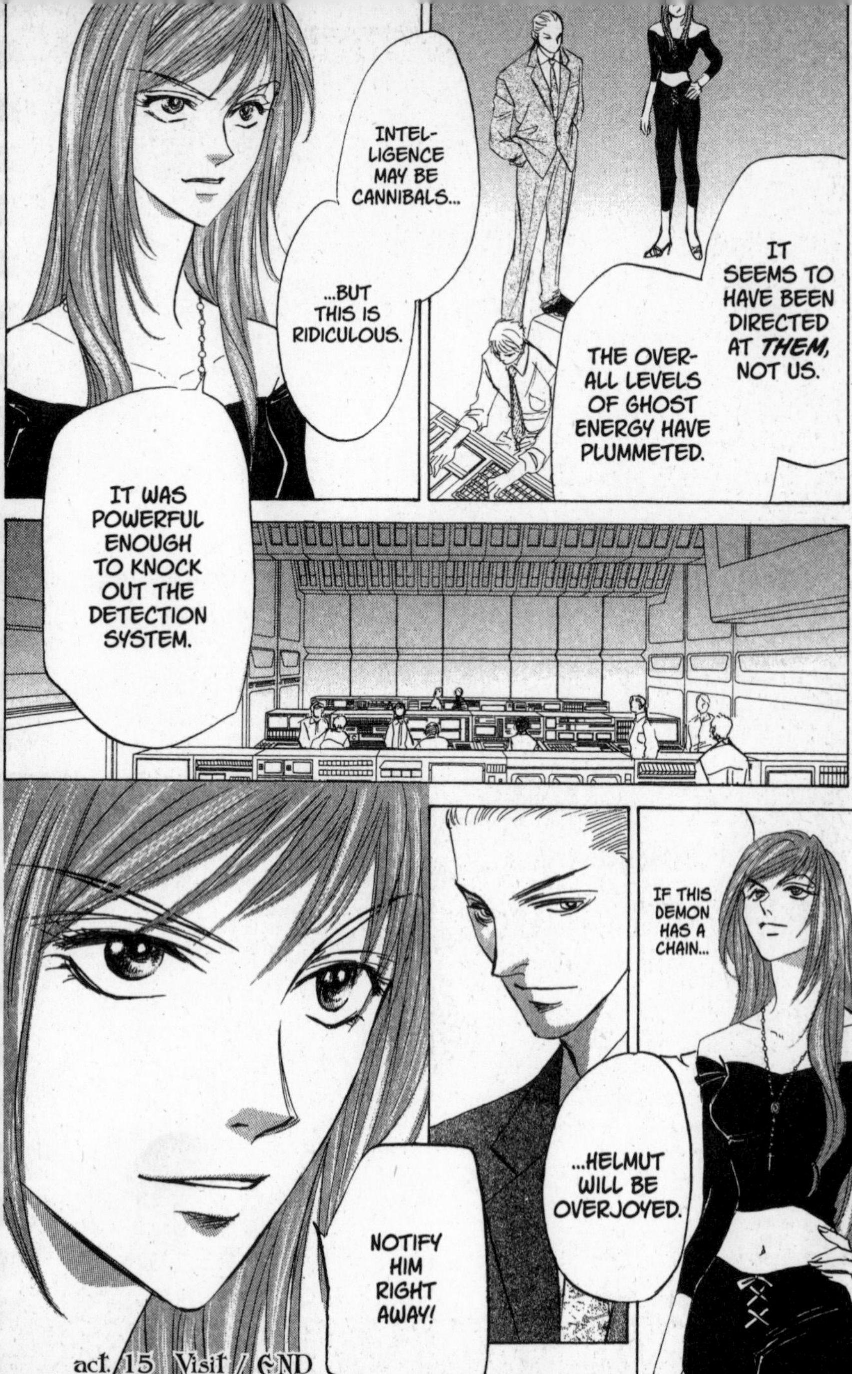
IT SEEMS TO HAVE BEEN DIRECTED AT *THEM,* NOT US.
THE OVERALL LEVELS OF GHOST ENERGY HAVE PLUMMETED.
INTELLIGENCE MAY BE CANNIBALS...
...BUT THIS IS RIDICULOUS.
IT WAS POWERFUL ENOUGH TO KNOCK OUT THE DETECTION SYSTEM.
IF THIS DEMON HAS A CHAIN...
...HELMUT WILL BE OVERJOYED.
NOTIFY HIM RIGHT AWAY!
act. 15 Visit / END

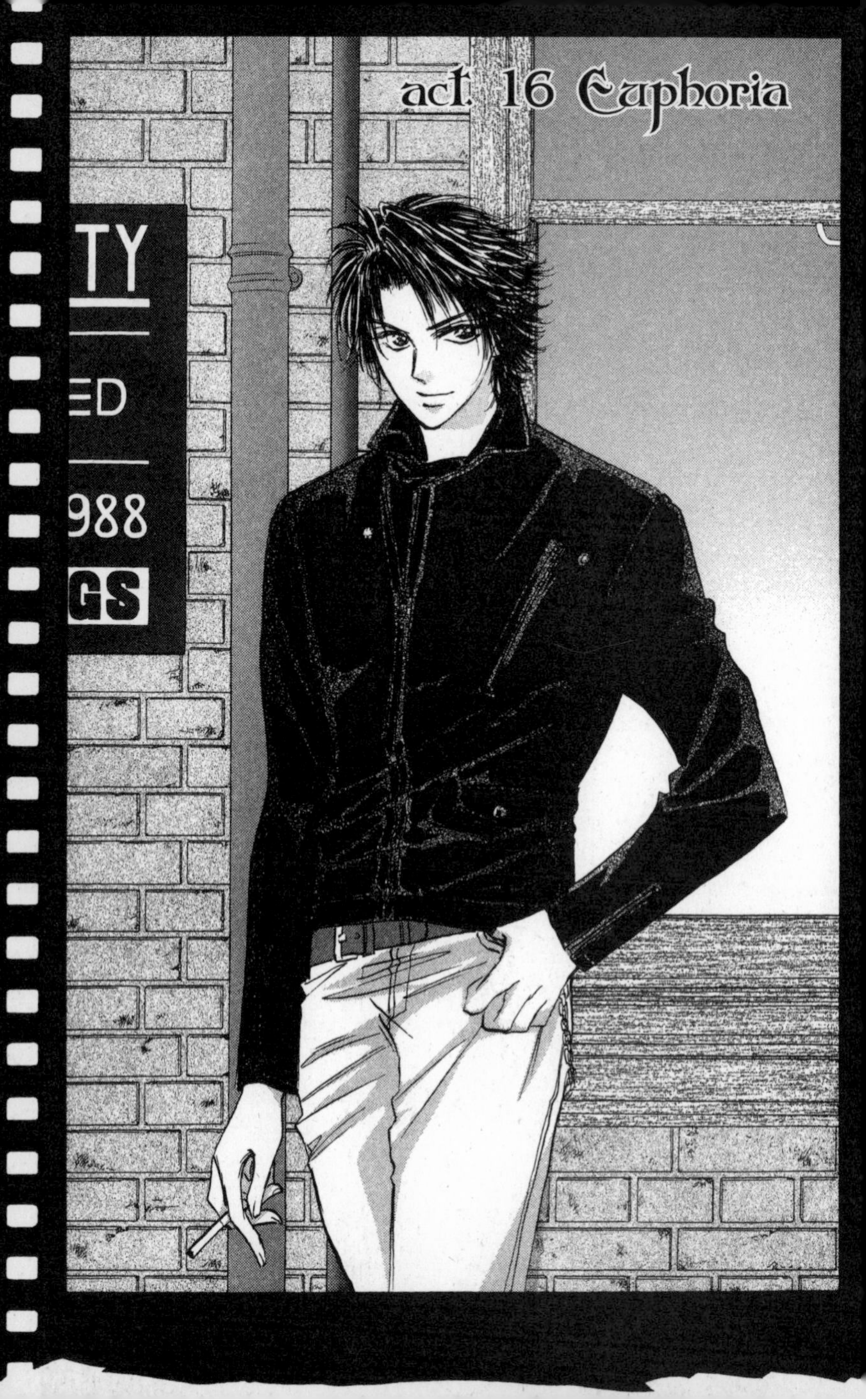
act. 16 Euphoria
TY
ED
988
GS

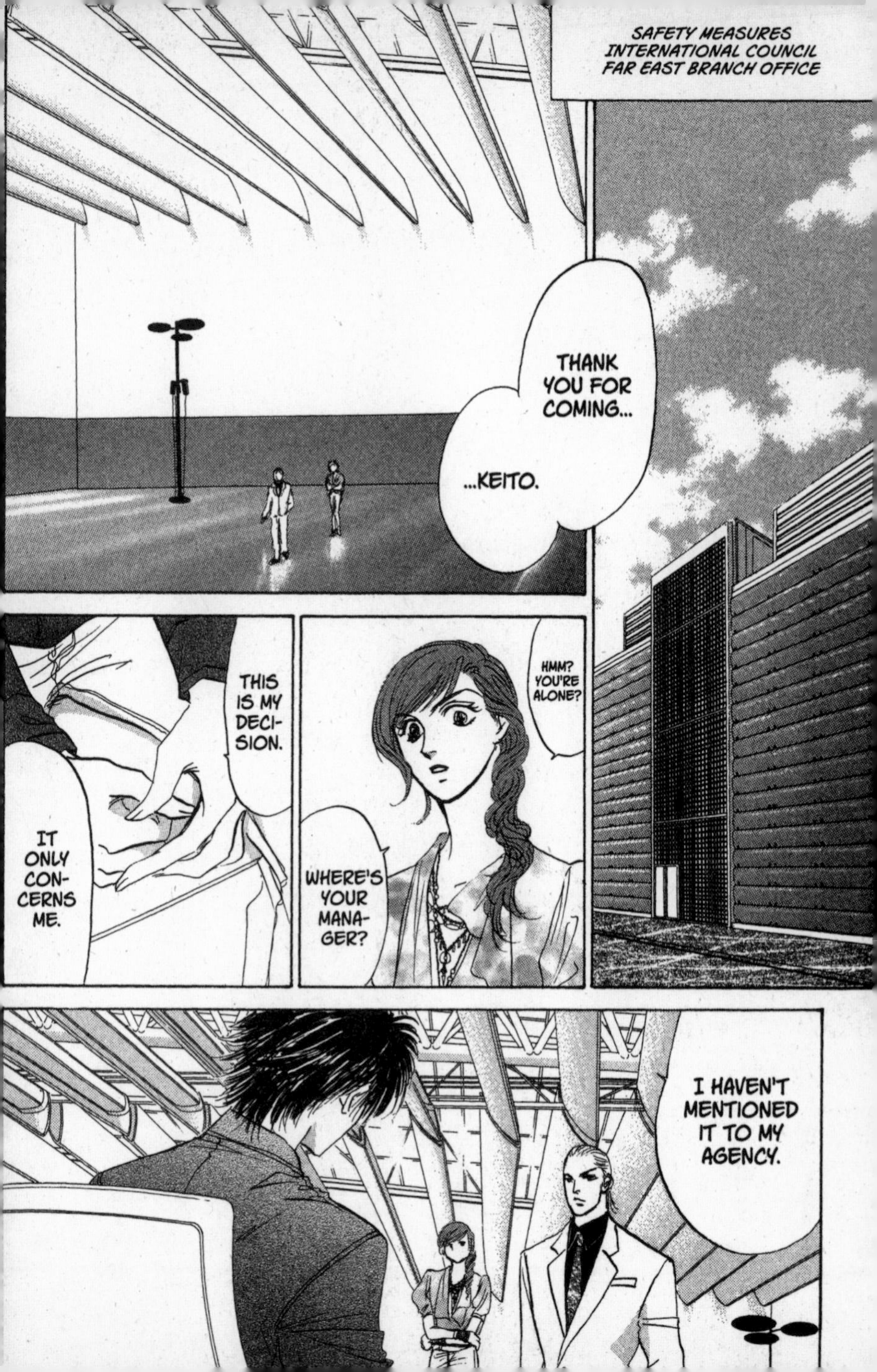
SAFETY MEASURES INTERNATIONAL COUNCIL FAR EAST BRANCH OFFICE
THANK YOU FOR COMING...
...KEITO.
HMM? YOU'RE ALONE?
WHERE'S YOUR MANA-GER?
THIS IS MY DECI-SION.
IT ONLY CON-CERNS ME.
I HAVEN'T MENTIONED IT TO MY AGENCY.

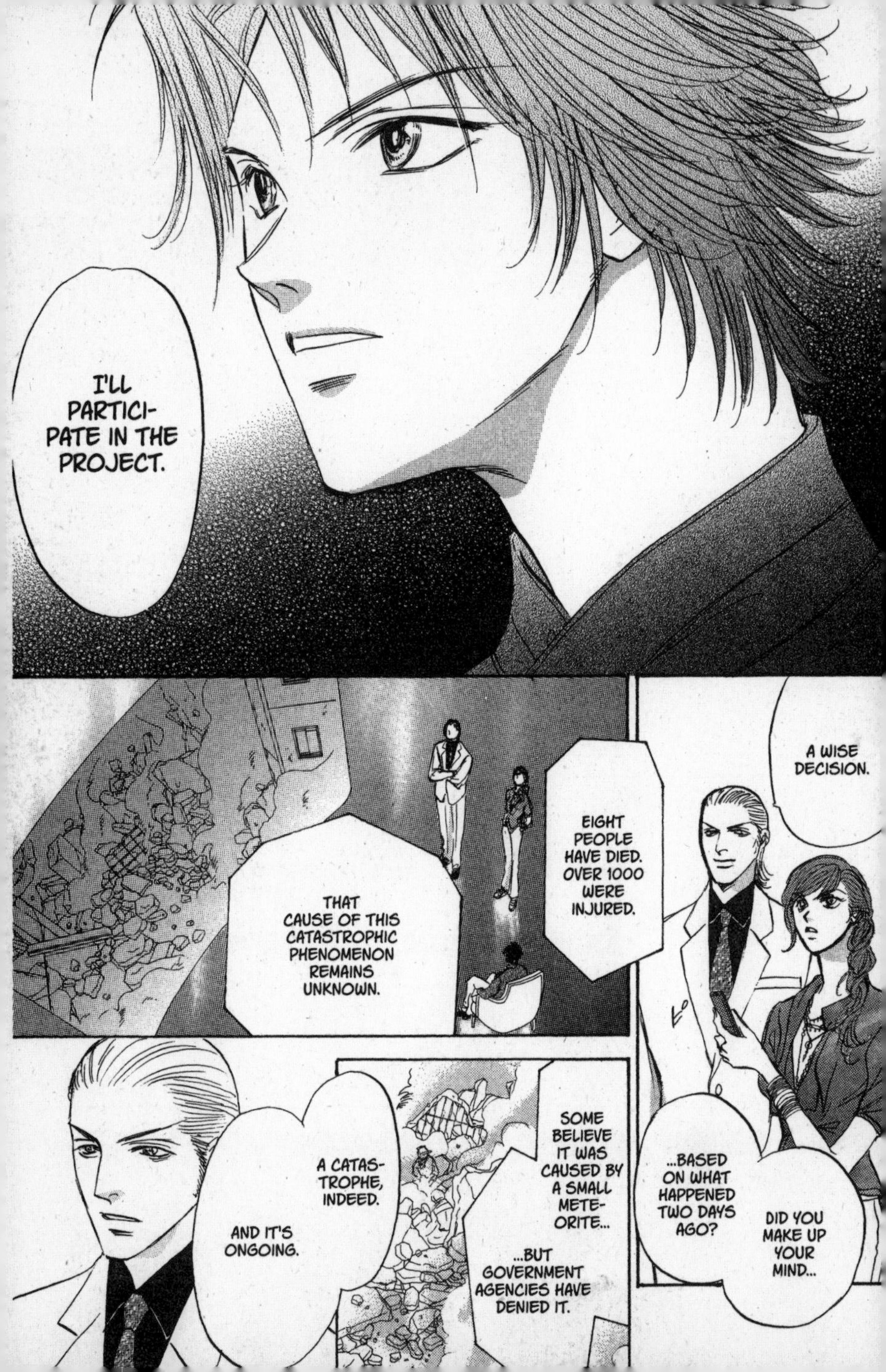
I'LL PARTICIPATE IN THE PROJECT.
A WISE DECISION.
DID YOU MAKE UP YOUR MIND...
...BASED ON WHAT HAPPENED TWO DAYS AGO?
EIGHT PEOPLE HAVE DIED. OVER 1000 WERE INJURED.
THAT CAUSE OF THIS CATASTROPHIC PHENOMENON REMAINS UNKNOWN.
SOME BELIEVE IT WAS CAUSED BY A SMALL METEORITE...
...BUT GOVERNMENT AGENCIES HAVE DENIED IT.
A CATASTROPHE, INDEED.
AND IT'S ONGOING.

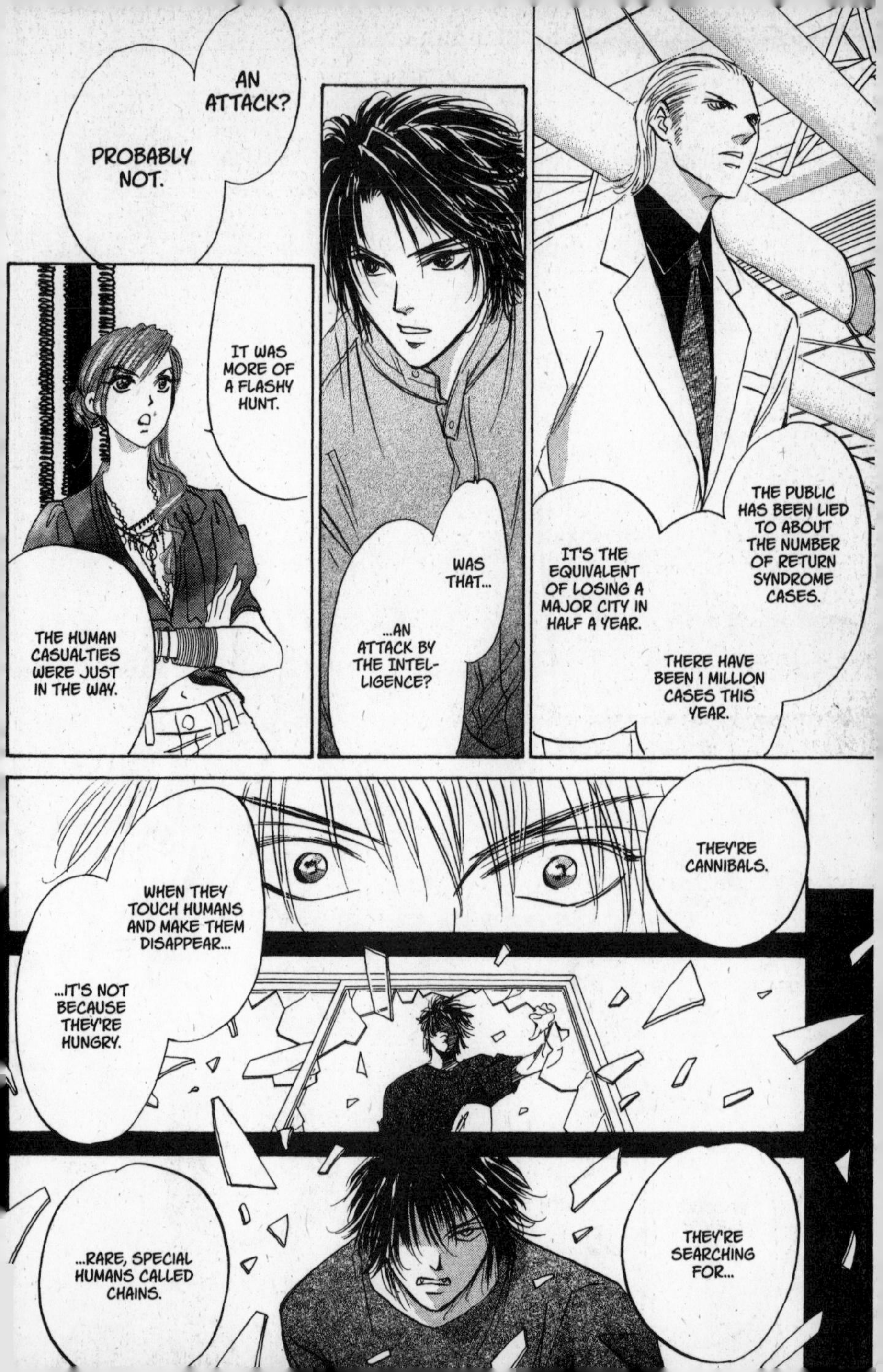
THE PUBLIC HAS BEEN LIED TO ABOUT THE NUMBER OF RETURN SYNDROME CASES.
THERE HAVE BEEN 1 MILLION CASES THIS YEAR.
IT'S THE EQUIVALENT OF LOSING A MAJOR CITY IN HALF A YEAR.
WAS THAT...
...AN ATTACK BY THE INTEL-LIGENCE?
AN ATTACK?
PROBABLY NOT.
IT WAS MORE OF A FLASHY HUNT.
THE HUMAN CASUALTIES WERE JUST IN THE WAY.
THEY'RE CANNIBALS.
WHEN THEY TOUCH HUMANS AND MAKE THEM DISAPPEAR...
...IT'S NOT BECAUSE THEY'RE HUNGRY.
THEY'RE SEARCHING FOR...
...RARE, SPECIAL HUMANS CALLED CHAINS.

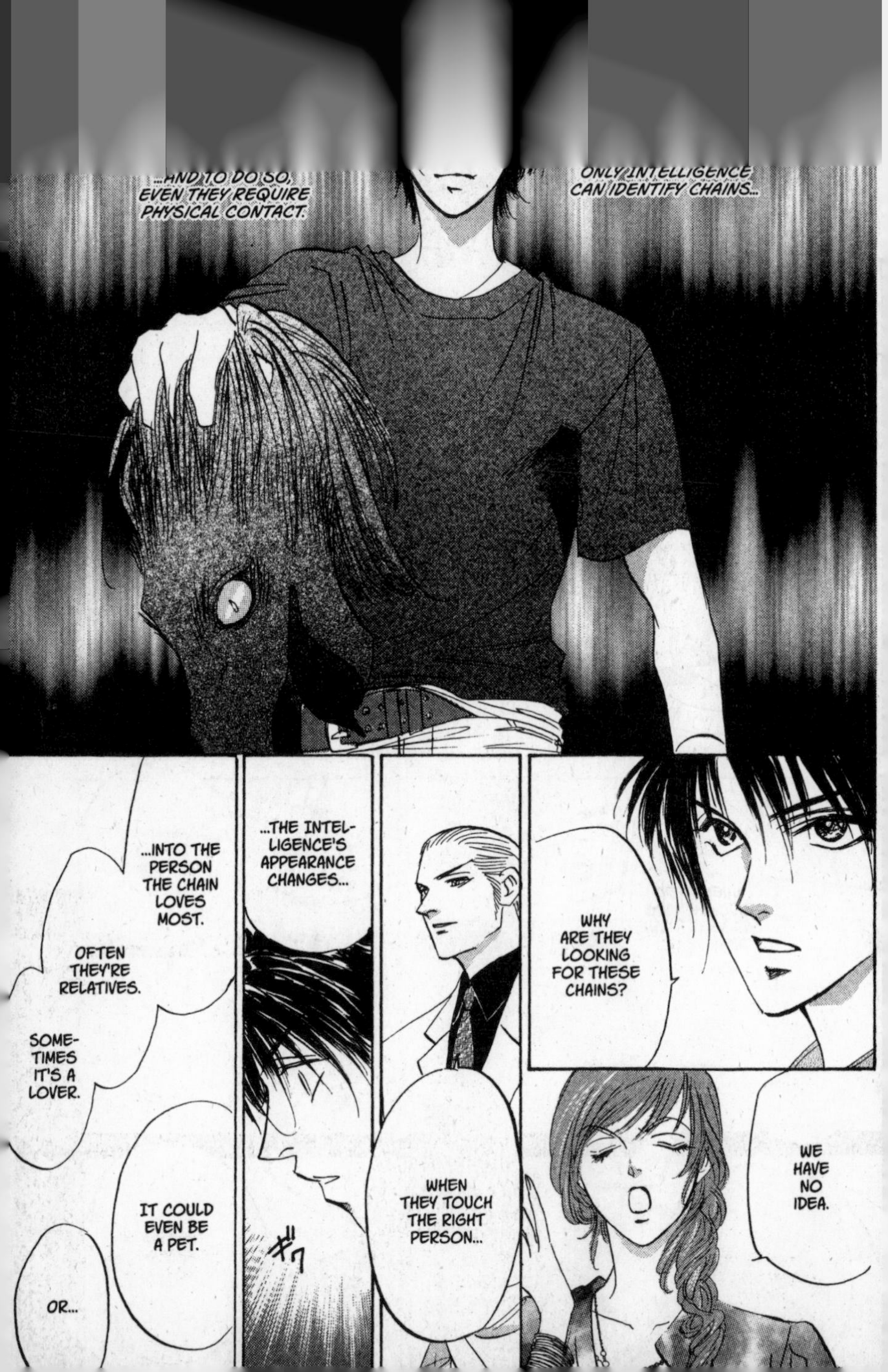
ONLY INTELLIGENCE CAN IDENTIFY CHAINS...
...AND TO DO SO, EVEN THEY REQUIRE PHYSICAL CONTACT.
WHY ARE THEY LOOKING FOR THESE CHAINS?
WE HAVE NO IDEA.
WHEN THEY TOUCH THE RIGHT PERSON...
...THE INTEL-LIGENCE'S APPEARANCE CHANGES...
ギク
...INTO THE PERSON THE CHAIN LOVES MOST.
OFTEN THEY'RE RELATIVES.
SOME-TIMES IT'S A LOVER.
IT COULD EVEN BE A PET.
OR...

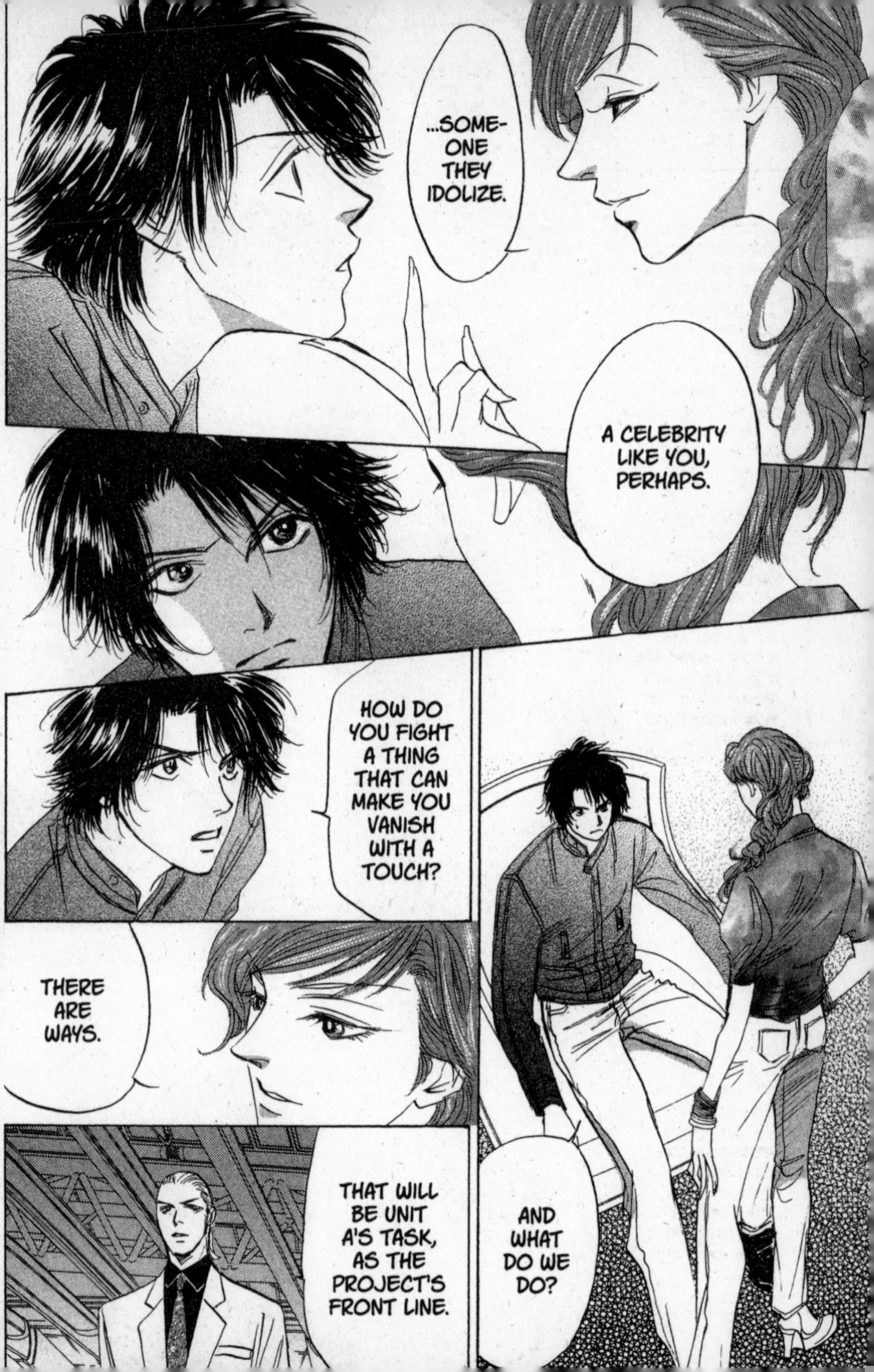
...SOME-ONE THEY IDOLIZE.
A CELEBRITY LIKE YOU, PERHAPS.
HOW DO YOU FIGHT A THING THAT CAN MAKE YOU VANISH WITH A TOUCH?
THERE ARE WAYS.
AND WHAT DO WE DO?
THAT WILL BE UNIT A'S TASK, AS THE PROJECT'S FRONT LINE.

FREE TALK
<4>

Let me digress for a moment. In volume 5 the relentless Zophie and the intense Helmut will be far more visible. Shinobu-kun is utterly trapped between these two overwhelming individuals.

I feel awful for him. I feel worse every day! He's such an intellectual, cerebral type that he couldn't possibly compete with the likes of them no matter how much blood they shared. (He tries, though!) On top of that, he has to keep an eye on K2. I guess the two girls are his oasis--the ones who sustain his spirit.

Starting in the next volume, Keito-kun will become more involved in the story. In some ways, all of the important characters are the protagonists. It would be entirely fair to say that volume 5 belongs to Keito. See you then!

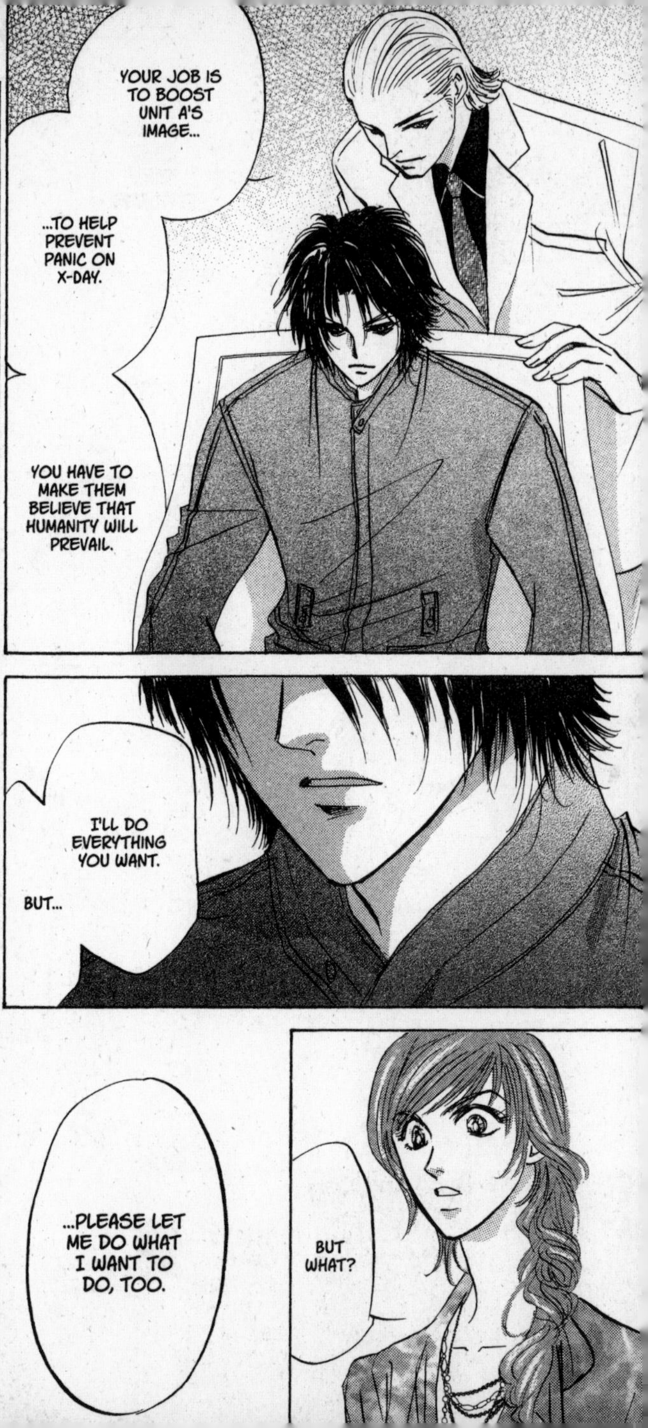
YOUR JOB IS TO BOOST UNIT A'S IMAGE...
...TO HELP PREVENT PANIC ON X-DAY.
YOU HAVE TO MAKE THEM BELIEVE THAT HUMANITY WILL PREVAIL.
I'LL DO EVERYTHING YOU WANT.
BUT...
BUT WHAT?
...PLEASE LET ME DO WHAT I WANT TO DO, TOO.

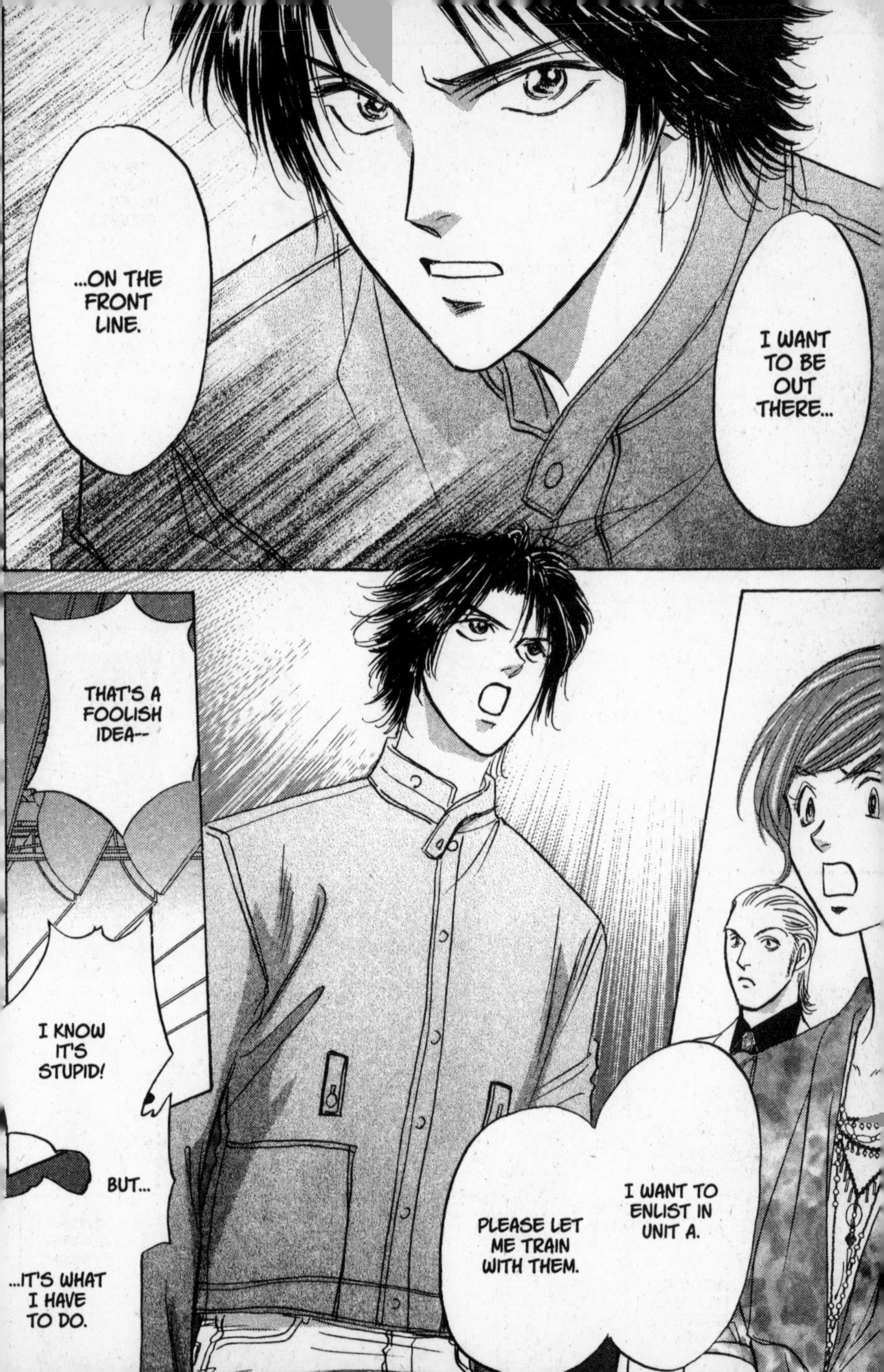
I WANT TO BE OUT THERE...
...ON THE FRONT LINE.
I WANT TO ENLIST IN UNIT A.
PLEASE LET ME TRAIN WITH THEM.
THAT'S A FOOLISH IDEA--
I KNOW IT'S STUPID!
BUT...
...IT'S WHAT I HAVE TO DO.

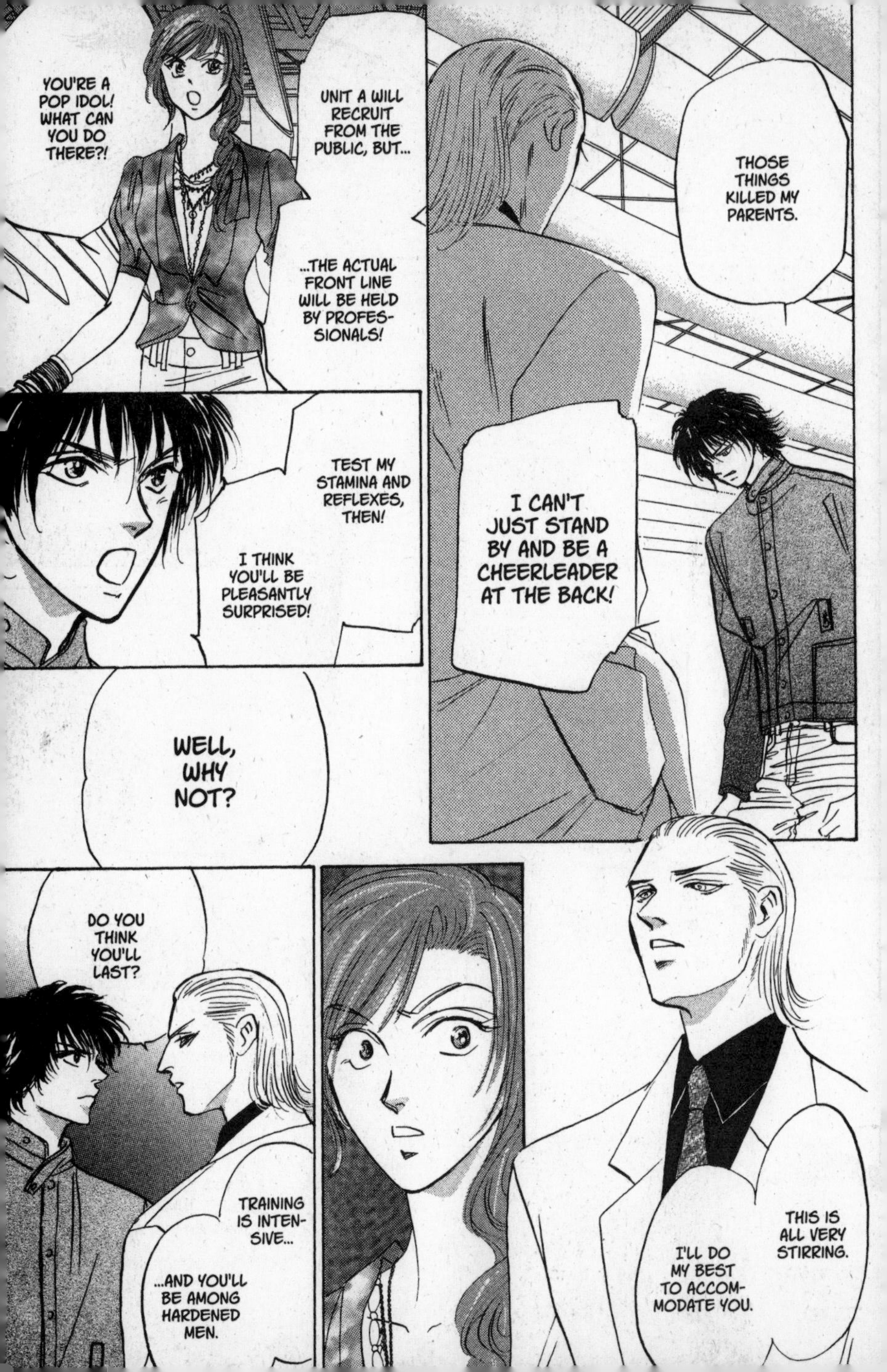
THOSE THINGS KILLED MY PARENTS.
I CAN'T JUST STAND BY AND BE A CHEERLEADER AT THE BACK!
UNIT A WILL RECRUIT FROM THE PUBLIC, BUT...
...THE ACTUAL FRONT LINE WILL BE HELD BY PROFES-SIONALS!
YOU'RE A POP IDOL! WHAT CAN YOU DO THERE?!
TEST MY STAMINA AND REFLEXES, THEN!
I THINK YOU'LL BE PLEASANTLY SURPRISED!
WELL, WHY NOT?
THIS IS ALL VERY STIRRING.
I'LL DO MY BEST TO ACCOM-MODATE YOU.
DO YOU THINK YOU'LL LAST?
TRAINING IS INTEN-SIVE...
...AND YOU'LL BE AMONG HARDENED MEN.

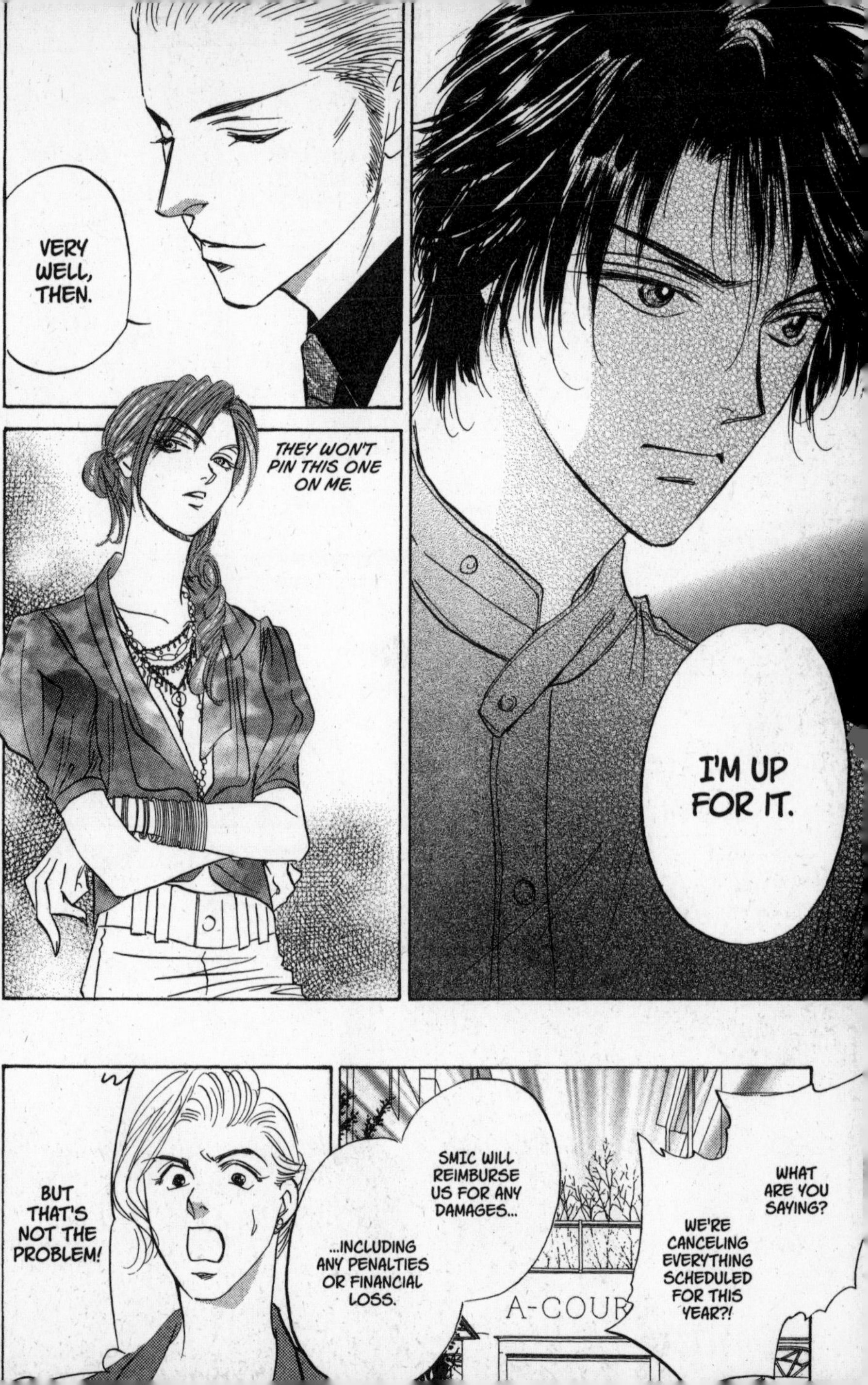

I'M UP FOR IT.
VERY WELL, THEN.
THEY WON'T PIN THIS ONE ON ME.
WHAT ARE YOU SAYING?
WE'RE CANCELING EVERYTHING SCHEDULED FOR THIS YEAR?!
SMIC WILL REIMBURSE US FOR ANY DAMAGES...
...INCLUDING ANY PENALTIES OR FINANCIAL LOSS.
BUT THAT'S NOT THE PROBLEM!

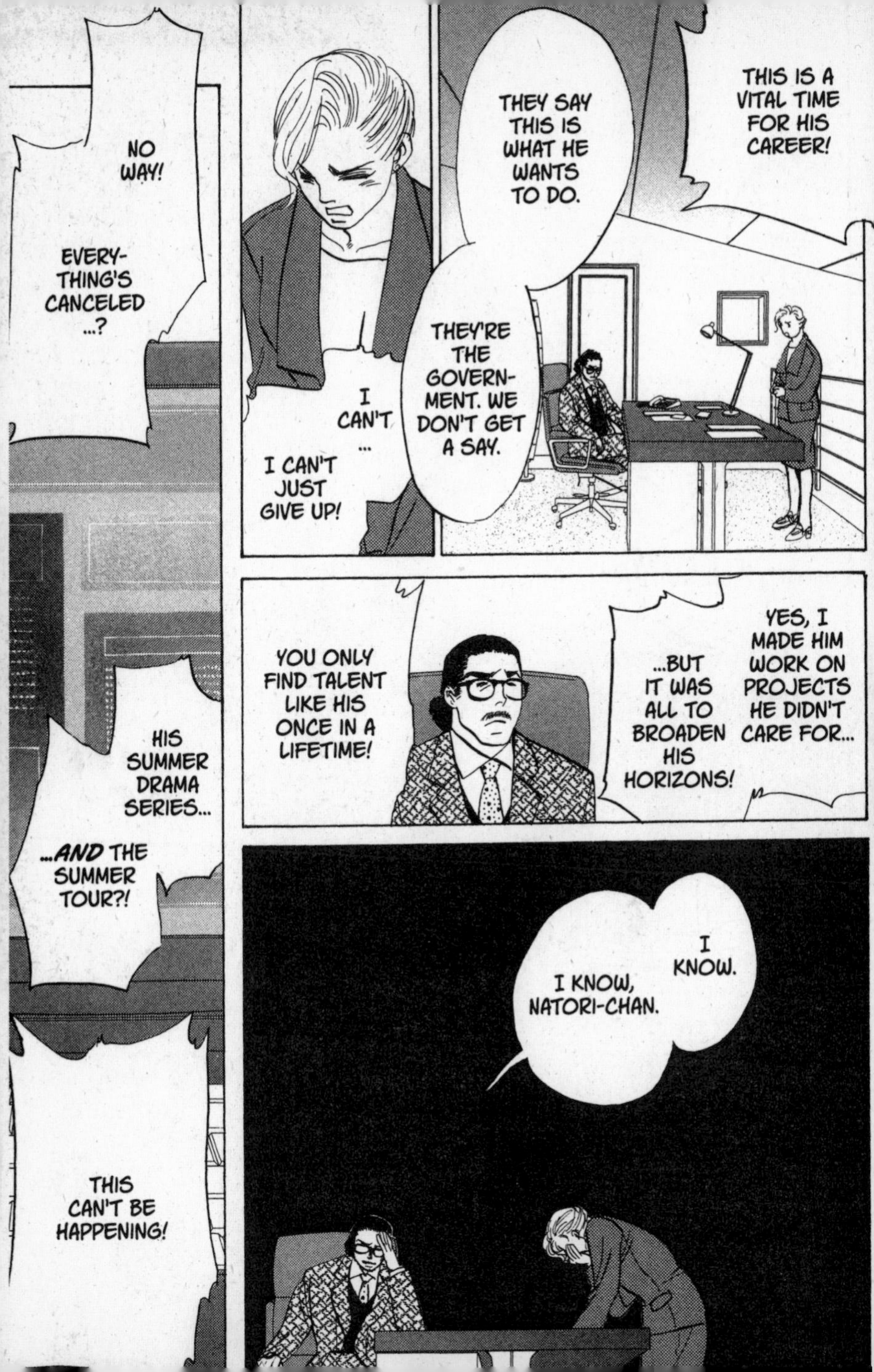
THIS IS A VITAL TIME FOR HIS CAREER!
THEY SAY THIS IS WHAT HE WANTS TO DO.
THEY'RE THE GOVERNMENT. WE DON'T GET A SAY.
I CAN'T...
I CAN'T JUST GIVE UP!
YES, I MADE HIM WORK ON PROJECTS HE DIDN'T CARE FOR...
...BUT IT WAS ALL TO BROADEN HIS HORIZONS!
YOU ONLY FIND TALENT LIKE HIS ONCE IN A LIFETIME!
I KNOW.
I KNOW, NATORI-CHAN.
NO WAY!
EVERYTHING'S CANCELED...?
HIS SUMMER DRAMA SERIES...
...*AND* THE SUMMER TOUR?!
THIS CAN'T BE HAPPENING!

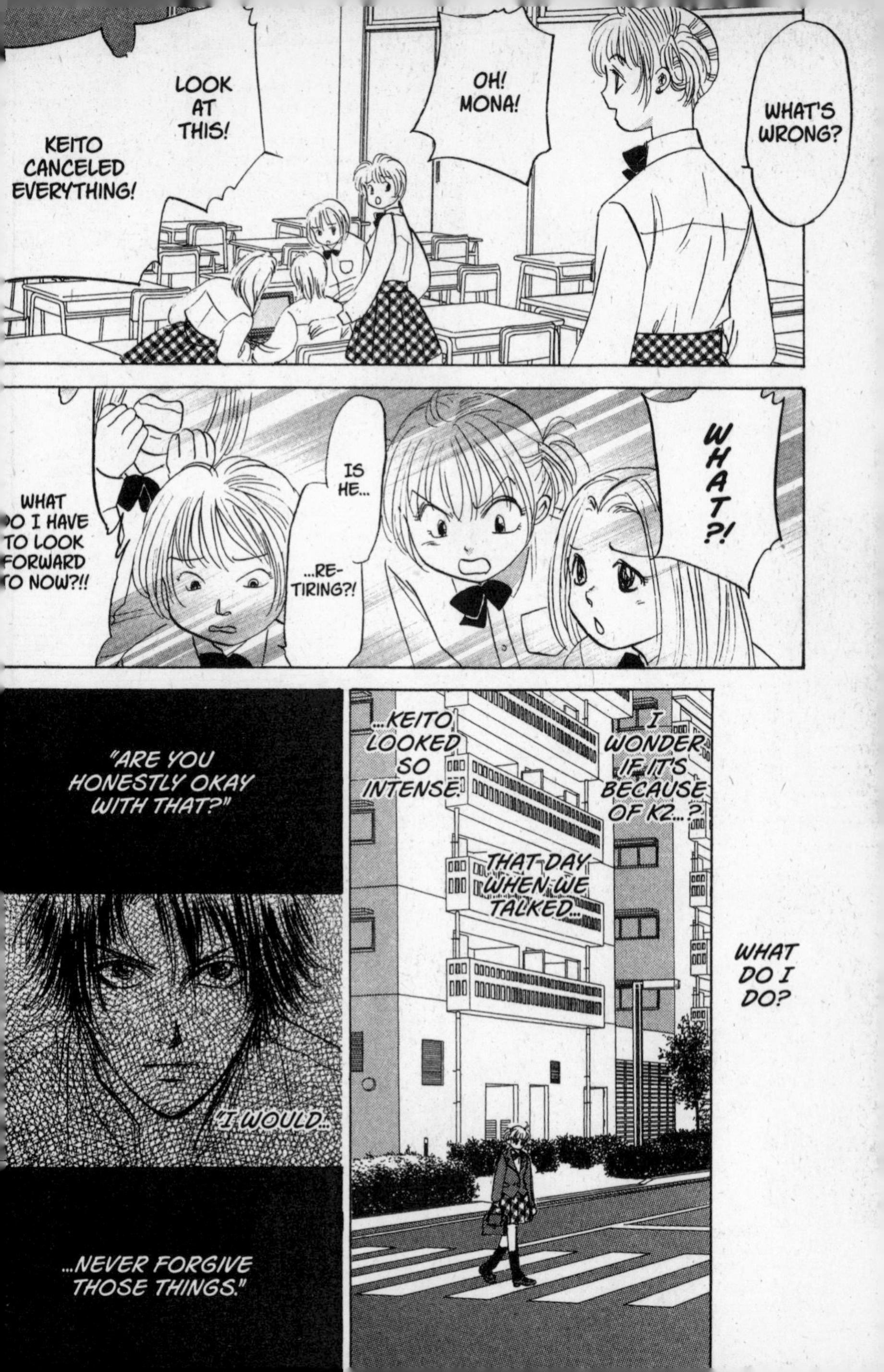
WHAT'S WRONG?
OH! MONA!
LOOK AT THIS!
KEITO CANCELED EVERYTHING!
WHAT?!
IS HE...
...RE-TIRING?!
WHAT DO I HAVE TO LOOK FORWARD TO NOW?!!
WHAT DO I DO?
I WONDER IF IT'S BECAUSE OF K2...?
...KEITO LOOKED SO INTENSE.
THAT DAY WHEN WE TALKED...
"ARE YOU HONESTLY OKAY WITH THAT?"
"I WOULD...
...NEVER FORGIVE THOSE THINGS."

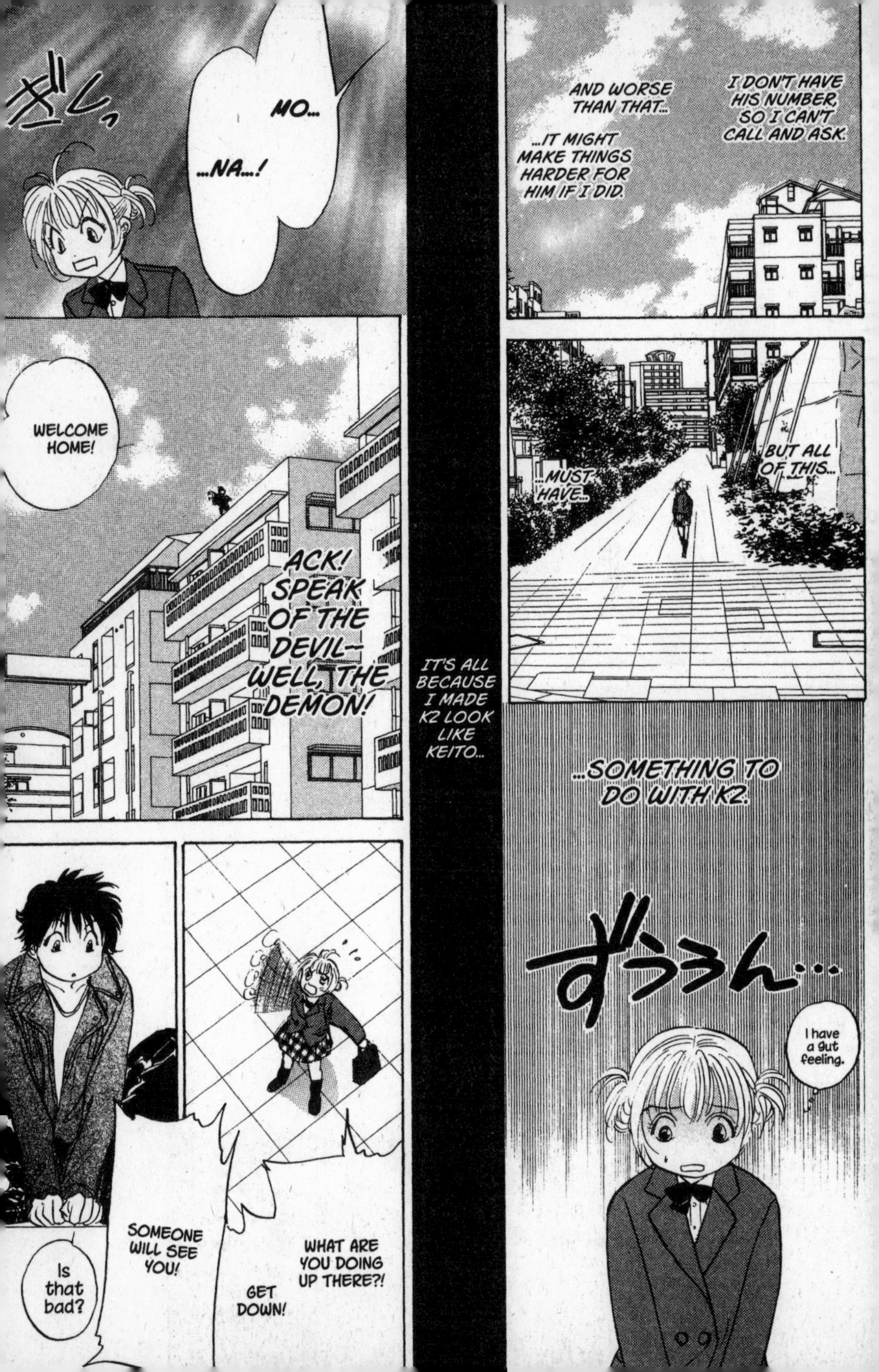
I DON'T HAVE HIS NUMBER, SO I CAN'T CALL AND ASK.
AND WORSE THAN THAT...
...IT MIGHT MAKE THINGS HARDER FOR HIM IF I DID.
BUT ALL OF THIS...
...MUST HAVE...
...SOMETHING TO DO WITH K2.
ずううん…
I have a gut feeling.
IT'S ALL BECAUSE I MADE K2 LOOK LIKE KEITO...
MO...
...NA...!
WELCOME HOME!
ACK! SPEAK OF THE DEVIL--WELL, THE DEMON!
WHAT ARE YOU DOING UP THERE?!
GET DOWN!
SOMEONE WILL SEE YOU!
Is that bad?

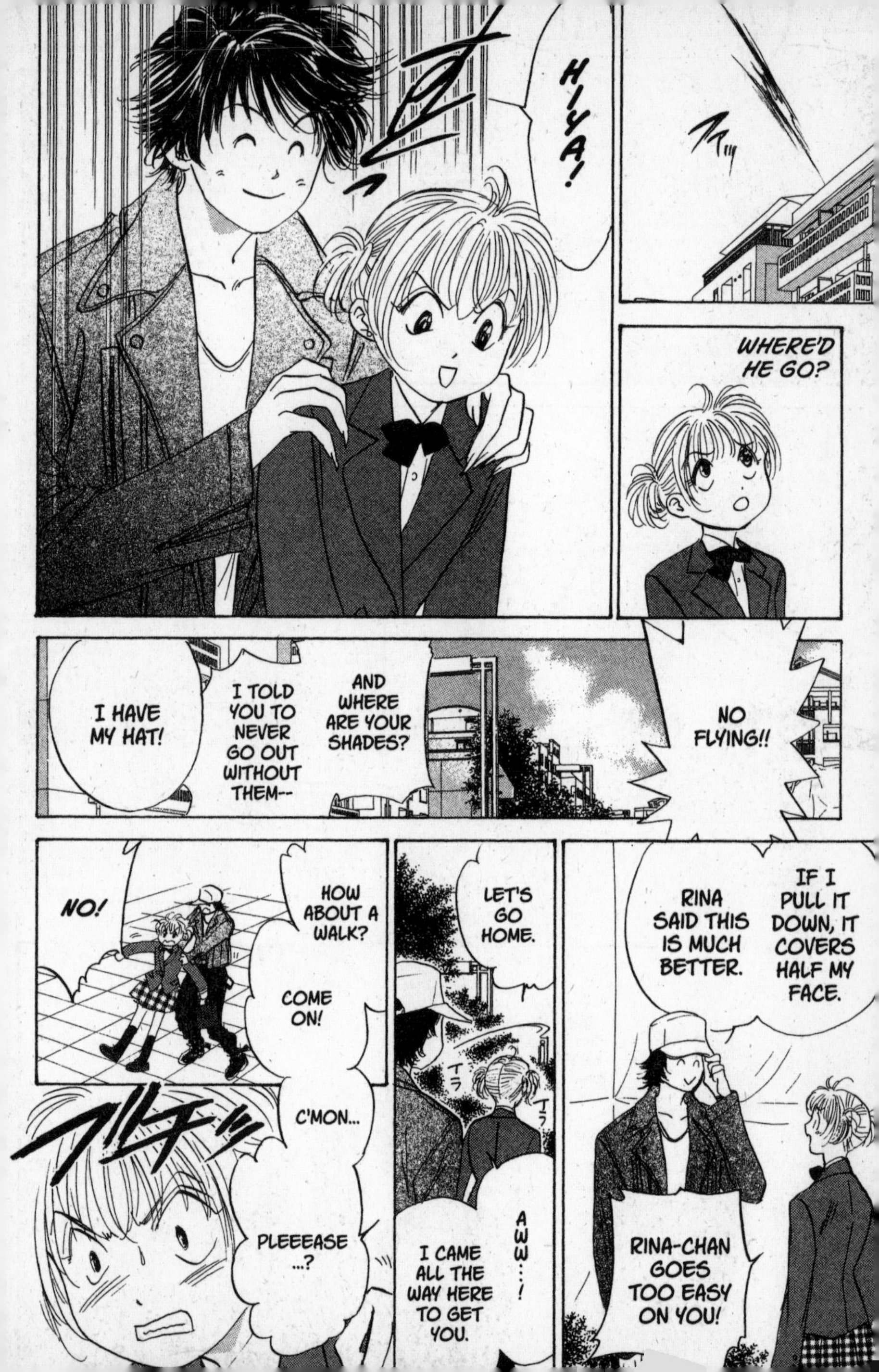
WHERE'D HE GO?
HIYA!
NO FLYING!!
AND WHERE ARE YOUR SHADES?
I TOLD YOU TO NEVER GO OUT WITHOUT THEM--
I HAVE MY HAT!
IF I PULL IT DOWN, IT COVERS HALF MY FACE.
RINA SAID THIS IS MUCH BETTER.
RINA-CHAN GOES TOO EASY ON YOU!
LET'S GO HOME.
AWW...!
I CAME ALL THE WAY HERE TO GET YOU.
HOW ABOUT A WALK?
NO!
COME ON!
C'MON...
PLEEEASE ...?

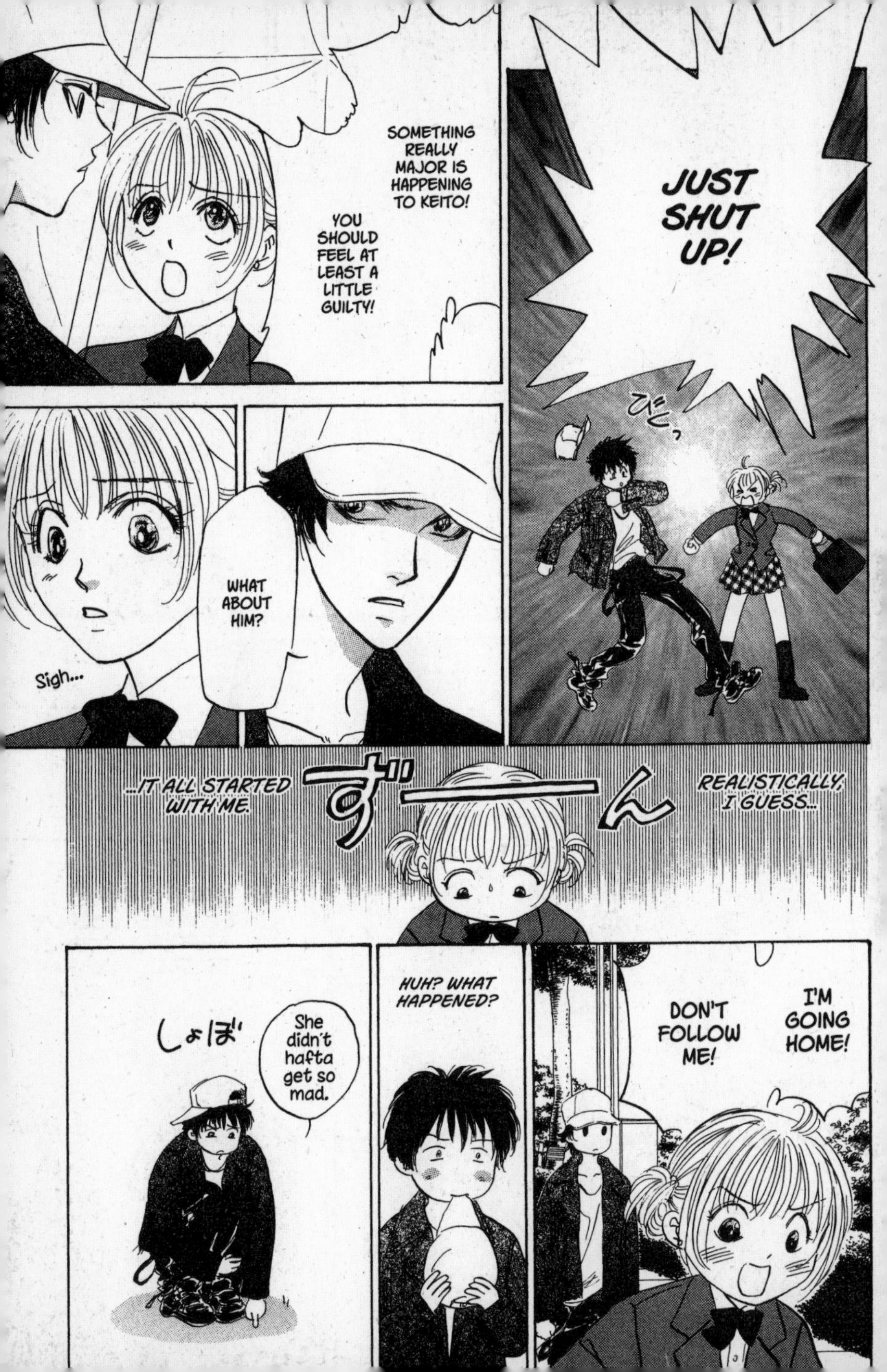
JUST SHUT UP!
ひくっ
SOMETHING REALLY MAJOR IS HAPPENING TO KEITO!
YOU SHOULD FEEL AT LEAST A LITTLE GUILTY!
WHAT ABOUT HIM?
Sigh...
REALISTICALLY, I GUESS...
ずーーん
...IT ALL STARTED WITH ME.
I'M GOING HOME!
DON'T FOLLOW ME!
HUH? WHAT HAPPENED?
She didn't hafta get so mad.
しょぼ

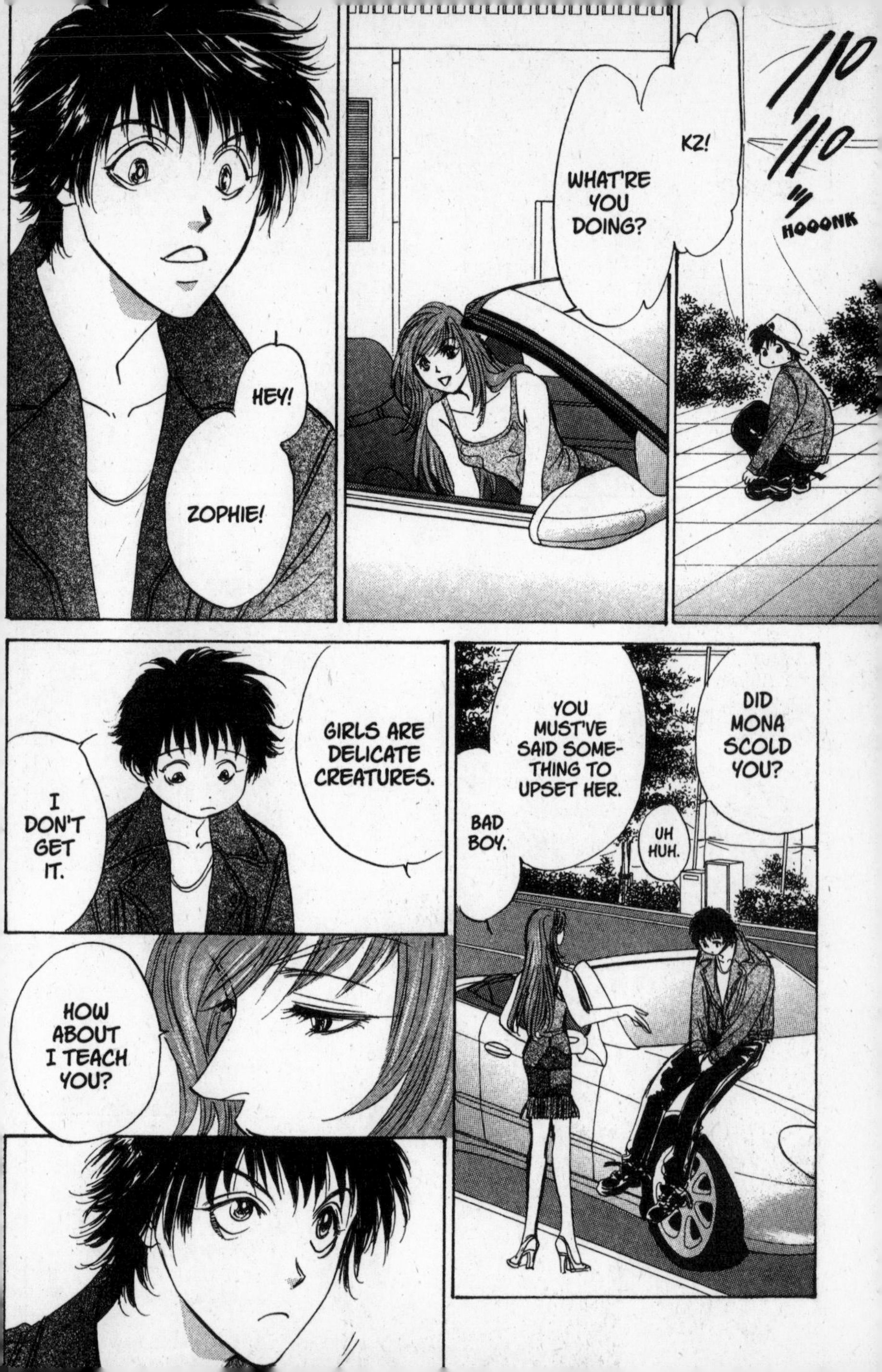
HOOONK
KZ!
WHAT'RE YOU DOING?
HEY!
ZOPHIE!
DID MONA SCOLD YOU?
UH HUH.
YOU MUST'VE SAID SOME-THING TO UPSET HER.
BAD BOY.
GIRLS ARE DELICATE CREATURES.
I DON'T GET IT.
HOW ABOUT I TEACH YOU?

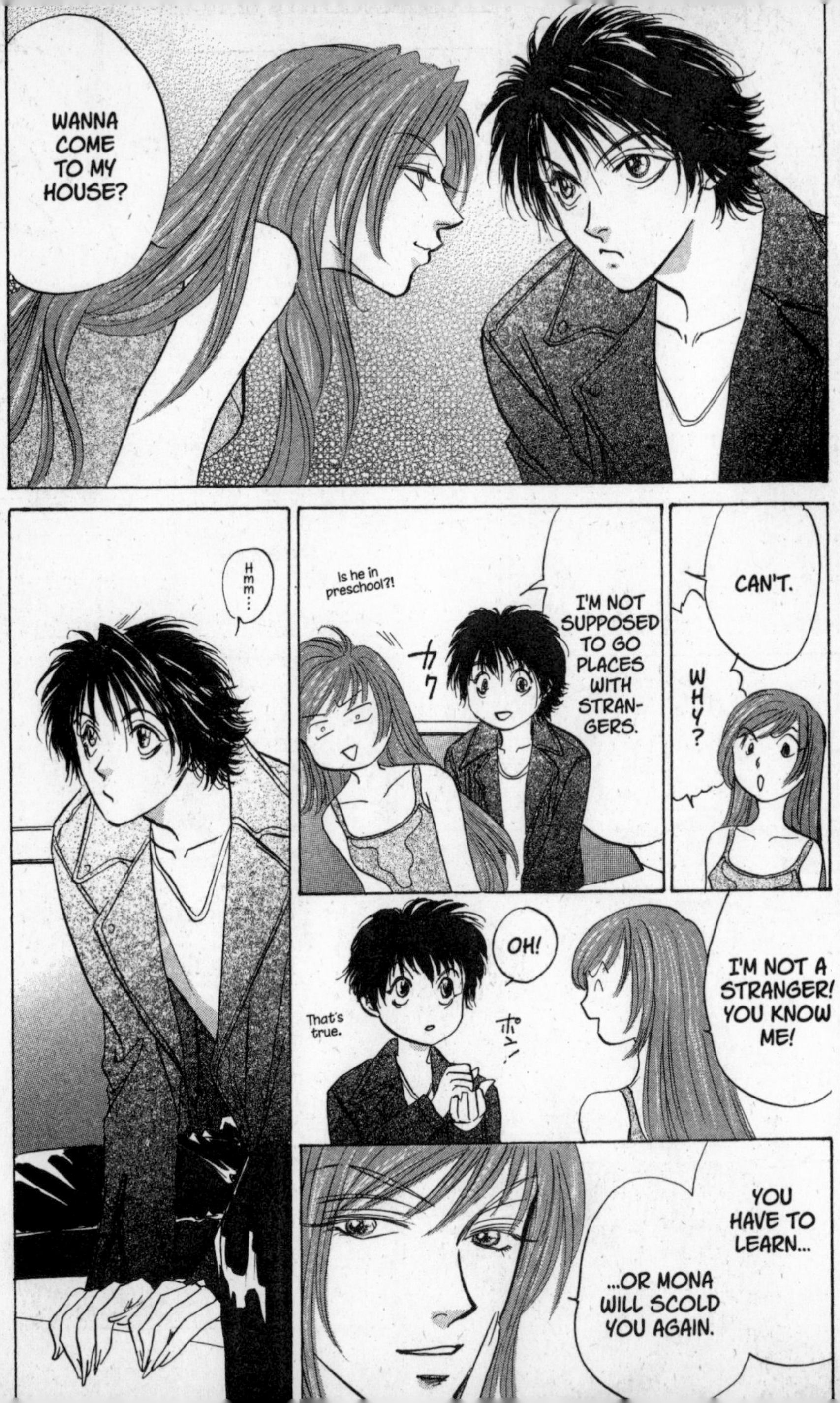
WANNA COME TO MY HOUSE?
CAN'T.
WHY?
I'M NOT SUPPOSED TO GO PLACES WITH STRANGERS.
Is he in preschool?!
カク
I'M NOT A STRANGER! YOU KNOW ME!
OH!
That's true.
YOU HAVE TO LEARN...
...OR MONA WILL SCOLD YOU AGAIN.
Hmm...

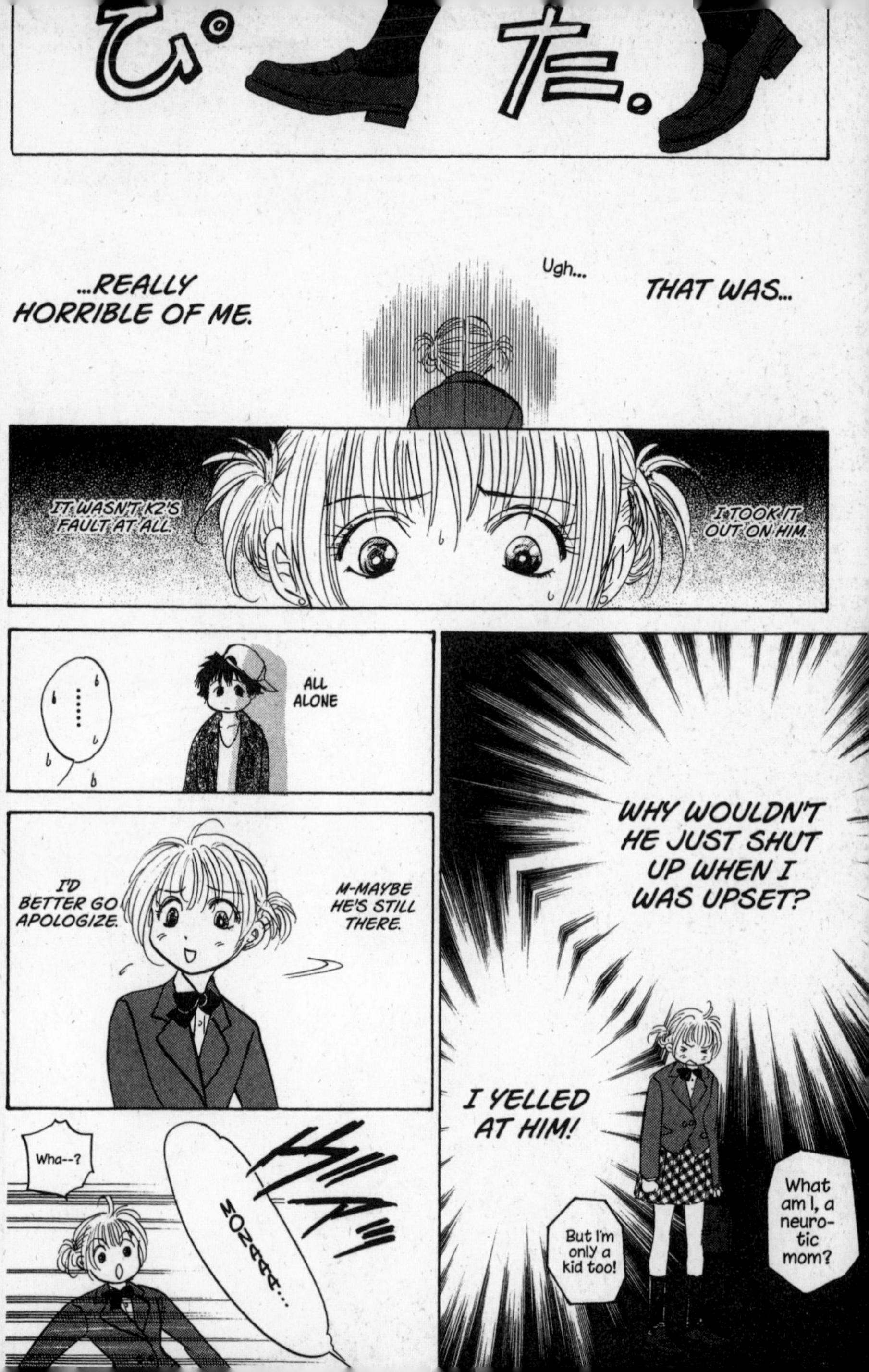
ぴた。
THAT WAS...
Ugh...
...REALLY HORRIBLE OF ME.
I TOOK IT OUT ON HIM.
IT WASN'T KZ'S FAULT AT ALL.
WHY WOULDN'T HE JUST SHUT UP WHEN I WAS UPSET?
I YELLED AT HIM!
What am I, a neurotic mom?
But I'm only a kid too!
ALL ALONE
......
M-MAYBE HE'S STILL THERE.
I'D BETTER GO APOLOGIZE.
MONAAAA...
Wha--?

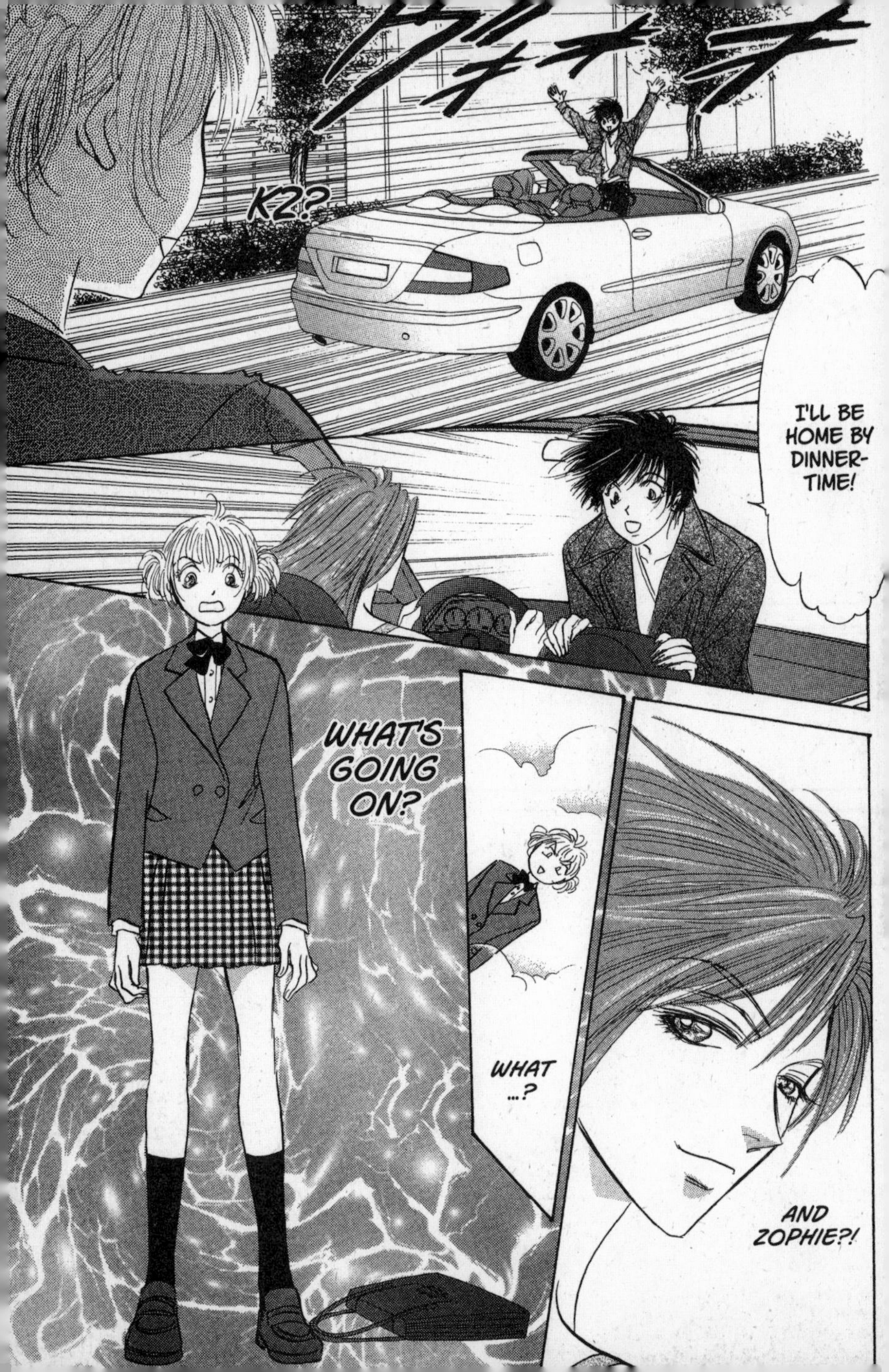
K2?
I'LL BE HOME BY DINNER-TIME!
AND ZOPHIE?!
WHAT ...?
WHAT'S GOING ON?

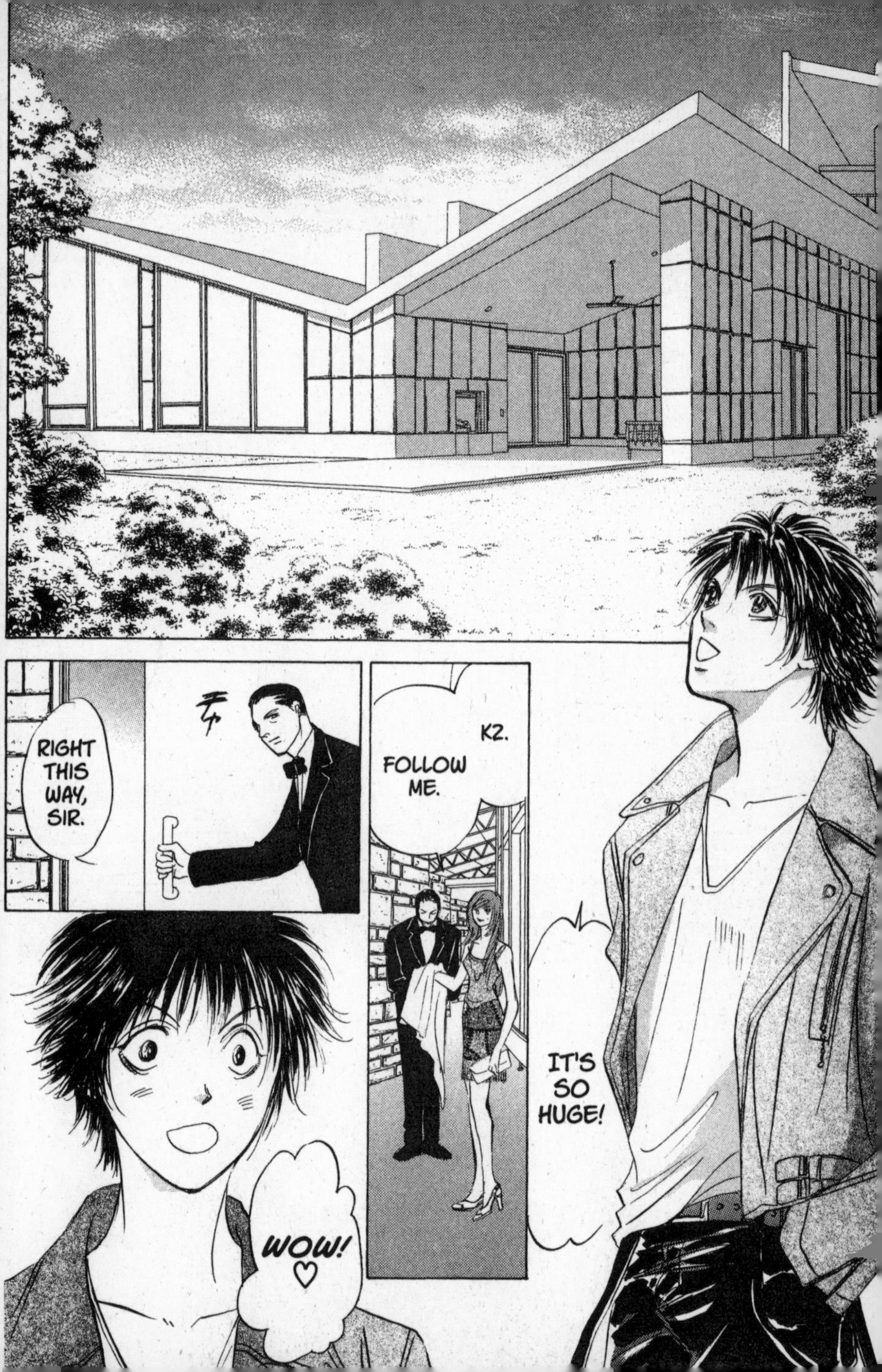
IT'S SO HUGE!
K2.
FOLLOW ME.
RIGHT THIS WAY, SIR.
WOW! ♥

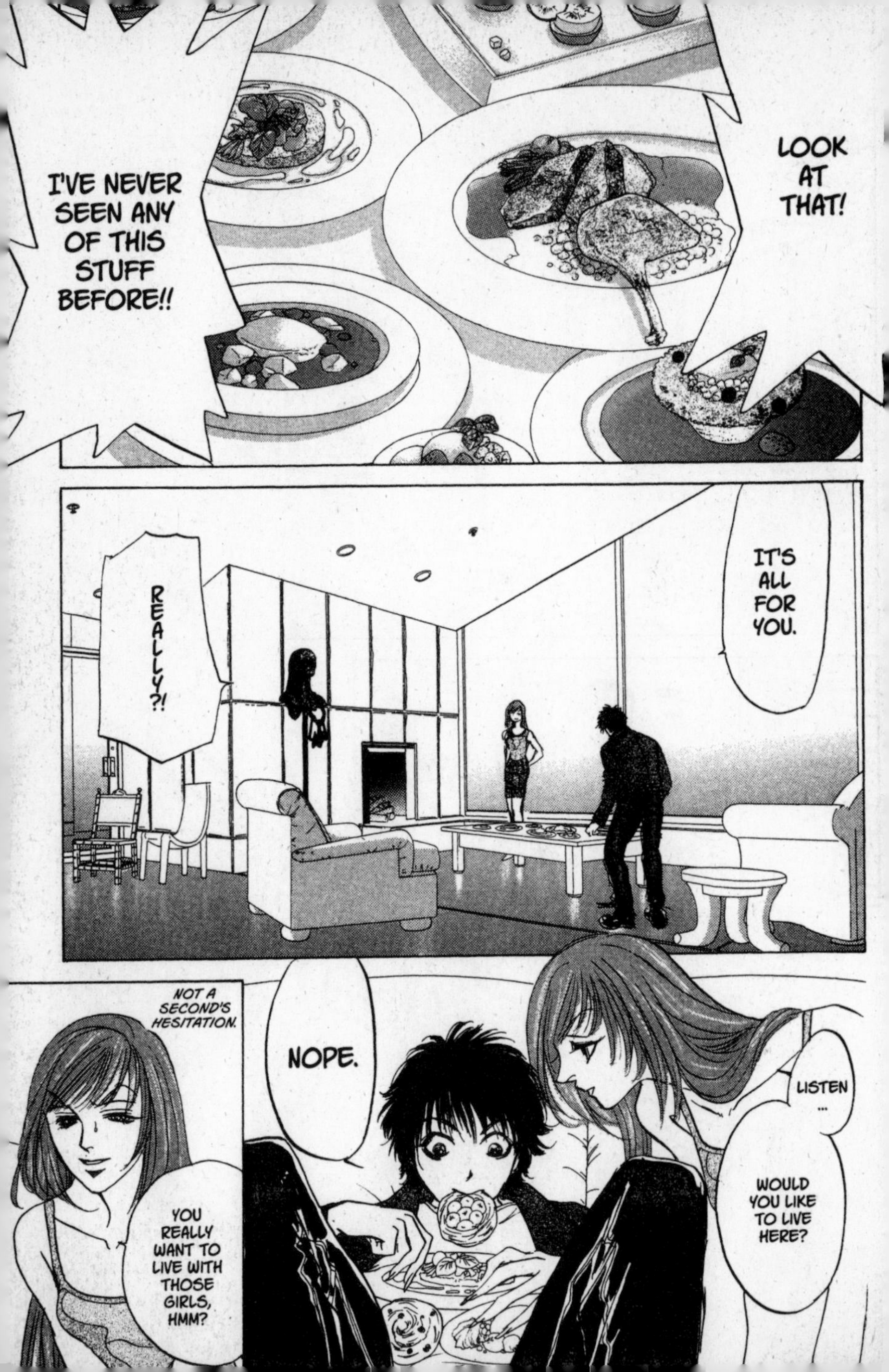
LOOK AT THAT!
I'VE NEVER SEEN ANY OF THIS STUFF BEFORE!!
IT'S ALL FOR YOU.
REALLY?!
LISTEN ...
WOULD YOU LIKE TO LIVE HERE?
NOPE.
NOT A SECOND'S HESITATION.
YOU REALLY WANT TO LIVE WITH THOSE GIRLS, HMM?

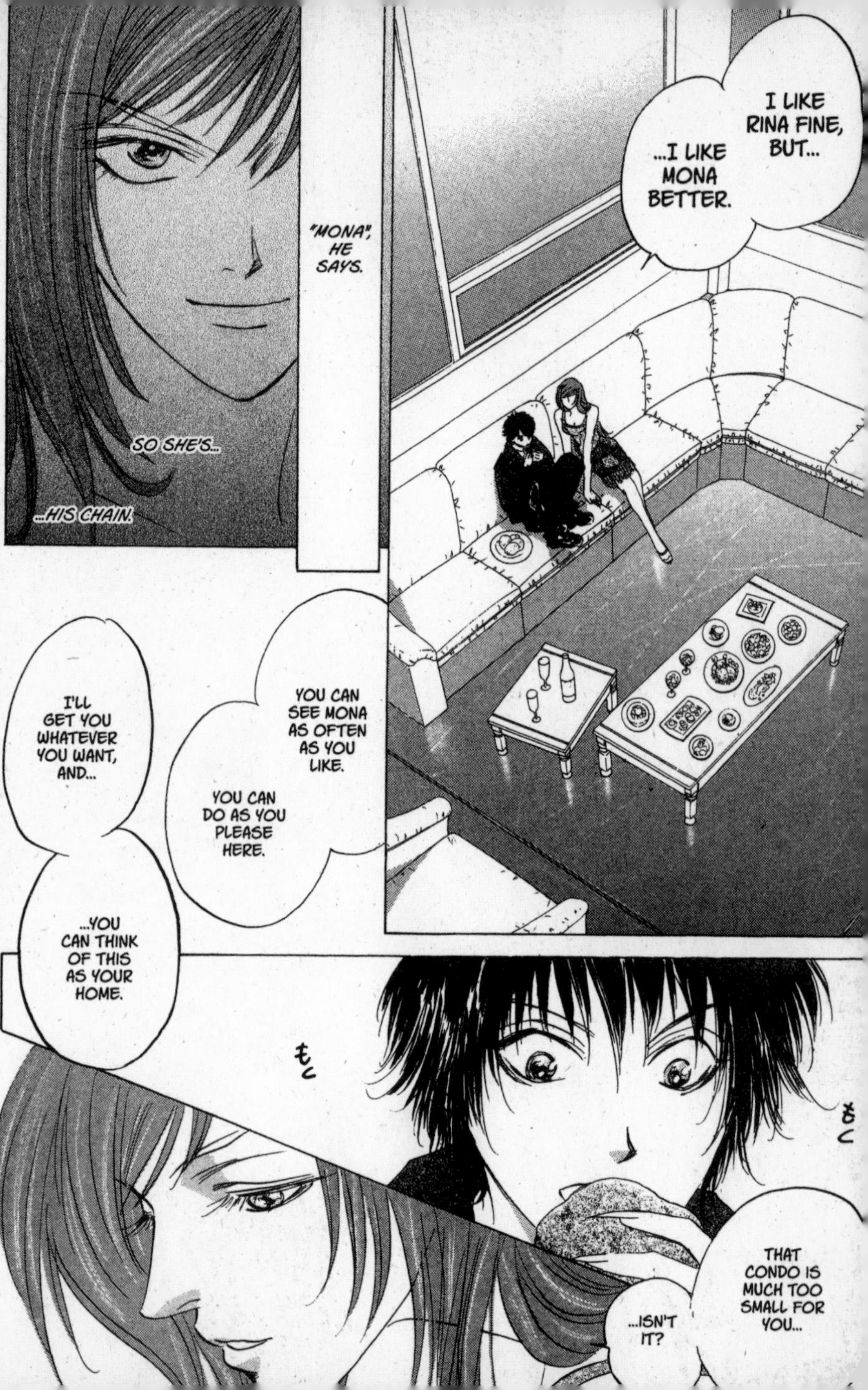
I LIKE RINA FINE, BUT...
...I LIKE MONA BETTER.
"MONA", HE SAYS.
SO SHE'S...
...HIS CHAIN.
YOU CAN SEE MONA AS OFTEN AS YOU LIKE.
YOU CAN DO AS YOU PLEASE HERE.
I'LL GET YOU WHATEVER YOU WANT, AND...
...YOU CAN THINK OF THIS AS YOUR HOME.
もぐ
もぐ
THAT CONDO IS MUCH TOO SMALL FOR YOU...
...ISN'T IT?

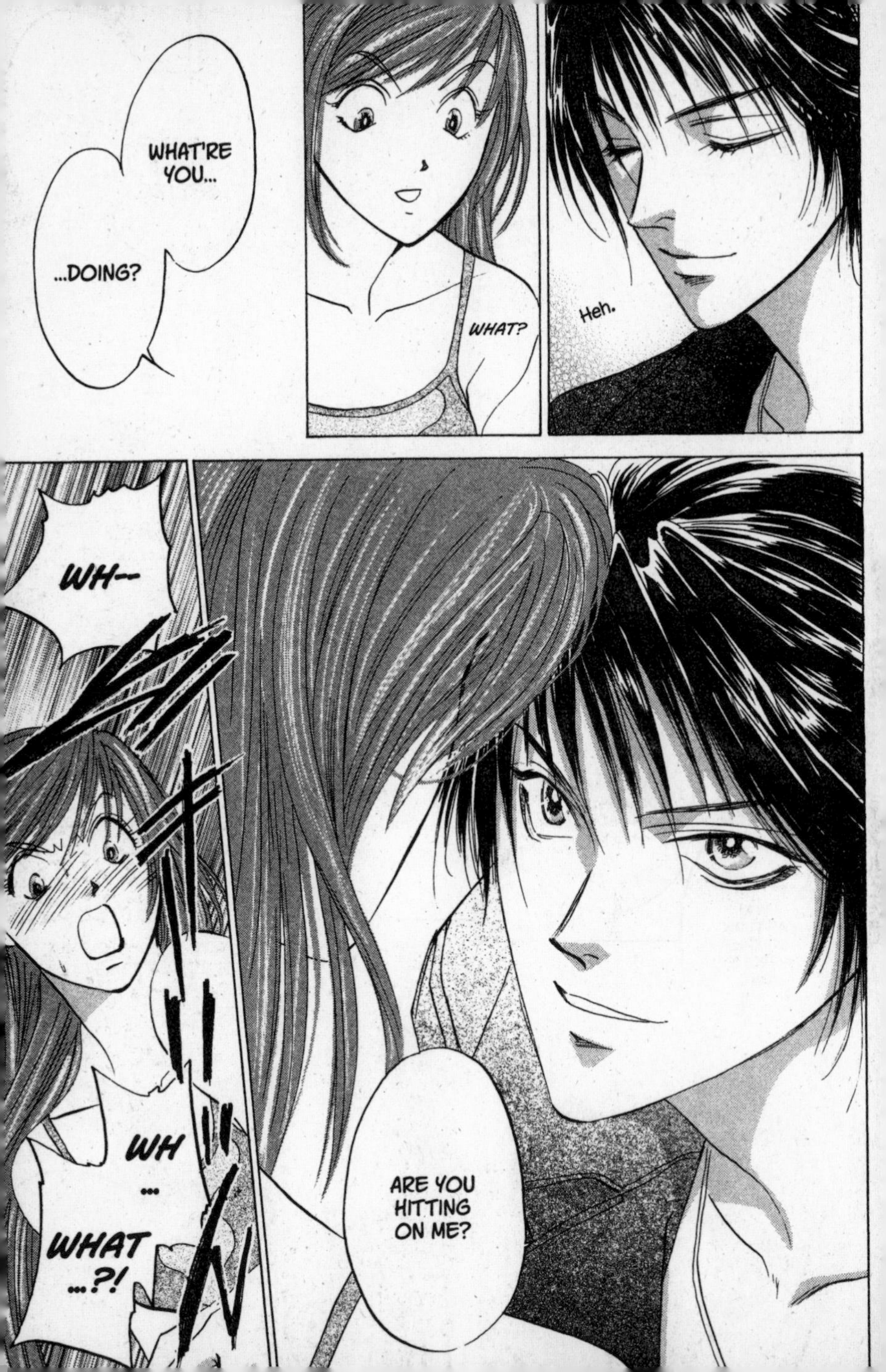
Heh.
WHAT?
WHAT'RE YOU...
...DOING?
ARE YOU HITTING ON ME?
WH--
WH ... WHAT ...?!

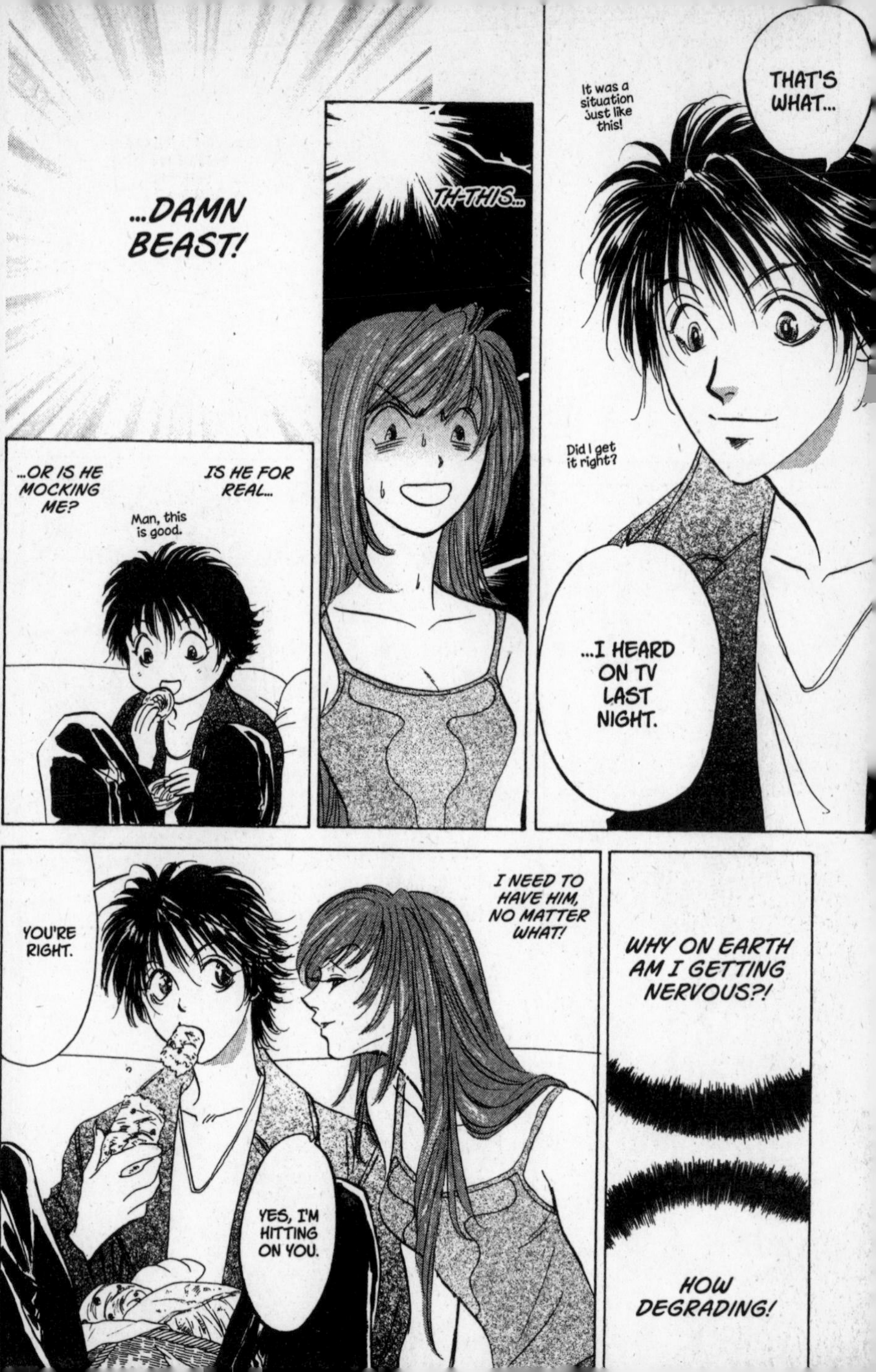
THAT'S WHAT...
It was a situation just like this!
Did I get it right?
...I HEARD ON TV LAST NIGHT.
TH-THIS...
...DAMN BEAST!
IS HE FOR REAL...
...OR IS HE MOCKING ME?
Man, this is good.
WHY ON EARTH AM I GETTING NERVOUS?!
HOW DEGRADING!
I NEED TO HAVE HIM, NO MATTER WHAT!
YOU'RE RIGHT.
YES, I'M HITTING ON YOU.

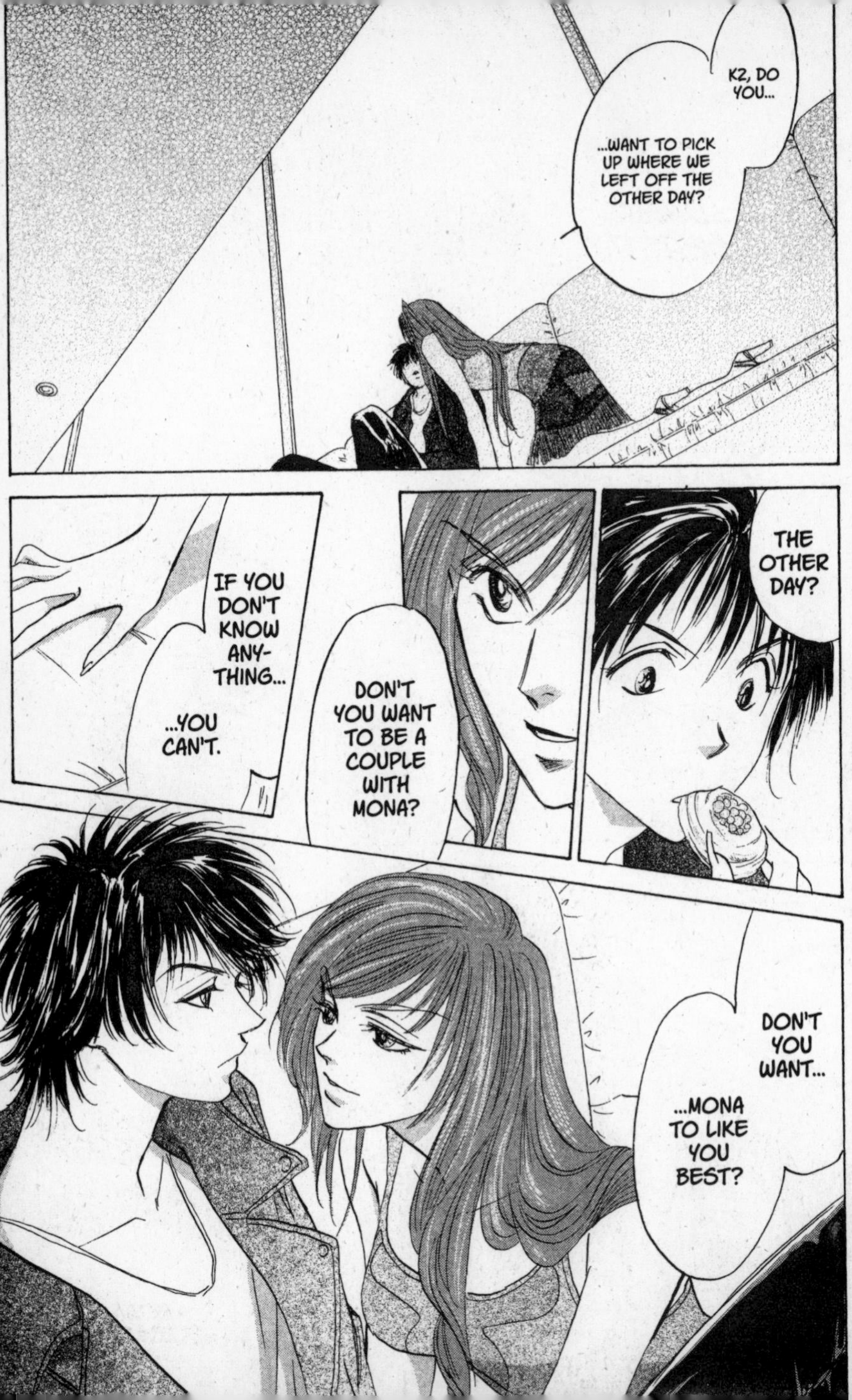
K2, DO YOU...
...WANT TO PICK UP WHERE WE LEFT OFF THE OTHER DAY?
THE OTHER DAY?
DON'T YOU WANT TO BE A COUPLE WITH MONA?
IF YOU DON'T KNOW ANY-THING...
...YOU CAN'T.
DON'T YOU WANT...
...MONA TO LIKE YOU BEST?

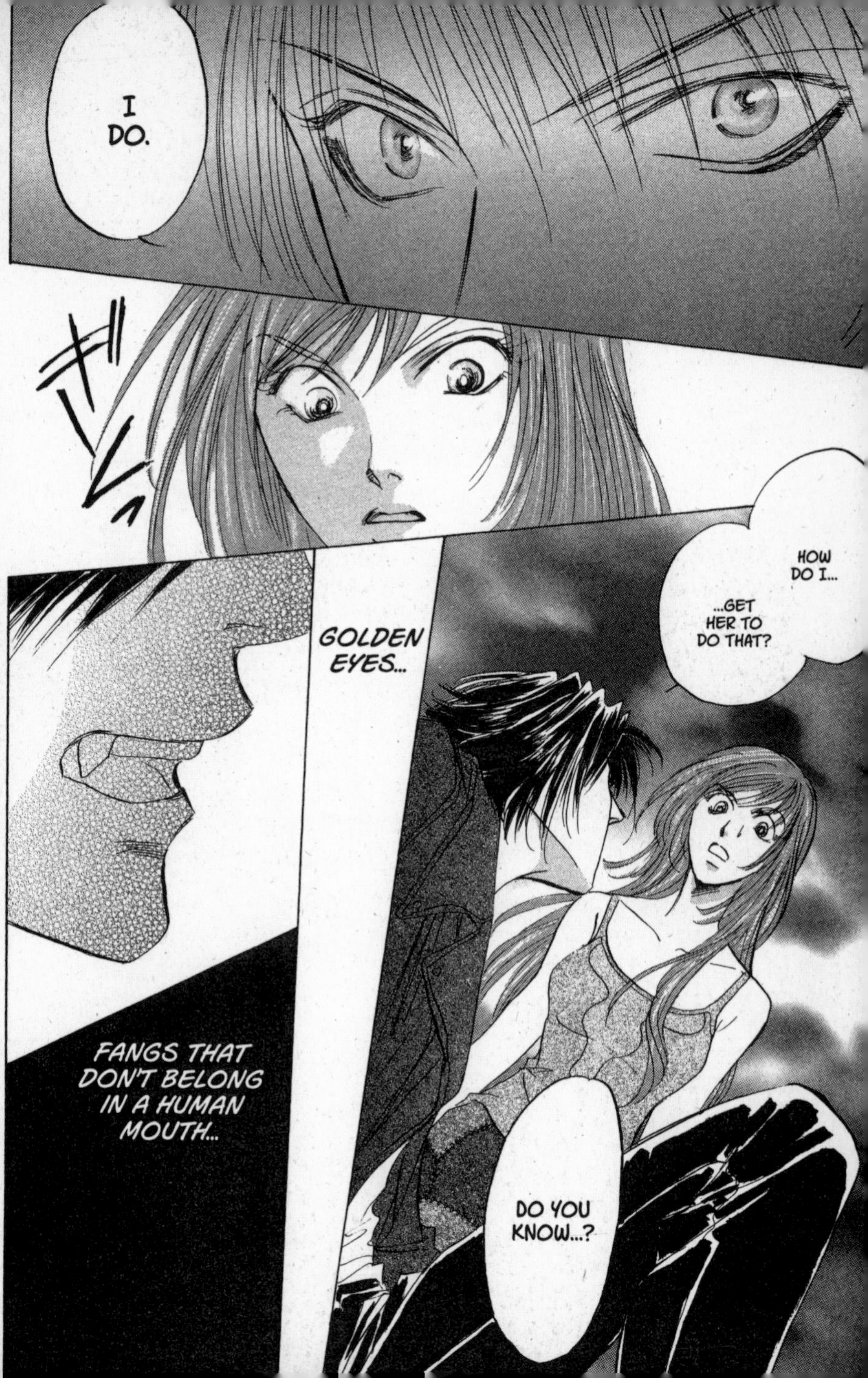
I DO.
HOW DO I...
...GET HER TO DO THAT?
DO YOU KNOW...?
GOLDEN EYES...
FANGS THAT DON'T BELONG IN A HUMAN MOUTH...

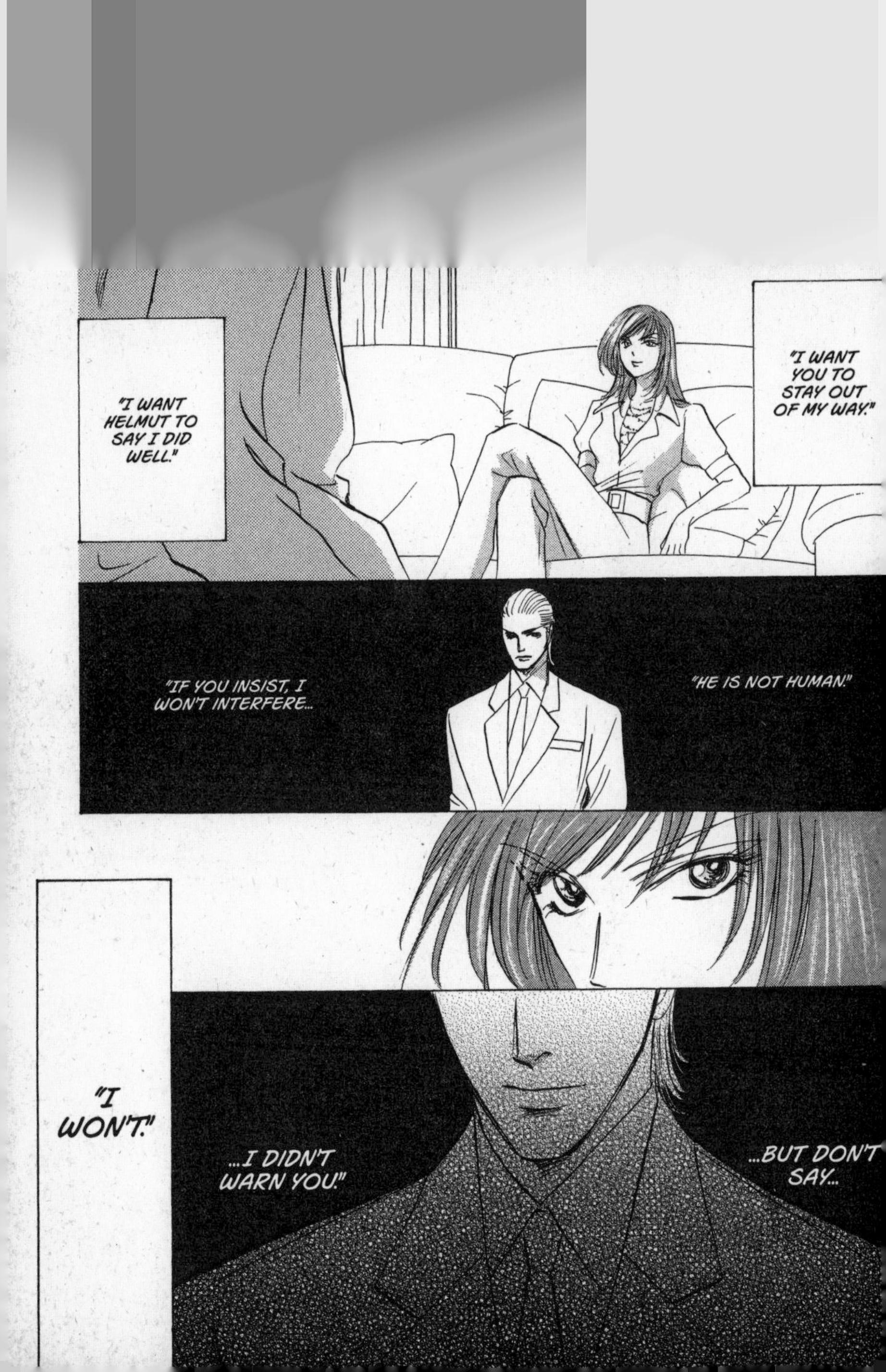
"I WANT YOU TO STAY OUT OF MY WAY."
"I WANT HELMUT TO SAY I DID WELL."
"HE IS NOT HUMAN."
"IF YOU INSIST, I WON'T INTERFERE...
...BUT DON'T SAY...
...I DIDN'T WARN YOU."
"I WON'T."

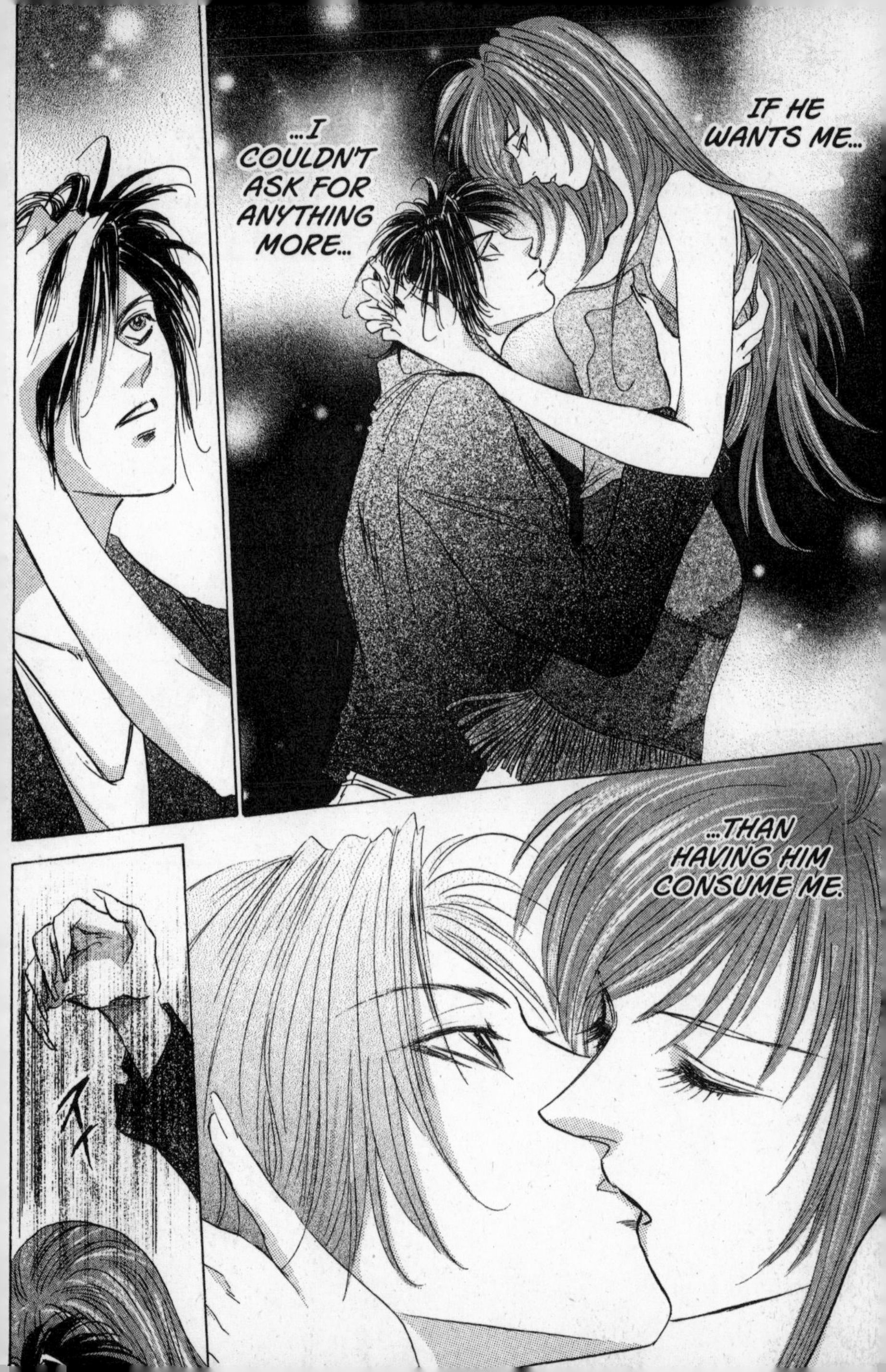
IF HE WANTS ME...
...I COULDN'T ASK FOR ANYTHING MORE...
...THAN HAVING HIM CONSUME ME.

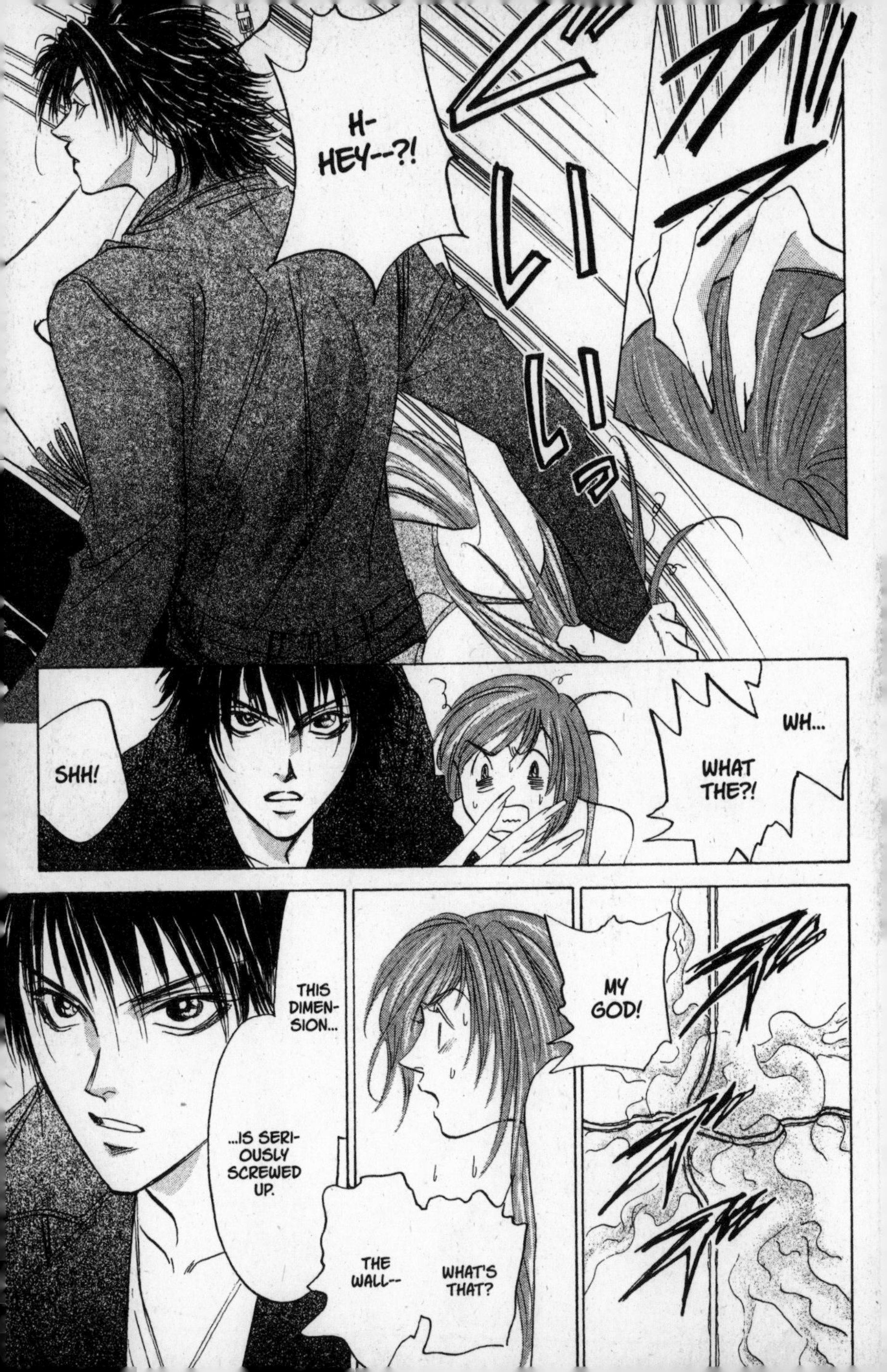
H- HEY--?!
WH... WHAT THE?!
SHH!
MY GOD!
WHAT'S THAT?
THE WALL--
THIS DIMENSION...
...IS SERIOUSLY SCREWED UP.

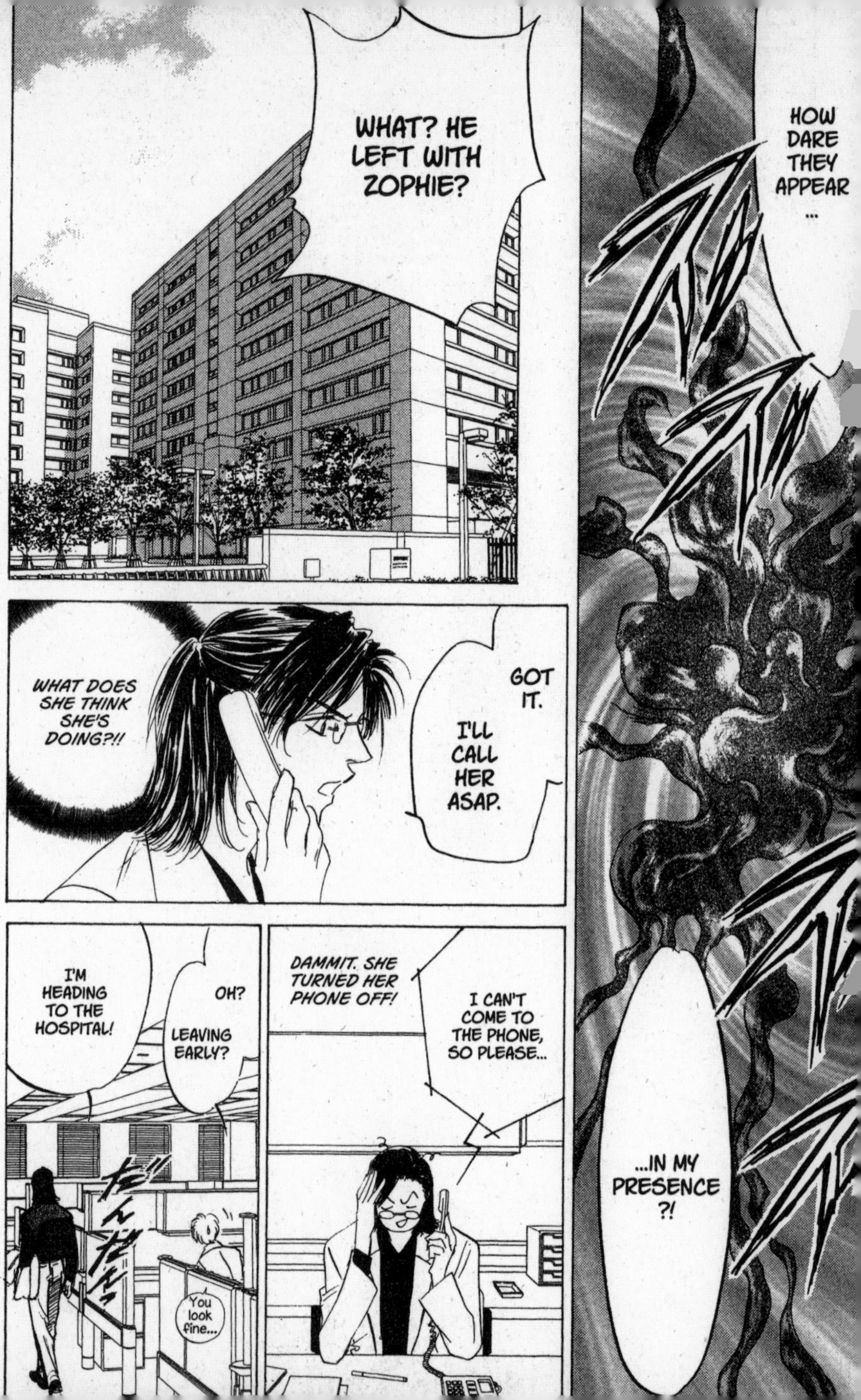
HOW DARE THEY APPEAR ...
...IN MY PRESENCE ?!
WHAT? HE LEFT WITH ZOPHIE?
GOT IT.
I'LL CALL HER ASAP.
WHAT DOES SHE THINK SHE'S DOING?!!
I CAN'T COME TO THE PHONE, SO PLEASE...
DAMMIT. SHE TURNED HER PHONE OFF!
I'M HEADING TO THE HOSPITAL!
OH?
LEAVING EARLY?
You look fine...

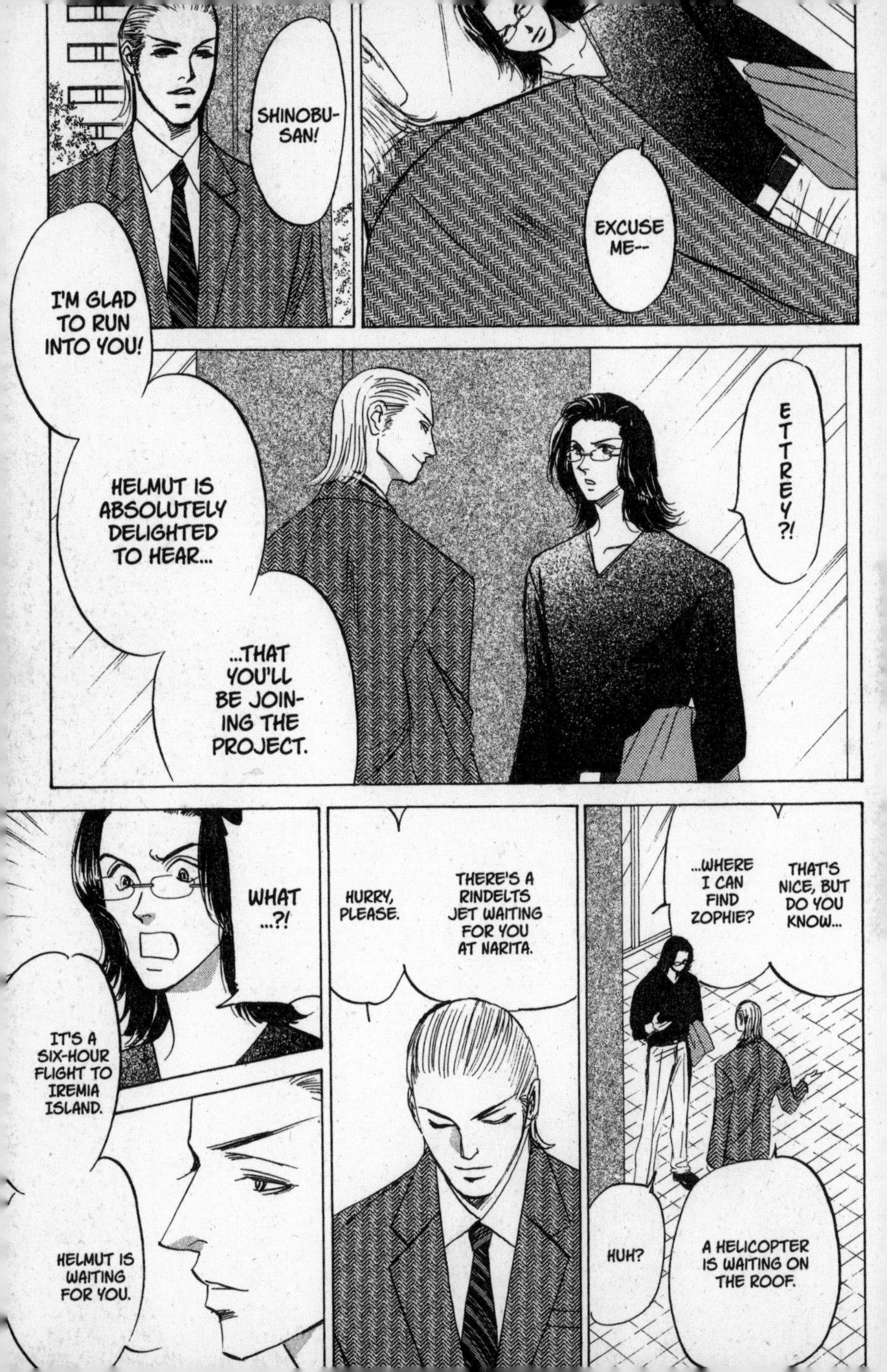
EXCUSE ME--
SHINOBU-SAN!
I'M GLAD TO RUN INTO YOU!
ETTREY?!
HELMUT IS ABSOLUTELY DELIGHTED TO HEAR...
...THAT YOU'LL BE JOINING THE PROJECT.
THAT'S NICE, BUT DO YOU KNOW...
...WHERE I CAN FIND ZOPHIE?
HUH?
A HELICOPTER IS WAITING ON THE ROOF.
THERE'S A RINDELTS JET WAITING FOR YOU AT NARITA.
HURRY, PLEASE.
WHAT ...?!
IT'S A SIX-HOUR FLIGHT TO IREMIA ISLAND.
HELMUT IS WAITING FOR YOU.

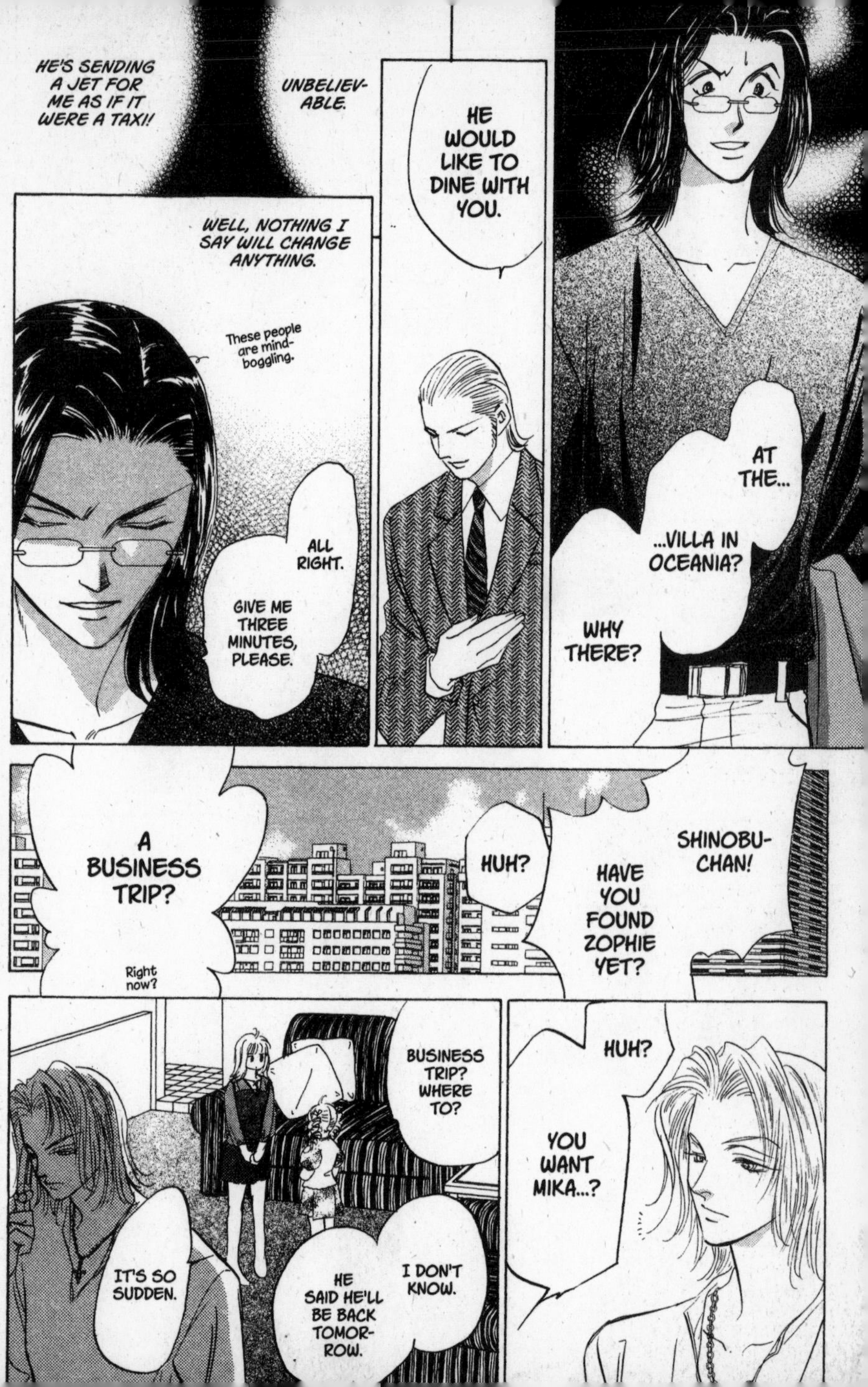
AT THE...
...VILLA IN OCEANIA?
WHY THERE?
HE WOULD LIKE TO DINE WITH YOU.
UNBELIEVABLE.
HE'S SENDING A JET FOR ME AS IF IT WERE A TAXI!
WELL, NOTHING I SAY WILL CHANGE ANYTHING.
These people are mind-boggling.
ALL RIGHT.
GIVE ME THREE MINUTES, PLEASE.
SHINOBU-CHAN!
HAVE YOU FOUND ZOPHIE YET?
HUH?
A BUSINESS TRIP?
Right now?
HUH?
YOU WANT MIKA...?
BUSINESS TRIP? WHERE TO?
I DON'T KNOW.
HE SAID HE'LL BE BACK TOMORROW.
IT'S SO SUDDEN.

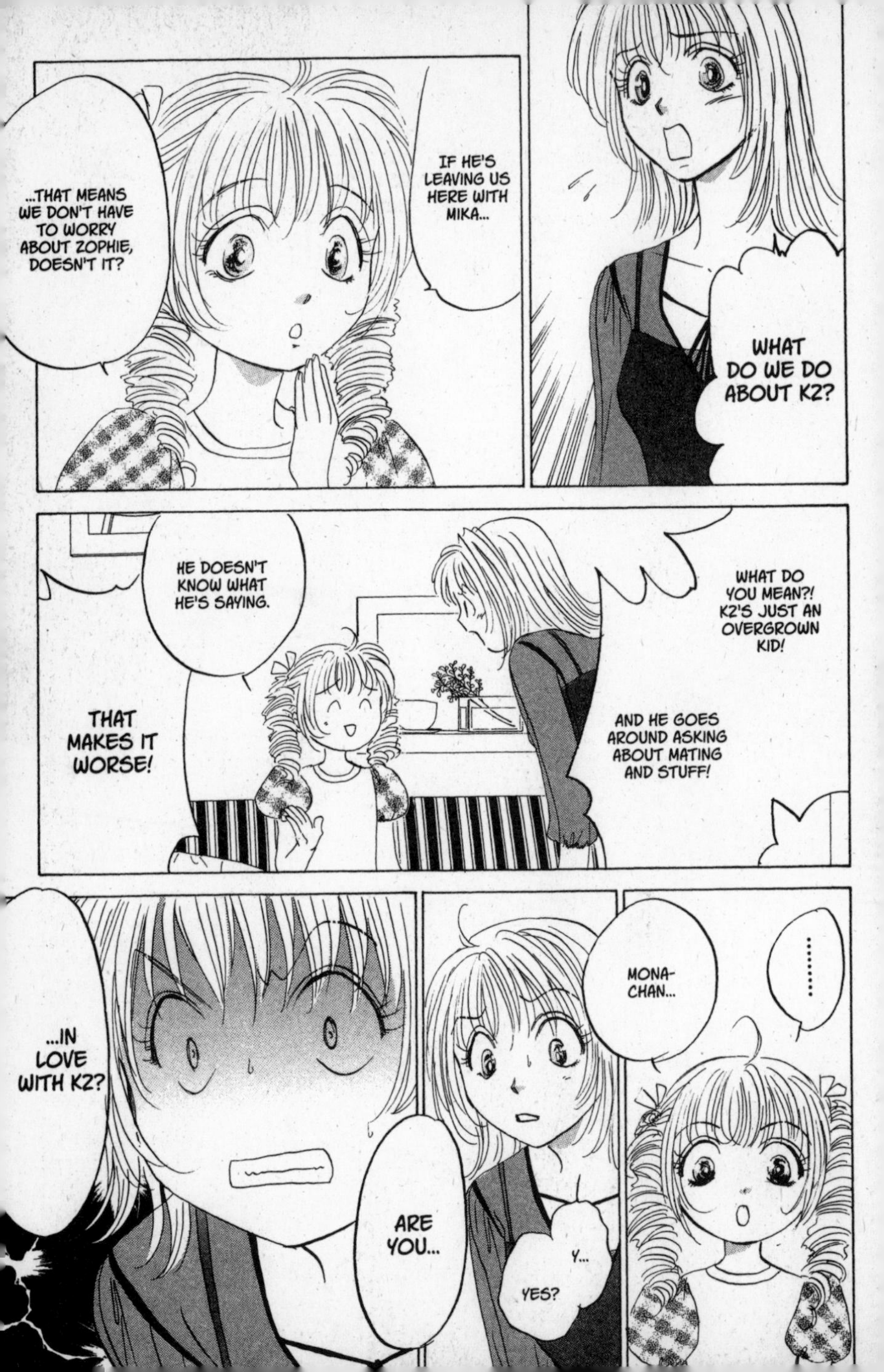
WHAT DO WE DO ABOUT K2?
IF HE'S LEAVING US HERE WITH MIKA...
...THAT MEANS WE DON'T HAVE TO WORRY ABOUT ZOPHIE, DOESN'T IT?
WHAT DO YOU MEAN?! K2'S JUST AN OVERGROWN KID!
AND HE GOES AROUND ASKING ABOUT MATING AND STUFF!
HE DOESN'T KNOW WHAT HE'S SAYING.
THAT MAKES IT WORSE!
....
MONA-CHAN...
ARE YOU...
...IN LOVE WITH K2?
Y...
YES?

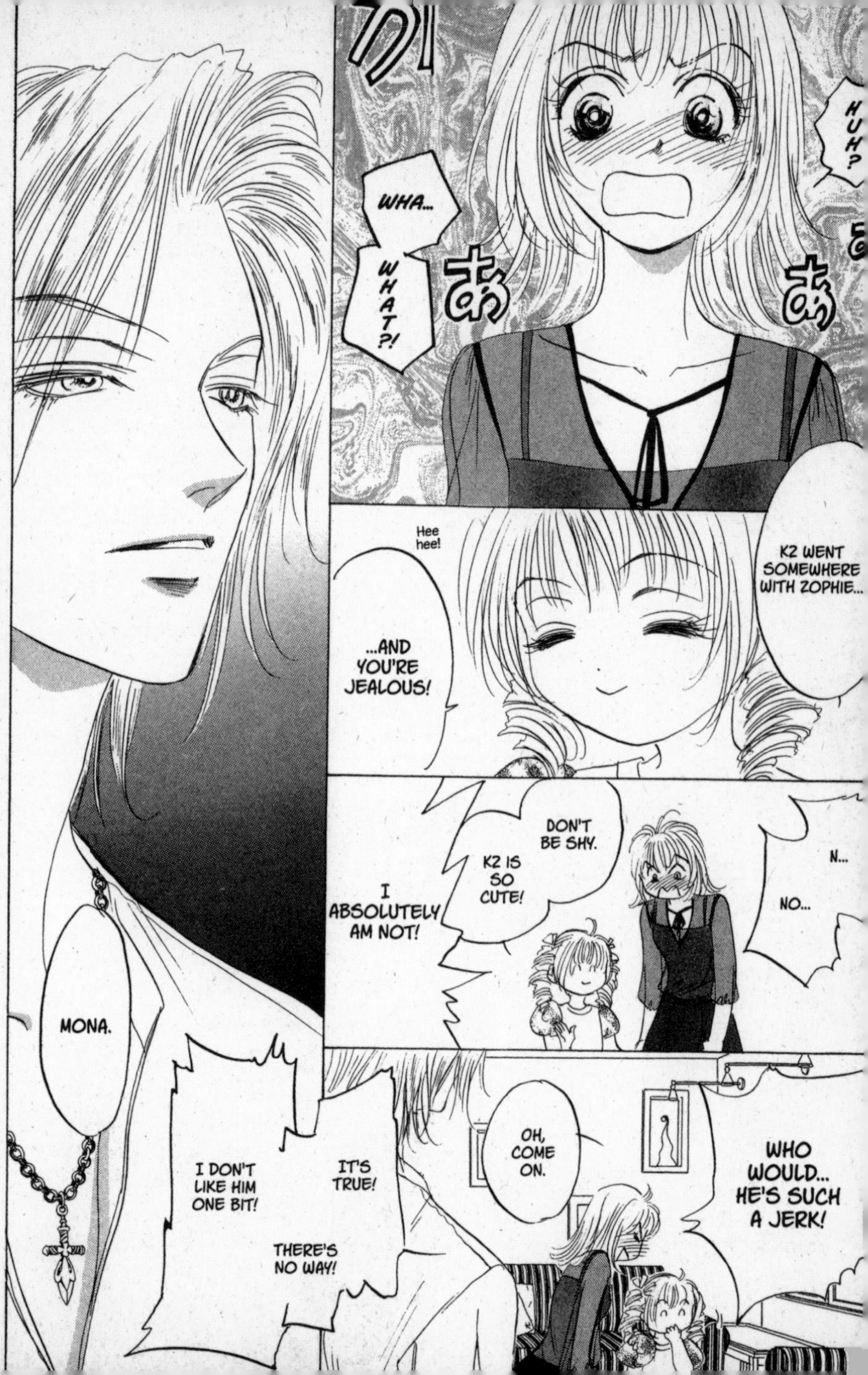
HUH?
WHA...
WHAT?!
K2 WENT SOMEWHERE WITH ZOPHIE...
Hee hee!
...AND YOU'RE JEALOUS!
N...
NO...
DON'T BE SHY.
K2 IS SO CUTE!
I ABSOLUTELY AM NOT!
WHO WOULD... HE'S SUCH A JERK!
OH, COME ON.
IT'S TRUE!
I DON'T LIKE HIM ONE BIT!
THERE'S NO WAY!
MONA.

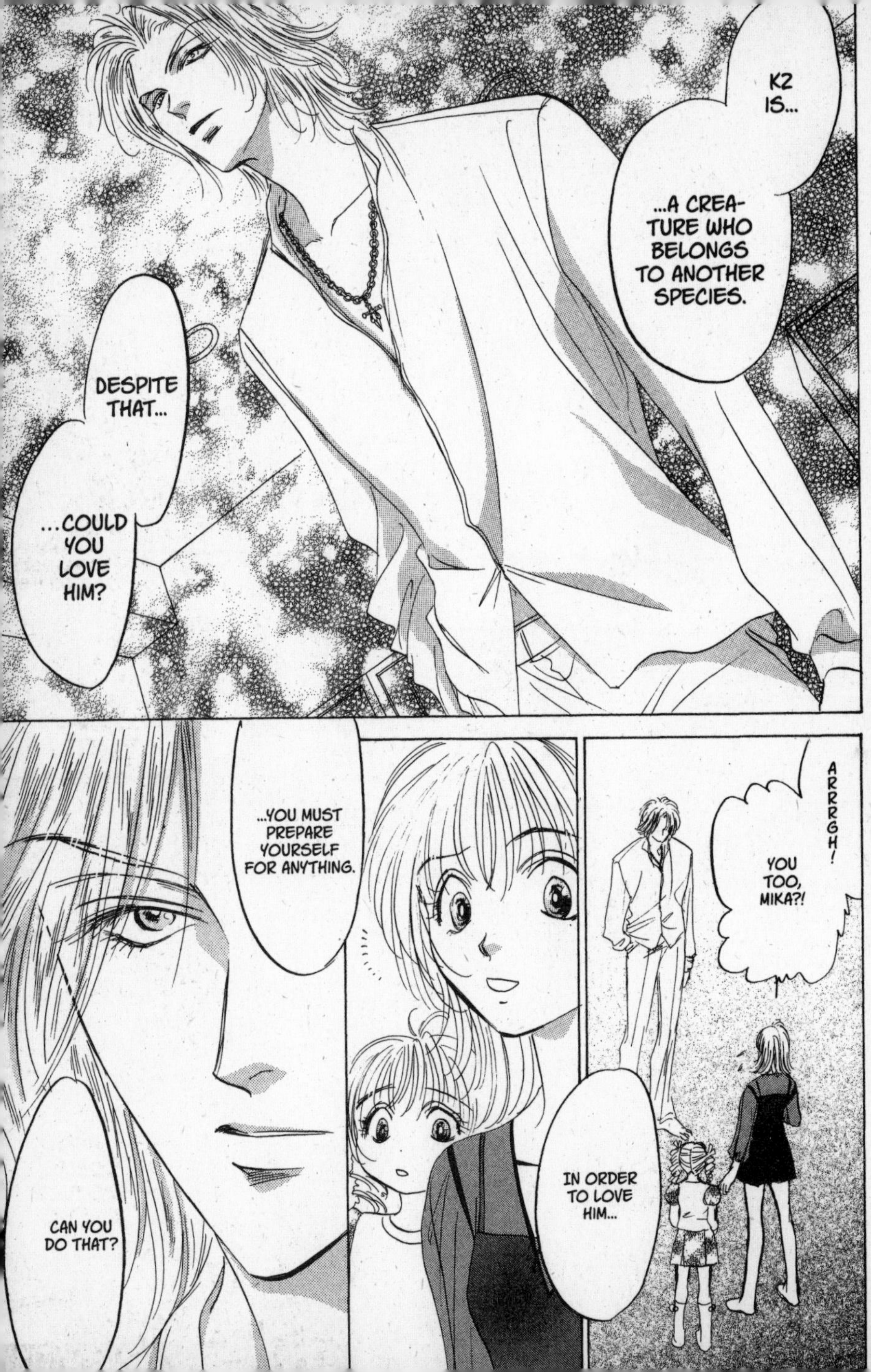
K2 IS...
...A CREATURE WHO BELONGS TO ANOTHER SPECIES.
DESPITE THAT...
...COULD YOU LOVE HIM?
ARRRGH!
YOU TOO, MIKA?!
IN ORDER TO LOVE HIM...
...YOU MUST PREPARE YOURSELF FOR ANYTHING.
CAN YOU DO THAT?

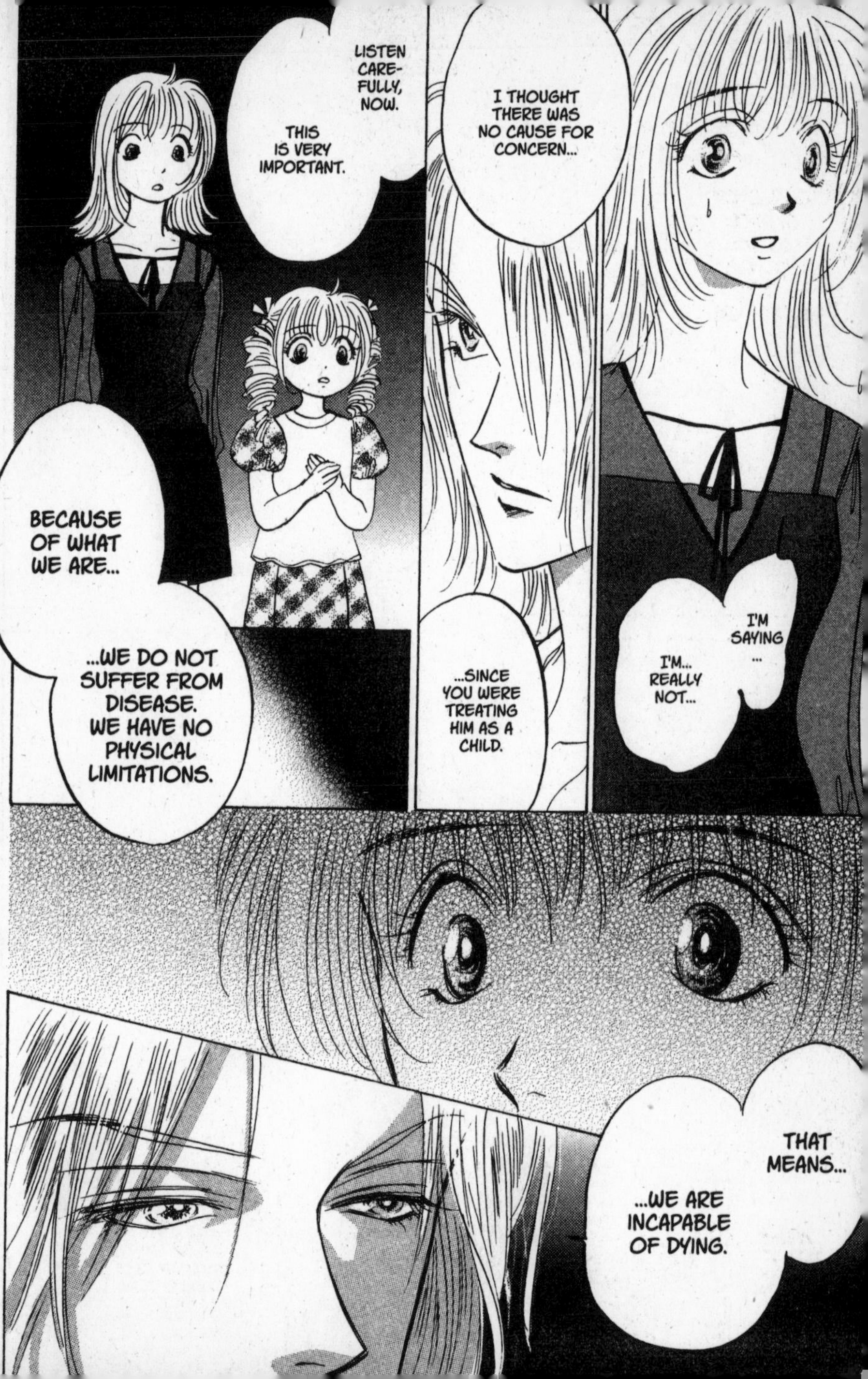
I'M SAYING...
I'M... REALLY NOT...
I THOUGHT THERE WAS NO CAUSE FOR CONCERN...
...SINCE YOU WERE TREATING HIM AS A CHILD.
LISTEN CARE-FULLY, NOW.
THIS IS VERY IMPORTANT.
BECAUSE OF WHAT WE ARE...
...WE DO NOT SUFFER FROM DISEASE. WE HAVE NO PHYSICAL LIMITATIONS.
THAT MEANS...
...WE ARE INCAPABLE OF DYING.

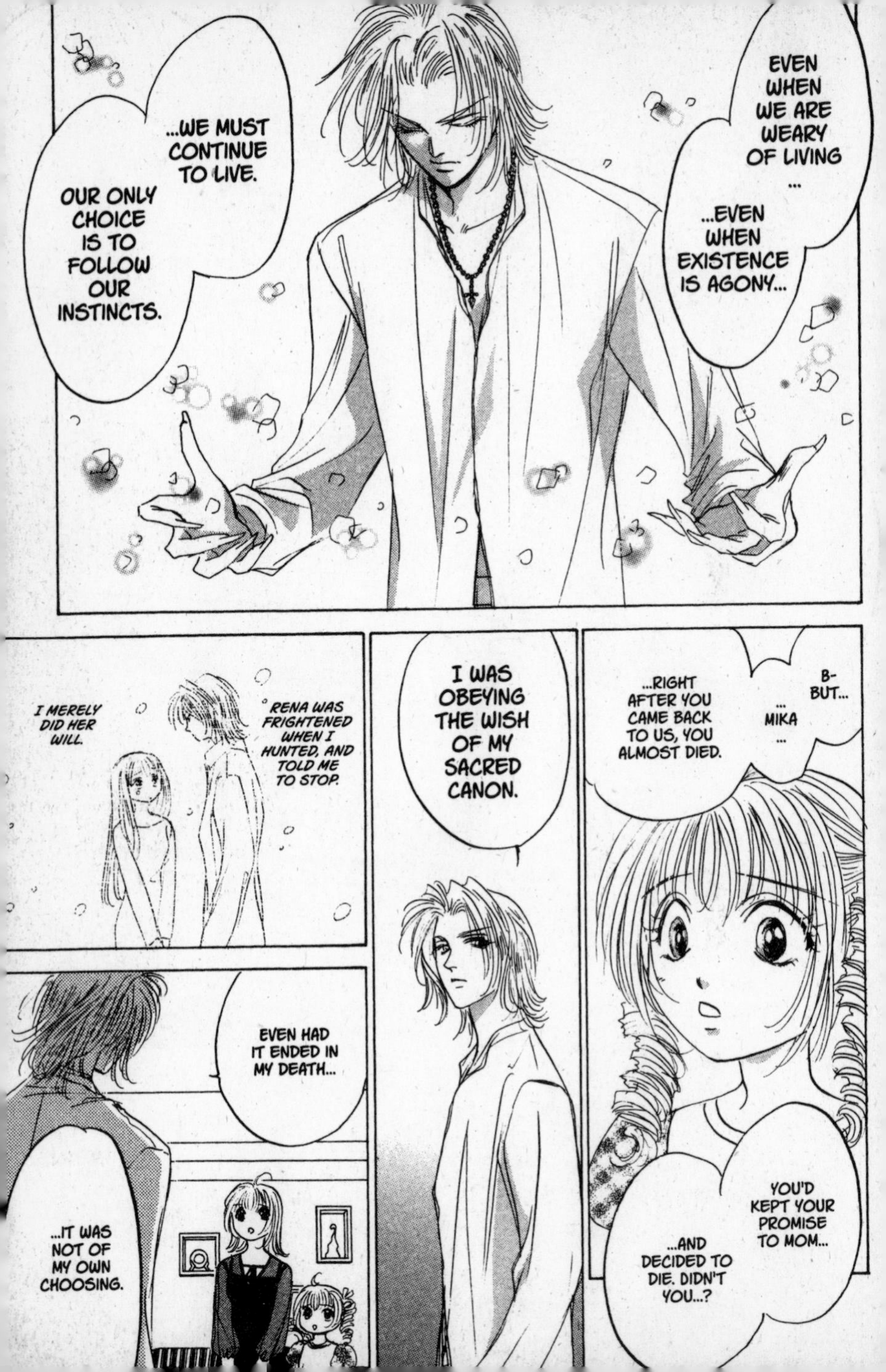
EVEN WHEN WE ARE WEARY OF LIVING ...
...EVEN WHEN EXISTENCE IS AGONY...
...WE MUST CONTINUE TO LIVE.
OUR ONLY CHOICE IS TO FOLLOW OUR INSTINCTS.
B-BUT...
... MIKA ...
...RIGHT AFTER YOU CAME BACK TO US, YOU ALMOST DIED.
YOU'D KEPT YOUR PROMISE TO MOM...
...AND DECIDED TO DIE. DIDN'T YOU...?
I WAS OBEYING THE WISH OF MY SACRED CANON.
RENA WAS FRIGHTENED WHEN I HUNTED, AND TOLD ME TO STOP.
I MERELY DID HER WILL.
EVEN HAD IT ENDED IN MY DEATH...
...IT WAS NOT OF MY OWN CHOOSING.

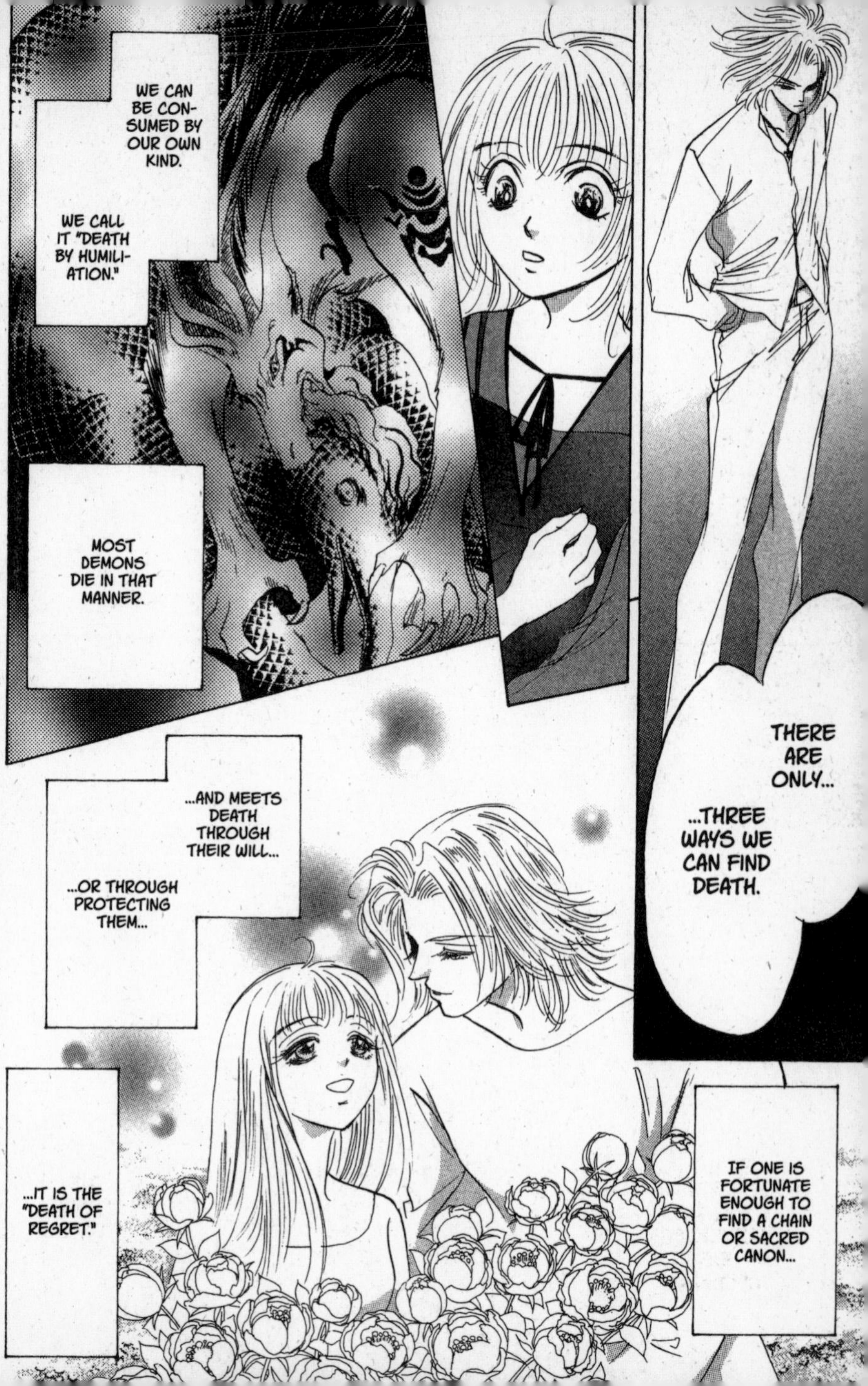
THERE ARE ONLY...
...THREE WAYS WE CAN FIND DEATH.
WE CAN BE CON-SUMED BY OUR OWN KIND.
WE CALL IT "DEATH BY HUMILI-ATION."
MOST DEMONS DIE IN THAT MANNER.
IF ONE IS FORTUNATE ENOUGH TO FIND A CHAIN OR SACRED CANON...
...AND MEETS DEATH THROUGH THEIR WILL...
...OR THROUGH PROTECTING THEM...
...IT IS THE "DEATH OF REGRET."

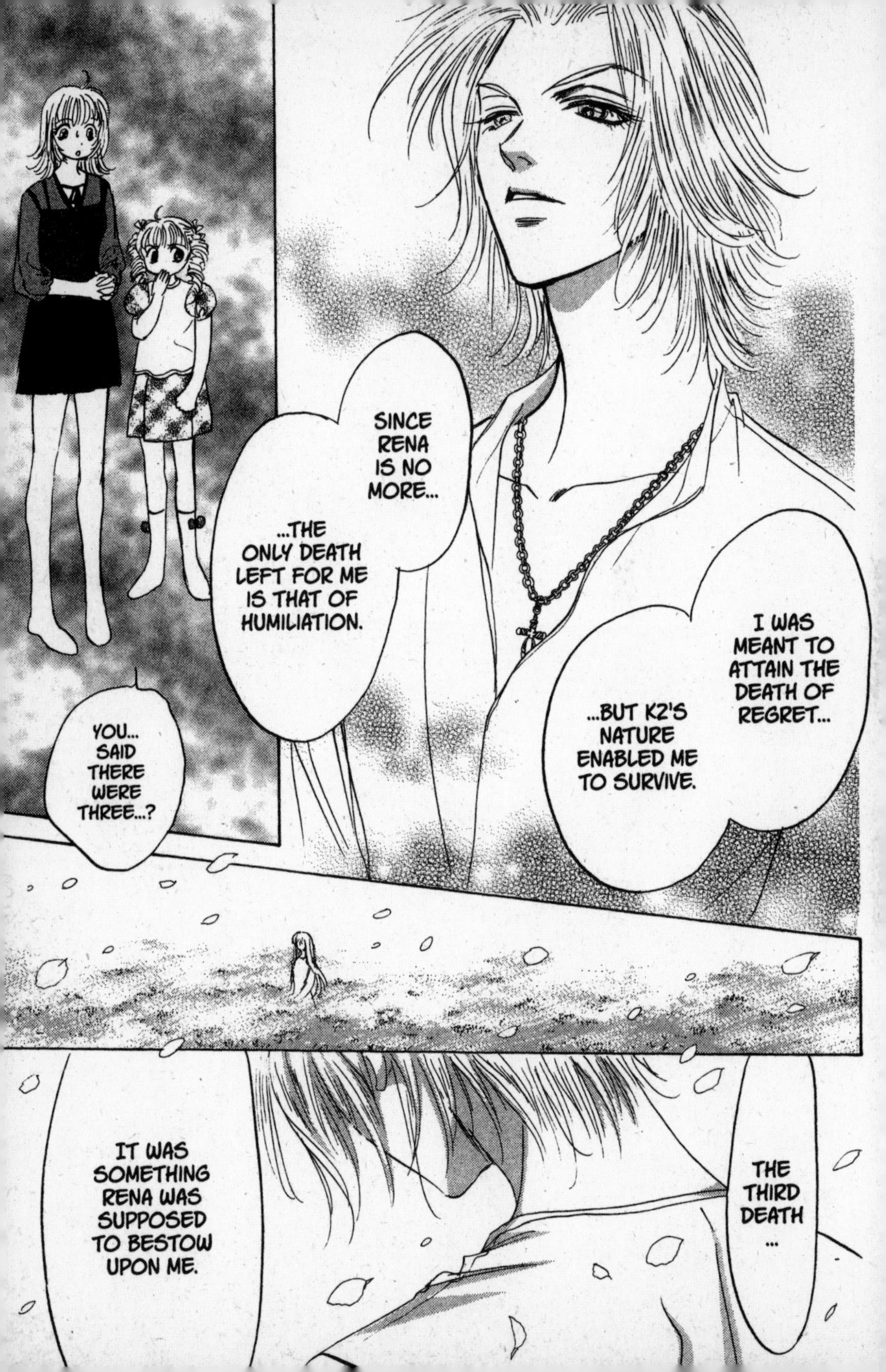
I WAS MEANT TO ATTAIN THE DEATH OF REGRET...
...BUT K2'S NATURE ENABLED ME TO SURVIVE.
SINCE RENA IS NO MORE...
...THE ONLY DEATH LEFT FOR ME IS THAT OF HUMILIATION.
YOU... SAID THERE WERE THREE...?
THE THIRD DEATH ...
IT WAS SOMETHING RENA WAS SUPPOSED TO BESTOW UPON ME.

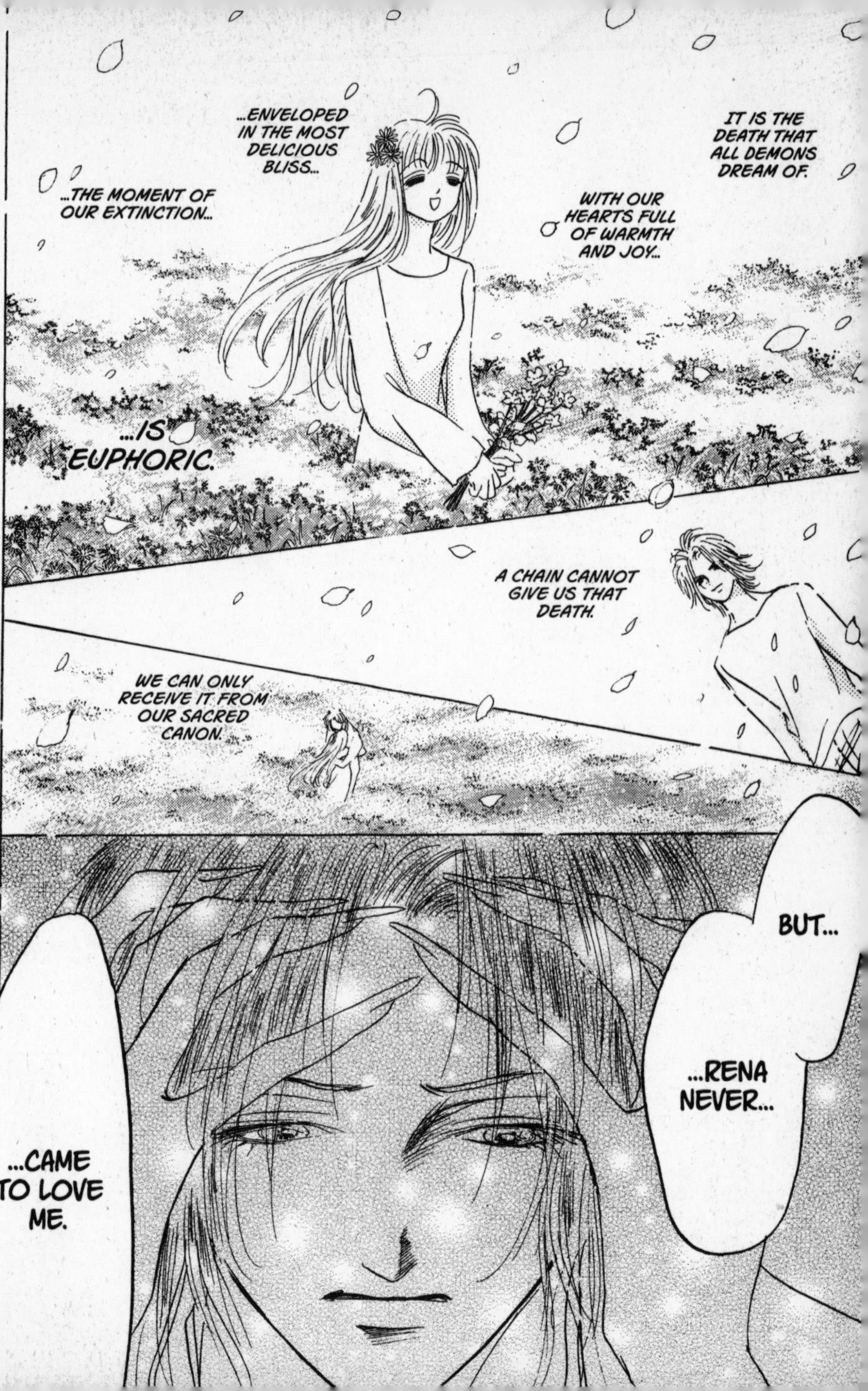
IT IS THE DEATH THAT ALL DEMONS DREAM OF.
WITH OUR HEARTS FULL OF WARMTH AND JOY...
...ENVELOPED IN THE MOST DELICIOUS BLISS...
...THE MOMENT OF OUR EXTINCTION...
...IS EUPHORIC.
A CHAIN CANNOT GIVE US THAT DEATH.
WE CAN ONLY RECEIVE IT FROM OUR SACRED CANON.
BUT...
...RENA NEVER...
...CAME TO LOVE ME.

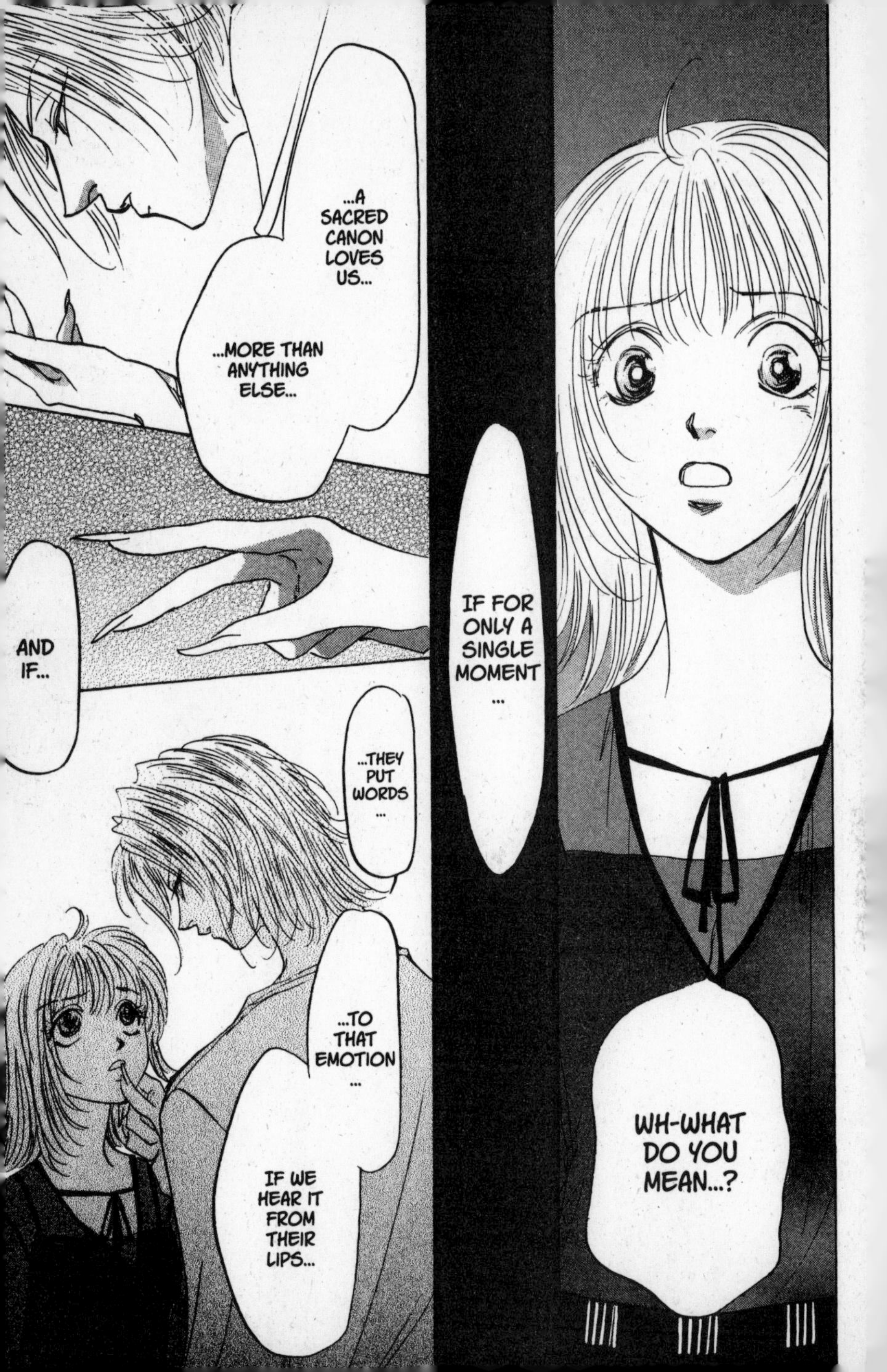
IF FOR ONLY A SINGLE MOMENT ...
WH-WHAT DO YOU MEAN...?
...A SACRED CANON LOVES US...
...MORE THAN ANYTHING ELSE...
AND IF...
...THEY PUT WORDS ...
...TO THAT EMOTION ...
IF WE HEAR IT FROM THEIR LIPS...

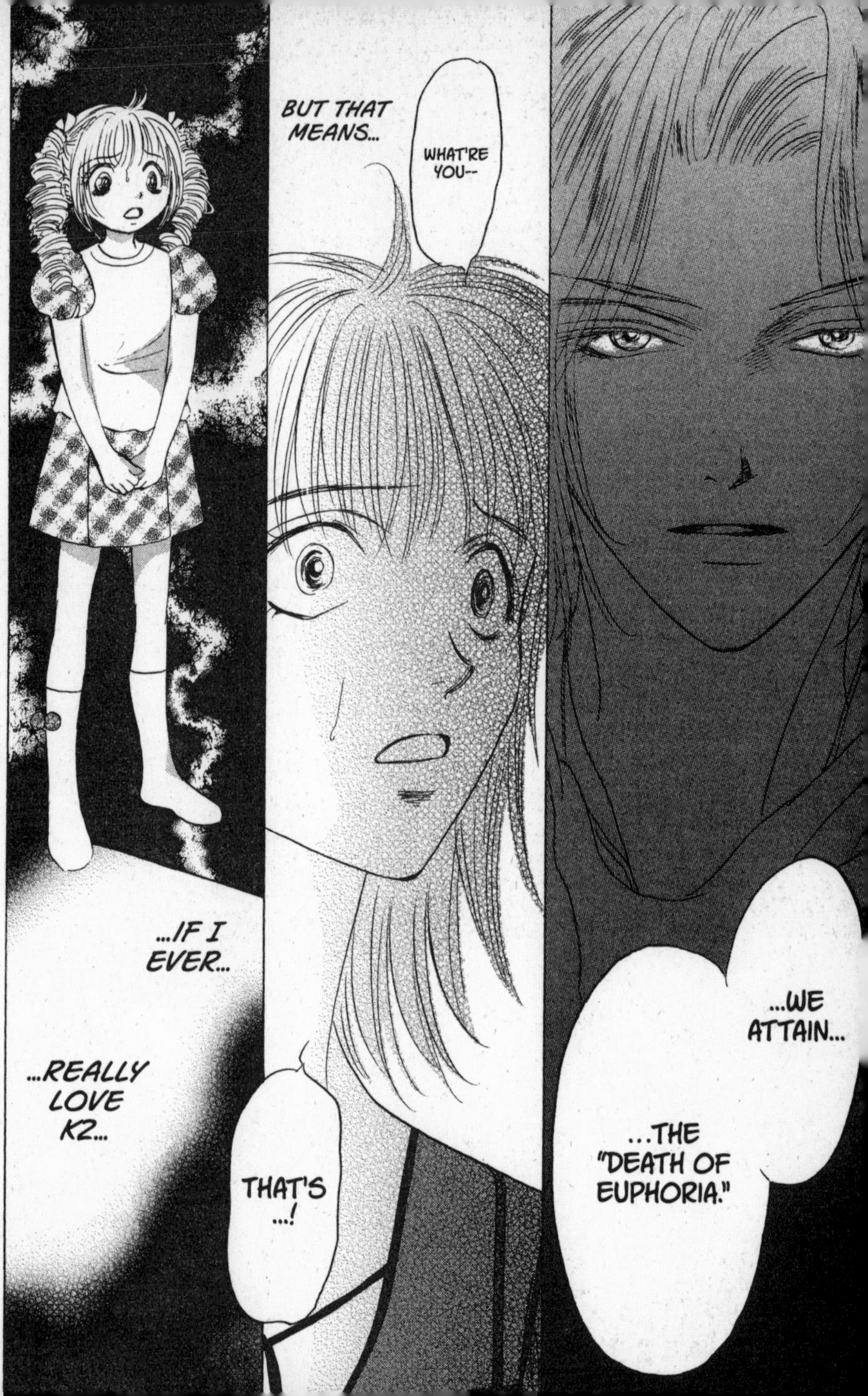
...WE ATTAIN...
...THE "DEATH OF EUPHORIA."
WHAT'RE YOU--
BUT THAT MEANS...
THAT'S ...!
...IF I EVER...
...REALLY LOVE KZ...

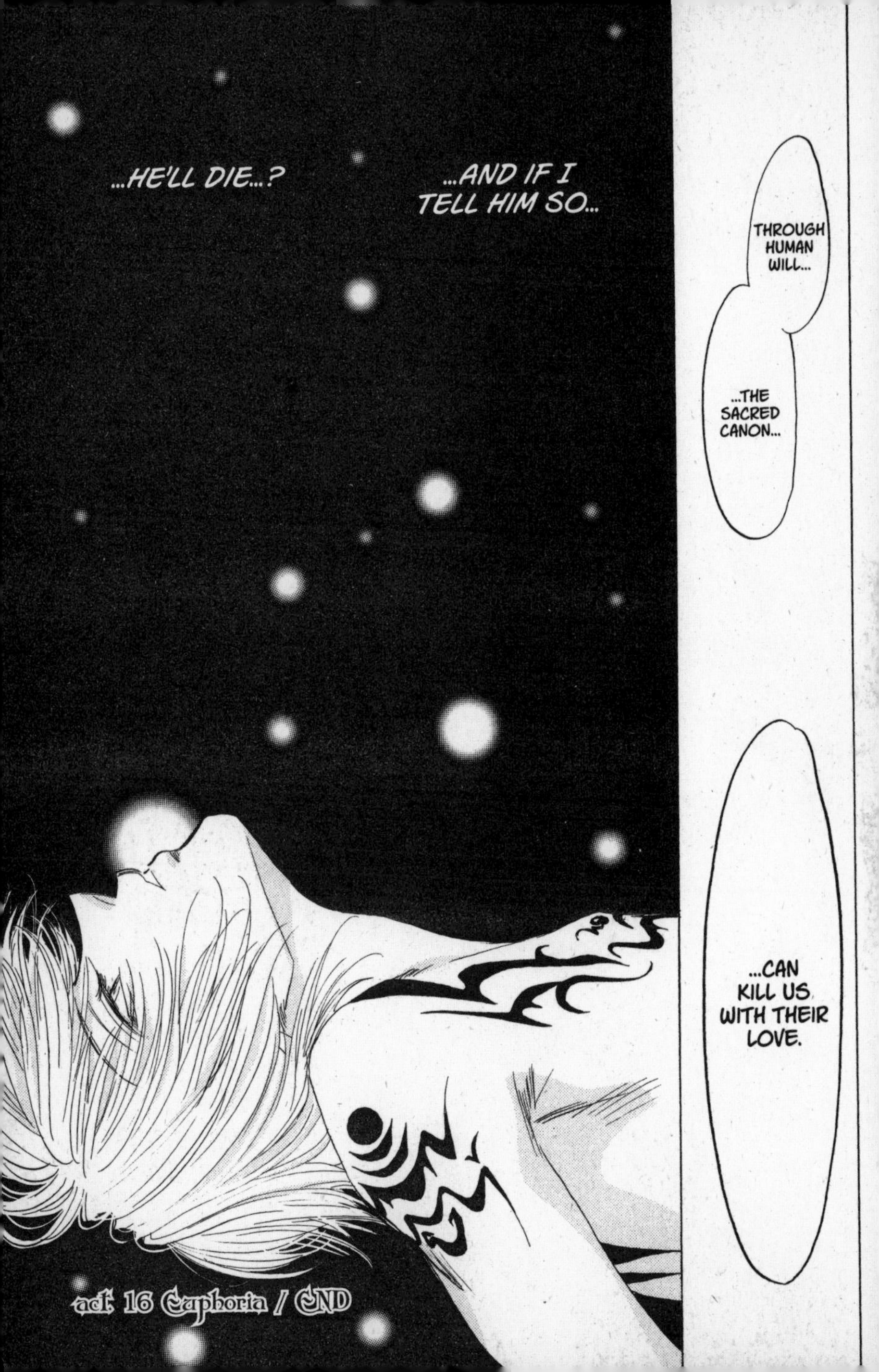
THROUGH HUMAN WILL...
...THE SACRED CANON...
...CAN KILL US WITH THEIR LOVE.
...AND IF I TELL HIM SO...
...HE'LL DIE...?
act. 16 Euphoria / END

Breakfast with the Koigusa Family

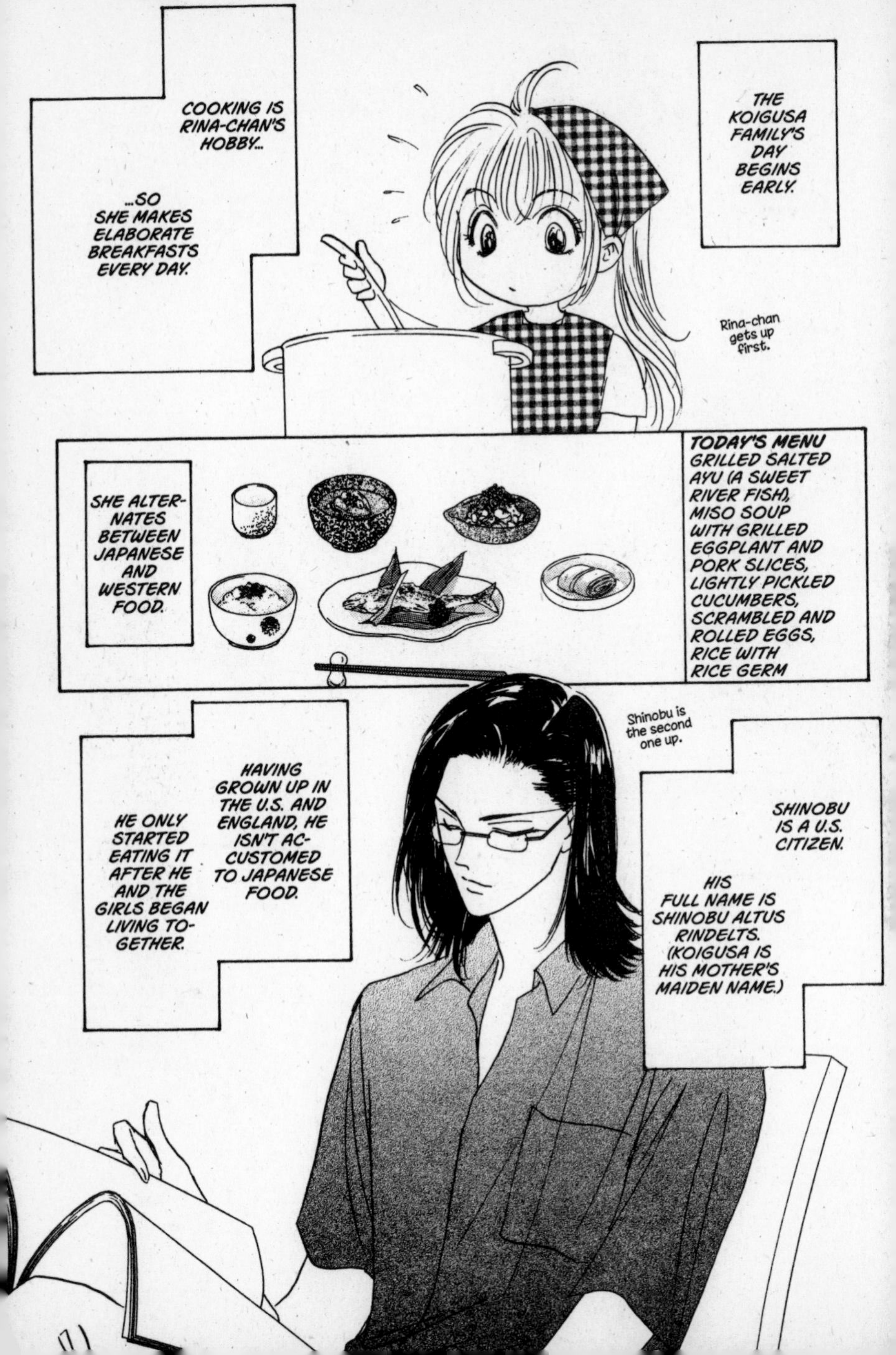
THE KOIGUSA FAMILY'S DAY BEGINS EARLY.
Rina-chan gets up first.
COOKING IS RINA-CHAN'S HOBBY...
...SO SHE MAKES ELABORATE BREAKFASTS EVERY DAY.
TODAY'S MENU
GRILLED SALTED AYU (A SWEET RIVER FISH), MISO SOUP WITH GRILLED EGGPLANT AND PORK SLICES, LIGHTLY PICKLED CUCUMBERS, SCRAMBLED AND ROLLED EGGS, RICE WITH RICE GERM
SHE ALTERNATES BETWEEN JAPANESE AND WESTERN FOOD.
Shinobu is the second one up.
SHINOBU IS A U.S. CITIZEN.
HIS FULL NAME IS SHINOBU ALTUS RINDELTS. (KOIGUSA IS HIS MOTHER'S MAIDEN NAME.)
HAVING GROWN UP IN THE U.S. AND ENGLAND, HE ISN'T ACCUSTOMED TO JAPANESE FOOD.
HE ONLY STARTED EATING IT AFTER HE AND THE GIRLS BEGAN LIVING TOGETHER.

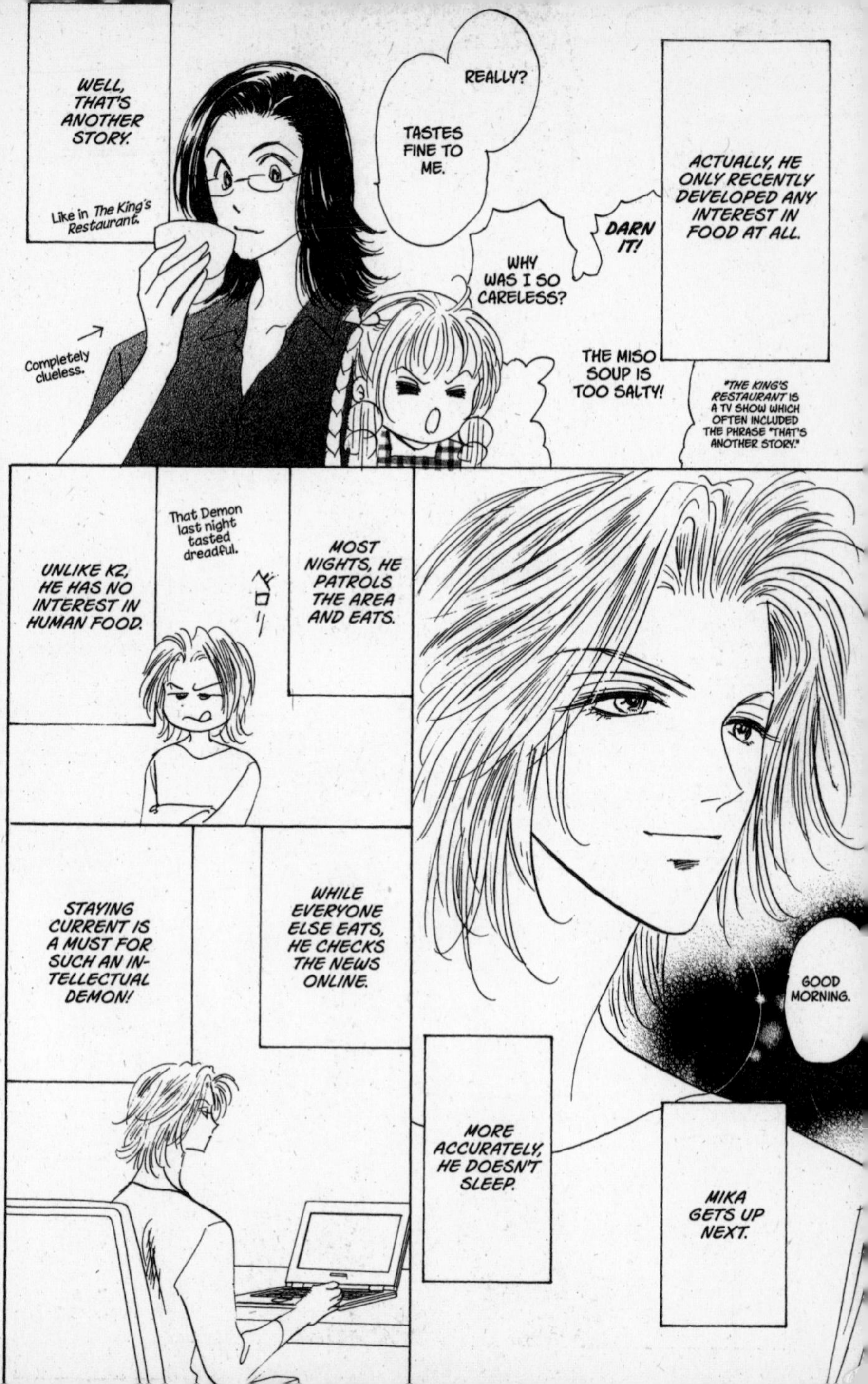
ACTUALLY, HE ONLY RECENTLY DEVELOPED ANY INTEREST IN FOOD AT ALL.
REALLY?
TASTES FINE TO ME.
DARN IT!
WHY WAS I SO CARELESS?
THE MISO SOUP IS TOO SALTY!
WELL, THAT'S ANOTHER STORY.
Like in The King's Restaurant.
Completely clueless.
*THE KING'S RESTAURANT IS A TV SHOW WHICH OFTEN INCLUDED THE PHRASE "THAT'S ANOTHER STORY."
GOOD MORNING.
MIKA GETS UP NEXT.
MORE ACCURATELY, HE DOESN'T SLEEP.
MOST NIGHTS, HE PATROLS THE AREA AND EATS.
That Demon last night tasted dreadful.
UNLIKE K2, HE HAS NO INTEREST IN HUMAN FOOD.
WHILE EVERYONE ELSE EATS, HE CHECKS THE NEWS ONLINE.
STAYING CURRENT IS A MUST FOR SUCH AN IN-TELLECTUAL DEMON!

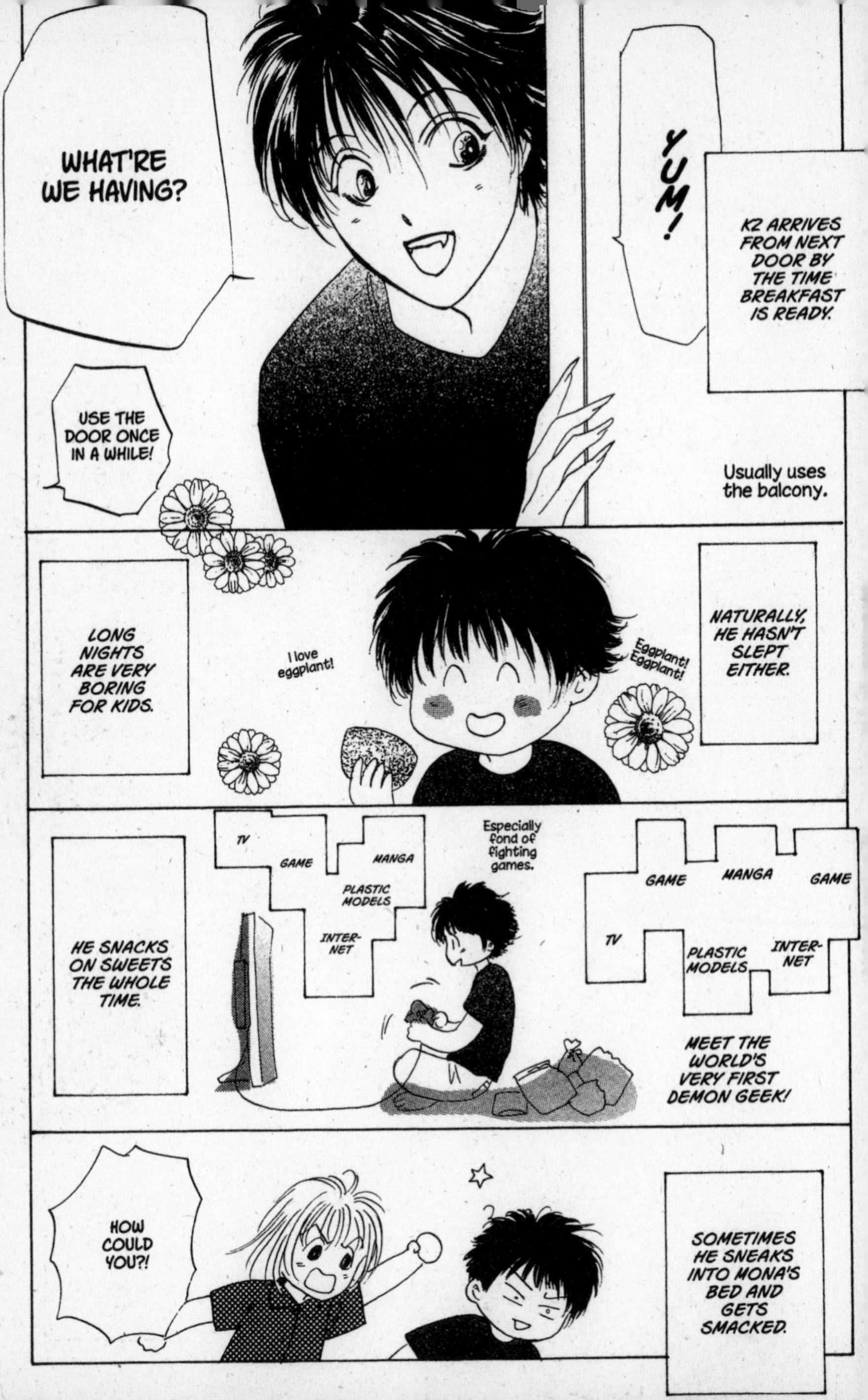

K2 ARRIVES FROM NEXT DOOR BY THE TIME BREAKFAST IS READY.
YUM!
Usually uses the balcony.
WHAT'RE WE HAVING?
USE THE DOOR ONCE IN A WHILE!
NATURALLY, HE HASN'T SLEPT EITHER.
Eggplant! Eggplant!
I love eggplant!
LONG NIGHTS ARE VERY BORING FOR KIDS.
GAME
MANGA
GAME
TV
PLASTIC MODELS
INTER-NET
MEET THE WORLD'S VERY FIRST DEMON GEEK!
Especially fond of fighting games.
TV
MANGA
GAME
PLASTIC MODELS
INTER-NET
HE SNACKS ON SWEETS THE WHOLE TIME.
SOMETIMES HE SNEAKS INTO MONA'S BED AND GETS SMACKED.
HOW COULD YOU?!

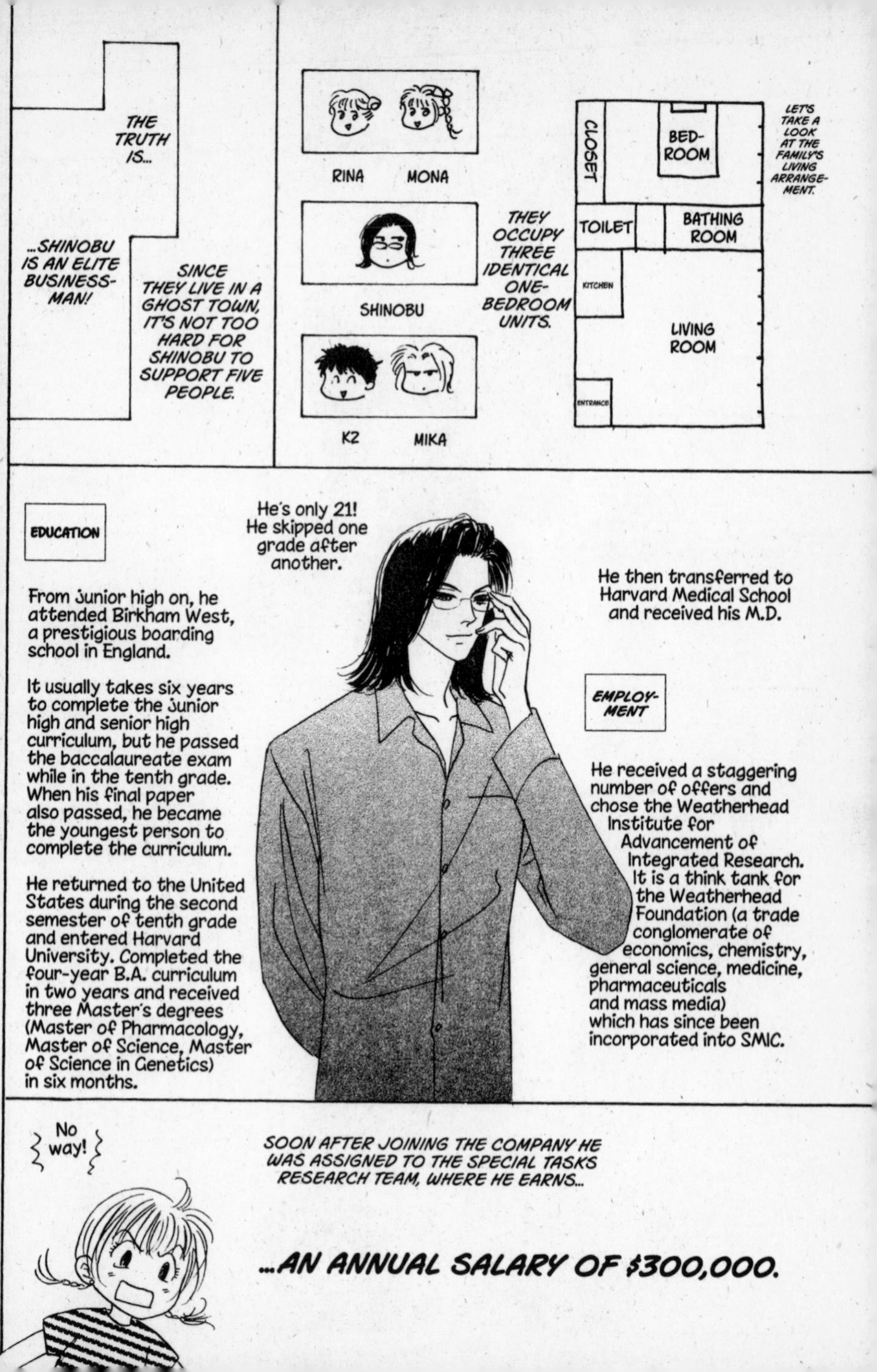

LET'S TAKE A LOOK AT THE FAMILY'S LIVING ARRANGEMENT.
CLOSET
BED-ROOM
TOILET
BATHING ROOM
KITCHEN
LIVING ROOM
ENTRANCE
THEY OCCUPY THREE IDENTICAL ONE-BEDROOM UNITS.
RINA
MONA
SHINOBU
KZ
MIKA
THE TRUTH IS...
...SHINOBU IS AN ELITE BUSINESS-MAN!
SINCE THEY LIVE IN A GHOST TOWN, IT'S NOT TOO HARD FOR SHINOBU TO SUPPORT FIVE PEOPLE.
He's only 21! He skipped one grade after another.
EDUCATION
From junior high on, he attended Birkham West, a prestigious boarding school in England.
It usually takes six years to complete the junior high and senior high curriculum, but he passed the baccalaureate exam while in the tenth grade. When his final paper also passed, he became the youngest person to complete the curriculum.
He returned to the United States during the second semester of tenth grade and entered Harvard University. Completed the four-year B.A. curriculum in two years and received three Master's degrees (Master of Pharmacology, Master of Science, Master of Science in Genetics) in six months.
He then transferred to Harvard Medical School and received his M.D.
EMPLOY-MENT
He received a staggering number of offers and chose the Weatherhead Institute for Advancement of Integrated Research. It is a think tank for the Weatherhead Foundation (a trade conglomerate of economics, chemistry, general science, medicine, pharmaceuticals and mass media) which has since been incorporated into SMIC.
SOON AFTER JOINING THE COMPANY HE WAS ASSIGNED TO THE SPECIAL TASKS RESEARCH TEAM, WHERE HE EARNS...
...AN ANNUAL SALARY OF $300,000.
No way!

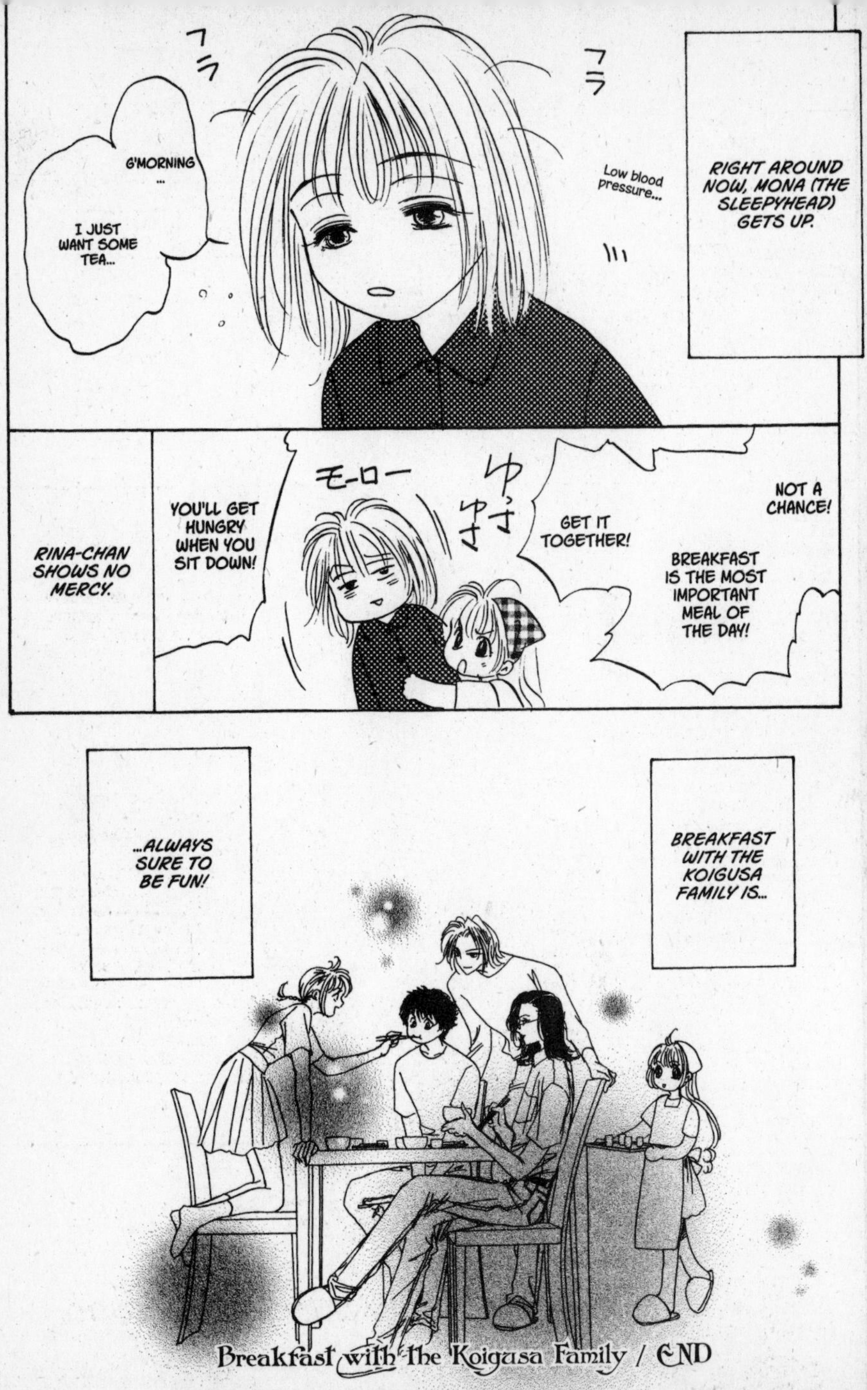
RIGHT AROUND NOW, MONA (THE SLEEPYHEAD) GETS UP.
Low blood pressure...
フラ
フラ
G'MORNING ...
I JUST WANT SOME TEA...
NOT A CHANCE!
BREAKFAST IS THE MOST IMPORTANT MEAL OF THE DAY!
GET IT TOGETHER!
ゆさゆさ
モーロー
YOU'LL GET HUNGRY WHEN YOU SIT DOWN!
RINA-CHAN SHOWS NO MERCY.
BREAKFAST WITH THE KOIGUSA FAMILY IS...
...ALWAYS SURE TO BE FUN!

Breakfast with the Koigusa Family / END

Story&Art

ITSUKI, Natsumi

Assistants

IZUTSU, Ai
OGAWA, Makiko
TAKADA, Chiyo
TANAKA, Sayoko
TANEDA, Tomoko
NOCHIOKA, Sumiko
HIROI, Michiko

Consultant Manager

ASANUMA, Yuko

Editor

SATO, Kazuya(LaLa)
MASUI, Akihito(LaLa)

Editorial Agent

OKUBO, Tomofumi(NAHT)
TAKEMURA, Toshiko(NAHT)

NATSUMI ITSUKI'S OFFICIAL WEBSITE - NATSUMIKAN
HTTP://INA-INC.JP/

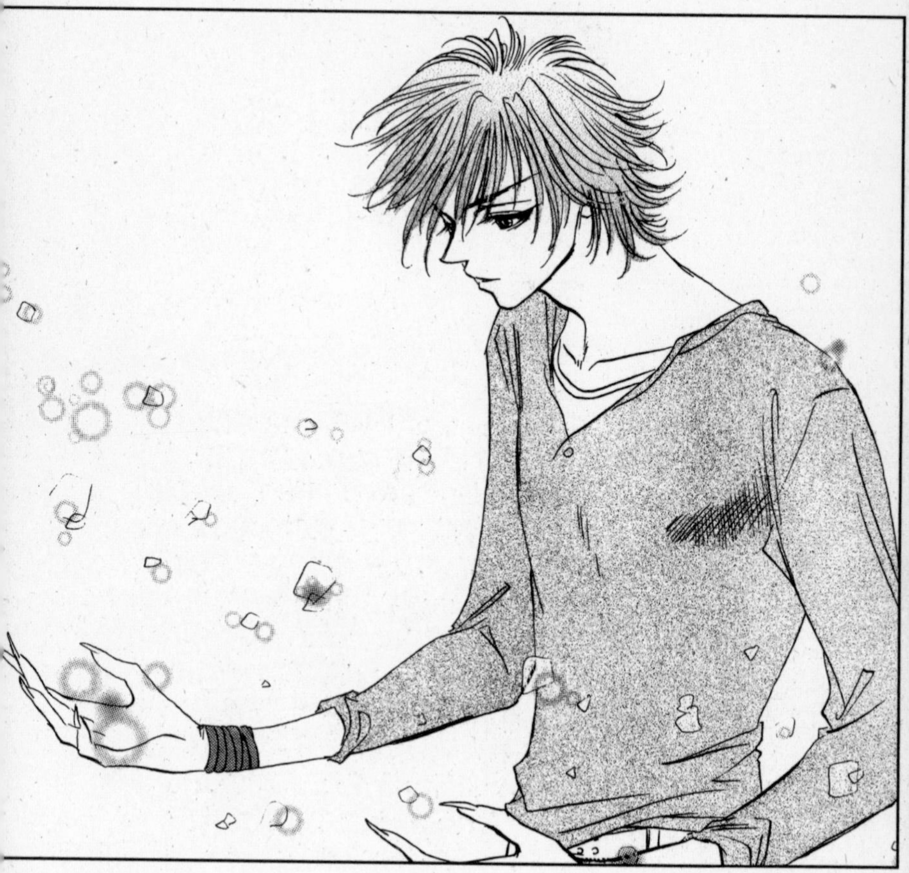

In the next volume of...

DEMON SACRED

WHAT DEMON WOULD DEAR TO
CHALLENGE "THE BEAST OF THE
APOCALYPSE," K2!? ...AND JUST WHEN
THINGS WERE HEATING UP BETWEEN HIM
AND ZOPHIE TOO. WHILE ZOPHIE GETS
MORE THEN SHE BARGAINED FOR--
SHINOBU IS JUST TRYING TO SURVIVE
THE MANIPULATIONS OF HIS OLDER HALF-
BROTHER WHILE KEEPING THE PRECIOUS
GIRLS IS HIS CARE SAFE. IN THE CHAOS,
UNIT A FINALLY MAKES THEIR MOVE...
WHO WILL BE THEIR FIRST TARGET?

DOWNLOAD THE REVOLUTION.

Get the free TOKYOPOP app for manga, anytime, anywhere!

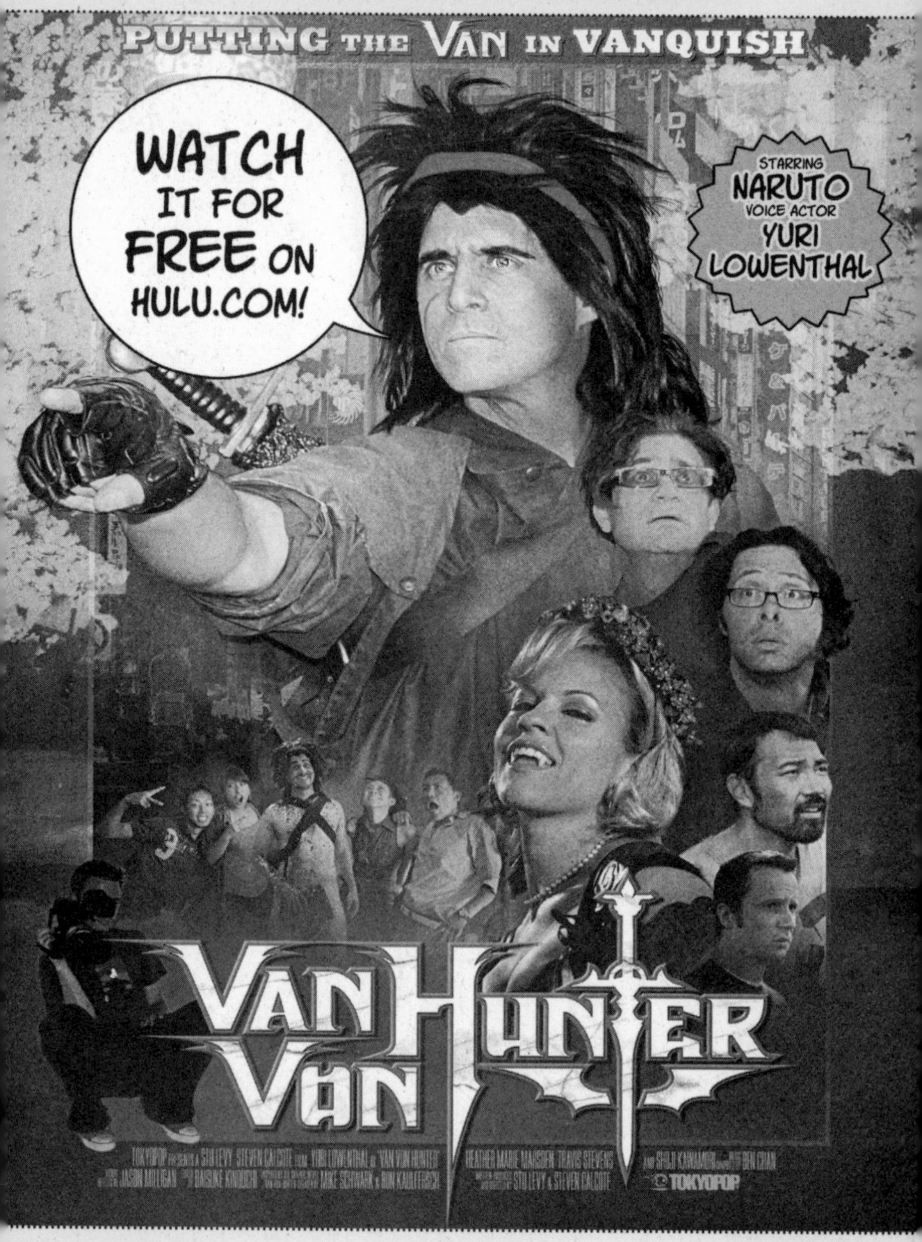
PUTTING THE VAN IN VANQUISH
WATCH IT FOR FREE ON HULU.COM!
STARRING NARUTO VOICE ACTOR YURI LOWENTHAL
VAN VON HUNTER
TOKYOPOP PRESENTS A STU LEVY STEVEN CALCOTE FILM YURI LOWENTHAL "VAN VON HUNTER" HEATHER MARIE MARSDEN TRAVIS STEVENS AND SHUJI KANAMORI BEN CHAN
JASON MILLIGAN DAISUKE KINOUCHI MIKE SCHWARK RON KAUFFERSCH STU LEVY STEVEN CALCOTE
TOKYOPOP

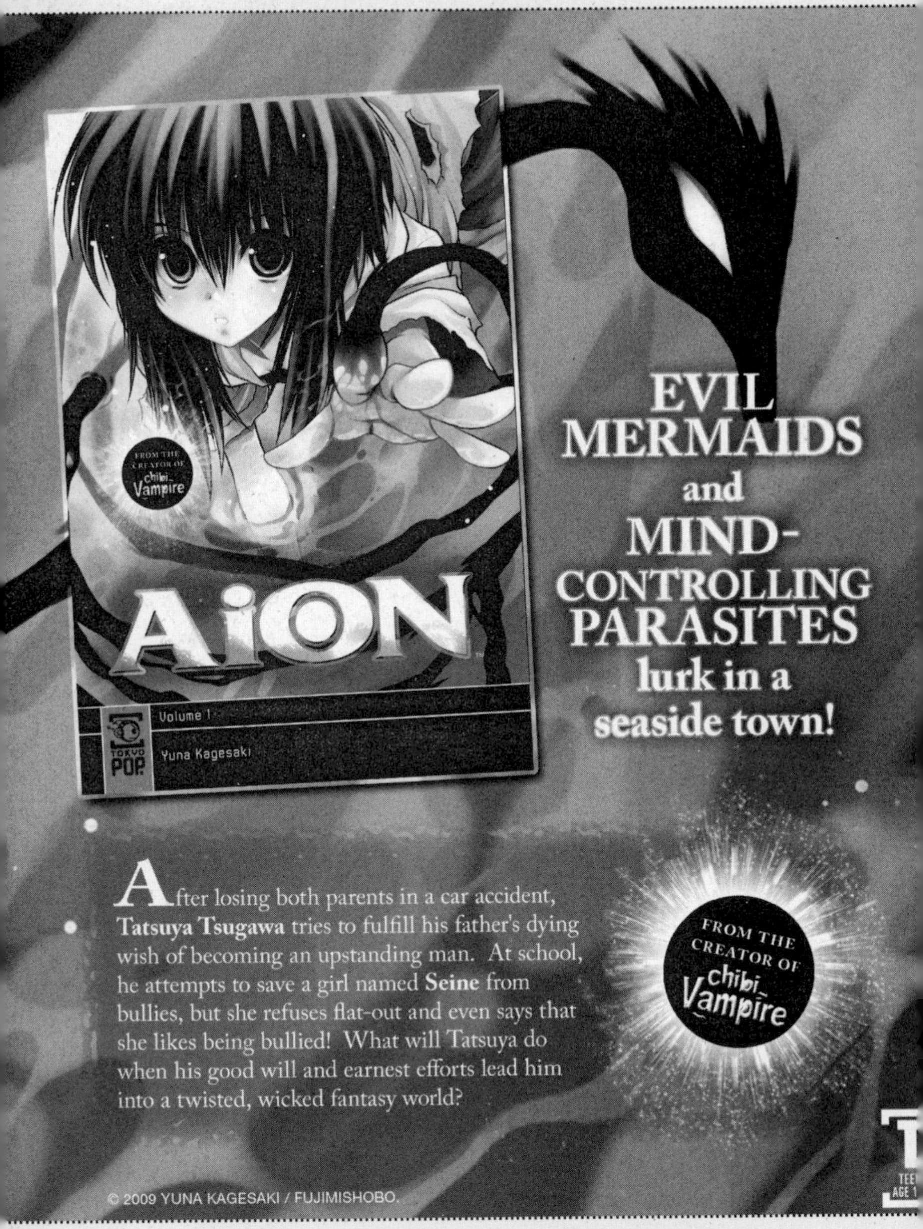
FROM THE CREATOR OF chibi Vampire
AiON
Volume 1
Yuna Kagesaki
TOKYOPOP
EVIL MERMAIDS and MIND-CONTROLLING PARASITES lurk in a seaside town!
After losing both parents in a car accident, Tatsuya Tsugawa tries to fulfill his father's dying wish of becoming an upstanding man. At school, he attempts to save a girl named Seine from bullies, but she refuses flat-out and even says that she likes being bullied! What will Tatsuya do when his good will and earnest efforts lead him into a twisted, wicked fantasy world?
FROM THE CREATOR OF chibi Vampire
© 2009 YUNA KAGESAKI / FUJIMISHOBO.

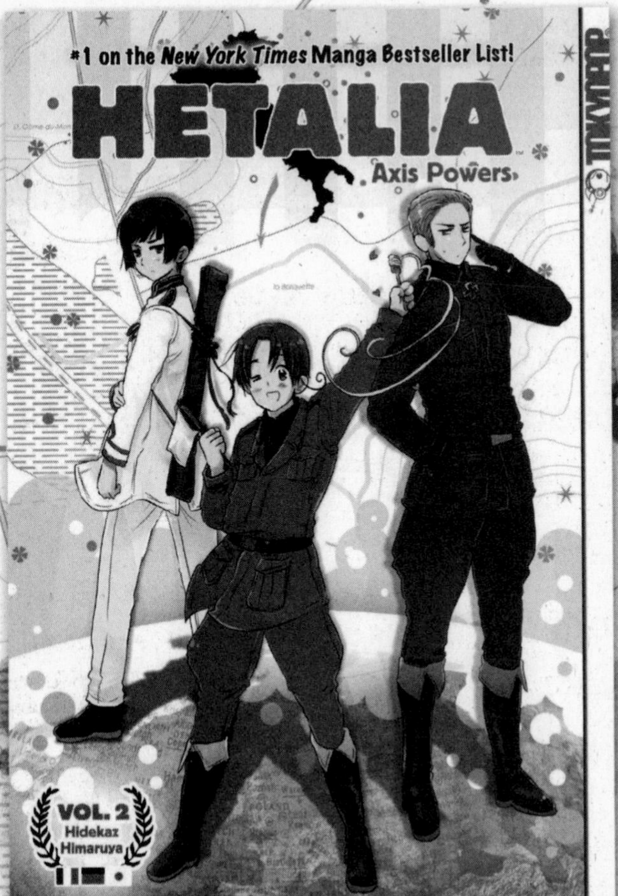
#1 on the New York Times Manga Bestseller List!
HETALIA
Axis Powers
TOKYOPOP
VOL. 2
Hidekaz Himaruya

Will Tomo find
treasure or *true love?*

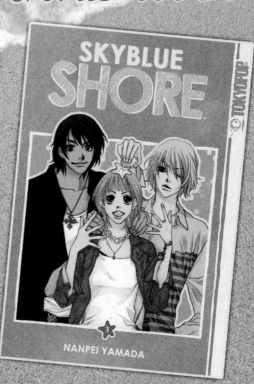

SKYBLUE SHORE

NANPEI YAMADA

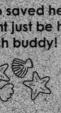 After her parents' divorce, Tomo always longed to return to the ocean to find her long-lost friend. A chance encounter with a molester leaves her dreaming about the attractive man who saved her and might just be her old beach buddy!

Sand, sun and love triangles!

ROMANCE · 0 OLDER AGE

STOP!

This is the back of the book.
You wouldn't want to spoil a great ending!

This book is printed "manga-style," in the authentic Japanese right-to-left format. Since none of the artwork has been flipped or altered, readers get to experience the story just as the creator intended. You've been asking for it, so TOKYOPOP® delivered: authentic, hot-off-the-press, and far more fun!

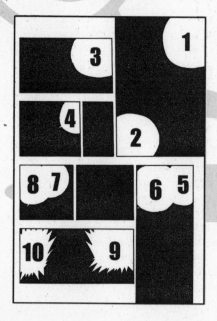

DIRECTIONS

If this is your first time reading manga-style, here's a quick guide to help you understand how it works.

It's easy... just start in the top right panel and follow the numbers. Have fun, and look for more 100% authentic manga from TOKYOPOP®!